IMAG

SOCIAL PROBLEMS AND SOCIAL ISSUES

An Aldine de Gruyter Series of Texts and Monographs

SERIES EDITOR

Joel Best

Southern Illinois University at Carbondale

IMAGES OF ISSUES

Typifying Contemporary Social Problems

Second Edition

JOEL BEST
Editor

ALDINE DE GRUYTER

New York

About the Editor

Joel Best is Professor and Chair of the Department of Sociology at Southern Illinois University at Carbondale. Specializing in social problems and deviance, his books include *Troubling Children* (Aldine de Gruyter), *Threatened Children*, and *Organizing Deviance* (with David F. Luckenbill). He received his Ph.D. from the University of California, Berkeley.

ALDINE DE GRUYTER
A division of Walter de Gruyter, Inc.
200 Saw Mill River Road
Hawthorne, New York 10532

This publication is printed on acid free paper ∞

Library of Congress Cataloging-in-Publication Data

Images of issues : typifying contemporary social problems / Joel Best,
    editor. — 2nd ed.
        p.   cm.
    Includes bibliographical references and index.
    ISBN 0-202-30538-4 (lib. bdg. : acid-free paper). — ISBN
0-202-30539-2 (pbk. : acid-free paper)
    1. Social problems.   2. Sociology.   I. Best, Joel.
HN28.I46   1995
361.1—dc20   94–47575
                                                                                    CIP

Manufactured in the United States of America

10 9 8 7 6 5 4 3 2 1

Contents

AFTERWORD

Preface to the Second Edition

During the past 20 years, constructionism emerged as an influential orientation among sociologists who study social problems. The body of constructionist studies of social problems continues to grow, and awareness of the constructionist stance has spread to other disciplines, including history, political science, law, criminology, social work, and evaluation research. Yet relatively few social problems courses introduce students to this exciting perspective.

In part, this may be because the key constructionist works seem to address scholars, rather than students. The first edition of *Images of Issues* sought to fill this gap with a collection of papers, written in relatively accessible prose, that offered an introduction to the constructionist perspective, dealt with timely issues, and contributed to the growing body of constructionist theory and research. But the substantive topics addressed in that 1989 edition quickly became dated as societal concerns shifted. Some issues, highly visible in the 1980s, dropped off the front pages in the 1990s, while new social problems attracted public attention.

This new edition reflects some of these shifts in concern. Only one of the substantive chapters—John M. Johnson's discussion of child abuse horror stories—is reprinted unchanged. Two other chapters—Craig Reinarman and Harry G. Levine on crack and Shirley A. Scritchfield on infertility—have been revised and updated. The remaining chapters represent recent work on new topics, including chapters on hate crimes, stalking, fathers' rights, multiculturalism in education, and other issues that moved into the limelight since the first edition's publication. Finally, the first edition's afterword—which rather casually introduced the distinction between strict and contextual constructionism—has been extensively revised to discuss the theoretical debate among constructionists more systematically.

I want to acknowledge some of the people who helped me prepare this edition: the scholars and teachers who provided encouragement when they told me they found the first edition useful; the folks at Aldine de Gruyter—particularly Richard Koffler and Arlene Perazzini—who helped turn my second thoughts into a book; Donna Maurer, who handled some of the editorial chores; and Sue Treece, who managed the conversion of the various manuscripts into a single word-processing format.

INTRODUCTION

1

Typification and Social Problems Construction

What do we mean when we speak of social problems? At first, the answer seems obvious: We mean such things as crime and discrimination and poverty. This book's table of contents gives other examples of this sort. Each chapter in this book concerns a particular social problem: child abuse, stalking, alcoholism, and so on. We usually answer the question "What are social problems?" by pointing to such examples.

But we might try to develop a more abstract definition, one that fits all our examples. For instance, we might say that social problems are trouble spots within society—social arrangements that do not work properly. Sociologists often define social problems along these lines. Thus, Bassis, Gelles, and Levine's (1982:2) textbook *Social Problems* gives this definition; "A social problem is a social condition that has been found to be harmful to individual and/or societal well-being." Another recent text states: "A social problem, then, can be defined as a condition that: (1) is widely regarded as undesirable or as a source of difficulties; (2) is caused by the actions or inactions of people or of society; [and] (3) affects or is thought to affect a large number of people" (Farley, 1987:2).

OBJECTIVIST DEFINITIONS AND THEIR LIMITATIONS

These definitions suggest that the essence of social problems lies in objective social conditions and that some conditions are problems. Thus, someone armed with Bassis et al.'s (1982) definition could evaluate various social conditions, deciding that Condition X is indeed harmful to either individuals or society, and therefore is a social problem, while Condition Y—which fails to meet the criterion of harm—is not a social problem. Such definitions are called *objectivist* because they define social problems in terms of objective conditions.

While they fit our common-sense notion of what social problems are,

3

objectivist definitions have two key flaws. First, *they minimize or even ignore the subjective nature of social problems.* Not all harmful conditions are considered social problems. Consider nutrition. Medical authorities argue that the typical American diet contains undesirable levels of fats and cholesterol. This condition clearly fits Bassis et al.'s definition of a social problem: This diet endangers the well-being of individuals, who face greater risks of heart disease and other medical disorders; and it also threatens societal well-being by forcing Americans to devote a growing share of their national income to health care. Yet the nutritional inadequacies of the American diet rarely appear on lists of social problems,[1] even though the condition fits most objectivist definitions. This reveals the subjective nature of social problems: Social problems are what people view as social problems.

Histories of particular social problems reveal the importance of subjective judgments. For example, the contemporary feminist movement began to gain public attention around 1970. The movement aimed to get people thinking differently; it challenged traditional, taken-for-granted assumptions about women's place in society. By the early 1970s, some women were joining "consciousness-raising" groups, where they discussed issues in their lives. Women encouraged one another to "make the personal political"—to understand that the difficulties individual women faced at home or at work were part of larger, societal problems, and that those problems needed to be addressed. Feminists began bringing these issues before the public; they held demonstrations, gave press conferences, wrote books and articles, and lobbied government officials. New terms began to appear in the press: sexism, wife abuse, sexual harassment, pay equity, and so on. Where pre-1970 textbooks on social problems rarely mentioned these issues, post-1970 texts routinely included one or more chapters on sexism and sex discrimination. Obviously, the objective conditions feminists attacked were not new; they had been around for a long time. The change was subjective. After 1970, people began including sexism, sex discrimination, and the like on their lists of social problems.

Our sense of what is a social problem is inevitably subjective. This is true, even when the problem seems purely objective. Thus, most scientists now agree that certain manufactured chemicals damage the ozone layer in the Earth's atmosphere, a process that threatens to increase the incidence of skin cancer, to damage crops, etc. This might seem to be a clear example of a harmful objective condition. But, again, this social problem has a subjective history. Scientists had to spot the loss in ozone, identify its cause, and bring it to public attention. The chemical industry resisted these claims, denying that there was a serious problem or that their chemicals were responsible. Politicians and the press began paying attention to the debate. In other words, people developed a subjective sense that this was a social problem. Suppose that no one noticed the declining ozone levels, or that politicians and the press refused to take the issue seriously. The objective condition (diminishing ozone) still would have had effects (more cancer, etc.) but it would not be on anyone's list of social problems. No condition is a social problem until someone considers it a social problem.

There is a second flaw in objectivist definitions of social problems: *The objective conditions that people define as social problems have relatively little in common.* Suppose we agree on a list of harmful conditions such as the typical American diet, sexism, the threatened ozone layer, crime, poverty, and the arms race. What do we do next? What do these conditions have in common? Very little—other than the fact that they are all somehow harmful.

This is why, until recently, sociologists rarely used the concept "social problems" in their research. Objectivist definitions of social problems inevitably lead to a hodge-podge list of topics with little in common. These problems do not have the same sorts of causes, and they do not have the same sorts of effects. Sociologists studying crime need to ask very different questions from those studying sexism. Saying that both are social problems does not offer a useful direction for research.

To be sure, sociologists seem to use the concept in their teaching. Most sociology departments offer a course in social problems. Typically, textbooks for these classes have a standard structure. There is a single introductory chapter, which presents an objectivist definition, followed by a dozen chapters examining specific conditions that the authors designate as social problems (sexism, crime, and so on). These chapters have little relationship to the introductory chapter (the term "social problem" rarely appears in the later chapters) or to one another. These texts lack integration simply because objectivist definitions of social problems do not lead to a better understanding of social problems in general. If we equate social problems with harmful objective conditions, we quickly discover that those conditions do not have much else in common. How does understanding the objective condition of crime help us understand the objective condition of sexism? The answer is not clear.

In short, objectivist definitions of social problems are common, and it is easy to see why. Equating social problems with objective conditions fits our common-sense notion of what social problems are. But objectivist definitions have two important limitations: They fail to recognize that the identification of any condition as a social problem is inevitably subjective; and they cannot guide our thinking about social problems because the conditions identified have so little in common.

THE CONSTRUCTIONIST PERSPECTIVE

As the limitations of objectivist definitions of social problems have become increasingly apparent, some sociologists have sought to develop an alternative, subjectivist approach to studying social problems. Their approach focuses on the processes by which people designate some social conditions as social problems. The most influential statement of this perspective is a short book, *Constructing Social Problems*, by Malcolm Spector and John I. Kitsuse (1977).[2] Although their approach is sometimes called subjectivist, Spector and Kitsuse are more often referred to as constructionists because they speak of the "social construction of social problems."[3] What does this mean? Simply that our sense of what is or is not a social problem is a product, something that has been produced or constructed through social activities. When activists hold a demonstration to attract attention to some social condition, when investigative reporters publish stories that expose new aspects of the condition, or when legislators introduce bills to do something about the condition, they are constructing a social problem.

Constructionists define social problems in terms of these activities. Spector and Kitsuse use the term "claims-making." They define social problems as "the activities of individuals or groups making assertions of grievances and claims with respect to some putative conditions" (Spector and Kitsuse, 1977:75). Note that this definition emphasizes the activities, the claimsmaking. In this view, social problems are not conditions; conditions are merely the subjects of claims. In fact, Spector and Kitsuse argue that the objective status of those conditions is irrelevant. People make claims about alleged or putative conditions. It does not matter whether the conditions exist; it matters only that people make claims about them.

It is important to understand that objectivism and constructionism use the term "social problems" to refer to very different things. For objectivist sociologists, social problems are conditions; for constructionists, social problems are claimsmaking activities. To be sure, objectivists may acknowledge that subjectivity plays a role, that we do not recognize social problems until the objective conditions come to people's attention. But, having said that, objectivists return their attention to the troublesome social conditions. In contrast, constructionists focus on claimsmaking; they view social conditions as little more than subjects for claimsmaking, as being of little interest in their own right.[4] Constructionists examine what claimsmakers say about conditions, not the conditions themselves. It is a mistake to think of objectivism and constructionism as being two sides of the same coin, or slightly different perspectives on the same topic. Because the two approaches define social problems in completely different ways, they are best understood as dealing with two distinct topics.

Constructionists, then, use the term "social problems" very differently from the way in which we use it in everyday life. Are there any advantages to this peculiar usage? How does it help to view social problems in terms of claimsmaking? The principal advantage is for sociological theory. Remember that objectivism's critics argue that the various social conditions objectivists call social problems have little in common. In contrast, by focusing on claimsmaking, constructionists draw attention to something all social problems have in common. The focus on claimsmaking suggests questions for further research. What sorts of claims get made? When do claims get made, and what sorts of people make them? What sorts of responses do claims receive, and under what conditions? Questions such as these guide constructionist research; they provide a framework for a theory of social problems.

Constructionist studies of social problems are relatively new. Thus far, most of this research has taken the form of case studies, in which a sociologist examines how a particular problem came to be constructed. For example, Stephen J. Pfohl's (1977) article, "The 'Discovery' of Child Abuse," traces the history of public concern about child abuse. Pfohl concentrates on the early 1960s, when some physicians—particularly pediatric radiologists—identified the "battered-child syndrome." Pfohl wants to explain why these physicians became the initial claimsmakers, and why their claims emerged when they did. He suggests that the victims' family doctors were reluctant to accuse abusive parents who, after all, paid the doctors' bills. In contrast, most pediatric radiologists worked as researchers or hospital staff physicians; they had little to lose (reporting abusive parents would have little effect on their practices) and much to gain (particularly greater prestige within their profession).

Case studies like Pfohl's offer the basis for a comparative theory of social problems construction. Sociologists might build on Pfohl's study by comparing child abuse to other instances where medical professionals were the leading claimsmakers. A comparison of several such cases—as well as contrasting instances where physicians did not take the lead—may help other sociologists develop a theory specifying the circumstances under which medical authorities are likely to make claims.[5] In turn, still other sociologists can test the theory's propositions in further research.

TYPIFICATION

Constructionists, then, argue that our views of social problems are social constructions. But claimsmakers do more than simply draw attention to particular social conditions. Claimsmakers shape our sense of just what the problem is. Any social condition is a potential subject for claimsmaking, or rather for several kinds of claimsmaking. Each social condition can be constructed as many different social problems.

Consider, for instance, the large number of young, poor, unmarried women having and raising babies. (This condition is the product of several changes. A larger proportion of young people has become sexually active—so that more young women are at risk of becoming pregnant. A young, unmarried woman's pregnancy is less likely to lead to a "shotgun wedding"—so that there are more unwed mothers. And fewer unwed mothers give their infants up for adoption—so that more children are raised in these households.) But notice that there are many ways to construct this condition as a social problem. Should we understand this as a moral problem—a result of young people's failure to honor values of chastity and marital sanctity? Is it an educational problem, stemming from our reluctance to teach sex education? Or should we concentrate on the young mother's lost chances, given the likelihood that she will need to quit school and have less opportunity for a fulfilling career? Is the treatment of young mothers simply another instance of a patriarchal society placing women at a disadvantage? Or are the babies the principal victims—born in poverty, raised by mothers who are immature and ill-prepared for the responsibilities of parenthood? Or should we focus on the costs to society as a whole—on the loss of potentially productive workers, the burden of growing welfare rolls, and the emergence of a cycle of poverty as the children of young mothers begin having babies of their own?

This is not just a matter of claimsmakers drawing our attention to a condition. Claimsmakers inevitably choose to focus on particular aspects of the condition. They do not merely say that Condition X is a problem; they characterize X as a problem of a particular sort. Even the names claimsmakers give a problem can reflect their stances toward it. Thus, speaking of "teen promiscuity" highlights the morality of sexual activity among the young, and people who use this term are likely to advocate policies that will promote abstinence. In contrast, those concerned with "teen pregnancy" focus on pregnancy as the problem, and they are more likely to try to reduce pregnancies by giving young women access to contraception and abortion.

Naming is just one way claimsmakers typify social problems. *Typification occurs when claimsmakers characterize a problem's nature.* Typification can take many forms. One of the most common forms is to give an orientation toward a problem, arguing that a problem is best understood from a particular perspective. Thus, claimsmakers assert that X is really a ____ (moral, medical, criminal, political, etc.) problem. Each orientation emphasizes different aspects of X. Typically, an orientation locates the problem's cause and recommends a solution. Thus, moral problems revolve around individuals' decisions to violate moral standards; ordinarily we hold people responsible for immoral acts. Claimsmakers who adopt a moral orientation typically advocate giving people guidance to discourage immorality and punishing those who violate moral standards. In contrast, medical problems are viewed as diseases, conditions for which individuals should not be held responsible. The solutions promoted by medical claimsmakers feature treatment by medical professionals. Another common form of typification involves illustrating a problem through the use of examples. Particular cases often shape our sense of social problems, and claimsmakers draw attention to examples that seem to justify their claims. Consider two very different portraits of women who have abortions. Abortion's defenders—pro-choice advocates—tend to demonstrate the need for abortion by pointing to pregnant victims of rape or incest, and asking whether these women should be forced to complete their pregnancies. In contrast, abortion's opponents—pro-life advocates—characterize women who choose abortion as acting callously, perhaps having multiple abortions, merely for their own convenience. Our attitudes toward social problems often reflect our reactions to such "typical" cases; the example comes to represent the larger problem.

Typification is an integral part of social problems construction. Claimsmakers inevitably characterize problems in particular ways: They emphasize some aspects and not others, they promote specific orientations, and they focus on particular causes and advocate particular solutions. While all claims involve typification, and while constructionist research often describes typification, typification is not usually the focus of the analysis. That is the task of this book. The individual chapters explore the nature of typification. Each presents a case study of contemporary claimsmaking, focusing on how a particular social problem was constructed and typified. The chapters are grouped around four themes: claims, claimsmakers, connections, and policies.

A careful reading of these chapters may raise some additional questions about constructionism as an approach to studying social problems. While each chapter concerns claimsmaking, the authors adopt somewhat different stances; they begin with different assumptions, rely on different sorts of evidence, and draw different conclusions. This reflects the diversity—and debate—among constructionists. Those sociologists who consider themselves constructionists agree about the limitations of the objectivist approach to social problems, but they disagree about just what the constructionist approach should be. The debate over the nature of constructionism is explored in this book's afterword.

NOTES

1. To be fair, Bassis, Gelles, and Levine (1982:451–453) have a brief section on preventive health care that alludes to the benefits of an improved diet.

2. Criticism of objectivist definitions of social problems is not new; Spector and Kitsuse (1977) trace the history of this debate. Other works that have influenced recent subjectivist research include Blumer (1971), Gusfield (1981), and Holstein and Miller (1993).

3. When sociologists speak of "social construction," they draw attention to the processes by which people assign meaning to the world. All the things we know are socially constructed. The term gained wide currency following the publication of Berger and Luckmann's *The Social Construction of Reality* (1966).

4. This does not mean that constructionists are unconcerned about the social conditions that people call social problems. As citizens, they may have deep personal concerns about particular issues, and, as sociologists, they may sometimes study objective social conditions. However, when they study the social construction of social problems, their attention shifts away from the conditions themselves, focusing instead on the claimsmaking about those conditions.

5. In other words, constructionist theory tends to be inductive. The analyst compares several cases and develops general theoretical principles based on those comparisons. For a detailed discussion of the logic involved, see Glaser and Strauss (1967).

REFERENCES

Bassis, M. S., R. J. Gelles, and A. Levine. 1982. *Social Problems*. New York: Harcourt, Brace Jovanovich.

Berger, P. L., and T. Luckmann. 1966. *The Social Construction of Reality*. Garden City, NY: Doubleday.

Blumer, H. 1971. "Social Problems as Collective Behavior." *Social Problems* 18:298–306.

Farley, J. E. 1987. *American Social Problems*. Englewood Cliffs, NJ: Prentice-Hall.

Glaser, B. G., and A. L. Strauss. 1967. *The Discovery of Grounded Theory*. Chicago: Aldine.

Gusfield, J. R. 1981. *The Culture of Public Problems: Drinking-Driving and the Symbolic Order*. Chicago: University of Chicago Press.

Holstein, J., and G. Miller (eds.). 1993. *Reconsidering Social Constructionism*. Hawthorne, NY: Aldine de Gruyter.

Pfohl, S. J. 1977. "The 'Discovery' of Child Abuse." *Social Problems* 24:310–323.

Spector, M., and J. I. Kitsuse. 1977. *Constructing Social Problems*. Menlo Park, CA: Cummings.

PART I

Claims

Claimsmaking is an act of communication. Claimsmakers address different audiences: Some hope to identify and organize the people directly harmed by the conditions described in their claims; others try to educate the general public; and still others approach the policymakers who can do something about the conditions. While some meet their audiences face-to-face, many contemporary claimsmakers use the mass media to reach their audiences. If the press can be convinced that their claims are newsworthy, the media will help spread their message.

Whatever the audience and however claimsmakers approach them, claimsmaking attempts to persuade. Claimsmakers want to convince others that X is a social problem or that Y offers the solution. Claimsmakers' success depends partly upon whether their claims persuade their audiences. In other words, claimsmaking is a rhetorical activity, and we can use rhetoric—the study of persuasion—to analyze claims (Best 1987). Several chapters in this book examine the content of claims and how claimsmaking rhetoric typifies social problems.

Claims often begin with dramatic examples. This is particularly true when the press presents claims. Consider the opening paragraphs in a front page *Los Angeles Times* story about a gang intervention program:

> Everything about him said it was no big deal: How he kicked back in his chair. How he tossed his blue gang-rag on the table in the interrogation room. Threatening to kill a woman—so what?
>
> The woman was a sixth-grade teacher. The suspect, the case-hardened veteran sitting across from Detective Jeffrey Greer, was 11 years old.
>
> "I thought that was, like, the worst," Greer remembered thinking. (Morrison, 1988:I-1)

This is what journalists call "a grabber"; it is a conventional, but very effective, way to begin a story, particularly one describing a social problem. The example captures the reader's attention, it links the larger, abstract problem of gangs to a specific image—an unrepentant 11-year-old. Note that the reporter does not claim that this is a typical case; in fact, the story suggests that it may be "the worst." Beginning with a dramatic example is a standard technique in newsmagazine cover stories, television news feature stories, and newspaper articles. Because we encounter them first, and because they are vivid, these examples play an important role in typifying social problems. Examples shape our sense of just what is the problem, of what needs to be done about it. In Chapter 2, John M. Johnson describes the role played by dramatic examples—what he calls horror stories—in the construction of the child abuse problem.

Claimsmakers choose typifying examples because they illustrate particular features of social problems. There are always alternative ways to typify social problems, but those alternatives are not always apparent unless an issue is contentious. When there is open debate about a social problem, rival claimsmakers may offer competing—often very different—typifying examples. For instance, advocates of expanded programs for the homeless might plead for sympathy for homeless children whose parents cannot find work; in contrast, critics of such programs might point to a homeless alcoholic, arguing that society should not be responsible for housing someone who continues to drink. But, for many claimsmakers, indifference is a greater obstacle than opposition. Audiences ignore many claims until claimsmakers develop a rhetorically powerful way of typifying the problem. But these alternative typifications are not always obvious until they evolve. For example, in Chapter 3, Kathleen Lowney and Joel Best trace the recent history of claims about stalking. They show that early typifications of this problem attracted little attention, and that stalking had to be redefined and retypified before it achieved widespread recognition as a social problem.

In our society, it has become common to use a medical model to typify social problems. Medicalization refers to the process of defining issues as medical matters: a problem is a "disease," that displays "symptoms," that must be "diagnosed" by medical professionals, who apply appropriate "treatments," in hopes of "curing" the condition (Conrad and Schneider 1992). During the twentieth century, such medical language, originally applied to measles, smallpox, and other disorders of the body, was applied increasingly to troubling behavior. Thus, psychiatrists and other medical authorities claimed that a wide range of behaviors, including criminality, sexual deviance, eating disorders, and poor school performance, needed to be recognized as medical problems. While not all of medicalized claims achieved complete acceptance, the notion that some behaviors might be "sick" and evidence of a "disease" became widespread. In Chapter 4, Lynn M. Appleton suggests such medicalization extends beyond the claims made by medical professionals. The use of medical language to describe problem drinking—that is, claims about "the disease of alcoholism"—has become routine, even though physicians pay little attention to and make few claims about alcoholism. Appleton explains this apparent contradiction by suggesting that sociologists define medicine too narrowly.

The doctor struggling against disease is just one way to characterize social problems, but most social problems claims draw upon equally familiar cultural imagery. Chapter 5, by Shan Nelson-Rowe, points to another popular typifying model—melodrama. Melodramatic claims typify social problems in terms of victims who are exploited by villains and who must be rescued by heroes. The melodramatic model is perhaps most often applied to crime problems, but Nelson-Rowe shows that it has other applications. He argues that the campaign to promote multiculturalism in education routinely uses melodramatic rhetoric to typify educational issues.

REFERENCES

Best, J. 1987. "Rhetoric in Claims-Making." *Social Problems* 34:101–121.

Conrad, P., and J.W. Schneider. 1992. *Deviance and Medicalization.* Expanded edition. Philadelphia: Temple University Press.

Morrison, P. 1988. "Ounce of Prevention Vs. Weight of Gang Influence." *Los Angeles Times* (May 29): I-1, 25–26.

2

Horror Stories and the Construction of Child Abuse

JOHN M. JOHNSON

Everyone recognizes that the mass media's power extends beyond the mere transmittal of information. Their power (and some of their mystery) also derives from their ability to elicit emotions. Eliciting emotions often paves the way for action. We recognize the importance of this process at a common-sense level. The Civil Rights Movement of the 1960s, for example, gained much support and momentum from the publication of emotionally provocative photographs and accounts of the brutalities at Selma and Montgomery, Alabama. Press coverage helped shape public action, leading to subsequent civil rights reforms. The Vietnam War—"the first mass media war"—offers another good example. The pervasive newspaper stories and television accounts of daily battle scenes were important influences at all stages of the war, for both its supporters and detractors. More recently, press coverage of the rioting in South Africa is seen as an important influence on U.S. policy.

Sociologists recognize the relevance and importance of emotionally provocative mass media accounts for creating new social problems. Sensationalized mass coverage often is an important aspect of social problems claimsmaking (Spector and Kitsuse 1977). Examples include the construction of "crime waves" (Fishman 1978), various problems of juvenile justice (Bortner 1984; Cavender 1981; Zatz 1985), foreign policy (Altheide 1985), corporate homicide (Swigert and Farrell 1980), and missing children (Best 1987), among others. This chapter analyzes mass media's use of child abuse horror stories, emotionally provocative stories about violence to children. Such horror stories have played an important role in the political, social, and institutional success of the child maltreatment movement in the United States.

THE EMERGENCE OF CHILD ABUSE AS A SOCIAL PROBLEM

Child battering, child abuse, and child neglect (now commonly sub-sumed under the term *child maltreatment*) are relatively new terms, even though injuries and fatalities to children are as old as recorded history. Dr. S. West published the first medical documentation of systematic, intentional injuries to children in 1888 (Solomon 1973:774). Researchers continued reporting important information about nonaccidental child-hood traumas to the medical professions long before child abuse emerged as a social problem and political issue in the early 1960s (Caffey 1946; Wooley and Evans 1955).

In 1962, the research team headed by Dr. C. Henry Kempe and Dr. Ray Helfer published their now-famous article on "The Battered-Child Syndrome" in the *Journal of the American Medical Association*. This study, published in the medical profession's most prestigious and respected journal, was accompanied by an official editorial asserting the serious-ness of this new medical problem. The characteristic features of the syndrome included traumatic injuries to the head and long bones, com-monly done to children under 3 years of age by parents who were themselves beaten or abused as children. The parents commonly denied mistreatment of their children. The publication of this research article was an important step in legitimizing this problem as one demanding medical intervention.

The first state laws specifically formulated for child abuse intervention were passed in 1963; between 1963 and 1967, 47 of the 50 states passed some form of child abuse and/or neglect legislation (deFrancis 1963, 1967). The American Humane Association (AHA) and several profes-sional social work organizations provided expert testimony and played other active roles in advocating legislative initiative (deFrancis 1970). Technological advances, as well as certain features of pediatric radiology as an occupational specialty, played important roles in these early efforts to establish the child abuse and neglect movement (Pfohl 1977). These developments have increased significantly the number of officially rec-ognized and classified child abuse and neglect cases (Johnson 1986). In 1963, a study commissioned by the AHA could document only 662 cases of nonaccidental trauma to children for the entire United States but, by 1980, nearly 700,000 cases achieved official recognition and status.

Child abuse began as a relatively esoteric concern of a few medical researchers. But the dramatic article on "The Battered-Child Syndrome" by Kempe et al. (1962) attracted the mass media's attention. Barbara Nelson (1984:65–75) argues that professional and mass media publica-tions offered complementary coverage, which was critical to the early agenda-setting and political successes of the social movement. Initially, the emphasis was on physical abuse or "battering," but as the movement achieved legitimacy, the scope of both media and movement concern expanded to other areas, including child neglect, emotional abuse, and, eventually, incest and sexual abuse of children (Johnson 1986, 1987). The publication of child abuse horror stories has played a prominent role in the social, political, and institutional successes of the child maltreatment movement during the last 25 years. These horror stories are mass media reports of individual cases that involve dramatic or unusual injuries to children and that evoke an emotional response about the problem of child abuse or neglect. This chapter analyzes the formal properties of child abuse horror stories and the role they have played in the emergence and definition of this social problem.

NATURE OF THE RESEARCH

This chapter derives from a larger study of all newspaper stories on child abuse and neglect that appeared for 32 years in the *Arizona Republic* and the *Phoenix Gazette*, the two major newspapers in Arizona. The earliest newspaper files on these topics begin in 1948 under the headings cruelty to children, family problems, domestic disturbance, as well as various conventional criminal classifications involving victimized children. Arizona was not one of the 47 states to pass child abuse legislation in the early 1963–1965 period. Arizona passed its first laws in August 1970; they became effective at the beginning of 1971. After the 1970 legislative action, state news organizations began keeping files labeled "child abuse" and "child neglect," as both phenomena were defined in the early legislation. I examined news stories from 1948 to 1980 to study the relations between mass media reporting and legislative action, the role of local versus national wireservice reporting, and the stories' substance (Johnson 1981, 1982). In addition, I collected clippings from many other newspapers, magazines, and other media over a period of more than 10 years.

During 1948–1980, a total of 623 news stories about child abuse and neglect appeared in the Phoenix newspapers. There were 93 stories during 1948–1969, an average of slightly more than 4 per year. Arizona's first child abuse law passed in 1970, producing a 10-fold increase in the news stories about this topic (*N*-40). Between 1971 and 1980, the papers published an additional 490 stories concerning all aspects of child battering, abuse, neglect, and maltreatment, averaging almost 50 per year.

Much of this coverage featured child abuse horror stories. Of the 93 stories published during 1948–1969, 88 (95%) presented facts about an

individual case of childhood injury. Most of these were dramatic, horrific stories. While the proportion of child abuse horror stories fell after
1970, they remain the dominant form of newspaper report. Of the 623
stories published during 1948–1980, 436 (70%) placed primary emphasis
on reporting the facts of an individual case. Local (Arizona) stories ac-
counted for 350 (80%) horror stories; the remaining 86 (20%) stories
came from the AP and UPI national wireservices.

To better understand the nature of these horror stories, I conducted
an ethnographic content analysis (Altheide 1986), which is a method of
analyzing documentary evidence, based on the observer's or analyst's
insider understanding about a setting or phenomena (see Johnson 1975).
In this case, I analyzed the mass media reports on child abuse to identify
the formal properties of child abuse horror stories. Formal properties are
those analytical features of the newsreporting format that define it as a
type. The content analysis of child abuse horror stories reveals five
distinct properties of the form: (1) evocation of negative emotionality,
which is accomplished by the development of either (a) ironic contrast,
or (b) structural incongruity, (2) disembodiment of interaction, (3) decontextualization, (4) use of official sources, and (5) individualization of
causal agency.

FORMAL PROPERTIES OF CHILD ABUSE HORROR STORIES

Evoking Negative Emotionality

Ideally, parents love and protect children. Families are the source of
intimacy and selfhood, and, even though parents have more power than
their children, parents presumably use this power in the child's best
interests. Family experience is, for most people, largely favorable and
rewarding. For some, it is not, but few view their family experience with
emotional neutrality. Thus, stories about violence within the family
have a great potential to elicit an emotional response from their
audience.

Mass media accounts of domestic violence play upon our common
family experience, whether actual or desired, to elicit emotions. The
term *child abuse horror story* obviously suggests that such stories evoke
feelings of horror, but I use the concept more broadly, referring to stories that elicit strong negative feelings. Whether the specific feelings
evoked are horror, shock, revulsion, sadness, anger, tragedy, or some
other is less important than the fact that the feelings are strong ones for
most individuals. Stories about horrible injuries or gruesome circumstances may produce emotional reaction:

The Baltimore Police found Patty Saunders, 9, in the 23 × 52 inch closet where she had been locked for half her life. She weighed only 20 pounds, and stood less than three feet tall. Smeared with filth, scarred from parental beatings, Patty had become irreparably mentally retarded. (*Newsweek*, October 10, 1977:31)

The preceding story evokes negative feelings, not only by portraying inhuman treatment, but by specifying the terrible, life-long consequences. Another example:

Alyssa Dawn Wilson died at the age of six weeks in a Beauford, South Carolina clinic. An autopsy disclosed that the infant had a ruptured liver and spleen and eye injuries, a fractured knee, 14 broken ribs, bite marks on her cheeks, bruises on her stomach and back and alcohol in her bloodstream. Her father was arrested for murder. (*Newsweek*, October 10, 1977:32)

In both examples, the injuries are such that the reader can clearly see that they could not have been either unintentional or accidental. At a commonsense level, we impute moral responsibility or culpability for intentional or willful injuries. We commonly do not hold people blameworthy if it can be shown that their actions were unintentional or accidental. But only the foolhardy could believe that the injuries in these examples could have resulted "from an accident." It is the fact that they are intentionally inflicted, rather than their consequences, that makes these injuries so horrifying. Barbara Nelson (1984:65–73) observes that one of the ironies of press coverage of child abuse cases is that severe injuries often make "better news copy" than more dramatic acts that result in death, because severe injuries permit a longer follow-up by other reporters and, hence, additional stories. A child's death often precludes such extended coverage.

Negative emotions may be aroused by detailing the gruesome facts of the injury, or the consequences of the abuse, or even the circumstances surrounding the investigation:

The body of a missing two-month-old boy was found in a pile of rubble Tuesday, hours after the infant's parents were charged in connection with his death. The Marion couple earlier told police that their son was abducted while they completed last minute Christmas shopping. The nude body was found under some dirt, leaves, and cement in the foundation of a torn down house, about four blocks from the parents' home. "The location was given to us by the father," said Detective Larry Connors. Thus far, police do not know if the death was the result of child abuse that went too far, or the result of a deliberate slaying. (*Fort Wayne Journal Gazette*, December 27, 1978:3)

Child abuse horror stories use two journalistic conventions to elicit an emotional response from the reader: ironic contrast and structural incongruity. They are related and similar in some respects, but nevertheless distinct. The press prefers certain kinds of stories because they allow for a better display of the intrinsic properties of the medium. Newspaper reporters have a strong preference for "man bites dog" stories, for example, because the print medium and the linear display allow for a greater exploitation of ironic contrast. "Man bites dog" is a phrase that epitomizes ironic contrast. The phrase creates the image of man, often the unwitting victim of a dog's attack, uncharacteristically turning on the animal alleged to be man's best friend. Presenting the story in print maximizes its ironic possibilities.

Consider the ironic contrast in a 1981 story about Arizona's leading medical expert on virtually all forms of child abuse and neglect. Dr. Larry C. Rork, the 1979 winner of local awards for his expertise and service related to child abuse, was subsequently accused of multiple acts of child abuse and sexual molestation by three boys confined at Camelback Hospital. Even though subsequent investigations completely exonerated Dr. Rork, he committed suicide before the investigation's completion (see Johnson 1988). The juxtaposition of Rork's expertise and the charges against him provides the story's irony.

Another story, from the *Kansas City Star* for Tuesday, August 9, 1977, concerns Herbert Smith, Jr., who faced 5 years to life in prison for the fatal beating of his stepdaughter, whose death he tried to prevent through a law suit. Smith, 31, from Wichita, pleaded no contest to a charge of second-degree murder. His daughter fell into a coma, and Smith filed a civil suit to prevent doctors and the child's mother from unhooking the child's respirator. Smith claimed in the suit that he could face more serious charges if the machine were unhooked. The injunction was denied, and the respirator was unhooked. In this case, the irony comes from the fact that the person responsible for the injuries became the litigant to "save the child's life."

Structural incongruity need not involve a formal irony, but it usually does include some feature that strikes the reader as bizarre, strange, unusual, or "out of place." One well-known example is the now infamous case of the 1984 arrest of the grandmotherly (and 77-year-old) Virginia McMartin, founder and director of the McMartin Preschool in Manhattan Beach, California. Along with six relatives and co-workers, she was charged with nearly 300 counts of sexual abuse and molestation of the children in their care. A second example:

A nine-year-old girl was sexually molested by her father and uncle, an aunt and her brother's boyfriend over a seven year period without any of the suspects knowing the others were involved. Each suspect had been questioned separately, and then released into the lobby of the police station in this St. Louis suburb. "You should have seen the look on their faces," said Detective Don Gultz. It was "You too?!" The four adults were charged with 53 felony counts. (Overland, Missouri, United Press International, August 16, 1985)

The "shocking" details in such stories elicit negative emotions from readers.

Disembodiment of Interaction

Mass media reports of child abuse never report the interactional sequences leading to abuse. The "facts" of a story are presented as if they "speak for themselves," and reporters make no attempt to give the participant's perspective. This reporting strategy works because reports of statistically rare dramatic injuries or "horror stories" receive disproportionate attention. The typical case of child abuse is not very dramatic: a nonserious injury to a child under 3, committed by a young person (usually the mother), who is under much stress while having few resources to manage the exigent circumstances, and so on. Such cases— *the overwhelming majority of child abuse*—usually are not seen as "good news stories" by the press. Mass media reports disproportionately present the more dramatic cases, with the assumption that "the facts speak for themselves."

> A 40-year-old man has been charged with assaulting his 15-year-old daughter by hanging her upside down by her toes and then beating her. (*Arizona Republic*, March 18, 1979:22)
>
> A Tucson woman, convicted of dumping her four-year-old daughter into a tub of scalding water for telling a lie, was sentenced to three years in prison. (*Arizona Republic*, March 9, 1978:11)

These stories reflect a common journalistic convention: beginning a story with a shocking or provocative "grabber." A typical grabber presents dramatic details of a specific individual case, intended to grab and retain the reader's attention for the rest of the story. Beginning a story with a "grabber" reflects journalists' "recipe knowledge" used to manufacture news. In the preceding examples, it seems evident that the abuse could not have been "reasonable," so there is no attempt to place the action described within an interactional or social sequence, no attempt to tell the story from the various participants' points of view, no attempt to place the account into some intelligible, comprehensible context. In this way, abuse is typified as irrational and incomprehensible.

Decontextualization

News reports rip child abuse situations out of their social context. There are some good, understandable reasons for this. First, child abuse almost always occurs within the privacy of the home and is rarely witnessed by outsiders or third parties. So reports invariably reach outside agencies, whether police, social service, or mass media, after the fact. Second, newsworkers place great reliance on institutionalized news sources as their primary source of information on many stories (Altheide 1976, 1985; Gans 1979; Tuchman 1978). This makes the original social context of a child abuse incident extremely difficult to recapture, even if reporters were motivated to do so.

> Dianne Devanne, age 11, had a lot to look forward to; high school, perhaps college and a career or raising a family. But she never got the chance. Police say she was beaten to death by her father and stepmother. A rare case? Hardly. In nearly every state, laws are very loose, accurate models are scarce, and society is restive when faced with terminating parental rights. Dianne Devanne returned home in August to Braintree, Massachusetts, after two years of living in foster homes and institutions. Everyday for two weeks prior to her death, she was beaten for such acts as spilling the salt or not doing the dishes quickly enough. The beatings increased to one an hour on the last day of her life. Her father, claiming she had fallen down the stairs, took her to the local hospital where she was pronounced dead from a blow to the head. A blood clot lodged in her brain. The following day, Dianne's father and stepmother were charged with murder. (*Los Angeles Times*, December 3, 1978:34)

This account displays a common reporting strategy for child abuse horror stories, that is, to describe injuries that could not be "reasonable" by any standard. If there is a counterclaim to the allegations (e.g., Mr. Devanne's claim that she had fallen down stairs), it can be easily neutralized or discredited, usually with a reference to some official source of information (e.g., the hospital's judgment that Dianne died from a blow to the head). This leads to the next property of child abuse horror stories, the reliance on and use of official sources of information.

Reliance on Official Sources

For stories on child abuse, newspapers and television news rely on official sources of information, including police, prosecutors, social welfare departments, hospitals, school officials, and so on. Official sources play prominent roles in many other kinds of stories (Altheide 1976, 1985; Gans 1979; Altheide and Johnson 1980; Tuchman 1978; Gitlin 1980). The reasons for relying on official sources are clear; official sources can help solve a daily practical problem of newsworkers: the need to generate enough material to fill a paper or news program. But, for stories on child abuse, there is another reason for relying on official sources: It is the official intervention and assessment of the actor's intent that *defines a particular act as abusive or neglectful*. For this reason, it would be implausible (if not impossible) for newsworkers to define some parental act as abusive or neglectful independent of an official assessment of the actor's behavior. News accounts of child abuse invariably rely on official sources of information, and they take the official perspective toward the act being reported. The following story is interesting because it shows the use of four official sources in writing the story (police, social services, courts, and official criminal records):

> Allen Madden was pummeled for perhaps four hours before he died, at times with fists, at times with a wooden club wrapped with gauze and labeled "The Big Stick." He was five years old. Police found his frail body on the living room floor, his blond hair red with blood, his hands bruised from trying to deflect the blows. "Probably, he did something an average little kid does, write on the wall or something. That's all it takes," said a former social worker who had urged that the shy kindgartner not be returned to home because she feared "there's going to be a dead kid." Allen died January 10. His mother and boyfriend are charged with murder. Allen's mother, Pam Berg, quit high school, married a sometime factory worker, Gerald Madden. . . . The Madden marriage ended shortly after Allen was born, each parent accusing the other in court of beating the children. (Quincy, Illinois, Associated Press, January 22, 1979:1)

This is not an example of the routine, ordinary child abuse case that crosses the desk of the average Child Protective Services worker who investigates such matters or that constitutes the overwhelming statistical majority of abuse cases. Most child abuse cases do not involve serious injuries. Few produce death. Few perpetrators have prior criminal records. Few such allegations result in some kind of court proceeding (about 10% nationally). The routine child abuse case does not make very good "copy" for news reporting. What makes good copy is a more dramatic case, such as the example here, and when these are reported on, official sources provide the newsworthy facts, and newsworkers invariably adopt the official perspective in presenting them.

Front line reporters at the local level tend to be young and, unlike seasoned news veterans, unreflective about adopting the official or bureaucratic view about some problem. It often takes years to learn about the deeper realities and meanings of some event or phenomenon, to recognize the hidden organizational interests that lie behind some rational, scientistic rhetoric. This is true in the child abuse field; many local news reporters are seduced by the bureaucratic reporting of a horrific story and rush to news judgment without realizing how the dissemination of these unrepresentative stories promotes vested bureaucratic, agency, or political interests. That two *Denver Post* reporters would win a Pulitzer Prize for exposing the myths and hidden promotive interests in the "missing children" issue is one small indication that the unexamined assumptions of the mass media are changing.

Individualization of Causal Agent

Most reporters and editors have been formally educated; they know the myths and some of the realities of domestic violence. Commonly held beliefs include the following: Abused children grow up to abuse their own children; unemployment places great stresses upon the unemployed individual and the family; drinking problems and alcoholism are frequently involved in domestic disputes; arguments over money and other practical matters are commonplace and frequently severe, etc. Nevertheless, when confronted with the prospect of interpreting the facts of an individual case, reporters rarely refer to such factors. It is much easier to sustain a complicated, mixed sense of social responsibility for other acts, including certain war crimes, employee theft, certain forms of organizational deviance, and some forms of "sexual deviance" (or sexual preference). Despite the fact that virtually all of us have some familial experience, the mass media accounts promote the idea that individuals bear total, absolute responsibility. Whatever the stressful conditions or circumstances that confront the individual, the press treats that individual as responsible for what occurs. Consider the following account:

> "Filth of just about any kind of description" throughout a Huron Street house prompted City County Health officials to charge a woman Thursday morning with neglect of a dependent child. It was the second time this year that Westerman was charged with neglect of the children. Allen Family Relations Court suspended a one-year sentence August 20 after a March 8 arrest because of similar conditions in the two-story house, Holly said. Neglect of a dependent is a felony. Health officials said they found the house filled with rubbish, garbage and excrement. Holly explained that he and Bonnie Rafert, a health inspector, went to the residence Thursday morning with a Board of Works crew to clear rubbish and garbage from the yard. The Health Department has received numerous complaints about the yard, he said. Westerman has been charged at least seven times since 1974 because the condition of the yard violated city ordinances. While Rafert was supervising the removal of the rubbish-filled van from the property, Westerman swung a bat at her, causing a door of the van to

slam in front of her, Holly said. When Holly attempted to arrest her, she ran into the house. Holly said he called the police for assistance. When he and the officers entered the house to make an arrest, the cluttered condition was evident. (*Fort Wayne Journal Gazette*, September 21, 1979:B1,2)

From this account, it seems reasonable to think that Westerman is economically poor (apparently not even having a first name!), having lived in the same residence for at least 5 years, but with few material resources for home repairs or other improvements, having interpersonal skills and a lifestyle that are at variance with middle-class standards and/or the official expectations of police, social workers, health inspectors, etc. And yet, the reporter seems to assume that official suspicions warrant the label "felony," and there is no attempt to assess the relationship between Westerman's material circumstances and their consequences on parental supervision. Whatever these circumstances might be, they apparently do not mitigate the absolute responsibility for maintaining a clean yard. Consider the following story. It asserts that the mother's knowledge was an intentional, willful knowledge, even though the grounds for this judgment are not spelled out to the reader. It concerns the story of a 20-year-old mother charged with neglect of a dependent child in connection with the July 7, 1979 death of her infant, Christopher Swenson, aged 2.

"Mindy Swenson was well aware that Christopher was being mistreated by Timothy Carpenter," the Allen Superior Court affidavit said. Carpenter was charged with murder, an habitual offense in the case, and lived with the mother and the child for several months prior to the death. The mother was booked at the City County lockup Wednesday and is being held at the Allen County Jail under $2,000 bond. She had been staying at the home of Carpenter's foster father in rural Auburn, Indiana. (*Fort Wayne Gazette*, July 10, 1979)

There is a general view about child abuse and neglect that pervades all of the mass media accounts. This view holds that child abuse and/or neglect is an entirely individualistic phenomenon, an act for which an individual is solely responsible. Rarely do stories refer to the wide range of stresses that can influence individuals, including such factors as absent partners, alcoholism, unemployment, financial difficulties, drug problems, stigmatization from prior arrests and/or prison records, poor occupational or school preparation, and a wide range of social–psychological difficulties. Even when such factors are cited or alluded to in mass media reports, they are not seen as mitigating personal responsibility. Society and its institutions are not seen as causal agents in producing child abuse and neglect; rather, the press takes the view that society and its institutions represent functional responses to the problem tending to control it. This is, of course, in keeping with larger trends involving the individualization and medicalization of a wide range of social problems (Newberger and Bourne 1979; Conrad and Schneider 1980).

THE ROLE OF HORROR STORIES IN THE CONSTRUCTION OF CHILD ABUSE AS A SOCIAL PROBLEM

Publishing child abuse horror stories serves a wide range of uses. One of the most obvious is that it fits the organizational needs and interests of news organizations. Barbara Nelson (1984) notes that child abuse stories have a great human interest potential, and that human interest stories have become increasingly important to the organizational needs and interests of mass media:

> The reporting of child abuse follows a fairly consistent pattern in which unwholesomely criminal cases where the child survives are preferred to what might be considered the more serious, but somehow more routine cases where the child dies. The titillation of bizarre brutality accounts, in part, for this pattern, but other factors also contribute to the newspapers' preference for this type of story. Part of this preference can be traced to the organizational needs of newspapers. From the perspective of news managers, more information unfolds in a case of brutality than in one where the child victim dies. This fact, in itself, sustains coverage. (Nelson 1984:71)

More than just news organizations are involved. The publication of child abuse stories also helps many professional and occupational groups, social science and medical researchers, and various private and nonprofit agencies. These agencies establish agendas for the child abuse movement. They are invariably tied to requests for more resources and more public funds. The crowning achievement of this political effort would have to be the passage of "The Mondale Bill," in 1974, which established the National Center for the Treatment and Prevention of Child Abuse and Neglect and infused $80,000,000 into child abuse programs during the ensuing 3-year period (see Hoffman 1979).

It would be a mistake to see child abuse as merely a creation of the media. News organizations played a creative role in the process; some would argue a major role. But, just as important, news organizations *responded* to a sense of urgency created by other groups, agencies, and sectors of the public. The press occasionally stimulated government action and legislative initiative, sometimes on their own, but more commonly at the bidding of other parties. Either way, the mass media reports of child abuse and neglect seem to have played a strong role in legitimizing this problem, serving at all phases to present the official conception and definition of child abuse, as well as promoting existing or planned official interventions, policies, programs, and budgetary requests. It is easy to see that the mass media perspective on child abuse is that promulgated by official agencies and their professional supporters. Insofar as the press criticizes official definitions or agencies, its criticism is coupled to the plea that officials do not have the resources they need to do a better job.

It is very important to understand that there is a larger cultural and historical context within which child abuse horror stories have appeared. Many of our contemporary social welfare and criminal justice institutions originated in the Progressive Era of the 1880s to the 1920s, a time of great optimism for institutional solutions to social problems. Today, we seem to have entered a New Progressive Era, characterized by significant cultural optimism about the capabilities of the welfare state to resolve social problems. The mass media organizations that have disseminated child abuse horror stories have, in addition, published many stories on incest, sexual abuse of children, child prostitution, drugs, crime of all sorts, pornography, drunk driving, etc. Such coverage has proliferated to such an extent that psychologist Robert J. Lifton has coined the term "psychological numbing" to refer to the feeling of being overwhelmed or inundated by such problems, even to the point of apathy or cynicism on the part of many citizens.

Educated persons who follow press coverage will feel the "psychological numbing" of which Lifton speaks, and so we will understand the existence of apathy and cynicism. Such feelings, however understandable, are transitory and situational for most people and do not reflect the kind of long range commitment to solving social problems that readers of a book such as this are likely to share. For us, it is important to have a realistic and informed basis of knowledge about modern mass media, definitions of social problems, and welfare state operations to make the best choices we can for a better future.

ACKNOWLEDGMENTS

I would like to express my gratitude and indebtedness to Diana Bohon-Bustamente who assisted with some of the data collection for this research and to John W. Johnson who has, over a period of many years, supplemented my own data collection by clipping newspaper stories on child abuse and neglect from midwestern newspapers. I am also grateful to the following individuals for commenting on earlier drafts of this chapter: Patti Adler, Peter Adler, David

Altheide, Gray Cavender, Mike Dornan, Jaber Gubrium, John Hepburn, Paul Higgins, Nancy Jurik, Pat Lauderdale, Robert Snow, and Carol Warren.

REFERENCES

Altheide, D. L. 1976. *Creating Reality*. Beverly Hills: Sage.
———. 1985. *Media Power*. Beverly Hills: Sage.
———. 1986. "Ethnographic Content Analysis." *Qualitative Sociology* 9 (Summer):55–72.
Altheide, D. L., and J. M. Johnson. 1980. *Bureaucratic Propaganda*. Boston: Allyn and Bacon.
Best, J. 1987. "Rhetoric in Claims-Making: Constructing the Missing Children Problem." *Social Problems* 34:101–121.
Bortner, M.A. 1984. "Media Images and Public Attitudes Toward Crime and Justice." Pp. 15–30 in *Justice and the Media: Issues and Research*, edited by R. Surette. Springfield, IL: Thomas.
Caffey, J. 1946. "Multiple Fractures in the Long Bones of Infants Suffering from Chronic Subdural Hematoma." *American Journal of Roentgenology* 56:163–173.
Cavender, G. 1981. "Scared Straight: Ideology and the Media." *Journal of Criminal Justice* 9(6):431–439.
Conrad, P., and J. W. Schneider. 1980. *Deviance and Medicalization*. St. Louis: Mosby.
deFrancis, V. 1963. "Parents Who Abuse Children." *PTA Magazine* 58 (November):16–18.
———. 1967. "Child Abuse—The Legislative Response." *Denver Law Journal* 44:3–41.
———. 1970. *Child Abuse Legislation in the 1970s*. Denver, CO: American Humane Association.
Fishman, M. 1978. "Crime Waves as Ideology." *Social Problems* 25:531–543.
Gans, H. J. 1979. *Deciding What's News*. New York: Pantheon.
Gitlin, T. 1980. *The Whole World Is Watching*. Berkeley: University of California Press.
Hoffman, E. 1979. "Policy and Politics: The Child Abuse Prevention and Treatment Act." Pp. 157–170 in *Critical Perspectives on Child Abuse*, edited by R. Bourne and E. Newberger. Lexington, MA: Lexington Books.
Johnson, J. M. 1975. *Doing Field Research*. New York: Free Press.
———. 1981. "Program Enterprise and Official Cooptation in the Battered Women's Shelter Movement." *American Behavioral Scientist* 24:827–842.
———. 1982. "Mass Media Reporting of Child Abuse." Unpublished paper.
———. 1986. "Symbolic Salvation." *Studies in Symbolic Interaction*, 6:289–305.
———. 1987. "The Changing Concept of Child Abuse and its Impact on Family Life." Pp. 257–275 in *The American Family and the State*, edited by J. R. Peden and F. R. Glahe. San Francisco: Pacific Research Institute for Public Policy.
———. 1988. "Media Manslaughter." *Studies in Symbolic Interaction* 9:255–264.

Kempe, C. H., F. N. Silverman, B. F. Stelle, W. Droegemuller, and H. K. Silver. 1962. "The Battered-Child Syndrome." *Journal of the American Medical Association* 181:17–24.

Nelson, B. J. 1984. *Making an Issue of Child Abuse*. Chicago: University of Chicago Press.

Newberger, E. H., and R. Bourne. 1979. "The Medicalization and Legalization of Child Abuse." Pp. 139–156 in *Critical Perspectives on Child Abuse*, edited by R. Bourne and E. H. Newberger. Lexington, MA: Lexington Books.

Pfohl, S. J. 1977. "The Discovery of Child Abuse," *Social Problems* 24:310–323.

Radbill, S. X. 1968. "A History of Child Abuse and Infanticide." Pp. 1–12 in *The Battered Child*, edited by R. E. Helfer and C. Henry Kempe. Chicago: University of Chicago Press.

Solomon, T. 1973. "History and Demography of Child Abuse." *Pediatrics* 51:773–776.

Spector, M., and J. I. Kitsuse. 1977. *Constructing Social Problems*. Menlo Park, CA: Cummings.

Swigert, V. L., and R. A. Farrell. 1980. "Corporate Homicide: Definitional Processes in the Creation of Deviance." *Law and Society Review* 15:161–182.

Tuchman, G. 1978. *Making News*. New York: Free Press.

Wooley, P. V., and W. A. Evans, Jr. 1955. "Significance of Skeletal Lesions in Infants Resembling Those of Traumatic Origin." *Journal of the American Medical Association* 158:539–543.

Zatz, M. S. 1985. "Los Cholos: Legal Processing of Chicano Gang Members." *Social Problems* 33:13–30.

3

Stalking Strangers and Lovers: Changing Media Typifications of a New Crime Problem

KATHLEEN S. LOWNEY and JOEL BEST

Like other social problems, crime problems are social constructions, brought to public attention through claimsmaking by activists, officials, or the press (Spector and Kitsuse 1977; Holstein and Miller 1993). Claims about a new crime usually characterize—or *typify*—the offender, the victim, and the crime itself. Claimsmakers describe offenders and victims as particular types of people—what Loseke (1993) calls person-categories. Thus, claimsmakers may argue that offenders or victims have distinctive motives, psychological profiles, or behavior patterns, or that they can be characterized in terms of gender, age, race, social class, or other background variables. Similarly, claimsmakers typify the timing, location, interaction patterns, and consequences of crimes. Claims thus define types of crime in terms of both their actors and the nature of the activity.

Studies of social problems construction usually examine successful claims, claims that attract media coverage, affect public opinion, and receive policymakers' attention. But successful claims are often the product of a prolonged, largely unsuccessful sequence of claimsmaking. Claimsmakers compete within a social problems marketplace (Best 1990; Hilgartner and Bosk 1988). There are always many claimsmakers trying to testify before Congress, attract press coverage, appear on talk shows, and otherwise bring their causes to the fore. Inevitably, many of these efforts fail, and claimsmakers struggle to develop rhetoric that will draw attention and lead to action. This often requires reframing or repackaging a problem, offering new typifications. Because constructionist research tends to focus on claims that succeed in the social problems marketplace, most analysts neglect the earlier phases of claimsmaking campaigns, when claimsmakers revise and alter their typifications. These

early phases may involve dissension and debate among claimsmakers promoting rival typifications and interpretations. Usually, claims that succeed
reflect a particular construction of the problem, which becomes seen as
authoritative, and those claimsmakers achieve "ownership" of the problem (Gusfield 1981). A successful typification is taken for granted by press,
public, policymakers—and all too often constructionist analysts—who
lose sight of the earlier, unsuccessful claims. This chapter extends constructionist analysis by exploring how earlier, unsuccessful typifications
evolved into the successful construction of stalking as a crime problem.

Stalking—"men and women who are repeatedly followed, harassed,
or physically threatened by other persons" (Gilligan 1992:285)—was recently and successfully constructed as a crime problem. California
passed the first antistalking law in 1990. Three years later, 48 states and
the District of Columbia had such laws, and several states were consid-
ering further legislation to expand or toughen their statutes. As one
legislator put it:

> Michigan and its sister States are creating a new crime. We are defining it,
> essentially, one unknown to the common law. We are making conduct
> illegal which has been legal up until now, and we are using the most
> serious proscription our society can devise, the deprivation of liberty,
> through a felony penalty. This is experimental legislation. (Perry Bullard
> in U.S. Senate 1992:64)

Claims that stalking was a large and growing problem led to hearings
before the U.S. Senate (1992, 1993); the National Institute of Justice (1993)
developed a Model Anti-Stalking Code for States. By late 1993, claims
about stalking had become familiar, and reports of strangers attacking
women (e.g., the kidnap/murder of Polly Klaas, or the assault on figure-
skater Nancy Kerrigan) often assumed that stalkers committed the crimes
(Toobin 1994; Ingrassia 1994). Less than 5 years after the term "stalking"
emerged, stalking had widespread recognition as a crime problem.

Print and electronic news reports are a principal source of information
about unfamiliar crime problems. The press helps construct new problems
by giving typifying examples, citing statistics, and quoting experts, thereby explaining what is at issue. Many constructionist studies examine
media claims. However, like most constructionist research, analyses of
claimsmaking in the media usually focus on successful claims. While some
studies note competing typifications, packages, or frames for controversial
(Gamson and Modigliani 1989) or weakly established (Best 1991) issues,
few researchers measure how media typifications change over time.

The media play various roles in social problems construction. Studies
of the construction of crime problems suggest that the press sometimes
serves as the primary claimsmaker, making the initial claims (e.g., claims-

making about urban violence [Brownstein 1991; Fishman 1978] and freeway violence [Best 1991]). Other problems emerge through secondary
press reports of claimsmaking by social activists (e.g., drunk driving
[Reinarman 1988], battering [Loseke 1992], and rape [Rose 1977]), professionals (e.g., child abuse [Pfohl 1977] and computer crimes [Hollinger
and Lanza-Kaduce 1988]), or criminal justice officials (e.g., serial murder
[Jenkins 1994]). Which claimsmakers play leading roles can affect a campaign's outcome. Because media attention is fleeting, crime problems
constructed by the press have a short spell in the spotlight (Best 1991).
For example, freeway violence received national coverage for less than a
month during 1987; when no other interest group adopted the issue and
continued to make claims about it, freeway violence faded from view.

Media coverage of stalking reveals a different pattern: various largely
unsuccessful typifications preceded the construction that finally gained
acceptance. The stalking problem came under public scrutiny after 1989,
through press coverage of sensational crimes involving celebrity victims
stalked by obsessed fans. However, for at least the previous decade,
there had been complaints about the very behaviors that would later
constitute the crime of stalking, although those claims neither evoked
great public concern nor led to antistalking laws. Moreover, stalking did
not vanish as a social issue because media attention shifted to other
issues. Rather, social activists, particularly in the victims' and battered
women's movements, assumed ownership of this new crime problem
and kept the issue alive by making fresh claims about stalking. Their
claims reconstructed the stalking problem, offering new characterizations of offenders, victims, and the crimes.

Following the discussion of our methods, we first describe early, unsuccessful claims about what would later be called stalking (1980–1988).
We next discuss the importance of celebrity victims during the emergence of the stalking problem (1989–1991), and then examine how the
definition of stalking changed as the press, legislators, and activists
began linking stalking to domestic violence (1992–1994). Our analysis
combines qualitative interpretation with quantitative data on changing
typifications of stalking. Finally, we explain how a new set of typifying
claims mobilized cultural and organizational resources, making possible
the successful construction of stalking as a new crime problem.

METHODS

We examined several dozen examples of claimsmaking about stalking,
including videotapes and transcripts of television news broadcasts and

talk shows; articles from newspapers, popular magazines, law reviews, and scholarly journals; and transcripts of Congressional proceedings. Although we could not examine everything written or broadcast about stalking, we searched several standard indexes for references to this crime problem, and we believe that our sources reflect the range of claims about the stalking problem.

These claims provide our analytic focus: rather than trying to assess the objective nature of stalking, we ask how claimsmakers depicted this crime problem. After collecting and examining claims about stalking, we sought to identify key elements in the typifications of offenders, victims, and the offense (e.g., whether the victim was a celebrity, the relationship between victim and offender prior to the stalking, whether the stalking led to homicide, and so on). As we identified key analytic dimensions, we systematically reexamined our collection of claims along those dimensions. By comparing individual claims with one another, we identified patterns and trends in our data, developing generalizations through this comparative process.

Our analysis includes quantitative data from stalking coverage in 24 U.S. popular magazine articles and 47 nationally televised news and information broadcasts between 1980 and June 1994. We chose these media for quantitative analysis because they reach national audiences and have reasonably thorough indexes. Magazine indexes (e.g., the *Reader's Guide to Periodical Literature*) are a staple source of constructionist data. Although there is no adequate single index of television programming, it has become possible to identify and retrieve broadcasts for news and information programming, ranging from the networks' evening news programs to talk shows. We located most of the magazine articles by searching the *Reader's Guide*, although our sample includes a few articles that appeared in magazines not indexed there. *Television News Index and Abstracts* indexes the evening network news broadcasts; Journal Graphics (a television transcript clearinghouse that began in 1981) listed many other television programs (e.g., talk shows, CNN broadcasts, and morning shows, and we also checked for transcripts of major talk shows (e.g., *Oprah*) not indexed by Journal Graphics. Since "stalking" did not become common parlance until after 1989, we searched the indexes under various headings, including crimes against women, following, harassment, and sexual harassment; of course, many of the stories indexed under these headings were not about stalking and are not included in our analysis. Our data do not provide a perfect measure of magazine and television coverage: we may have missed relevant stories that were not indexed or indexed under other headings; and the indexes' coverage changed over time (in particular, the number of programs indexed by Journal Graphics grew). Still, our analysis includes every relevant magazine story and television program we located. In each article or broadcast, we identified typifying examples (Best 1990)—cases used to illustrate the problem of stalking. All but one of the articles and broadcasts featured one or more examples. Some cases, usually involving victims who were either celebrities or active in the movement for antistalking laws, were described two to eight times. Since each description served as a typifying example in a different story or broadcast, we included each in the sample. The full sample contained 215 typifying examples.

BEFORE STALKING: OBSESSION AND PSYCHOLOGICAL RAPE, 1980–1988

Between 1980 and 1986, national magazines published seven articles describing women being followed or harassed with letters, telephone calls, or unwanted gifts. Some of the annoying behaviors continued for years; some women were physically assaulted. Any female could be a victim: although most of the victims knew their harassers as colleagues at work (Winter 1980), ex-husbands (Anonymous 1980), or ex-boyfriends (Mithers 1982), some of the men were strangers (Wilcox 1982).

The articles called these behaviors "a form of sexual harassment," "obsession," or "psychological rape" (Wilcox 1982; Mithers 1982). One psychiatrist, interviewed shortly after John Hinckley tried to assassinate President Reagan, said that psychological rape "has linked such celebrities as Jodie Foster and Caroline Kennedy to ordinary women who've found themselves pursued by men who claim to be in love with them" (Wilcox 1982:233).

The articles described the harassers, all males, as obsessive, compulsive, often passive in nature, with a limited range of sexual expression and low self-esteem (Heil 1986; Wilcox 1982). Many had "only protective feelings [toward their victim], and believe that their actions may shield their loved ones from imagined 'enemies' such as the Mafia or CIA" (Wilcox 1982:293). The term psychological rape reflected "the nonviolent nature of the harassment—letters, obscene phone calls and persistent shadowing are its most common forms" (Wilcox 1982:233). Most harassers were "lovesick" (Heil 1986:128), although a few might become violent.

The articles held the harasser responsible for his behavior. A female attorney described harassment as "plain male possessiveness" (Anonymous 1980:39). A more psychological explanation held that some men were more susceptible to rejection by women with whom they were

romantically linked. The psychological rapist, however, does not acknowledge his problems; rather, he blames his victim. One harasser was
quoted: "*I'll* say I have a problem, the woman I love doesn't love me. It's
the worst thing that can happen to anyone" (Wilcox 1982:293). Some
psychological experts held victims partially responsible for subtly encouraging their harassers:

> [T]hey can often get away with it because their ex-girlfriends unwittingly
> allow them to. . . . Kate [harassed for over a decade] admits that even
> while Will [her former boyfriend] was harassing her with phone calls and
> driving by her house in the middle of the night, she gave him a scarf she
> had knitted for him. (Heil 1986:138)

The articles portrayed victims as confused by the harassers' attention;
some women acknowledged partial culpability: "He said I'd provoked
him into anger last night and I had the guilty uneasy feeling that maybe
that was partially true" (Anonymous 1980:34). The articles warned that
common social scripts for ending relationships often do not work with
psychological rapists: "It's hard to turn your back on a former lover
who's obviously in pain, and it may seem cruel to avoid all contact with
him. In the end, however, there's no other way" (Mithers 1982:36).

The victims in these articles complained of the criminal justice system's failure to protect them. Police often did not treat harassment as
serious, even when it involved criminal behavior. But victims reported
feeling terrified:

> Basically, the psychological rapist works by gradually reducing the num-
> ber of places a woman feels safe or functional in her daily life. This is why
> relatively harmless behavior, repeated over months or years, can inspire
> real terror. (Wilcox 1982:233)

Victims claimed the criminal justice system did not understand their
terror, and that this precluded their cases being handled properly. A Los
Angeles prosecutor explained that these cases were hard to prosecute: "A
jury will want to know why *emotional* harassment is damaging when the
victim is never touched. . . . I see only six prosecutable cases of emotional
harassment each year" (Wilcox 1982:295—emphasis in original).

Thus, early magazine articles depicted female victims of male harassers. (In 1987, the popular movie *Fatal Attraction* [about a harassing
female] inspired an article in *People* describing three men harassed by
women [Kunen 1987]). Experts typified the harassers' behaviors as non-
violent, and sometimes portrayed victims as coresponsible for their
plight. Victims complained they felt terror, but got little help from the
criminal justice system. In retrospect, these articles can be seen as early

claims about what would become the stalking problem, although only one article used that word (among others) (Heil 1986). While occasional press coverage viewed the behavior as problematic, the issue had not yet been packaged and presented so as to command public attention.

STALKING EMERGES: STAR-STALKERS AND CELEBRITY VICTIMS, 1989–1991

Stalking became a visible issue in 1989 following the sensational murder of actress Rebecca Schaeffer, killed by fan Robert Bardo, a stranger who became obsessed with her, attempted to contact her, then shot her (Axthelm 1989). Her murder received widespread publicity as "The case that galvanized the public: the fatal attraction of a disturbed young man for an up-and-coming actress" (Dan Rather in *48 Hours* 1992:2). Schaeffer was not the first celebrity victim; John Hinckley stalked actress Jodie Foster before attempting to assassinate President Reagan in 1991, and a fan stalked and stabbed actress Theresa Saldana in 1982. However, claims about stalking rarely drew on these examples until Schaeffer's murder. The stalking problem did not, then, simply emerge following a well-publicized crime against a celebrity victim. Yet Schaeffer's murder became the typifying example for what the media now termed "star-stalking" (Cosgrove 1990; *Geraldo* 1990).

The construction of star-stalking as a crime problem typified victims as celebrities—actors and actresses, television personalities, and political figures. Claimsmakers referred to such celebrity victims as talk show hosts David Letterman and Johnny Carson, author Stephen King, actor Michael J. Fox and actresses Jodie Foster, Theresa Saldana, and Sharon Gless, singers Olivia Newton-John and Sheena Easton, and musician John Lennon (Cosgrove 1990; *Geraldo* 1990). Several of these examples were not current; the harassment had occurred years earlier. During 1989 and 1990, national magazine articles and television broadcasts presented 16 typifying examples of stalking; 11 (69%) involved celebrity victims. In every other year, celebrity victims were a minority among the examples.

Claimsmakers depicted star-stalkers as mentally disturbed, inappropriately obsessed with their celebrity victims. Psychiatrist John Stalberg, who interviewed Robert Bardo, described him:

> On a scale of zero to 10, among schizophrenics, he's a 10—one of the sicker people I've seen. . . . With Rebecca Schaeffer, he found a—an obsession. She was the answer to his lonely, depressed, miserable life. (*48 Hours* 1992:3–4)

Another psychiatrist described a range of involvement running from ordinary fans through obsessed people to celebrity killers:

> Dr. Danto: A fan is somebody who admires a star. . . .
> Geraldo: . . . Let's go [to the] erotomanic worshiper. What does that mean?
> Dr. Danto: Well, this is a person who has a love delusion, where they develop a feeling that the star is either singing to them or speaking to them. . . .
> Geraldo: Now, as they deteriorate get worse. Controller?
> Dr. Danto: Yeah. They, who are usually unemployed, want to start running the life of the star, advising them on financial matters or career matters. . . . The next one gets very frustrated for his lack of recognition. There's been no response and starts to use something that will get him attention. Violence.
> Geraldo: And obviously, the bottom of the list there.
> Dr. Danto: The death threatener is somebody who's really becoming very angry and very agitated and wants . . . the attention of that star.
> Geraldo: And somebody who gets the attention usually becomes—
> Dr. Danto: Is the killer, and the killer may either involve himself with the star or go into a lambing method where he looks for a sacrificial lamb. . . . (*Geraldo* 1990:14)

The stalker's interest in the celebrity victim appears inexplicable to others. Stalking, then, emerged as an irrational, essentially random crime:

> Moriarty [reporter]: Why do you think you've been singled out?
> Andrea Evans [actress]: Yeah, I wish I knew. . . . But I have no way of knowing that. (*48 Hours* 1992:9)

As in other random offenses, the victim is blameless; the offender bears the responsibility.

Some discussions of star-stalking referred to the psychiatric disorder "erotomania" (Cosgrove 1990). First described in 1921, erotomania entered the American Psychiatric Association's (1987) *DSM-III-R* as "delusional (paranoid) disorder, erotomanic type":

> The central theme of an erotic delusion is that one is loved by another. . . .
> The person about whom this conviction is held is usually of higher status, such as a famous person or a superior at work, and may even be a complete stranger. Efforts to contact the object of the delusion, through telephone calls, letters, gifts, visits, and even surveillance and stalking are common. (American Psychiatric Association 1987:199)

Erotomania usually affects women (Segal 1989), and discussions of star-stalking often mentioned the women who had harassed David Letterman, Michael J. Fox, and Sharon Gless.

A primary difference between earlier claims about psychological rape and the more successful campaign against star-stalking was the redefinition of the behavior as *violent*. The stalker's behavior, which might be threatening or merely inappropriate, needed to be seen as potentially violent (Dietz et al. 1991a, 1991b). Some claimsmakers (e.g., the interview quoted above between Geraldo Rivera and Dr. Danto) suggested that stalkers "deteriorated," becoming increasingly capable of violence. Unpredictable and possibly lethal, stalking was a form of random violence.

While earlier claimsmakers criticized the criminal justice system's failure to halt psychological rape, their claims produced no legislation. However, concern over star-stalking led to California passing an antistalking law; claimsmakers linked Schaeffer's murder, the 1982 stabbing of Theresa Saldana (in the news because her attacker was about to be paroled), and the deaths of four Orange County women within a 6-week period (each killed by a man against whom she had a restraining order) (Morville 1993). These cases became typifying examples, evidence of the need for an antistalking law. Supported by peace officers' associations and the Screen Actors Guild (SAG), California's law passed in 1990 (*Pacific Law Journal* 1990:500). When it took effect, the Los Angeles Police Department established a six-person Threat Management Unit (TMU) to investigate stalking cases. Both SAG's lobbying and the creation of a TMU in Los Angeles (with its many show business celebrities) reveal that concern over star-stalking fostered the initial antistalking law.

STALKING REDEFINED: FAILED RELATIONSHIPS AND MALE VIOLENCE, 1992–1994

In 1992, other states began following California's example. Often, a highly publicized attack inspired lawmakers: "Behind almost every state stalking bill has been at least one local tragedy" (Morville 1993:929, n47). Twenty-nine states passed antistalking laws (many modeled on California's law) in 1992; 18 other states and the District of Columbia followed suit in 1993 (National Institute of Justice 1993:12). Also in 1992, Senator William Cohen (R—Maine) began calling for federal action, and the national media dramatically increased their coverage of stalking. Between 1980 and 1988, national magazines and television broadcasts averaged one story about stalking per year; during 1989–1991 (when star-stalking attracted attention) the average more than doubled to 2.3

stories per year; but there were 22.0 stories per year—another, nearly 10-fold increase—during 1992 through June 1994. Some stories achieved high visibility: *Washington Post* reporter George Lardner (1992) received a Pulitzer Prize for reporting on his daughter's murder by a stalker, and the award triggered additional press coverage; in 1993, Kathleen Krueger, wife of U.S. Senator Bob Krueger (D—Texas), used her own experiences as a stalking victim to campaign for a federal antistalking law (Ellis 1993; U.S. Senate 1993).

These new claims reframed stalking as a women's issue, a widespread precursor to serious violence, typically committed by men against former spouses or lovers. The term "stalking"—now the consensus replacement for such earlier labels as psychological rape, star-stalking, and erotomania—implied deliberate intent to harm the victim:

> The verb "stalk" is defined as: (1) "to move threateningly or menacingly;" (2) "to pursue by tracking;" and (3) to go stealthily towards an animal "for the purpose of killing or capturing it." These definitions say much about the crime of stalking, suggesting that a stalker is a hunter, is dangerous, and thus should be avoided if at all possible. (Perez 1993:265)

In this new construction, stalking was a common problem. An often-repeated estimate suggested that there were 200,000 stalkers. We do not know the origin of this statistic. It first appears in our sample of national media coverage in *U.S. News and World Report*'s February 17, 1992 issue: "researchers suggest that up to 200,000 people exhibit a stalker's traits" (Tharp 1992:28). Like other statistical estimates of social problem magnitude, this number soon took on a life of its own; it was often repeated, but never examined or explained (Best 1990). Other claimsmakers suggested that 200,000 was an underestimate:

> There are an estimated 200,000 stalkers in the United States, and those are only the ones that we have track of. (Sally Jessy Raphael in *Sally Jessy Raphael* 1994:3)
>
> Some two hundred thousand people in the U.S. pursue the famous. No one knows how many people stalk the rest of us, but the figure is probably higher. (Sherman 1994:198)
>
> Four million women that we know about—know about each year are beaten and terrorized and stalked by somebody they know. (Oprah Winfrey in *Oprah* 1994:12)

Claimsmakers variously estimated that lifetime victimization by stalkers would affect one American in 40 (Safran 1992), or 30 (Tharp 1992), or 20 (*CNN Prime News* 1993). The numbers varied, but there was agreement that stalking was increasing, "a national epidemic" (Gilligan 1992:337).

Most claimsmakers also agreed that stalking was a form of domestic violence against women. To be sure, occasional claimsmakers asserted that "the violent ending is actually very rare" (psychologist Daniel Martell in *Maury Povich Show* 1992:8), that "men are stalked just as many times as women" (former victim Kathleen Baty in *Donahue* 1992:5), or that the stalker was "often a total stranger" (Safran 1992:266). But most claims typified stalking as "almost exclusive to women" (*John and Leeza* 1993), and "often preced[ing] violent acts, from assault to rape, child molestation, and murder" (Beck 1992:60). In this construction, stalkers were not strangers ("as many as 75 or 80 percent of cases involve people who were once married or dating" [Ingrassia 1993:28]), and their victims were not celebrities ("38 percent . . . are ordinary Americans" [Goodwin 1993:50]).[1]

Linking Stalking to Domestic Violence

This new construction connected stalking to a well-established social problem—domestic battering: "'the majority of battered women experience stalking in some form,' says Vickie Smith, head of the Illinois Coalition Against Domestic Violence" (Miller 1993:18). The battered women's movement had long complained that the criminal justice system failed to protect women trying to escape abusive partners, that restraining orders were ineffective (Loseke 1992). By reframing these women's problems as stalking, a visible issue with connotations of extreme violence, battered women's claimsmakers could move their concerns to the top of the policy agenda.

During the intense claimsmaking of 1992–1993, there were only two published scholarly studies of stalkers: an examination of LAPD TMU files—"erotomanic and obsessional subjects in a forensic sample" (Zona, Sharma, and Lane 1993), and a typology of "criminal stalkers" (Holmes 1993). Neither offered much original data. However, antistalking claimsmakers routinely borrowed data from research on domestic violence to characterize stalking:

> Approximately 50 percent of all females who leave their husbands for reasons of physical abuse are followed, harassed, or further attacked by their former spouses. This phenomenon is known as "separation assault.". . . . The broader concept is called "stalking." (Bradburn 1992:271)
>
> Studies in Detroit and Kansas City reveal that 90 percent of those murdered by their intimate partners called police at least once. (Senator William Cohen in *Congressional Record* 1992:S9527)
>
> Nearly one third of all women killed in America are murdered by their husbands or boyfriends, and, says Ruth Micklem, codirector of Virginians

Against Domestic Violence, as many as 90 percent of them have been
stalked. (Beck 992:61)

The juxtaposition of the latter two quotes reveals how evidence used in
claimsmaking evolves: Senator Cohen cited a finding that 90% of wom-
en killed by husbands or lovers had previously called the police; when
later claimsmakers repeated that statistic, they equated having called the
police with being stalked, ignoring the likelihood that many women
called to complain about abuse by partners living in the same residence
(and therefore not stalkers). Presumably similar assumptions lay behind
U.S. Representative Joseph Kennedy's claim that, "Nine women a day
are killed by stalkers in our country" (*Larry King Live* 1994:3). Claimsmakers described antistalking laws as "an effective deterrent to domestic
abuse" (Furio 1993:90); West Virginia's original law narrowly defined
victims as "those who either cohabitated or had intimate relationships
with their stalkers" (Perez 1993:267).

Claims that many stalkers were former husbands or boyfriends cast
virtually all women as potential victims: "We're not idiots up here that
asked to be victims. This happens to anybody period" (former victim
Stephanie in *Sally Jessy Raphael* 1993b:7). Here, as in earlier claims about
star-stalking, victims bear no responsibility; claimsmakers emphasized
that most victims did nothing to encourage their stalkers. (One exception was a talk show devoted to women harassing former boyfriends;
the host repeatedly suggested that the men encouraged stalking [*Sally
Jessy Raphael* 1993c]). In most ways, stalking's typification resembled that
of domestic violence: "wife abuse is a label for severe, frequent, and
continuing violence that escalates over time and is unstoppable. Such
violence is that in which unrepentant men intentionally harm women
and where women are not the authors of their own experiences which
they find terrifying" (Loseke 1992:20). Once they linked stalking to battering, claimsmakers had little difficulty attributing the same characteristics to both crimes.

This link became apparent in state legislative proceedings. Illinois
lawmakers, for example, justified antistalking legislation by pointing to
four recent cases of victims murdered by former husbands or boyfriends
in Chicago suburbs. The *Chicago Tribune*'s (1991) editorial endorsing an
antistalking law shared this frame: "Hundreds of women are threatened
and harassed and intimidated by ex-boyfriends or ex-husbands. . . .
[An antistalking law has] the potential to be a helpful weapon against
domestic violence." Supported by the Illinois Coalition Against Domestic Violence, the bill received unanimous support in both legislative
houses; mothers of two of the dead victims were on hand when the bill
was signed into law. Both state and national branches of the battered
women's movement and the victims' rights movement supported anti-

stalking bills. The National Victim Center lobbied in more than a dozen states, and Theresa Saldana (a former stalking victim and the founder of Victims for Victims) campaigned in behalf of the laws. In Nebraska, for instance, both the Nebraska Coalition for Victims of Crime and the Nebraska Domestic Violence-Sexual Assault Coalition supported anti-stalking legislation. Stalking was now a form of both violent crime and domestic violence.

Patterns in Media Typification

Media coverage of stalking reflected this new construction. Table 3.1 compares the typifying examples—the cases illustrating the stalking problem—in national magazine articles and television broadcasts from 1980–1988, 1989–1991, and 1992–mid-1994. While stalking was always depicted as something male offenders did to female victims, this characterization intensified over time. Celebrity victims received more attention during 1989–1991, when claimsmakers focused on star-stalking. In 1992–1994, typifying examples were slightly more likely to feature victims who had been engaged or married to their stalkers, and less likely to depict stalkers who were strangers to their victims. And, perhaps most dramatically, later claimsmaking used more examples that ended

Table 3.1. Characteristics of Typifying Examples in Magazine Articles and Television Broadcasts about Stalking, 1980–1994[a]: Percentage of Examples with Different Characteristics[b]

	1980–1988 (%)	1989–1991 (%)	1992–June 1994 (%)	χ^{2c}
Victim is female	86	83	94	n.s.
Victim is a celebrity	18	48	16	0.002
Stalker is male	82	78	90	n.s.
Victim and stalker have been engaged or married	14	5	18	n.s.
Victim and stalker were strangers	24	68	19	0.001
Stalking leads to homicide	5	10	30	0.008
	(n = 22)	(n = 23)	(n = 170)	

[a] 1994 sources January through June only.
[b] Calculations do not include missing values.
[c] Statistical significance of χ^2 test

in homicide. Stalking was reconstructed as a serious, violent crime, often committed against women by former or current husbands or lovers.

Earlier constructions of the stalking problem fell under joint owner- ship (Gusfield 1981); the media consulted experts from both law and medicine. While lawyers and criminal justice system agents spoke of the law's difficulty in stopping stalkers, psychiatrists and psychologists in- terpreted stalking as mental disorder. Even after stalking's boundaries expanded to include much domestic abuse, most claims continued to depict stalking as a psychological problem: "Ninety percent of stalkers suffer from mental disorders" (Ellis 1993:63). Oprah Winfrey offered this "profile" of stalkers: "low self-esteem, feelings of dependency, views people as possessions, fears abandonment, severely jealous, easily irri- table and 40 percent of them have alcohol problems" (*Oprah* 1994:9).

But claimsmakers denied that psychological problems absolved stalkers of responsibility. Some labeled stalkers "essentially evil" (psy- chologist Rick Shuman in *Oprah* 1992:13) or located stalking within a context of male domination of women:

> They're not so much crazy men as slightly exaggerated men. They have a view that women should be controlled. . . . They tend to view women as property. . . . They target women because women are targets of oppor- tunity in our society. (psychiatrist Peter Breggin in *Larry King Live* 1990:5)
>
> Another group . . . does this because it has something to do with men's privilege and they think it is OK to do this to women, and while I wouldn't call them well-balanced people, I wouldn't call them crazy. (victim Jane McAllister in U.S. Senate 1992:60)

While claimsmakers after 1991 might not agree on a single model of stalkers' psychology, there was no hint—as there had been in some earlier claims about psychological rape—that female victims might bear any responsibility for being stalked. Typifying examples featuring chil- dren or adolescents as victims made the pedophile/stalker's respon- sibility especially clear (Safran 1992; *Sally Jessy Raphael* 1993a).

After 1991, the medical model became less important in constructing the stalking problem. As Table 3.2 indicates, during both 1980–1988 and 1989–1991, the media turned to medical authorities as often as legal authorities. In contrast, only one pre-1992 story cited a representative of the battered women's or the victims' movements. After 1992, media discussions of stalking referred to mental health experts less often, while citations to representatives from the legal system remained stable, and references to experts from the battered women's and the victims' rights movements increased. (Because there were few articles and broadcasts before 1992, none of these findings is statistically significant.) This shift reflects the reconstruction of the stalking problem: the media asked legal

Table 3.2. Authorities Cited in Magazine Articles and Television Broadcasts about Stalking, 1980–1994[a]: Percentage of Articles or Broadcasts Citing Different Authorities[b]

	1980–1988 (%)	1989–1991 (%)	1992–June 1994 (%)
Medical, mental health experts	44	71	36
Legal, criminal justice experts	44	71	65
Women's, victims' movement experts	11 ($n = 9$)	0 ($n = 7$)	22 ($n = 55$)

[a] 1994 sources January through June only.
[b] Because an article or broadcast could cite more than one type of authority, percentages do not total 100%.

authorities for assessments of the new antistalking laws, while members of the victims' and battered women's movements became relevant experts once stalking was linked to domestic violence.

The stalking problem, then, was not constructed all at once. After 1992, the press portrayed stalking as a violent crime against women, typically committed by former husbands or lovers. This construction built upon earlier (1989–1991) concern about star-stalking by men and women suffering from erotomania. And the issue of celebrity stalking had precursors in still earlier claims about harassment, obsession, and psychological rape, claims that, in retrospect, resemble the later claims about stalking.

RETYPIFICATION AND THE MOBILIZATION OF CULTURAL AND ORGANIZATIONAL RESOURCES

These shifting typifications raise questions for constructionist analysis. Early constructionist statements outlined natural histories for social problems construction (Blumer 1971; Spector and Kitsuse 1977). Most case studies emphasize either claimsmaking rhetoric (e.g., Gusfield 1981; Best 1990) or the organization of claimsmaking campaigns (e.g., Pfohl 1977; Rose 1977). These approaches let the analyst take the claimsmakers' success for granted and pay little attention to earlier, unsuccessful claims. When analysts do address the timing of success, their explanations tend to be post hoc accounts focused on dramatic, precipitating events.

The case of stalking demonstrates the complexity of successfully constructing new social problems. Preceded by earlier, less successful typifications, the successful construction of stalking combined three elements: (1) typifying claims, which mobilized both (2) cultural resources and (3) organizational resources.[2]

Typifying Claims

The raw material for the stalking problem—people who objected to being harassed, harassment sometimes ending in homicide, even well-publicized cases with celebrity victims—existed long before claimsmakers began talking about "stalking." Presumably, the stalking problem might have been constructed much earlier than it was.

A key step in social problems construction is linking a troubling event to a problematic pattern, defining a particular *incident* as an *instance* of some larger problem. In the case of stalking, this juxtaposition of event and pattern occurred at several points, producing various typifications. While some media reports described the harassment of lone individuals (e.g., Winter 1980; Safran 1992), others juxtaposed several cases, suggesting they were all instances of psychological rape (Wilcox 1982) or fatal attractions (Kunen 1987) or star-stalking (*Geraldo* 1990). Of course, the key juxtaposition occurred in Southern California after 1989, when claimsmakers linked Rebecca Schaefer's murder with the attacks on Theresa Saldana and the four women killed in Orange County.

Table 3.3 summarizes this sequence of typifications, noting some of the characteristics claimsmakers associated with psychological rape (1980–1988), star-stalking (1989–1991), and stalking (1992–1994). Although our analysis links these different claims, arguing that they dealt with essentially the same phenomenon, it is interesting to note how the typifications differed in their characterizations of the gender of both victim and offender, the victim's responsibility and celebrity, the nature of the offender's psychological problem, the prior relationship between victim and offender, and the prospect of violence.

Claimsmakers rarely offer formal definitions. Rather, they illustrate a problem's nature through typifying examples. We have already noted how typifying examples presented in the media changed. By 1992, claimsmakers offered other evidence to support the current typification of stalking, including statistical claims (e.g., the number of stalking cases, the frequency of stalking-related homicides, the proportion of victims whose stalkers were former intimates). This represented domain expansion (Best 1990): stalking claims expanded what had been a relatively narrow focus on star-stalking to include much domestic violence.

Table 3.3. Elements in the Construction of Stalking as a Crime Problem

Period	Typifying claims	Cultural resources	Organizational resources	Results
1980–1988	Psychological rape: males harass females; usually not violent; victim may share responsibility; obsessed offender	Vulnerability to harassment Women heading households		Occasional media coverage
1989–1991	Star-stalking: celebrity victim; offender can be either gender; offender may suffer from erotomania; offender may deteriorate; violence and homicide as outcomes; victim not responsible	Vulnerability to harassment Random violence	Screen Actors Guild lobbying Celebrity protection services	Increased media coverage California law passed
1992–1994	Stalking: males harass females; often former intimates; form of domestic violence; victim not responsible; statistical claims; homicide as outcome	Vulnerability to harassment Victimization of women Male violence Pedophilia	Crime victims' movement Battered women's movement LAPD TMU	Frequent media coverage Laws in other states Federal attention

Cultural Resources

Not all claims receive ratification from press, public, and policymakers. Constructionist analysts suggest that claims attract notice when they "relate to deep mythic themes" (Hilgartner and Bosk 1988:64), have "cultural resonance" (Gamson and Modigliani 1989:5–6), or draw upon "cultural resources" (Best 1991). Claims can be packaged in ways more or less likely to elicit favorable responses, and the cultural themes that claims evoke are a key element in this packaging.

Consider a central theme in stalking claims: the victim's inability to make the harasser stop. These claims routinely emphasized the victims' emotions, e.g., their frustration and anxiety over the continuing harassment and their uncertainty and fear over what might happen next. The obsessive pursuit of another is a standard theme in American popular culture; many movies, novels, and popular songs center around obsessive love. The treatment can be comic or romantic (e.g., the would-be lover who won't give up until love is reciprocated, as in *The Graduate*), but it is often central to horror or suspense stories (e.g., *Fatal Attraction*, *The Bodyguard*). This suggests widespread cultural recognition of the troubling qualities of such pursuit. Of course, the relationship between cultural resources and claimsmaking is not one-way. Claimsmakers draw upon available cultural resources, but their claims also inform and shape popular culture (Best 1990). For example, one 1994 suspense novel borrows heavily from stalking claims: the hero, a police detective in Beverly Hills' TMU, discusses the psychological and social patterns of stalkers (Woods 1994).

It is more difficult to prove a link between other, less specific cultural resources and the success of stalking claims. For instance, concern over stalking may have reflected the growing proportion of households headed by women, to the degree that women not living with a man seemed more vulnerable to a stalker's harassment. And concerns expressed in other claimsmaking campaigns seem consistent with the emergence of stalking as a social problem. These include concern over random violence (found in claims about serial murder, freeway shootings, drive-by shootings, carjacking, and other crimes), male violence and the victimization of women (forcible rape, date and acquaintance rape, and domestic violence), and pedophilia. When claimsmakers typified stalking as random or unpredictable, violent, or gendered, they drew upon cultural resources that might encourage a favorable response to their claims. If stalking was somehow "like" other, well-established problems, then claims about stalking became more credible.

Organizational Resources

Claims also vary in the degree to which specific organizations promote them. In a competitive social problems marketplace, whether well-
publicized claims lead to policy changes depends less on press coverage
than upon organized pressure to propose, pass, and implement new
policies. During its brief moment in the national spotlight in 1987, freeway violence attracted more intense press coverage than stalking ever
received, yet the issue faded within a few weeks (Best 1991). Press
coverage drew attention to freeway violence, but when the media's
attention shifted, no one continued promoting the problem.

Prior to 1989, claims about psychological rape lacked significant organizational support, and these issues never attracted prolonged attention. Mobilization of organizational resources occurred only after
Rebecca Shaeffer's murder and the retypification of the problem as star-
stalking. Key actors in promoting star-stalking had ties to the entertainment industry: the media's appetite for dramatic news about celebrities
ensured increased coverage; individuals who specialized in providing
security services for celebrities (e.g., Gavin de Becker) discussed their
work with the media (e.g., Bacon 1990; *Geraldo* 1990); and the SAG
lobbied for California's antistalking law.

But antistalking laws spread only when other social movements supported the new legislation. In particular, the battered women's movement and the victims' rights movement campaigned for laws modeled
on the California statute. Linking their cause with the visible problem of
star-stalking gave the battered women's movement a fresh face. Coup-
ling longstanding complaints about ineffective restraining orders to the
lethal menace of stalking turned a tired topic into a hot issue. Antistalking laws put reform of the restraining order process on the public agenda, promising to give an established system of control new teeth. Media
coverage of stalking increasingly cited experts from such organizations
as Virginians Against Domestic Violence (Beck 1992). These statewide
groups had links to the National Victim Center, Victims for Victims, and
other victims' rights organizations. Like other long-term social movements, the victims' rights movement must continually reframe their
claims in fresh ways. Opposition to stalking linked both the battered
women's movement and the victims' rights movement to a new, dramatic, highly visible problem. By assuming ownership and using their
resources to continue promoting the stalking problem, these movements kept stalking before the public and policymakers.

Mobilizing organizational resources helped pass antistalking legislation, but the absence of organized opposition may have been equally

important. Violent, even murderous crimes by vengeful ex-husbands or mentally disturbed fans had few defenders; the campaign for antistalking laws met little opposition. While civil libertarians questioned the laws' constitutionality, the consensus deplored stalking.

The Role of Contingency

Constructions of social problems become successful when typified in ways consistent with the larger culture's concerns, and when they mobilize significant organizational support. Stalking became an established social problem when these conditions were fulfilled, and not before. This is important, because there were earlier opportunities to construct stalking as a social problem.

Consider the 1982 stabbing of actress Theresa Saldana. The crime was well publicized, as was Saldana's recovery and her founding the self-help group Victims for Victims (Reilly 1982). Saldana played herself in a 1984 NBC made-for-TV movie, *Victims for Victims*, and she wrote a book about her experiences (Saldana 1986). Her case attracted new publicity in 1989, when California prepared to parole her attacker (who had continued to make threats against her) (Bacon 1989). This new attention to her case coincided with the murder of Rebecca Schaeffer and, following Schaeffer's death, Saldana's case became a typifying example in claims about first star-stalking and later stalking.

Yet before 1989, discussions of Saldana's case treated it as an example of violent crime and crime's effects on victims. There was no particular emphasis placed on Saldana's awareness, prior to the attack, that she was being pursued and that she might be in danger. In other words, before Schaeffer's murder, Saldana's experience was not constructed in terms of its stalking-like qualities. In retrospect, we can imagine stalking (or at least star-stalking) being constructed as a social problem following the attack on Saldana. Saldana was an articulate celebrity-victim, willing to speak out, and her attack came only a year after the news about John Hinckley following Jodie Foster. Following her attack, Saldana became an example, but she typified the problem of violent crime, not the threat posed by stalking. In spite of its potential as a typifying example, Saldana's case did not precipitate the construction of the stalking problem.

Saldana's case suggests the role of contingency in social problems construction. Some contingencies are external, e.g., the distribution of media resources, or other claims competing for attention (Hilgartner and Bosk 1988). But other contingencies are internal: How do claimsmakers choose to typify the problem? Does that typification take advantage of cultural resources? Can organizational resources be mobilized to promote the cause? Such considerations explain the timing of claimsmakers' success.

CONCLUSION: STALKING'S SIGNIFICANCE

We completed this chapter in mid-1994, while stalking remained the subject of intense claimsmaking, and the problem's future was uncertain. Dozens of law review articles examined antistalking laws; critics warned that appellate courts might rule that the laws were unconstitutionally vague or overbroad, or that the laws might be applied in ways their authors had not intended, e.g., to control strikers or antiabortion protesters (Faulkner and Hsaio 1994). The national attention to stalking charges filed against a man who sent electronic mail messages suggested that the crime's boundaries were not yet clear (*CNN World Today* 1994). Still, the laws seemed to promise that stalking would endure as an institutionalized crime category. Moreover, the sensational murder of Nicole Brown Simpson inspired claims reaffirming stalking's ties to battering (e.g., Lewin 1994). At least in the law and in the media, stalking had been successfully constructed.

The history of the stalking problem demonstrates that such success is problematic and requires explanation. The current typification followed less successful claims that typified the problem in very different terms. Success required a typification that both drew upon cultural resources and attracted significant organizational support. The case of stalking suggests that this combination of typifying claims, cultural resources, and organizational resources is essential to successful claimsmaking. Still, the precise elements in a successful typification and the timing of the claims' success depend upon contingencies.

The construction of stalking as a new crime problem parallels the recent success of other claims about victimization. Many of these involve male violence against women. Others came to public attention through claimsmaking by victims seeking to redefine criminality and victimization. These broader shifts in public definitions of crime and victimization demand attention, but their analysis will require an analytic reconstruction of the changing typifications that led to the successful construction of specific crimes, such as stalking.

ACKNOWLEDGMENTS

Partial support for this research came from a 1992 Faculty Research Grant from Valdosta State College and a 1993 Special Projects Grant from Southern Illinois

University at Carbondale. We benefited from comments on earlier drafts by Robert A. Fein, Philip Jenkins, Donileen R. Loseke, David F. Luckenbill, and T. Memoree Thibodeau.

NOTES

1. This figure of 38%—often repeated—apparently came from an unpublished study of the first 74 case files from the LAPD's TMU. The study classified victims as highly recognized celebrities (17%), lesser known entertainment figures (32%), former employers or other professionals (13%), and ordinary citizens (38%) (Morin 1993:127–128). However, the published version of this research did not include this classification (Zona et al. 1993). Although "none of the [study's] cases involved domestic violence situations" (Zona et al. 1993:896), claimsmakers routinely used the 38% figure as evidence of the link between stalking and domestic violence.

2. Our argument is analogous to the resource mobilization approach to studying social movements (e.g., Zald and McCarthy 1987). Resource mobilization theorists argue that the emergence of social movements cannot be attributed to grievances, because grievances are a more-or-less constant part of the cultural landscape. Instead, resource mobilization theory suggests that movements emerge when organizations mobilize members, funding, and other necessary resources.

REFERENCES

American Psychiatric Association. 1987. *Diagnostic and Statistical Manual of Mental Disorders* (3rd ed., revised). Washington, DC: American Psychiatric Association.

Anonymous. 1980. "My Ex-Husband Won't Leave Me Alone." *Good Housekeeping* 190 (March):32–34, 39, 42

Axthelm, P. 1989. "An Innocent Life, a Heartbreaking Death." *People* 32 (July 31):60–62, 64, 66.

Bacon, D. 1989. "Vicious Crime, Double Jeopardy." *People* 31 (June 5):44, 46–49.

———. 1990. "When Fans Turn into Fanatics. . . ." *People* 33 (February 12):103, 105–106.

Beck, M. 1992. "Murderous Obsession." *Newsweek* 120 (July 13):60–62.

Best, J. 1990. *Threatened Children*. Chicago: University of Chicago Press.

———. 1991. "'Road Warriors' on 'Hair-Trigger Highways'." *Sociological Inquiry* 61:327–345.

Blumer, H. 1971. "Social Problems as Collective Behavior." *Social Problems* 18:298–306.

Bradburn, Wayne E., Jr. 1992. "Stalking Statutes." *Ohio Northern University Law Review* 19:271–288.

Brownstein, H. H. 1991. "The Media and the Construction of Random Drug Violence." *Social Justice* 18(4):85–103

Chicago Tribune. 1991. "Police Need Help to Stop Stalkers" (editorial). (November 18):I.18.

CNN Prime News. 1993. "Michigan Legal System Takes Stalking Very Seriously." (January 1):Journal Graphics transcript 273.

CNN World Today. 1994. "Michigan Investigates Cyberspace Stalking." (May 27):Journal Graphics transcript 778.

Congressional Record. 1992. Senate (July 1):S9527.

Cosgrove, S. 1990. "Erotomania." *New Statesman & Society* 3(July 27):31–32.

Dietz, P. E., D. B. Matthews, D. A. Martell, T. M. Stewart, D. R. Hrouda, and J. Warren. 1991a. "Threatening and Otherwise Inappropriate Letters to Members of the United States Congress." *Journal of Forensic Sciences* 36:1445–1468.

Dietz, P. E., D. B. Matthews, C. Van Duyne, D. A. Martell, C. D. H. Parry, T. Stewart, J. Warren, and J. D. Crowder. 1991b. "Threatening and Otherwise Inappropriate Letters to Hollywood Celebrities." *Journal of Forensic Sciences* 36:185–209.

Donahue. 1992. "Love Stalkers Would Rather See Ex Dead than with Someone Else." (November 25):Journal Graphics transcript 3607.

Ellis, D. 1993. "Nowhere to Hide." *People* 39(May 17):62–66, 68, 71–72.

Faulkner, R. P., and D. H. Hsiao. 1994. "And Where You Go I'll Follow." *Harvard Journal on Legislation* 31:1–62.

Fishman, M. 1978. "Crime Waves as Ideology." *Social Problems* 25:531–543.

48 Hours. 1992. "Stalker." (March 4). Transcript from Burrelle's Information Services.

Furio, J. 1993. "Can New State Laws Stop the Stalkers?" *Ms.* 3(January):90–91.

Gamson, W., and A. Modigliani. 1989. "Media Discourse and Public Opinion on Nuclear Power." *American Journal of Sociology* 95:1–37.

Geraldo. 1990. "Tracking the Star Stalkers." (March 20):Journal Graphics transcript 654.

Gilligan, M. J. 1992. "Stalking the Stalker." *Georgia Law Review* 27:285–342.

Goodwin, M. 1993. "Stalked?" *Woman's Day* 56(March 16):49–50, 52.

Gusfield, J. R. 1981. *The Culture of Public Problems.* Chicago: University of Chicago Press.

Heil, A. 1986. "Lovesick." *Mademoiselle* 92(December):128–130, 136–138.

Hilgartnner, S., and C. L. Bosk. 1988. "The Rise and Fall of Social Problems." *American Journal of Sociology* 94:53–78.

Hollinger, R. C., and L. Lanza-Kaduce. 1988. "The Process of Criminalization." *Criminology* 26:101–126.

Holmes, R. M. 1993. "Stalking in America." *Journal of Contemporary Criminal Justice* 9:317–327.

Holstein, J. A., and G. Miller (eds.). 1993. *Reconsidering Social Constructionism.* Hawthorne, NY: Aldine de Gruyter.

Ingrassia, M. 1993. "Stalked to Death?" *Newsweek* 122 (November 1):27–28.

————. 1994. "Open to Attack." *Newsweek* 123 (January 17):46–47.

Jenkins, P. 1994. *Using Murder*. Hawthorne, NY: Aldine de Gruyter.

John and Leeza. 1992. Videotaped broadcast (December).

Kunen, J. S. 1987. "The Dark Side of Love." *People* 28(October 26):89–98

Lardner, G., Jr. 1992. "The Stalking of Kristen." *Washington Post* (November 22):C1–C3.

Larry King Live. 1990. "Telephone Terrorism." (September 10):Journal Graphics transcript 126.

————. 1994. "What About Nicole Simpson?" (June 22):Journal Graphics transcript 1153.

Lewin, T. 1994. "Case Might Fit Pattern of Abuse, Experts Say." *New York Times* (June 19):20.

Loseke, D. R. 1992. *The Battered Woman and Shelters*. Albany: State University of New York Press.

————. 1993. "Constructing Conditions, People, Morality, and Emotion." Pp. 207–216 in *Constructionist Controversies*, edited by G. Miller and J. A. Holstein. Hawthorne, NY: Aldine de Gruyter.

Maury Povich Show. 1992. "A Stalker's Victim Discusses her Ordeal." (August 20):Journal Graphics transcript 247.

Miller, B. 1993. "Thou Shalt Not Stalk." *Chicago Tribune Magazine* (April 18):14–16, 18, 20.

Mithers, C. L. 1982. "Can a Man be Too Mad about You?" *Mademoiselle* 88 (October):36.

Morin, K. S. 1993. "The Phenomenon of Stalking." *San Diego Justice Journal* 1:123–162.

Morville, D. A. 1993. "Stalking Laws." *Washington University Law Quarterly* 71:921–935.

National Institute of Justice. 1993. *Project to Develop a Model Anti-Stalking Code for States*. Washington, DC: U.S. Department of Justice.

Oprah. 1992. "Stalking." (May 1). Transcript from Burrelle's Information Services.

————. 1994. "Women in Fear for their Lives." (January 21). Transcript from Burrelle's Information Services.

Pacific Law Journal. 1990. "Selected 1990 Legislation." 22:500–501.

Perez, C. 1993. "Stalking." *American Journal of Criminal Law* 20:264–280.

Pfohl, S. 1977. "The 'Discovery' of Child Abuse." *Social Problems* 24:310–323.

Reilly, S. 1982. "A Rising Star Lives to Shine Again. . . ." *People* 18 (November 8):155–156.

Reinarman, C. 1988. "The Social Construction of an Alcohol Problem." *Theory and Society* 17:91–120.

Rose, V. M. 1977. "Rape as a Social Problem." *Social Problems* 25:75–89.

Safran, C. 1992. "A Stranger was Stalking our Little Girl." *Good Housekeeping* 215(November):185, 263–266.

Saldana, T. 1986. *Beyond Survival*. New York: Bantam.

Sally Jessy Raphael. 1993a. "A Pervert Is Stalking my Small Child." (February 25):Journal Graphics transcript 1274.

———. 1993b. "I was Stalked Like an Animal." (May 19):Journal Graphics transcript 1227.

———. 1993c. "If I Can't Have Him No One Can." (June 22):Journal Graphics transcript 1254.

———. 1994. "Miss America Stalked." (February 15):Journal Graphics transcript 1420.

Segal, J. 1989. "Erotomania Revisited." *American Journal of Psychiatry* 146:1261–1266.

Sherman, W. 1994. "Stalking." *Cosmopolitan* 216 (April):198–201.

Spector, M., and J. I. Kitsuse. 1977. *Constructing Social Problems*. Menlo Park, CA: Cummings.

Tharp, M. 1992. "In the Mind of a Stalker." *U.S. News and World Report* 112(February 17):28–30.

Toobin, J. 1994. "The Man Who Kept Going Free." *New Yorker* 70 (March 7):38–48, 53.

U.S. Senate. 1992. Antistalking legislation. Hearings held by the Committee on the Judiciary. September 29.

———. 1993. Antistalking proposals. Hearing held by the Committee on the Judiciary. March 17.

Wilcox, B. 1982. "Psychological Rape." *Glamour* 80(October):232–233, 291–296.

Winter, P. D. 1980. "Notes on a Death Threat." *Ms.* 8(January):60–65.

Woods, S. 1994. *Dead Eyes*. New York: HarperCollins.

Zald, M. N., and J. D. McCarthy. 1987. *Social Movements in an Organizational Society*. New Brunswick, NJ: Transaction.

Zona, M. A., K. K. Sharma, and J. Lane. 1993. "A Comparative Study of Erotomanic and Obsessional Subjects in a Forensic Sample." *Journal of Forensic Sciences* 38:894–903.

4

Rethinking Medicalization: Alcoholism and Anomalies

LYNN M. APPLETON

In their influential *Deviance and Medicalization: From Badness to Sickness* (1980), Peter Conrad and Joseph Schneider synthesized the scattered literature on medicalization into a compelling argument about its nature and extent in modern American society. Through five compelling case studies, they identified a process of medicalization through which "[d]eviant behaviors that were once defined as immoral, sinful, or criminal have been given medical meaning" (1980:1). Their work won wide acclaim and, during the 1980s, sociologists produced numerous medicalization studies on topics ranging from menopause to gambling (Conrad 1992).

Alcoholism was one of the first cases of medicalization to be studied (Conrad and Schneider 1980),[1] and many sociological writings use it as an example of medicalization. For example, Calhoun, Light, and Keller's popular introductory sociology text explains that "[a]n important by-product of the growth of the health-care industry and the prestige of physicians . . . is an increase in the number of conditions that are thought to be of medical concern" (1994:384). They continue, "People who were addicted to alcohol or drugs were once considered sinners or weaklings. Now such addictions are considered illnesses" (1994:384). Similarly, Macionis's popular introductory sociology text discusses how "[g]radually . . . alcoholism was redefined as a medical problem. Thus, alcoholism is now generally considered to be a disease, and alcoholics are defined as 'sick' rather than 'bad'" (1989:216). Kurtz and Chalfant's *The Sociology of Medicine and Illness* (1991) devotes an entire chapter to the medicalization of deviance, with special attention to alcoholism. And Andrew Abbott, a leading sociological analyst of the professions, asserts that "medicine has recently seized alcoholism" (Abbott 1988:9).

Although many sociologists accept the contention that "alcoholism has been medicalized," their apparent agreement hides a fundamental problem in the theory of medicalization. The problem emerged because

59

the theory's originators and popularizers assumed that the definition of "medicine" was unproblematic. They assumed that "medicine" was the practitioners and institutions of allopathic[2] medicine. But this assumption has produced theoretical and empirical problems that have undermined medicalization theory.

THE ROLE OF MEDICINE IN MEDICALIZATION

In the 1970s, few sociologists doubted the tremendous power of medicine. Popular culture deified physicians, and critical sociologists gloomily predicted that medicine was the emerging center of a new and subtle form of social control (Illich 1976). In this intellectual setting, sociologists looked to the institution of medicine for an explanation of why the label of "disease" was applied to an increasingly broad range of phenomena.

In most of *Deviance and Medicalization* (1980), Conrad and Schneider imply that medicalization necessarily involves conventional medical institutions. They write: "[t]his book examines how increasing forms of deviant behavior have been defined as medical problems and thereby properly under medical control. We examine how medicine achieved the authority to define problems as 'sickness' rather than 'badness' and analyze the consequences of this transformation" (1980:8–9). Years later, Conrad (1992:211) notes that

> [m]edicalization occurs when a medical frame or definition has been applied to understand or manage a problem; this is as true for epilepsy as for 'gender dysphoria' (transsexualism). The interest in medicalization has predominantly focused on previously nonmedical problems that have been medicalized (and, often, thought to be inappropriately medicalized), but actually medicalization must include all problems that come to be defined in medical terms.

Conrad and Schneider never define what they mean by "medicine," but they imply that it is the practice of allopathic medicine by legally certified physicians. For example, their theoretical chapter on the "Historical and Conceptual Background" of medicalization begins with a discussion of the Enlightenment and the scientific method, examines how these gave birth to allopathic medicine, and focuses on medicine's "greatest clinical achievement," the germ theory of disease, and the "actual control of infectious disease . . . along with the consolidation and monopolization of medical organization and practice about the turn of the century that enabled the medical profession to achieve a position of social and professional dominance" (1980:262).

By "medicine," Conrad and Schneider refer to what physicians do, what allopathic medical schools teach, and what medical researchers affiliated with such schools conclude. They exclude "alternative" medicines and "folk" medicines: chiropractic medicine, Christian Science, crystal healing, shamanic ritual, sweat lodges, and homeopathy (Freund and McGuire 1991). When they define "medicalization" as the "emergence of medicine as the dominant definer of deviance," a reasonable reader concludes that medicalization involves physicians, their associations, and the hospitals with which they affiliate.

But Conrad and Schneider do not argue that all medicalizing entrepreneurs are medical personnel. Discussing alcoholism, they note that "the medical profession has rarely been in the vanguard of the disease forces" (1980:106) and "the rise for [sic] the disease concept of alcoholism illustrates that the process of collective medical definition need not necessarily be sustained primarily by medical personnel" (1980:73). But their original model of medicalization proposes that, regardless of a definitional crusade's beginnings, it successfully concludes when the medical definition is legitimated and institutionalized inside mainstream medicine (1980:269–271). Medical legitimacy consists of "securing medical turf," which generally involves both medicine's and law's embrace of the medicalized definition of some deviance. When a prior criminal definition existed, medicalization requires that the state grant medicine "the right to a particular social control turf. Medicine, in fact, may become the agent of social control for the state, as with opiate addiction and child abuse, or replace problematic parts of the state control apparatus, as with chronic drunkenness" (1980:270).

Once the authoritative institutional gatekeepers legitimate the definition, the final stage of medicalization is the "fixity and semipermanence" of institutionalization. Conrad and Schneider identify two types of institutionalization: codification, as part of the "official medical and/or legal classification system" in diagnostic manuals and criminal codes; and bureaucratization, through large social control bureaucracies such as the National Institute of Alcohol Abuse and Alcoholism (NIAAA). And, underscoring the centrality of medical professionals in successful medicalization, they note that public acceptance lags behind professional acceptance of medicalization, so that "[t]he public remains more skeptical about medical designations than professionals, especially in the cases of alcoholism, opiate addiction, and homosexuality" (1993:271).

But, although Conrad and Schneider's early work assumes that medicine is essential to medicalization, their later work (1992:277–292; Conrad 1992) abruptly drops that assumption. It denies that the involvement of medical practitioners and institutions is either a necessary or sufficient condition for medicalization. And it puts them in the peculiar position of arguing that medicalization can occur without the involvement of any medical personnel or institutions.

This peculiar argument is an attempt to bring medicalization theory into agreement with the 1980s literature on medicalization. According to Conrad (1992:218), this literature "centers on the degree to which physicians and the medical profession are active in the medicalization process." Much of that literature finds that medicalization crusades frequently do not involve medical professionals.

Alcoholism is a good example of an ostensibly medicalized deviance that does not involve medical institutions. Medical doctors and medical institutions have made only the most tentative of commitments to alcoholism and addiction to other drugs as "medical problems." Conrad (1992:210) concedes that "in certain instances [of medicalization], the medical profession is only marginally involved or even uninvolved (e.g., alcoholism)." But he does not confront the irony of arguing that medicalization can proceed without the involvement of medical institutions or medical professionals (see also Conrad and Schneider 1992:281–282).

Instead of looking at their theory's basic assumptions to see if they need modification, Conrad and Schneider tinkered with the theory in ways that produce serious conceptual problems. In their "Afterword" to the second edition of *Deviance and Medicalization* (1992), they argue that medicalization is not primarily a phenomenon of "[w]hat doctors do and control." Rather, "medicalization is primarily a definitional phenomenon—that is, one of how a problem is collectively defined, by whom, and with what consequences" (1992:278). And Conrad (1992:211) writes:

> The key to medicalization is the definition issue. Medicalization consists of defining a problem in medical terms, using medical language to describe a problem, adopting a medical framework to understand a problem, or using a medical intervention to "treat" it. This is a sociocultural process that may or may not involve the medical profession.

But even "a sociocultural process" must involve actors. If it does not involve the medical profession, then who does it involve? And with what legitimacy do they propose this medical definition or intervention?

Conrad does not clarify the issue when he offers a distinction among three levels of medicalization (1992:211):

> Medicalization can occur on at least three distinct levels: the conceptual, the institutional, and the interactional. On a conceptual level a medical vocabulary (or "model") is used to "order" or define the problem at hand; few medical professionals need be involved, and medical treatments are not necessarily applied. On the institutional level, organizations may adopt a medical approach to treating a particular problem in which the

organization specializes. Physicians may function as gatekeepers for benefits that are only legitimate in organizations that adopt a medical definition and approach to a problem, but where the everyday routine work is accomplished by nonmedical personnel. On the interactional level, physicians are most directly involved. Medicalization occurs here as part of doctor-patient interaction.

Consider the implications of this. Conrad and Schneider argue that a behavior can be medicalized on a "conceptual" level even if it is not medicalized on the level of doctor/patient interaction; they say that something can be "medicalized" even if doctors do not see it or treat it as such. This, they assert, is the case with alcoholism. But, is it meaningful to argue that a behavior can be medicalized on the conceptual but not on the institutional or interactional level? Whose claims that "X is a medical problem" find acceptance if those claims are not buttressed by any doctor's support? If every autoworker in Detroit argues that buying a non-American-made car is a crime, have they thereby criminalized the act?

Certainly, nonmedical "moral entrepreneurs" might launch a campaign to persuade both medical workers and the lay public that "X is a medical problem." But, if medical professionals fail to be persuaded, is it reasonable to say that X is "medicalized on a conceptual level"? Most sociologists of medicine would agree that "[n]o other occupational group in the United States has held the type of dominance and autonomy in its field that the medical profession has for the past century" (Kurtz and Chalfant 1991:99). Even with recent decreases in its power (Cockerham 1988; Starr 1982), the medical profession retains the high degree of authority and self-regulation that is the essence of the traditional definition of a "profession" (Abbott 1988). So, if doctors deny or ignore a medicalization claim, how could that claim be successful?

Arguably, Conrad and Schneider could be saying that some conditions "really" are diseases, regardless of what doctors say or do. A similar argument in critical criminology is that many legally ignored actions by corporations and their executives are "really" crimes (Taylor, Walton, and Young 1975). But most such arguments try to show that some law on the books is not being enforced. In the absence of an unenforced law or a new interpretation of an existing law, the claim "X is a crime" must reduce to the argument that "X should be a crime." And, of course, the latter is the province of the moralist rather than the sociologist or jurisprudent.

Conrad and Schneider do not intend to be moralists. Indeed, they work from a theoretical tradition that is the antithesis of moralism. Social constructionism, by arguing that all morality is a social construction, eschews Platonic discussions of the ahistorical Good or Bad. So, when Conrad and Schneider argue that medicalization can be achieved without medicine's compliance, they are not arguing that behavior X "really" is an illness. Instead, they mean that some group believes that behavior X is an illness. But, given the power of the medical profession, they do not make a convincing case for any nonmedical group's authority to make medical claims. Instead, they beg the question of medical authority.

Conrad and Schneider believe that they can advance the theory of medicalization by removing medicine from it. But their approach risks the Humpty Dumpty syndrome (Carroll 1942:196):

> "When I use a word," Humpty Dumpty said, in rather a scornful tone, "it means just what I choose it to mean—neither more nor less."
>
> "The question is," said Alice, "whether you can make words mean so many different things."
>
> "The question is," said Humpty Dumpty, "which is to be master— that's all."

It is easy to understand Conrad and Schneider's temptation to remove "medicine" from "medicalization." If medicalization involves extending the medical profession's activities to some new area, then alcoholism is only weakly medicalized: few medical schools teach about alcoholism, few doctors make diagnoses of alcoholism, few doctors (and fewer nurses) treat alcoholism, and the popular "disease" concept of alcoholism does not embrace the Western medical model (Freund and McGuire 1991:6–7). But Conrad and Schneider have tried to revise the medicalization thesis to recognize the ways in which alcoholism seems to *be* medicalized: especially among educated laypeople, the "disease" model is the dominant one; and the disease model dominates in treatment centers, self-help settings, and that amorphous fellowship often dubbed "the recovering community."

But, rather than waiving the requirement of medical involvement in the medicalization process, medicalization theory should modify its conceptualization of medicine itself. In what follows, I will argue that adherents of the disease model of alcoholism favor an alternative medicine, one with a relationship to allopathic medicine analogous to that of Christian Science or chiropractic. The apparent anomaly of "medicalization without medicine" is resolved when medicalization theory adopts a constructionist view of medicine as well as of deviance.

SCIENCE AND MEDICINE AS SOCIAL CONSTRUCTIONS

Ironically, Conrad and Schneider's theoretical conundrum might have been forestalled if they had adopted a constructionist view of science and medicine. Constructionist sociologists of science (Knorr-Cetina 1981) argue that science is a constructed set of rules for defining "truth." Multiple scientific worlds coexist, although some command more legitimacy and resources. In a similarly constructionist tradition, many critical sociologists of medicine argue that all healing systems are socially constructed, and that allopathic medicine is just one medicine among many (McGuire 1981). These critics do not assume that allopathic medicine's legal stranglehold on the words "medicine," "medical doctor," and "reimbursable medical procedure" is a consequence of its monopoly on the ability to heal. Instead, they explain this monopoly by focusing on the "collective mobility project" of the allopathic medical professions and on the routes through which M.D.s amassed cultural and political power (Friedson 1970; Starr 1982).

But the legitimacy of conventional science and medicine is such that it suborns even sociologists. Like Conrad and Schneider, most sociologists think only about conventional allopathic medicine when they think about "medicine." And allopathic medicine has been indifferent to the "disease model" created and promulgated through Alcoholics Anonymous (AA) and the "recovering community."

MAINSTREAM MEDICINE AND ALCOHOLISM

Mainstream allopathic medicine generally has ignored attempts to medicalize alcoholism. Nevertheless, medicalization popularizers and AA adherents make much of its official pronouncements that grudgingly make concessions to the disease model. For example, a recent statement in the *Journal of the American Medical Association* recognized alcoholism as "an heterogenous disease involving bio-psycho-social factors" and noted a "genetic vulnerability" in many individuals (ASAM 1992). But such official statements are products of furious politicking among a small minority of a profession (Kirk and Kutchins 1992), and they have little relationship to professional practice.

Despite all public pronouncements about alcoholism as a disease, medical practice rejects treating it as such. Not only does alcoholism not follow the model of a "disease," it is not amenable to standard medical treatment, and alcoholics rarely are willing to become even minimally acceptable "patients."

The disease theory of alcoholism violates every one of the assumptions that Freund and McGuire (1991) identify as basic to the biomedical model. First, that model assumes a clear dichotomy between the mind and the body. It also takes the standpoint of physical reductionism, assuming "that illness can be reduced to disordered bodily (biochemical or neurophysiological) functions" (1991:226). In contrast, the "disease theory of alcoholism" characterizes alcoholism as a physical, psychological, and spiritual illness. These three dimensions of human existence are not hierarchically ordered; one is not the "primary" realm, and all are equally important to the person's health. Second, the biomedical model assumes that each disease has a single and potentially identifiable cause. The "disease theory" of alcoholism spends little time on the issue of causality, but adherents of the disease theory identify a wide range of different factors that might be involved in alcoholism's etiology (Heather and Robertson 1989; Kinney and Leaton 1987). Third, the biomedical model draws an analogy between the body and the machine; as with the repair of a machine, a part of the body can be repaired in isolation from the rest of the body. But the disease theory of alcoholism is intimately tied to an approach to "recovery" that insists upon the relatedness of all aspects of a person's life. Alcoholism is an illness of the whole person; consequently, recovery must be the recovery of the whole person.

In both the explanation and treatment of alcoholism, the disease model includes a consideration of "spirituality" that is inimical to biomedicine:

> Spirituality is the identification with that which is the deepest, most profound, and permanent element of being human. The chemically dependent person needs this unadulterated type of spirituality, having profoundly experienced a lack of wholeness, a fragmentation, a fracturing, a disintegration, a going to pieces; thus, the addict cries out desperately for wholeness, for healing and mending, for integration and integrity. It is a life or death choice. For the AA person, it is a matter of survival. (McElrath 1987:152)

The "disease model of alcoholism" fits poorly with the biomedical model of disease because the former developed independently of the latter. The disease model of alcoholism was not pioneered by medical doctors, except in the limited sense that one of the founders of Alcoholics Anonymous (AA) was a physician.[3] True, the beginning of AA's "Big Book" is a 1930s letter from a Dr. William Silkworth in which he proposes that "the action of alcohol on these chronic alcoholics is a manifestation of an allergy . . . the phenomenon of craving is limited to this class and never occurs in the average temperate drinker" (Alcoholics Anonymous 1976:xxvi). But the "Big Book" generally ignores the causes of alcoholism, except to say that they are "obscure" (Alcoholics Anonymous 1976:24). Much more of the book is devoted to discussing spiritual change than the origins of alcoholism. As the "Big Book" puts it (Alcoholics Anonymous 1976:50) in the chapter addressed to agnostics: "deep down in every man, woman, and child, is the fundamental idea of God. . . . For faith in a Power greater than ourselves, and miraculous demonstrations of that power in human lives, are facts as old as man himself." Only a Higher Power is capable of stopping the alcoholic from drinking, because alcoholics by definition have "no power of choice in drink" (Alcoholics Anonymous 1976:24). Only the Higher Power can "accomplish those things for us which we could never do by ourselves" (Alcoholics Anonymous 1976:25).

AA's disease model is somewhat inchoate, but asserts that alcoholics are physically, mentally, and spiritually "different" from nonalcoholics. This "difference" makes them susceptible to liquor in ways that other people are not. They are not alcoholics because they drink too much; they drink too much because they are alcoholics. AA's disease model eschews seeing alcoholism as a "symptom" of some underlying psychological problem; the AA model is even reluctant to support "dual diagnoses" (e.g., a diagnosis of alcoholism and a personality disorder) in formal treatment. Alcoholism is the alcoholic's primary problem, and abstinence through "the program" is the only solution. But, just as alcoholism is more than a behavior, to be "in recovery" is more than abstinence from liquor. Rudy (1986:46) quotes one AA member as explaining, "When I stopped drinking, I wasn't sober—just dry. In the beginning, I was drunk and I wasn't even drinking. So you see, alcoholism has to be more than just physical."

Not only does the disease theory of alcoholism fail to correspond with mainstream medicine's concept of a disease, but alcoholism itself resists standard medical interventions. The biomedical model and its associated medical institutions developed around the diagnosis and treatment of acute illness: people "caught" diseases like dysentery or diphtheria; doctors identified the diseases and prescribed medicines to cure them. But alcoholism is more like a chronic than an acute illness, and chronic illnesses are problematic for medical doctors and institutions. Maddox and Glass (1988:258) point out that many chronic illnesses are "incompatible with standard accepted conceptions of morbidity as self-limiting, acute in onset, and specific in course and treatment." Translated, this means that chronic illnesses do not resemble the illnesses that mainstream medicine is organized to see and to treat; the paradigmatic illness is an acute illness that goes away eventually (whether through death or recovery), is experienced as a radical departure from normal good health, is caused by a particular entity or event, and can be treated with a particular intervention. Chronic illnesses are a new and underdeveloped part of mainstream medical practice. So, as mainstream medicine deals poorly with chronic problems such as rheumatoid arthritis, its failure to treat the more stigmatized and difficult chronic problem of "alcoholism" should come as no surprise.

Another reason physicians avoid alcoholism is that alcoholics make poor patients. People decide to "seek the sick status" as a consequence of social factors rather than biological pressures (Kurtz and Chalfant 1991:76). Five factors influence whether or not people interpret some state as a "medical problem": (1) they experience a crisis that calls attention to the symptoms; (2) the symptoms may threaten some social activity valued by the individual; (3) someone sanctions the individual for the symptoms and often advises/insists upon a visit to a doctor; (4) the individual feels that the condition is threatening; and (5) the individual's symptoms are similar to others experienced in the past. But these factors are unlikely to produce a definition of "drinking alcohol" as a "medical problem." People do not enjoy shortness of breath, dizzy spells, or persistent digestive problems, but they do enjoy drinking alcohol. And many will work hard to organize their interpretation of the world in a way that permits them to continue drinking.

Alcoholics do not present themselves in doctors' offices with a list of symptoms that include, "I keep drinking even though I want to quit" and "My life is absolutely miserable because of problems caused by my drinking." They might say, "I have a pain right here" (cirrhosis) or "I have trouble catching my breath" (cardiac myopathy), but they are unlikely to describe behavioral problems. "Denial is part of the disease," say both AA and the most recent AMA pronouncement on alcoholism. But a patient who does not want to be treated is a difficult patient, a patient unlikely to comply with the physician's instructions. Doctors have plenty of eager, relatively compliant patients; they do not need to deal with the difficulty of the alcoholic. As Freund and McGuire (1991:243) put it:

> physicians particularly dislike situations, such as emphysema, senility, diabetes, arthritis, psychiatric conditions, and obesity, that challenge their faith in the potency of bioscientific medicine . . . they dislike conditions, such as back pain, chronic vague pains, headaches, and chronic fatigue, that offer little probability of cure while bringing their competence or diagnostic skills into question. Furthermore, they dislike conditions for which they believe the patient or others are responsible, such as sexual behavior [that produces medical complications], auto accidents, suicide attempts, and other self-inflicted injuries.

Further, physicians have a strong sense of time constraint. "Even when time is actually available for more medical work, doctors narrow the objectives of their routine (and typically uninteresting) practice by thinking not 'What can I do for this patient?' but 'What can I do for this patient in the next six minutes?'" (Freund and McGuire 1991:240). Alcoholism is not a diagnosis that will be accepted without a challenge, and nothing in most doctors' training makes the challenge worthwhile.

Medical doctors' rejection of the disease theory of alcoholism has a strong basis in the biomedical model underpinning most of their training and in the social dynamics of the doctor/patient relationship. It also finds support in the medical science that ostensibly underpins medical practice. In practice, of course, most medical doctors know little about medical research. Front-line medical practitioners learn about medical advances through a multistage process that is more social than intellectual. But medical research on alcoholism does not support the disease model; highly respected and influential medical authorities do not promote the theory and treatment of alcoholism as a disease. Similarly, medical research repeatedly has failed to find any genetic basis for alcoholism (Fingarette 1988; Heather and Robertson 1989; Peele 1989). Thus, medical students are not introduced to a biomedical model of alcoholism, and currently practicing physicians face no pressures to change their ideas about alcoholism and its place in their practice.

Although allopathic physicians and mainstream medical science are indifferent to the disease model, a significant segment of the population is not. Conrad and Schneider's struggle to consider alcoholism as "medicalized" largely rests on the passionate embrace of the disease model by a significant group: AA members, their (often Al-Anon) families, and persons in AA-based groups (e.g., Narcotics Anonymous, Cocaine Anonymous). Almost a decade ago, Norman Denzin (1987b:17) estimated that about 800,000 persons annually were involved in some AA-related process of "recovery."[4] If AA has continued to grow at the rapid pace at which it did in the 1980s (Robertson 1988:220), the AA philosophy is a part of the consciousness of an even larger proportion of the American population.

The AA-influenced "recovering community" is loyal to the disease concept and, largely through its efforts, the idea that "alcoholism is a disease" has spread. According to Gallup polls of adult Americans (cited in Peele 1989:60), almost two-thirds of late-1980s respondents to a random sample survey agreed that alcoholism can be hereditary; in 1982, only 40% agreed with that statement. Crawford's (1987:290) exhaustive literature review reports a growing American consensus on some elements of the disease model. And Heather and Robertson (1989:148) offer a similar summary: "the proportion of people found to agree with the bald statement that alcoholism is an illness or that the alcoholic is a sick person steadily increased after the Second World War."

But critics of the disease model argue that it is only weakly held by those who espouse it. Rudy (1986) reports that, in addition to the disease model, AA members generally have a psychological explanation for their alcoholism. Other researchers (Heather and Robertson 1989:150; Tournier 1979) conclude that disease adherents also hold a confusing

muddle of beliefs about the alcoholic as "weak willed," about environmental or psychological causes for alcoholism, and about the "responsibility" of the deviant drinker. But, for at least those disease adherents
who have been strongly affected by AA, these apparent contradictions
are not experienced as contradictions. Rather, from the AA perspective,
these beliefs are part of an integrated vision of human health and illness.
They are part of a system of alternative medicine, not a failed attempt to
transfer a concept from mainstream medicine to a new arena.

THE DISEASE MODEL AND ALTERNATIVE MEDICINE

Many unconventional medicines coexist with allopathic medicine.
But, because the political power of allopathic medicine is so great (Starr
1982), most of these are relatively unorganized, low-profile, and often
invisible (Murray and Rubel 1992). Consider, for example, the barely
concealed surprise of the authors of a recent, pathbreaking article in the
New England Journal of Medicine (Eisenberg et al. 1993:251) that found that
"the estimated number of visits made in 1990 to providers of unconventional therapy was greater than the number of visits to all primary care
medical doctors nationwide, and the amount spent out of pocket on
unconventional therapy was comparable to the amount spent out of
pocket by Americans for all hospitalization." Their study defined unconventional therapies as "medical interventions not taught widely at U.S.
hospitals" (1993:246). These included chiropractic, massage therapy,
commercial weight loss programs, biofeedback, hypnosis, imagery,
spiritual healing, lifestyle diets (e.g., macrobiotics), herbal medicine,
energy healing, self-help groups, exercise, prayer, homeopathy, and
acupuncture. But, as if dramatizing the bias of mainstream medicine,
these researchers resisted acknowledging that these "medical interventions" are part of systems of ideas and practices that are "alternative
medicines." They reserved the term "medicine" for mainstream medicine, writing about these "unconventional therapies" as if they were not
part of any larger system of ideas and practices. However, if we refuse to
be suborned by the power of allopathic medicine, we arrive at a different
conclusion. From this perspective, a system of medical knowledge is any
theory of illness and wellness that is coupled with the practice of interventions intended to restore health.

In a chapter in *Other Healers: Unorthodox Medicine in America* (1988),
Norman Gevitz notes a slow scholarly movement away from the presumption that only orthodox medicine is "real medicine." When researchers refuse to privilege the perspective of orthodox medicine, they

discover that many medical worlds coexist: chiropractic (Wardwell 1988), homeopathy (Kaufman 1988), Christian Science (Sheopfelin 1988), divine healing (Harell 1988), botanical medicine (Rothstein 1988), folk medicine (Hufford 1988), and more. Although Gevitz's book does not include Alcoholics Anonymous or the "recovery movement," it easily could have. AA and related fellowships also have created visions of the meaning of health, the origins of illness, and the nature of healing. Out of this alternative medical system, the "disease theory of alcoholism" emerged.

Most sociologists assume that the statement that "alcoholism is a disease" is analogous to the statement that "measles is a disease," and they have had one of two reactions to the former statement: most commonly, they accept the medicalization of alcoholism as another episode in "medical imperialism"; but some analysts have marshalled evidence to disprove the disease hypothesis and demonstrate the social causes of alcoholism. Thus, Heather and Robertson (1989) title the first part of their book, "Problem drinking is not a disease." But, as Rudy (1986) argues, the disease model is neither an hypothesis to be tested nor a statement of the outcome of scientific research. Rather, it is the "objectification" of "AA members' externalizations regarding their experiences as alcoholics" (Rudy 1986:92). Denzin (1987a:64–69) also argues that AA did not borrow its disease model from mainstream science, does not seek legitimacy from mainstream science, and is uninterested in how mainstream science evaluates its perspective on alcoholism:

> much of modern behavioral science builds upon the Cartesian dualism that posits an objective world that can be studied, interpreted, and controlled by the methods of modern inquiry. Alcoholics Anonymous denies this dualism. It denies also an objective view of the world, locating the alcoholic subject, instead, in a world that is intersubjective, noncausal, spiritual, collective, and distinctly oriental, as opposed to western and occidental. (Denzin 1987a:65)

As people become part of AA, they reconstruct their own drinking history using AA's disease model. They develop a new way of thinking and feeling about their selves (Denzin 1987a, b), one that is consistent with the AA philosophy. Then, as they move into "twelfth step" work (i.e., into helping other alcoholics), they disseminate the model to others. Alcoholics "in recovery" through AA are the single largest group of persons possessing a well-developed ideology of alcoholism. Thus, they are a significant force in shaping others' attitudes toward alcoholism.

The impact of AA's model has intensified as inpatient treatment centers proliferated. For many years, persons "in recovery" have been the majority of front-line workers in alcoholism and drug dependency treatment centers (Brown 1991; Weiner 1981:221) and they have been a significant proportion of other treatment workers. Thus, AA's disease model dominates treatment "not only as a philosophy but also a method" (Tournier 1979:230): it dictates not only how treatment workers think about alcoholism, but how they treat it. Treatment philosophy is dominated by AA's insistence that alcoholism is a disease with a biological basis, albeit with other significant dimensions. For example, the *Encyclopedia of Alcoholism* (O'Brien and Chafetz 1991:88-89) notes that, "[t]he disease concept of alcoholism provides the basis for most of the current approaches to the treatment of alcoholism" and "most authorities still affirm the major elements of the disease concept." AA's Twelve Steps, which assume abstinence from liquor and focus on behavioral, emotional, and spiritual changes,[5] dominate treatment methods.

As the Twelve Steps indicate, the disease model is more than an unproven (and perhaps, from the perspective of mainstream science, unprovable) contention about biology. It is also a contention about the way that a disease resides in the whole person: body, mind, and spirit (AA 1976; Denzin 1987a; Rudy 1986). After examining the social thought of AA, Kurtz and Kurtz (1985:125) argue that AA's disease model is fundamentally antithetical to mainstream medicine's ideas of illness: "the alcoholic does not 'have' [alcoholism]—he *is* it. To be an alcoholic, then, is *not* to 'have alcoholism': it is to be an alcoholic." This holistic approach to disease requires an equally holistic approach to treatment.

AA warns alcoholics that they must make a leap of faith in order to live (Denzin 1987a:65). As AA's "Big Book" puts it, "The central fact of our lives [in recovery] today is the absolute certainty that our Creator has entered into our hearts and lives in a way which is indeed miraculous" (AA 1976:25). Because alcoholism is a disease of the whole person, it can be "cured" only by changes in the whole person. The body must stop drinking; the mind must change its beliefs; the spirit must rise to a new level of commitment to and awareness of a Higher Power.

In this regard, AA resembles many old and new alternative medicines. For example, in the late 1980s, physician Bernie S. Siegel produced two best-selling books on the significance of emotion and spirituality in causing and curing disease. His *Love, Medicine and Miracles* (1986) and *Peace, Love and Healing* (1989) underscore the market for the message that health is more than the absence of sickness, spirituality is an essential part of wellness, and mind/soul is a powerful factor in shaping health. But the message is as old as the century-old tradition of Christian Science, which rests on the premise that the patient's "true nature" is healthy (Schoepflin 1988:201–202).

AA resembles other holistic, alternative medical systems in its insistence that adversity is an opportunity for higher-level wellness. Siegel (1986) argues that "[t]he ultimate goal is to use your disease and affliction as a gift." The recovering person has the opportunity to create a more joyful, meaningful, and healthy life than that prior to the illness. Similarly, the individual "in recovery" is continually presented with an opportunity to move to a higher level of wellness. The recovering alcoholic is more self-conscious, reflective, honest, peaceful, and hopeful than the alcoholic before recovery.

Many analysts and critics of AA focus on its religious aspects, suggesting that it is a "religion" or even a "religious cult." But, as Rudy and Greil (1988) argue, AA provides its members with a remarkably consistent and useful rebuttal to this charge. AA literature and members argue that AA is a spiritual but not a religious organization, and they underscore that the "Higher Power" can be a traditional concept of God, a pantheistic idea of the AA fellowship, or any other force that transcends the individual human. In its emphasis on spirituality, AA demonstrates its continuity with nineteenth-century movements such as Christian Science and contemporary movements such as "mind/body" medicine (Borysenko 1987) and "quantum healing" (Chopra 1993). Mainstream medicine may have broken the link between transcendence and healing, but it strongly survives in alternative medicines (see the articles in Gevitz 1988). Spiritual healing practices continue to be widespread, even in modern Western societies (Eisenberg et al. 1993; Freund and McGuire 1991:196); the theory of medicalization would benefit from recognizing and studying them with as much care as it has devoted to conventional medicine.

FALSE PREMISES, FALSE CONCLUSIONS

The theory of medicalization originated in a decade when several inaccurate background assumptions shaped sociologists' work and blinded them to the existence of multiple medical worlds.

> Analysts have long pointed to social factors that have encouraged or abetted medicalization: the diminution of religion, an abiding faith in science, rationality, and progress, the increased prestige and power of the medical profession, the American penchant for individual and technological solutions to problems, and a general humanitarian trend in western societies. (Conrad 1992:213)

But this list tells only part of the story of the twentieth century in the western societies. Recent sociological research shows that none of these trends is as strong as earlier sociologists believed.

First, the assumption of secularization has had some significant challenges in recent years. An overwhelming proportion of the American population report believing in God and in an afterlife; many mid- and late-life adult Americans have a formal religious affiliation. A scan of the *New York Times* bestseller list over the past few years reveals the power of calls to spirituality: for example, Marianne Williamson's *Return to Love* (1992), based on "a course in miracles," teaches the power of prayer and the instrumental utility of the transcendent. Her work is paralleled by the spiritual content of similarly best-selling authors John Bradshaw (1988) and Deepak Chopra (1993).

Second, Americans' "abiding faith in science, rationality, and progress" has failed to abide with them. As Robert Nisbet pointed out in *History of the Idea of Progress*, the American idea of progress had toppled from its cultural centrality by the 1960s. In the post-Hiroshima and DDT era, "science" is as much associated with threat as with salvation. And rationality's triumph is mitigated by the deliberately nonrational embrace of AA, "inner child" work, crystal healing, late-night television's Psychic Friends' Network, and formal religion's influences.

Third, while Americans may continue to yearn for technological solutions to problems, they have tempered their individualism with novel forms of collective problem-solving. For every person who labels his affective disturbance as a "depression" to be medicated with Prozac, another likely interprets similarly ambiguous feelings as distress that can be resolved through "working the program" within some group. As Robert Wuthnow (1994) shows, self-help groups are remarkably numerous and, generally, reasonably effective settings within which individuals wrestle with the problems of self-esteem and self-knowledge. Groups that mirror AA's insistence on a Higher Power are a direct and often successful assault on Americans' ambivalent individualism (Bellah et al. 1991).

Based on erroneous assumptions about a strong and unilinear trend toward the unchallenged dominance of mainstream medicine, the medicalization thesis has offered an implicit criticism of the process of medicalization.[6] Although Conrad and Schneider list its social benefits (1980:246–248),[7] their discussion of medicalization's "darker side" (Conrad and Schneider 1980:248–252) dwarfs their discussion of its "lighter side." But, just as they were mistaken in their assumptions about mainstream medicine's power and the power of the trends that produced it, they made similar errors as they outlined their fears. For at least the disease model of alcoholism, the consequences of medicalization are far less threatening than imagined.

First, Conrad and Schneider allege that medicalization makes deviants less responsible for their actions. But, although the disease theory's account of alcoholism's origins denies that alcoholism is the "fault" of the alcoholic, the disease model's program for recovery stresses significant individual responsibility. The individual must confess his faults and make amends; he must commit himself to a continual process of moral inventory; he must "work the program." The alcoholic is not responsible for his alcoholism, but he is responsible for his recovery. The disease model of alcoholism has strong and evident roots in the cultural values of individual responsibility.

Second, they charge that medical language hides the value judgments made in defining even a medicalized deviance. But AA's world is not a world of moral neutrality. Compulsive, repetitive drinking is an undesirable state of affairs. And individuals are given increasing amounts of responsibility to discipline themselves to avoid such behavior. Consider Denzin's (1987b:130–131) discussion of AA's position on "slips" (i.e., on taking a drink while attempting recovery): "Alcoholics who drink after a long period [e.g., one year] of sobriety are seen as using their illness as an excuse for drinking. On the other hand, newcomers are seen as drinking because their illness causes them to drink."

Third, they argue that medicalization increases social domination by experts. Conrad and Schneider clearly believe that this is "bad," although the Progressives would have applauded it. In the case of alcoholism, of course, the point is moot: the diagnosis and treatment of alcoholism are not dominated by experts. Indirectly, of course, one might argue that any discussion of "diseases" increases the cultural power of medicine. But mainstream medicine is beleaguered from many sources and its domination is far from assured.

Fourth, they argue that medical social control is expanded. Because medicalization is *by definition* an extension of medical social control, this is a tautology. But it is presented as an empirical consequence of medicalization, and it is assumed to be "bad" because it contributes to the fifth dark dimension of medicalization: its contribution to the individualization of social problems. Conrad and Schneider (1980:25) argue that "[t]he medicalization of deviance is part of a larger phenomenon that is prevalent in our society: the individualization of social problems." But what hegemonic culture permits problems to be attributed to "the society" rather than to the individual deviants? Moreover, doesn't the individualization of social problems entail the demand that individuals be seen as responsible for their actions? If so, the first and fifth dark dimensions describe incompatible outcomes.

Is medical social control expanded? In the case of alcoholism, alcoholics themselves constructed, developed, and propagated the disease model. Its dissemination has not increased the power of mainstream medicine.

Is the individualization of social problems enhanced by medicalization? Perhaps. But, although the disease model explains that one becomes an alcoholic alone, one can recover from alcoholism only in a group and through "working the steps." Recovery through AA is organized around participation in AA groups, acknowledgment of interdependence with others, and the acceptance of responsibility for some parts of others' lives.

Conrad and Schneider's sixth and seventh negative consequences are the ones that ring truest for the disease model of alcoholism. They argue that medicalization depoliticizes deviant behavior by keeping "us from recognizing it as a possible intentional repudiation of existing political arrangements" (Conrad and Schneider 1980:251). But what form of social control doesn't? Indeed, a hallmark of social control is that it turns into "deviance" what might otherwise be "rebellion." Still, if doping and drinking are some kind of prepolitical rebellion, the disease model pulls attention away from their message.

And, finally, they argue that medicalization contributes to the exclusion of evil from the discourse of deviance and normalcy. Here, I believe, they are right. Although transcendence and spirituality thrive in the alternative medicines, evil forces and evil choices make less frequent appearances. God has survived, while the Devil is in retreat. The irony would make even Nietzsche grin.

THE FUTURE OF MEDICALIZATION THEORY

If medicalization theory ceases to privilege mainstream medicine, it will be in a better position to understand what it means for alcoholism to be medicalized. If biomedicine is no longer the measure of all that is medical, then we can begin to explore the vaguely articulated medical world that has produced the disease model of alcoholism and has won so many adherents. This exploration will help us understand more than alcoholism. It will help us understand the explosion of putative diseases that have arrived on TV talk shows and on the "self-help" shelves of our local bookstores. A revised approach to medicalization can permit us to see the alcoholics of AA, the "adult children" of Adult Children of Alcoholics, the codependents of CODA (Codependents Anonymous), the sex addicts, the gambling addicts, the workaholics, and the rest as more than social dupes who make up stories about their lives. Instead, we can begin to take those stories seriously and examine the storytellers' attempts to turn their stories into truths. We can examine the relative success of different diseases and consider the relationship that emerges among them. Each has its own set of knowledge-workers, of consumers, and of critics. And very few of them involve practitioners with white lab coats or "M.D." on their letterhead.

NOTES

1. For theoretical reasons, I should put "alcoholism" in quotes whenever I use it. But that practice is so awkward in a text that I would rather offer this blanket disclaimer: this chapter does not assume that "alcoholism" is any more (or less) real than "murder," "depression," or "masculinity." All are social constructions.

2. Allopathic medicine is medicine that seeks to cure by producing effects dissimilar to the disease that it seeks to treat. The term is an explicit contrast with homeopathy, medicine that cures by the principle of similarities. I use this term as a way of "making strange" the medicine that Americans take for granted. I could also call this medicine "conventional" or "orthodox."

3. AA was founded in 1935 by two alcoholics. Bill Wilson was an unsuccessful businessman with a longstanding drinking problem, and Dr. Bob Smith was a proctologist whose medical practice was menaced by his drinking. For this story, see Robertson (1988).

4. AA members are active members, attending regular meetings. In one recent survey, the average member attended four meetings a week. Although many analysts argue that some of those who cease attending meetings maintain their sobriety, no systematic data on dropouts are available (Institute of Medicine 1990:109).

5. The Twelve Steps are:

(1) We admitted that we were powerless over alcohol—that our lives had become unmanageable; (2) Came to believe that a power greater than ourselves could restore us to sanity; (3) Made a decision to turn our will and our lives over to the care of God *as we understood him*; (4) Made a searching and fearless moral inventory of ourselves; (5) Admitted to God, to ourselves, and to another human being the exact nature of our wrongs; (6) Were entirely ready to have God remove all these defects of character; (7) Humbly asked Him to remove our shortcomings; (8) Made a list of all persons we had harmed, and became willing to make amends to them all; (9) Made direct amends to such people wherever possible, except when to do so would injure them or others; (10) Continued to take personal inventory and when we were wrong promptly admitted it; (11) Sought through prayer and meditation to improve our conscious contact with God *as we understood Him*, praying only for knowledge of His will for us and the power to carry that out; (12) Having had a spiritual awakening as the result of these Steps, we tried to carry this message to alcoholics, and to practice these principles in all our affairs [italics in original]. (AA 1976)

6. Conrad (1992:210) notes that "[t]he term [medicalization] has been used more often in the context of a critique of medicalization (or overmedicalization) than as a neutral term."

7. The social benefits are: "the creation of humanitarian and nonpunitive sanctions; the extension of the sick role to some deviants; a reduction of individual responsibility, blame, and possibly stigma for deviance; an optimistic therapeutic ideology; care and treatment rendered by a prestigious medical profession; and the availability of a more flexible and often more efficient means of social control" (Conrad and Schneider 1980:248).

REFERENCES

Abbott, A. 1988. *The System of Professions: An Essay on the Division of Expert Labor*. Chicago: University of Chicago Press.

Alcoholics Anonymous. 1976. *Alcoholics Anonymous: The Story of How Many Thousands of Men and Women Have Recovered from Alcoholism*, 3rd ed. New York: Alcoholics Anonymous World Services, Inc.

ASAM (American Society for Addiction Medicine). 1992. *ASAM News* 7(5):1.

Bellah, R., R. N. Madsden, W. M. Sullivan, A. Swidler, and S. Tipton. 1991. *Habits of the Heart: Individualism and Commitment in American Life*. Berkeley: University of California Press.

Borysenko, J. (with L. Rothstein). 1987. *Minding the Body, Mending the Mind*. Reading, MA: Addison-Wesley.

Bradshaw, J. 1988. *Healing the Shame That Binds You*. Deerfield Beach, FL: Health Communications.

Brown, J. D. 1991. "The Professional Ex-: An Alternative for Exiting the Deviant Career." *Sociological Quarterly* 32:219–230.

Calhoun, C., D. Light, and S. Keller. 1994. *Sociology*, 6th ed. New York: McGraw-Hill.

Carroll, L. 1942. *Through the Looking Glass and What Alice Found There*. Boston: Books.

Chopra, D. 1993. *Ageless Body, Timeless Mind: The Quantum Alternative to Growing Old*. New York: Harmony Books.

Cockerham, W. C. 1988. "Medical Sociology." Pp. 575–600 in *Handbook of Sociology*, edited by N.J. Smelser. Newbury Park, CA: Sage.

Conrad, P. 1992. "Medicalization and Social Control." *Annual Review of Sociology* 18:209–232.

Conrad, P., and J. W. Schneider. 1980. *Deviance and Medicalization: From Badness to Sickness*. St. Louis: Mosby.

———. 1992. *Deviance and Medicalization: From Badness to Sickness*. Expanded Edition. Philadelphia: Temple University Press.

Crawford, A. 1987. "Attitudes about Alcohol: A General Review." *Journal of Drug and Alcohol Dependence* 19:279–311.

Denzin, N. K. 1987a. *The Alcoholic Self*. Newbury Park, CA: Sage.

———. 1987b. *The Recovering Alcoholic*. Newbury Park, CA: Sage.

Eisenberg, D. M., R. C. Kessler, C. Foster, F. E. Norlock, D. R. Calkins, and T. L. Delbanco. 1993. "Unconventional Medicine in the United States: Prevalence, Costs, and Patterns of Use." *New England Journal of Medicine* 328:246–252.

Fingarette, H. 1988. *Heavy Drinking: The Myth of Alcoholism as Disease*. Berkeley: University of California Press.

Freidson, E. 1970. *Profession of Medicine: A Study of the Sociology of Applied Knowledge*. New York: Dodd, Mead.

Freund, P. E. S., and M. B. McGuire. 1991. *Health, Illness, and the Social Body: A Critical Sociology*. Englewood Cliffs, NJ: Prentice-Hall.

Gevitz, N. 1988. "Three Perspectives on Unorthodox Medicine." Pp. 1–28 in

Other Healers: Unorthodox Medicine in America, edited by N. Gevitz. Baltimore: Johns Hopkins Press.

Harrell, D. E., Jr. 1988. "Divine Healing in Modern Protestantism." Pp. 215–227 in *Other Healers: Unorthodox Medicine in America*, edited by N. Gevitz. Baltimore: Johns Hopkins Press.

Heather, N., and I. Robertson. 1989. *Problem Drinking*, 2nd ed. Oxford: Oxford University Press.

Hufford, D. J. 1988. "Contemporary Folk Medicine." Pp. 228–264 in *Other Healers: Unorthodox Medicine in America*, edited by N. Gevitz. Baltimore: Johns Hopkins Press.

Illich, I. 1976. *Medical Nemesis: The Expropriation of Health.* New York: Pantheon Books.

Institute of Medicine. 1990. *Broadening the Base of Treatment for Alcohol Problems.* Washington: National Academy Press.

Kaufman, M. 1988. "Homeopathy in American: The Rise and Fall and Persistence of a Medical Heresy." Pp. 99–123 in *Other Healers: Unorthodox Medicine in America*, edited by N. Gevitz. Baltimore: Johns Hopkins Press.

Kinney, J., and G. Leaton. 1987. *Loosening the Grip: A Handbook of Alcohol Information.* St. Louis: Times Mirror/Mosby Publishing.

Kirk, S. A., and H. Kutchins. 1992. *The Selling of DSM: The Rhetoric of Science in Psychiatry.* Hawthorne, NY: Aldine de Gruyter.

Knorr-Cetina, K. D. 1981. *The Manufacture of Knowledge: An Essay on the Constructivist and Contextual Nature of Science.* New York: Pergamon Press.

Kurtz, E., and L. F. Kurtz. 1985. "The Social Thought of Alcoholics." *Journal of Drug Issues* 15:119–134.

Kurtz, R. A., and H. P. Chalfant. 1991. *The Sociology of Medicine and Illness*, 2nd ed. Boston: Allyn and Bacon.

Macionis, J. J. 1989. *Sociology*, 2nd ed. Englewood Cliffs, NJ: Prentice-Hall.

Maddox, G. L., and T. A. Glass. 1988. "Health Care of the Chronically Ill." Pp. 236–261 in *Handbook of Medical Sociology*, 4th ed., edited by H. E. Freeman and S. Levine. Englewood Cliffs, NJ: Prentice-Hall.

McElrath, D. 1987. *Hazelden: A Spiritual Odyssey.* Center City, MN: Hazelden Foundation.

McGuire, M. B. (with D. Kantor). 1988. *Ritual Healing in Suburban America.* New Brunswick, NJ: Rutgers University Press.

Nisbet, R. 1980. *History of the Idea of Progress.* New York: Basic Books.

O'Brien, R., and M. Chafetz. 1991. *Encyclopedia of Alcoholism*, 3rd ed. New York: Facts on File.

Peele, S. 1989. *The Diseasing of America: Addiction Treatment Out of Control.* Lexington, MA: Lexington Books.

Robertson, N. 1988. *Getting Better: Inside Alcoholics Anonymous.* New York: Morrow.

Rothstein, W. G. 1988. "The Botanical Movement and Orthodox Medicine." Pp. 29–51 in *Other Healers: Unorthodox Medicine in America*, edited by N. Gevitz. Baltimore: Johns Hopkins Press.

Rudy, D. R. 1986. *Becoming Alcoholic: Alcoholics Anonymous and the Reality of Alcoholism.* Carbondale: Southern Illinois University Press.

Rudy, D. R., and A. L. Greil. 1988. "Is Alcoholics Anonymous a Religious Organization?: Meditations on Marginality." *Sociological Analysis* 50:41–51.

Schoepflin, R. B. 1988. "Christian Science Healing in America." Pp. 192–214 in *Other Healers: Unorthodox Medicine in America*, edited by N. Gevitz. Baltimore: Johns Hopkins Press.

Siegel, B. S. 1986. *Love, Medicine and Miracles*. New York: Harper & Row.

———. 1989. *Peace, Love and Healing*. New York: Harper & Row.

Starr, P. 1982. *The Social Transformation of American Medicine*. New York: Basic Books.

Taylor, I., P. Walton, and J. Young. 1973. *The New Criminology*. New York: Harper & Row.

Tournier, R. E. 1979. "Alcoholics Anonymous as Treatment and as Ideology." *Journal of Studies on Alcohol* 40:230–239.

Wardwell, W. I. 1988. "Chiropractors: Evolution to Acceptance." Pp. 157–191 in *Other Healers: Unorthodox Medicine in America*, edited by N. Gevitz. Baltimore: Johns Hopkins Press.

Weiner, C. L. 1981. *The Politics of Alcoholism: Building an Arena around a Social Problem*. New Brunswick, NJ: Transaction Books.

Williamson, M. 1992. *A Return to Love*. New York: Harper Collins.

Wuthnow, R. 1994. *Sharing the Journey*. New York: Free Press.

5

The Moral Drama of Multicultural Education

SHAN NELSON-ROWE

Multicultural education is a social movement within education that seeks to transform the organization, practice, and ideological content of schooling. More specifically, the movement calls for greater cultural diversity in matters of curriculum, pedagogy, faculty, and other educational issues. Multicultural educators view themselves as representing subordinate cultural groups within schools in a challenge to the dominance of an institutional elite.

This chapter analyzes the claims made by multicultural educators with respect to the identities of the various groups involved in education: teachers, administrators, students, reformers, etc. These claims can be seen as key elements in the process of collective identity construction. My analysis focuses on the rhetorical uses of language in constructing collective identities. More specifically I examine how multicultural educators in particular have created identities that reflect a melodramatic view of the moral order, with victims, villains, and heroes.

DATA AND METHODS

I examined 123 journal articles, books, and organizational position statements on multicultural education published in the United States between 1969 and 1991. Articles and position statements about educational reform in the United States were selected from *Education Index*. These documents reveal what Gamson and Modigliani (1989:3) term "specialist's discourse," i.e., that discourse found in the "journals and other print media aimed at those whose professional lives involve them in the issue." The documents sample multicultural rhetoric from a broad range of professional educators and their organizations. *Education Index* included over 200 journals in 1969 and more than 350 journals in 1991, journals produced by and for professional educators and educational researchers. The sample includes articles by individual authors, as well as position statements by such professional organizations as the National Catholic Education Association, the National Council for the Social Studies, the American Association of Colleges for Teacher Education, the Association for Supervision and Curriculum Development, the Music Educators National Conference, and the National Coalition for Cultural Pluralism.

RHETORIC AND IDENTITY

I use the term rhetoric to mean the persuasive use of language. Rhetoric is "addressed" to an external audience, but also to claimsmakers themselves (Burke 1950:38). Consider, for example, the claims of antiabortion activists who blockade abortion clinics. Typically, these protestors claim they are preventing the "murder" of unborn babies, characterizing clinic staff and patients as uncaring, selfish, and brutal (Condit 1990; Luker 1984). On the one hand this rhetoric is directed at an audience of others, including those who consume the protest in the media. In this respect the protestors' claims are an effort to persuade this audience of the legitimacy of the blockade and perhaps to recruit new activists. On the other hand, the protestors themselves also are an audience for these claims. By characterizing themselves as defenders of unborn life, and others as murderers, the protestors reassure themselves of the importance and ultimate morality of their actions.

Sociologists define identity in terms of the personal characteristics attributed to individuals in the course of social interaction (McCall and Simmons 1966; Strauss 1959; Weinstein 1969). People, in ordinary interaction, ascribe or impute characteristics to themselves and those whom they encounter. These characteristics, to the extent they are accepted by participants in the encounter, constitute those participants' identities. Insofar as identities arise out of claimsmaking activities, they are subject to ongoing revision and reinterpretation.

"Identity bargaining" (Weinstein 1969:757), the process of constructing identities, involves an exchange of claims, verbal and nonverbal, about the identity of the self and the other. Goffman (1959) analyzed claims pertaining to the self in terms of rational, calculating efforts to use the "presentation of self" as a means of persuading others. Other claims, known as "altercasting," reflect the efforts of people to persuade the others to accept certain identities (Weinstein and Deutschberger 1963). As the term identity bargaining suggests, the identities claimed through self-presentation and altercasting do not go uncontested. Individuals may reject some or all of the identity claims made by others, and may also engage in self-presentation and altercasting of their own. Identities are constructed through this process of interaction in which participants negotiate competing identity claims until the participants arrive at mutually agreeable identities.

The concepts of presentation of self, altercasting, and identity bargaining were developed to analyze face-to-face, interpersonal relations. Here, I extend these concepts to the analysis of the construction of collective identities by social problems claimsmakers and social movement actors.

Collective identity bargaining is a process by which collective actors make competing identity claims about themselves and relevant others. Collective identity claimsmakers may be organizations or individuals. Organizations, for example, frequently issue position statements, white papers, manifestos, and so forth. These documents, much as individual claims about personal identity, are forms of self-presentation and altercasting. Individuals may likewise make collective identity claims in the name of organizations, movements, or solidary groups. The "resolution" of competing claims into a collective identity bargain is always temporary and subject to revision pending changes in the context of the claimsmaking.

Collective identity claims involve claims about four key attributes: power, interests, values, and motives. Claims about power usually concern the institutional position of individuals or groups, and the perceived authority, influence, or coercive resources attached to the position. Claims about interests convey claimsmakers' perceptions of the material interests of individual or collective actors. Claims about values describe the claimsmakers' perceptions of the actors' moral and ideological beliefs. Finally, claims about motives draw conclusions about the relationship between the alleged power, interests, and values of actors and their behavior. While collective identity claims address these four attributes, it is important to note that individual claimsmakers do not necessarily address all four at the same time. Some may focus on power, while others emphasize values or interests. An examination of sustained claimsmaking campaigns by numerous individuals and organizations, however, should reveal efforts to impute power, interests, values, and motives to collective actors.

In addition to constructing collective identities, claims about power, interests, values, and motives convey ideas and images of the moral order as seen by the claimsmaker, and the position of the claimsmaker and relevant others in that moral order. Claimsmaking rhetoric reveals, among other things, public notions about who has power, the uses and

Table 5.1.   The Melodramatic Moral Order

	Victim	Villain	Hero
Power	Weak	Strong	Strong
Interest	Overcoming domination	Dominating the weak	Preventing domination
Values	Positive	Negative	Positive
Motives	Alienated	Selfish	Altruistic

abuses of power, what kinds of interests are legitimate and illegitimate, hierarchies of values, and how people are motivated in their actions. The same rhetoric also reveals where actors place themselves and others within their moral order.

The melodrama is one kind of moral order typically constructed by social problems claimsmakers, including multicultural educators as I will show. In the melodramatic moral order, the principal identities are those of victim, villain, and hero. Melodramas portray power relations, interests, values, and motives in terms of good and evil, weak and strong characters (see Table 5.1). Victims are completely powerless to confront the villain, and need to be rescued or protected by the heroes. Villains are unremittingly evil and heroes are paragons of virtue. Villains pursue their victims out of selfishness and malevolence. Heroes are altruistically motivated by their benevolent values.

To sum up the argument thus far, social problems claimsmaking can be analyzed in terms of its role in the rhetorical construction of collective identities. Claimsmakers use a variety of rhetorical idioms to persuade themselves and others about the moral competence of various collective actors with respect to controversial issues. This occurs through a process of collective identity bargaining in which individuals and groups impute identities to themselves and others. Collective identity construction is characterized by imputations of power, interests, values, and motives, and these imputed attributes reveal ideas and imagery of the moral order in which claimsmakers act.

THE RHETORIC OF MULTICULTURAL EDUCATIONAL REFORM

Multicultural education (MCE) means different things to different people. The root idea, however, is that the United States contains culturally diverse groups, each with its own traditions, customs, and ways of living. Rather than viewing cultural diversity as a problem to be solved by creating a unified national culture, via "Anglo-conformity" or a "melting pot," multiculturalists see a resource to be preserved and celebrated. The problem, from their perspective, is that educational leaders in the United States traditionally have suppressed minority cultures because they viewed them as deficient next to the dominant Anglo-American culture. Multiculturalists claim the suppression of diversity leads minority pupils, who find their languages and heritages denigrated, to develop negative self-images and perform poorly in school. "Monocultural" education also perpetuates racial and ethnic tensions in society. To multiculturalists, the need for MCE is growing as demographic trends, including immigration, birth, and death rates, cause a decline in the Anglo-American population relative to Hispanic-, African-, and Asian-Americans. MCE advocates claim the reforms they promote are of paramount importance. This brief definition of MCE cannot do justice to the variety of beliefs about what it is and why it is necessary, but it does capture what the various reformers have in common.

Even in this rough sketch of the multiculturalists' position, we begin to see the identities they impute to themselves and others. For example, "educational leaders" have the power to suppress minority cultures. MCE rhetoric also involves claims about the power, interests, values, and motives of multiculturalists and others engaged in multicultural reform. Multiculturalists' discourse also constructs three principal collective identities—"culturally different students" as victims, "Anglocentric schools" as villains, and "multicultural educators" as protectors (see Table 5.2).

Casting "Culturally Different Students" as Victims

The most salient attribute MCE reformers assign to school children, especially those from ethnic and racial minority groups, is their powerlessness within schools. In his pioneering monograph, Jack Forbes described "Negroes, Indians, and Mexican-Americans and other racial-cultural minorities" as "guinea pigs for 'experiments' in monocultural, monolingual, 'vacuum ideology,' 'compensatory education'"(Forbes 1969:16). The National Catholic Education Association (1983:3) criticized the failure of education to match "reality" and "ideals, particularly in its treatment of the poor and powerless." This criticism highlights what multiculturalists view as the schools' dominant tendency to impose Anglo-American culture on all students regardless of their own cultural backgrounds.

Cultural imposition impedes the development of positive self-images among minority children. This is a crucial problem in American education, according to proponents of MCE, who tend to view self-esteem,

Table 5.2.   The Moral Drama of Multicultural Education

	Victim *Culturally different* *students*	*Villain* *Anglocentric* *schools*	*Hero* *Multicultural* *educators*
Power	Powerless in the face of school authorities	Powerful use of institutional resources	Powerful use of pedagogical knowledge and techniques
Interest	Developing ethnic pride and self-esteem	Maintenance of power and privilege in the status quo	General concern for human survival and welfare of subordinate groups
	Recognizing Anglocentric schools as cause of problems	Narrow self-interest	Altruistic
Values	Love of learning	Antidemocratic Racist WASP cultural superiority	Democracy Individual freedom Interracial harmony
Motives	Alienated indifference to school brought on by official ignorance and denigration of cultural diversity, and lack of MCE	Able but unwilling to make changes that would afford culturally different students a positive education	Able and willing to act in a morally responsible fashion to promote cultural diversity, equality, and MCE

ethnic or racial pride, and success in school as intimately bound together. "Culturally different students," writes one MCE advocate, "need to know that they are a legitimate part of society" (Baker 1983:45). Curricula, textbooks, and other school characteristics that exclude or denigrate racial and ethnic heritages send students "a message that does little to enhance self-esteem," says another reformist (Johnson 1991:4). Indeed, one critic suggests that ethnic pride and self-esteem "may decrease with increased stay in schools for many black children, regardless of their academic status" (Slaughter 1974:168). The National Council for Social Studies (1976:11) concurred, claiming the "psychic cost of assimilation . . . demands self-denial, self-hatred, and rejection of family ties." Disputes exist among MCE activists about how to go about reforming schools, but all agree that "monocultural" approaches to education fail to give minority children the self-esteem necessary to be confident of their power to act for themselves. Children become "victims of the culture of silence . . . [who] have lost faith in their ability to transform and alter their life circumstances" (Cross, Long, and Ziajka 1978:266).

Multiculturalists see minority youths' powerlessness as closely linked to student values. MCE advocates claim all children come to school with enthusiasm. The long struggle to gain admittance to unsegregated schools is offered as evidence. Poor student values cannot account for poor performance, rather schools themselves "are often guilty of destroying the passion for learning that people of color bring to school" (Grant 1988:16). In part this is due to "bland curricular approaches" that deprive all students of "opportunities to exchange ideas and experiences" (Soto 1989:145). But minority students are doubly victimized by teaching styles and curricula that do not take into account cultural differences in how people learn. As a result, culturally different students become alienated from school, and display behaviors white, middle-class teachers incorrectly interpret as evidence of negative attitudes toward learning (Forbes 1969; Slaughter 1974).

MCE advocates believe minority students have an interest in altering the system of schooling, but their very powerlessness prevents them from doing so. In part, they are powerless because they do not recognize their victimization. "Ethnic youths must be taught that they have been victimized by institutional racism" so that they can learn to blame the system rather than themselves for their difficulties in school. As victims of institutional racism in schools and elsewhere, minority youth also have an interest in learning how to "become effective and rational political activists." Students should be involved in "social action projects which will teach them how to influence and change social and political institutions" (Banks 1972:267). Most multiculturalists agree that MCE must "teach for participation in decision-making" (Davies and Clasby 1973:138), help students become "politically efficacious, and socially activist" (Gay 1975:178), and teach children to "make intelligent decisions" and "propose solutions" to the problems they face (Clothier, Gayles, Rackley, and Rackley 1978:11).

In short, the collective identity of "culturally different students" constructed by multiculturalists portrays the students as powerless, alienated victims of an educational system that either ignores or denigrates their cultural backgrounds, and crushes their enthusiasm for learning. Multicultural rhetoric also attributes to culturally different students an interest in changing how schools and other social institutions operate, and argues that MCE should empower these students to take action.

Multiculturalists use two principal rhetorical idioms to construct the collective identity of culturally different children: the rhetorics of endangerment and entitlement. The rhetoric of endangerment involves claims about threats to health and well-being (Ibarra and Kitsuse 1993:39). Multiculturalists invoke such threats metaphorically, speaking of racism as a "disease" and MCE as a cure. One writer describes racism as "one of the most crippling diseases" facing the United States (Kendall 1983:11). More literally, the notion that conventional educational practices threaten the self-esteem of culturally different students suggests that schools endanger the mental, if not physical, health and welfare of these pupils. Such rhetoric evokes a sense of moral urgency to safeguard the children's well-being.

The rhetoric of entitlement also calls forth a sense of moral urgency. This idiom "emphasizes the virtue of securing for all persons . . . equal institutional access as well as the unhampered freedom to exercise choice of self-expression" (Ibarra and Kitsuse 1993:38). MCE rhetoric features numerous appeals to democracy, individualism, freedom, and rights. The American Association of Colleges for Teacher Education's Commission on Multicultural Education, for example, supports "explorations in alternative and emerging lifestyles" (1973:264), while the Association for Supervision and Curriculum Development argues that MCE will improve the possibilities for developing individual "potential" (ASCD 1977:2). The National Council for the Social Studies similarly believes the absence of MCE serves to limit "the realization of human potential," and that this runs "counter to the democratic values of freedom of association and equality of opportunity" (NCSS 1976:11).

Appeals to the rights of culturally different students include the claim that they "may have different educational entitlements and needs," and that educational equality may require schools "to provide specialized services, programs, and instruction for these students" (Banks 1983:583). The underlying idea is that equality does not mean that all pupils have a right to receive the same education. Instead it means they have the right to receive an education that suits their "preferred modes of relating, communicating, motivation, and learning" (Castaneda 1974:65). The presumption of these rights requires developing MCE programs that reflect the cultural differences students bring to the classroom.

Casting "Anglocentric Schools" as Villains

The moral drama of multiculturalism casts "Anglocentric" schools as the villain. Multiculturalists' claims about schools criticize the melting pot ideology (e.g., Barnes 1979:419–423). This ideology claims that immigrants to the United States have all of their cultural differences melted down and combined into a new and uniquely American culture. MCE advocates, by contrast, believe that minority immigrants are compelled to adopt Anglocentric cultural practices and to abandon their own cultures. In criticizing schools the multiculturalists portray the vicious nature of the melting pot ideology as something to be taken for granted and not open to debate. "There is no need here to dwell extensively on the well-known litany of wrongs perpetrated on minority students" by schools imbued with the melting pot ideology (Arciniega 1975:164). Other critics decry the "Anglo-centric curriculum" (Banks 1981:8) as "dominated by white European facts, exploits and miracles" (Sizemore 1973:49).

This characterization of American schools attributes significant power to Anglocentric, or WASP (White, Anglo-Saxon, Protestant) educators, as they are often called. It does so by implication rather than by directly naming individuals or groups responsible for conditions in the schools. The quotations in the preceding paragraph, for example, focus on curriculum, as do many claims in the MCE literature (e.g., Cardenas and Fuller 1973; Garcia 1977; Leyba 1973). Other claims criticize "schools" as institutions for producing the "institutionalization of racism" through "the use of racially biased textbooks, the general lack of minority teachers and administrators . . . [and] the misuse of testing materials" (Grant 1975:185).

Attributing values to actors within biased schools is also indirect. MCE rhetoric attacks values embedded within Anglocentric schools rather than attributing values to specific individuals or groups: "What kind of democracy would utilize public schools to suppress the heritage of a minority simply because it is a minority . . . ? What kind of free society can use the schools as a means to diminish individual freedom and enforce conformity?" (Forbes 1969:43). Without naming names, this assigns to schools (and the society that produced them) values opposed to democracy and individual freedom, and committed to suppressing minority heritages and enforcing conformity. The theme that American schools are antidemocratic and authoritarian recurs throughout the MCE literature. One critic claims "schools preach a lot about democracy, freedom, and equality" but actually "promote values and behaviors . . . antithetical to these ideals" (Suzuki 1984:303-04). Others suggest schools reflect the values "of a rather narrow cultural elite" (Edson 1988:24), and seek "to impose the order of ethnic and cultural definitions on minority students" (Piper 1986:27).

Although MCE claims do not directly blame educators for creating a system that harms culturally different children, claimsmakers do hold educators morally and professionally responsible for reforming the schools. For most multiculturalists reform begins with changing teachers' training. Preservice and in-service training programs should instill multicultural awareness in teachers, and provide them with positive knowledge about the contributions of all cultural groups to United States and world history (e.g., Banks 1975; Bowen and Salsman 1979; Cox 1980). But reform must also reshape "the total educational environment" including the formal and hidden curricula, institutional norms, school policy, counseling programs, assessment and testing, teaching methods, and materials (see Banks 1981:21–23). Ultimately, school personnel have the "responsibility of providing equal educational opportunities" to culturally different children, and this requires a multicultural environment (Castaneda 1974:65).

Multiculturalists attribute inegalitarian interests and motives to educators who do not actively support MCE reforms. "Teachers . . . need to be willing to allocate opportunities to culturally diverse learners" (Soto 1989:145). Others suggest the failure to implement MCE rests not with the lack of knowledge or solutions, but instead with a lack of leadership, will, and commitment (Goodlad 1984; Kagan, Schreiber, and Zigler 1984). Taken together, these claims portray educators within Anglocentric schools as able but unwilling to promote more democratic schools committed to the freedom and individual expression MCE offers culturally different students.

In sum, the collective identity attributed to Anglocentric schools and, by implication, educators within them, is that of very powerful institutions committed to the preservation of a dominant culture and the elimination of diverse, less powerful cultures. Anglocentric schools and their leaders are hypocritical, insofar as they "preach" about democracy and individual freedom while acting to deny them to culturally different children. Although MCE claims do not explicitly attribute interests and motives to the school-villains, they rule out inability to act as an excuse and place moral responsibility on the schools to redress the injustices inflicted on culturally different students.

The construction of Anglocentric schools as villains reveals two interesting patterns. First, the idioms used to construct this identity are the same as those used to construct culturally different children as victims. Just as the idiom of endangerment portrayed minority youth as victims of psychological assault, the same idiom casts schools, and indirectly educators, as the source of the assault. Similarly, the idiom of entitlement claims the right to a culturally diverse education for minority children, and it portrays schools as subverting that same right.

Of equal interest is the construction of an institutional rather than a human villain. Why do MCE claimsmakers avoid directly identifying human villains in their rhetoric? And why do they fail to impute interests to human actors within the schools? In large part this may reflect the intended audience for the specific claims in my sample. Professional journals are read almost entirely by school teachers, principals, supervisors, and faculty of teachers' colleges. This audience includes some educators converted to the cause of MCE, some opposed to it, and some who may be persuaded to join the movement. By not directly blaming members of their audience, MCE educators may avoid alienating those in the third group whom they seek to enlist. At the same time MCE claims insist that the status quo is detrimental, and that change is needed. This rhetoric leaves the audience with the choice of supporting MCE, supporting a biased educational system, or constructing a counterrhetoric that undercuts the multiculturalists' claims. Perhaps more strident rhetoric could be found in claims addressed exclusively to other multiculturalists, where the goal is not to gain converts, but to exhort the faithful to maintain their commitment to MCE and their own collective identity.

Casting "Multicultural Educators" as Heroes

Multiculturalists' collective presentation of self defines their identity in opposition to that of Anglocentric schools and educators. For example, MCE advocates claim to have the power to change how schools teach children and shape children's identities, and thereby to reduce social problems outside the school. Emphasizing the power of classroom teachers, one critic claims that "sharp teachers can change the real curriculum" (Cuban 1972:273), implying that teachers who resist change are either dull or uncommitted to the goals of MCE. Education in world music has the power to help "students deepen their own cultural identities . . . and gain a better understanding of the identities of other students as well" (Gamble 1983:40). Such collective identity claims portray multicultural educators with the same level of power as Anglocentric educators. The difference is that multiculturalists can use their power to help students build positive identities and self-images.

Most of all, MCE advocates believe they have the power to reduce racial and ethnic hostility and promote harmony. The Task Force on Ethnic Studies Curriculum Guidelines of the National Council for the Social Studies (1976:4) claims that schools have "an important role to play in reducing the tensions and injustices, including the misgivings about self, that result from unexamined ethnic beliefs and attitudes." Similar rhetoric describes educators as "a powerful force," as being able to "play a part," and as "show[ing] promise for" eliminating racism and reducing tensions between ethnic, religious, and national-origin groups (Freedman 1984; Kendall 1983; Lee 1983).

Teachers of multicultural education can have these salutary effects by promoting understanding and tolerance of cultural differences. This claim depends on a fundamental belief that racial and ethnic hostilities are based on ignorance that MCE can reduce. Thus one writer suggests that MCE "should lead to a greater respect for [all] cultural groups . . . and fewer intergroup conflicts caused by ignorance and misunderstanding" (Gollnick 1980:14). Others suggest that MCE will help to "clarify moral imperatives and expand social consciousness," lead to a "greater tolerance and respect" for others, "deenergize the attitude that Western systems are the norm," and reduce the appeal of "persuasive racist propaganda" (Dodds 1983; Gamble 1983; O'Brien 1980; Perry 1975). In these claims, multicultural educators have the power to disabuse children of culturally biased beliefs, and to instill an attitude of tolerance, if not appreciation, for cultural differences.

Rhetorical claims about multiculturalists' power also reveal the values they impute to their collective identity. These values are defined in opposition to those imputed to Anglocentric educators. Multicultural-ists' values include "the value of the individual," a "humanistic spirit," and a "democratic heritage" (Clothier et al. 1978:1–7). More specifically, multicultural educators view their work in terms of values of cultural diversity, the importance of individual and cultural identity, the eradica-tion of cultural bias and discrimination, and the promotion of inter-cultural harmony (Cole 1984; Glenn 1989; Gollnick and Chinn 1983; Ramsey 1982). They reject the melting pot commitment to cultural unity in favor of what the Commission on Multicultural Education (1973) of the American Association of Colleges for Teacher Education termed "No One Model American." This view spurns the notion of an American archetype and the ideal of assimilation.

Their values frame the multiculturalists' view of culturally biased schools as an urgent social problem in need of reform. "Policies and programs must be guided primarily by our own value commitments" insofar as the research on minority youth and education is "thin, contradic-tory, and inconclusive" (Banks 1983:585). In the absence of firm evidence that one set of policies would be more effective than another, the urgency of the problem requires policies consistent with the values of MCE.

In portraying themselves as heroes, multiculturalists use the rhetoric of loss (Ibarra and Kitsuse 1993:37) to portray the eradication of diverse cultural beliefs, knowledge, and practices as a problem. They also use the rhetoric of calamity (Ibarra and Kitsuse 1993:39) by claiming the United States faces dire consequences if MCE reforms are not adopted.

The rhetoric of loss praises the protective actions of those who chal-lenge the devaluation of "sacred" objects, characterizing them as heroes or saviors. Thus, we have seen movements to save the whales, save the planet, and save our schools. Multiculturalists attack the loss or devalua-tion of cultures different from the dominant WASP culture in the United States. The Commission on Multicultural Education declares that "cul-tural diversity is a valuable resource" (1973:264), and the National Coali-tion for Cultural Pluralism claims that among "resources formerly and currently used to insure physical and social progress" for the nation, "the myriad ethnic, cultural, and racial" human resources have not been fully used to their advantage" (1974:149). Similarly, the National Council for the Social Studies argued that MCE would defuse hostilities and allow society to "benefit from its rich base of ethnic traditions and cultures" (1976:14).

The rhetorical presentation of cultural diversity as a threatened resource, and MCE as the means of preserving and extending that resource, casts the multiculturalists as protectors. This protector identity receives further support from claims about the changing demographic composition of the United States. In general, multiculturalists argue that the United States, while always a multicultural nation, is becoming even more so as a result of immigration, birth, and death rates. The National Catholic Education Association describes "an increasingly diverse population" of students (1983:02), and multiculturalists offer various estimates of population change:

> By 2010 there will be 62,644,000 school age children in the United States, over 38 percent of whom will be minority. (Haberman and Post 1990:32)
>
> The combined minority group population [in California] increased from 20.5% in 1970 to 43.6% in 1980. This trend can be expected to accelerate. One report estimates that 1990 minority population will reach 64%. (Cervantes 1984:278)
>
> In California . . . the Hispanic population has exceeded the white population since 1977. (Grant 1984:14)

These claims are not all consistent with each other, and some are questionable. But they are rhetorically powerful because they argue that a multicultural population demands educational reform.

Here, multiculturalists use the rhetoric of calamity. This idiom evokes imagery of unimaginable disaster, and calls for immediate action. MCE claimsmakers describe "intergroup conflict" as a "serious threat to our nation and the ideals of American democracy" (Banks 1973:750). "If we are to survive (literally!), we must learn to respect each other's strengths and weaknesses" (Barnes 1979:424). Multiculturalists also point to a perceived resurgence of the Ku Klux Klan (Lee 1983:406), and an increasingly technological and industrialized world (ASCD 1977; Barnes 1979; Corder and Quisenberry 1987) as ominous developments. The combined threats of racial wars and technological domination make MCE necessary for the "future of our planet and our own survival" (Corder and Quisenberry 1987:158), and to avoid "being alienated, bureaucratized, and depersonalized by the rationality of the ethos of industrial technology" (ASCD 1977:2). "The challenge is herculean. The odds are against us. The hour is late" (Banks 1973:750), but "we can't afford to ignore it" (Standifer 1987).

This rhetoric of calamity establishes the interests of multicultural educators as general rather than parochial. Their rhetoric appeals to a broad audience by proclaiming that MCE serves the interests of everyone in preventing race wars, depersonalization, and social destruction. Their claims use inclusive pronouns such as us, we, and our. MCE claims imply that Anglocentric educators are self-interested, seeking to preserve WASP power and privilege; in contrast, multicultural educators are concerned with the interests of all. Where human survival itself is at stake, no one can be disinterested, and no one can be selfish in acting to assure survival.

The combined power, values, and interests multicultural educators impute to themselves lead to very different conclusions about their motives in comparison with Anglocentric educators. Multiculturalists rhetorically construct schools as villains who are able but unwilling to help make MCE reforms. By contrast, multiculturalists impute to themselves the ability and willingness to act, and describe their motives in terms of MCE being "basically a moral and ethical issue" (Cheng, Brizendine, and Oakes 1979:273). They claim MCE is part of the "moral responsibility to provide children a meaningful education" (Butterfield, Demos, Grant, Moy, and Perez 1979:382), and prepare young people to be the next generation of leaders (Commission on Multicultural Education 1973). Insofar as the United States is composed of people from diverse cultures, and is becoming more so, it is the responsibility of educators to expose children to diversity, help them understand and appreciate it, and contribute to greater intercultural harmony (Codianni and Tipple 1980). Multiculturalists proclaim themselves willing to accept this responsibility.

In short, multiculturalists cast themselves as protectors, not only of cherished American values such as democracy, individual freedom, justice, and liberty, but also of the rights of children to receive an education that treats their cultural heritages with dignity. Multiculturalists give themselves the power to redefine how schools operate and to instill the value of cultural diversity in the curriculum, pedagogy, and other aspects of education. The power they wield is similar to that of Anglocentrists. The difference is that multiculturalists attribute to themselves motives guided by values and interests that will benefit humanity rather than parochial groups within society.

DISCUSSION

The concept of collective identity bargaining points to the ways in which collective actors construct identities for themselves and other salient actors in their moral worlds. Claims about power, values, interests, and motives reveal who the claimsmakers profess to be and where they place themselves in the moral order. For multiculturalists, the moral order is an essentially melodramatic one. There are clearly defined victims, villains, and heroes whose identities and actions are unambiguous. Anglocentric schools are uniformly corrupt. Culturally different children are uniformly eager to learn, only to become alienated by oppressive schools. Multiculturalists are uniformly motivated by egalitarian and democratic values. Multiculturalists construct a world in which power is abused by a dominant cultural group to subordinate less powerful cultural groups, especially the children within those groups. As the heroes of this melodrama, multiculturalists propose to use the power they have within educational institutions to empower the victims (culturally different children) to seize control of their own lives.

Ironically, the multiculturalists' melodramatic rhetoric undercuts their claim of empowering culturally different students. The victim identity assigned to these students makes them ultimately dependent upon the multicultural educator-heroes for their liberation. Moreover, for students to gain their own power they must accept the multiculturalists' construction of their problems. That is, culturally different students must learn to view themselves as victims and multicultural educators as their protectors. Only by doing so will these students become effective political activists.

Collective identity bargaining is an interactive process, yet I have focused on the identity claims of the multiculturalists alone. In doing so I have not addressed the response of the others, especially those labeled Anglocentric. Critics portray multiculturalists as "politically correct" authoritarians seeking to impose doctrinaire beliefs on school children. The same critics portray themselves as defenders of traditional knowledge against trendy reformers. On the face of it, these identity counterclaims suggest a similar melodramatic moral order in which the identities are reversed, one in which politically correct (not multicultural) educators are the villains, traditionalists (not Anglocentrists) are the heroes, and students, as well as tradition, are victims.

Claims and counterclaims by multiculturalists and traditionalists ignore the students' own construction of their identities. While educators on each side of the issue make claims about the effects of schooling on students' identities, neither group is particularly concerned with letting students speak for themselves. Allowed to do so, would culturally different students construct a moral order in which they claim the identity of victim? If so, would they identify their interests with multiculturalists or with traditionalists? The silencing of the students on these questions speaks to the power educators of all ideological perspectives have over the students they claim to serve.

ACKNOWLEDGMENTS

I would like to thank William A. Gamson, Scott A. Hunt, and Gary D. Jaworski for their valuable comments and suggestions.

REFERENCES

Arciniega, T. A. 1975. "The Thrust Toward Pluralism: What Progress?" *Educational Leadership* 33(December):163–167.
ASCD Multicultural Education Commission. 1977. "Encouraging Multicultural Education." Pp. 1–5 in *Multicultural Education: Commitments, Issues, and Applications*, edited by C. A. Grant. Washington, D.C.: Association for Supervision and Curriculum Development.
Baker, G. C. 1976. "Cultural Diversity: Strength of the Nation." *Educational Leadership* 33(January):257–260.
———. 1983. "Motivating the Culturally Different Student." *Momentum* 14(February):45–46.
Banks, J.A. 1972. "Imperatives in Ethnic Minority Education." *Phi Delta Kappan* 53:266–269.
———. 1973. "Teaching for Ethnic Literacy: A Comparative Approach." *Social Education* 37:738–750.
———. 1975. *Teaching Strategies for Ethnic Studies*. Boston: Allyn and Bacon.
———. 1981. *Multiethnic Education: Theory and Practice*. Boston: Allyn and Bacon.
———. 1983. "Multiethnic Education and the Quest for Equality." *Phi Delta Kappan* 64:582–585.
Barnes, W. J. 1979. "Developing a Culturally Pluralistic Perspective: A Community Involvement Task." *Journal of Negro Education* 48:419–430.
Bowen, E. M., and F. L. Salsman. 1979. "Integrating Multiculturalism into a Teacher Training Program." *Journal of Negro Education* 48:390–395.
Burke, K. 1950. *A Rhetoric of Motives*. New York: Prentice-Hall.
Butterfield, R. A., E. S. Demos, G. W. Grant, P. S. Moy, and A. L. Perez. 1979. "A Multicultural Analysis of a Popular Basal Reading Series in the International Year of the Child." *Journal of Negro Education* 48:382–389.
Cardenas, R., and L. W. Fuller. 1973. "Toward a Multicultural Society. *Today's Education* 62(Sept./Oct.):83–88.
Castaneda, A. 1974. "Persisting Ideological Issues of Assimilation in America." Pp. 56–70 in *Cultural Pluralism*, edited by E. Epps. Chicago: University of Chicago Press.
Cervantes, R. A. 1984. "Ethnocentric Pedagogy and Minority Student Growth." *Education and Urban Society* 16:274–293.
Cheng, C. W., E. Brizendine, and J. Oakes. 1979. "What Is an Equal Chance for Minority Children?" *Journal of Negro Education* 48:267–287.
Clothier, G., A. R. Gayles, L. G. Rackley, and S. W. Rackley. 1978. *New Dimensions in Multicultural Education*. Kansas City, MO: Midwest Educational Training and Research Organization.

Codianni, A. V., and B. E. Tipple. 1980. "Conceptual Changes in Ethnic Studies." *Viewpoints in Teaching and Learning* 56(Winter):26–37.

Cole, D. J. 1984. "Multicultural Education and Global Education: A Possible Merger." *Theory Into Practice* 23:151–154.

Commission on Multicultural Education. 1973. "No One Model American." *Journal of Teacher Education* 24:264–265.

Condit, C. M. 1990. *Decoding Abortion Rhetoric*. Urbana and Chicago: University of Illinois Press.

Corder, L. J., and N. L. Quisenberry. 1987. "Early Education and Afro-Americans: History, Assumptions and Implications for the Future." *Childhood Education* 63(February):154–158.

Cox, B. Y. 1980. "Multicultural Training: A Missing Link in Graduate Music Education—A Statement from the MENC Commission on Multicultural Awareness." *Music Educators Journal* 67(September):39–42.

Cross, D. E., M. A. Long, and A. Ziajka. 1978. "Minority Cultures and Education in the United States." *Education and Urban Society* 10:263–276.

Cuban, L. 1972. "Ethnic Content and 'White' Instruction." *Phi Delta Kappan* 53:270–273.

Davies, D., and M. Clasby. 1973. "The U. S. Office of Education and Cultural Pluralism." Pp. 137–140 in *Cultural Pluralism in Education: A Mandate for Change*, edited by M. D. Stent, W. R. Hazard, and H. N. Rivlin. New York: Appleton-Century-Crofts.

Dodds, J. B. P. 1983. "Music as a Multicultural Education." *Music Educators Journal* 69(May):33–34.

Edson, C. H. 1988. "Chicago: 1893." *Educational Studies* 19:1–29.

Forbes, J. D. 1969. *Education for the Culturally Different: A Multi-Cultural Approach*. Berkeley: Far West Laboratory for Educational Research and Development.

Freedman, P. I. 1984. "Multiethnic/Multicultural Education: Establishing the Foundations." *The Social Studies* 75:202–204.

Gamble, S. 1983 "A Multicultural Curriculum," *Music Educator's Journal* 69:39–41.

Gamson, W., and A. Modigliani. 1989. "Media Discourse and Public Opinion on Nuclear Power: A Constructionist Approach." *American Journal of Sociology* 95:1–37.

Garcia, F. C. 1977. "Politics and Multicultural Education Do Mix." *Journal of Teacher Education* 28(May-June):21–25.

Gay, G. 1975. "Organizing and Designing Culturally Pluralistic Curriculum." *Educational Leadership* 33 (December):176–183.

Glenn, C. L. 1989. "Just Schools for Minority Children." *Phi Delta Kappan* 70:777–779.

Goffman, E. 1959. *The Presentation of Self in Everyday Life*. Garden City, NJ: Doubleday.

Gollnick, D. 1980. "Multicultural Education." *Viewpoints in Teaching and Learning* 56:1–17.

Gollnick, D., and P.C. Chinn. 1983. *Multicultural Education in a Pluralistic Society*. St. Louis: C.V. Mosby.

Goodlad, J. 1984. "The Uncommon Common School." *Education and Urban Society* 16:243–252.

Grant, C. A. 1975. "Racism in School and Society." *Educational Leadership* 33(December):184–188.

———. 1988. "Race, Class, Gender and Schooling." *Education Digest* 54(December):15–18.

Grant, M. 1984. "One Opinion on Solving the Dropout Problem: Ethnicity, Si, Assimilation, No." *Thrust* 13(April):14–17.

Haberman, M., and L. Post. 1990. "Cooperating Teacher's Perception of the Aims and Goals of Multicultural Education." *Action in Teacher Education* 12(Fall):31–35.

Ibarra, P., and J. I. Kitsuse. 1993. "Vernacular Constituents of Moral Discourse: An Interactionist Proposal for the Study of Social Problems." Pp. 25–58 in *Constructionist Controversies: Issues in Social Problems Theory*, edited by J. A. Holstein and G. Miller. Hawthorne, NY: Aldine de Gruyter.

Johnson, P. 1991. "Traditional Offerings Won't Cut It." *American Teacher* 75(March):4.

Kagan, S., E. Schreiber, and E. Zigler. 1984. "Recognizing Commonalities— Respecting Differences." *Education and Urban Society* 16:382–389.

Kendall, F. E. 1983. "Presenting Multicultural Education to Parents." *Momentum* 14(February):11–13.

Lee, M. K. 1983. "Multiculturalism: Educational Perspectives for the 1980s." *Education* 103:405–409.

Leyba, C. F. 1973. "Cultural Identity: Problems and Dilemmas." *Journal of Teacher Education* 24(Winter):272–276.

Luker, K. 1984. *Abortion and the Politics of Motherhood*. Berkeley: University of California Press.

McCall, G. J., and J. L. Simmons. 1966. *Identities and Interactions*. New York: Free Press.

National Catholic Education Association. 1983. "Relishing 'The Stew' of Cultural Diversity." *Momentum* 14(February):2–3.

National Coalition for Cultural Pluralism. 1974. "Statement by the Steering Committee." Pp. 149–150 in *Cultural Pluralism in Education: A Mandate for Change*, edited by M. D. Stent, W. R. Hazard, and H. N. Rivlin. New York: Appleton-Century-Crofts.

National Council for the Social Studies. 1976. *Curriculum Guidelines for Multiethnic Education*. Arlington, VA: National Council for the Social Studies.

O'Brien, J. P. 1980. "Integrating World Music in the Music Appreciation Course." *Music Educators Journal* 67(Sept):39–42.

Perry, J. 1975. "Notes Toward a Multicultural Curriculum." *English Journal* 64: 8–9.

Piper, D. 1986. "Language Growth in the Multiethnic Classroom." *Language Arts* 63:23–36.

Ramsey, P. G. 1982. "Multicultural Education in Early Childhood." *Young Children* 37(January):13–24.

Sizemore, B. A. 1973. "Making the Schools a Vehicle for Cultural Pluralism." Pp.

43–54 in *Cultural Pluralism in Education: A Mandate for Change*, edited by M. D. Stent, W. R. Hazard, and H. N. Rivlin. New York: Appleton-Century-Crofts.

Slaughter, D. T. 1974. "Alienation of Afro-American Children." Pp. 144–174 in *Cultural Pluralism*, edited by E. Pipps. Chicago: University of Chicago Press.

Soto, L. D. 1989. "Enhancing the Written Medium for Culturally Diverse Learners Via Reciprocal Interaction." *The Urban Review* 21:145–149.

Standifer, J. A. 1987. "The Multicultural, Non-Sexist Principle: We Can't Afford to Ignore It." *Journal of Negro Education* 56:471–474.

Strauss, A. 1959. *Masks and Mirrors: The Search for Identity*. New York: Free Press.

Suzuki, B. H. 1984. "Curriculum Transformation for Multicultural Education." *Education and Urban Society* 16:294–322.

Weinstein, E. A. 1969. "The Development of Interpersonal Competence." Pp. 753–775 in *Handbook of Socialization Theory and Research*, edited by D. A. Goslin. Chicago: Rand McNally.

Weinstein, E. A., and P. Deutschberger. 1963. "Some Dimensions of Altercasting." *Sociometry* 26:454–466.

PART II

Claimsmakers

Claims cannot exist without claimsmakers. Claimsmakers both create claims and promote them. Claimsmaking can be difficult, frustrating work, and not everyone is willing to do it. Claimsmakers tend to be interested parties—individuals who stand to gain something if their claims are successful—but not all claimsmakers have similar interests.

Perhaps the most obvious type of claimsmaker is the *victim*. People who feel aggrieved vent their grievances and seek compensation. The membership in grass roots social movements often consists largely of such people: Southern blacks in the early stages of the civil rights movement, homosexuals in the movements for gay and lesbian rights, Vietnam veterans demanding compensation for health problems attributed to Agent Orange, and so on. Victims' claimsmaking rhetoric often includes references to their personal experiences: they can "tell it like it is." The horror stories in grass roots movements come from first-person testimony.

One problem with grass roots movements is that the members often lack sophisticated claimsmaking skills and resources. Effective claimsmaking campaigns may require organizing members, fundraising, public relations, grant writing, lobbying, and other complex tasks. While claimsmaking novices sometimes muddle through, experienced claimsmakers have clear advantages (McCarthy and Zald 1977). The college students who participated in civil rights demonstrations and voter registration drives during the early 1960s learned valuable skills. Some became *activists* and took their skills to new social movements, especially the antiwar and women's movements. Activists tend to be motivated by ideology; they join causes in which they believe. But ideology need not be important; claimsmakers can hire independent consultants who specialize in fundraising or public relations. These *specialists* may be less committed to the cause than activists, but they bring experience and skills to the cause.

Activists' expertise is in conducting claimsmaking campaigns. Another important type of claimsmaker is a different sort of expert. *Professionals*, such as scientists, lawyers, and doctors, lend the authority of their disciplines to claimsmaking. When their claims are successful, these professionals usually stand to increase their status, wealth, and power.

Often, of course, social problems construction features alliances among different types of claimsmakers. For example, in Chapter 6, Philip Jenkins analyzes the construction of clergy sexual abuse—particularly within the Catholic Church—as a social problem. Jenkins suggests that this campaign involved several sorts of claimsmakers, including victims of abuse, lawyers and therapeutic professionals, and activists seeking to change the Church.

In addition to trying to extend their influence to new social problems, professionals may seek to redefine problems already under their control. For instance, some of the most spectacular advances in medical science, such as organ transplants and open-heart surgery, involve sophisticated new technology. Such procedures can produce amazing cures, but they are costly, consuming scarce resources while helping relatively few patients. A growing emphasis on expensive, technologically sophisticated, curative medicine means a lower priority for educational and preventive medicine programs that might help more people at lower cost. Here, claimsmaking campaigns pit medical professionals representing different specialties (and often different philosophies of medicine) against one another. Shirley A. Scritchfield describes one such struggle—over the treatment of infertility—in Chapter 7.

Discussions of claimsmaking sometimes assume that claimsmakers are outsiders, struggling to get the attention of policymakers. But this is not always the case. *Pressure groups* "are ordinarily part of the polity, the set of groups that can routinely influence government decisions and can ensure that their interests are normally recognized in the decision-making process" (Useem and Zald 1982:144). Their claims are not always visible, because pressure groups often approach policymakers privately. *Officials* also engage in claimsmaking. Sometimes their claims serve to protect their turf from the encroachments of rivals; sometimes they hope to expand their influence. Often, these are bureaucratic conflicts, barely visible to people outside the government. But other campaigns are noisy affairs, with officials using their offices to attract maximum publicity. The noise level tends to rise when the cause is popular and uncontroversial. Thus, in Chapter 8, Craig Reinarman and Harry G. Levine argue that politicians (particularly in the Reagan and Bush administrations) played key roles in promoting the "crack" crisis and the War on Drugs.

REFERENCES

McCarthy, J. D., and M. N. Zald. 1977. "Resource Mobilization and Social Movements." *American Journal of Sociology* 82:1212–1241.

Useem, B., and M. N. Zald. 1982. "From Pressure Group to Social Movement." *Social Problems* 30:144–156.

6

Clergy Sexual Abuse: The Symbolic Politics of a Social Problem

PHILIP JENKINS

In the last decade, the issue of sexual abuse of minors by priests and ministers has come to be seen as a widespread social problem requiring urgent remedies (Berry 1992; Burkett and Bruni 1993; Rossetti 1990). The issue itself is by no means new; the stereotype of the pedophile priest has existed in anticlerical rhetoric for centuries, and it survives quite vigorously in popular humor (Bruce 1985a; Jenkins 1992b,c; Roberts 1990). In fact, sexual imagery and speculation formed a major component of the virulent anti-Catholicism that was so central to American politics during the nineteenth century (Bennett 1990; Davis 1986). However, such overt manifestations of religious conflict had subsided greatly during recent years, and it is remarkable to observe the vigor and alleged scale of the current "clergy sex abuse" problem, no less than the general acceptance that the charges have achieved.

In terms of social problem theory, the rapid success of these claims requires some explanation (Best 1989). We can identify several contributory factors, including changing media attitudes, and the new legal environment that offered rewarding opportunities for litigants alleging abuse by clergy. The claims also gained attention because the cases publicized offered a rich selection of symbolic messages with great utility for a variety of social and political interest groups. Claimants portrayed notorious instances of sexual exploitation by clergy as typical conduct for a large section of the clerical profession, especially the Roman Catholic priesthood. This caused the mobilization of sentiment against both the profession and the churches to which the clergy belonged, to discredit opinions and political stances held by those groups on contemporary social and moral issues. This transformed the issue from general concern about abuse by clergy into a specific attack on the Catholic church, a dimension that was by no means inevitable in the problem's original formulation. The whole affair thus illustrates the rhe-

105

torical manipulation of a social problem for the ideological benefit of particular claimsmakers (compare Jenkins 1994).

DISCOVERING CLERGY SEXUAL ABUSE

During the 1980s, the issue of child sexual abuse came to be seen as a pervasive threat that might explain numerous social difficulties and dysfunctions. At the end of the decade, concern about child abuse was increasingly focused on specific aspects of that problem, including "ritual abuse" allegedly committed by cults and satanic groups, and "clergy abuse," the molestation of children and young people by priests and ministers. The reality of ritual abuse was and is very controversial, but there is no serious dispute that the clergy abuse problem did have some basis in fact, and that at least some children had been sexually assaulted by "pedophile priests." In contrast to ritual abuse, the objective foundation of clergy abuse has been repeatedly established in both civil and criminal courts. The origins of the problem in the wider child abuse issue would be of great significance in establishing the issue as a topic worthy of public concern and attention, as clergy abuse inevitably inherited most or all of the stereotypical characteristics already associated with "child abuse" (Best 1990; Jenkins 1992a). There was thus little need for claimsmakers to prove certain facts essential to the development of a new problem or menace. It was taken for granted that clergy molestation was harmful and prevalent, and that such behavior could continue for many years without attracting notice.

"Clergy abuse" has been reported within most major Christian denominations, and the issue has been discussed in Jewish circles, though by far the largest number of stories have involved the Roman Catholic church. This is a critical point that rarely receives notice in the literature, either scholarly or popular, for "clergy abuse" has become synonymous with the issue of "pedophile priests," a convenient alliteration that appears to blame Catholic clergy as opposed to pastors, preachers, ministers, or rabbis. There is no central organization that tabulates reports of abusive clergy or ministers, but the major body providing liability insurance for religious institutions reports that in the last decade, there were several hundred known cases of clerical child abuse involving non-Catholic clergy, in addition to others involving sexual misconduct with adults (CNN 1993; see, for example, Smothers 1988). In the late 1980s, a series of sex scandals brought about the downfall of Protestant televangelists Jim Bakker and Jimmy Swaggart. However, the two best-known books on the clergy abuse issue are, respectively, subtitled "Catholic Priests and the Sexual Abuse of Children" (Berry 1992) and "Children, Sexual Abuse and the Catholic Church" (Burkett and Bruni 1993).

The centrality of Catholic priests in the construction of the problem will thus require explanation. Certainly, the media invariably emphasize the Catholic context in reporting on the phenomenon, generally focusing on one of several egregious cases in which individual priests or religious[1] were involved in molesting dozens or hundreds of children over a period of years. In modern times, the first widely publicized incident involved Catholic priest Gilbert Gauthe, charged in 1984 with repeated attacks committed over several years in Louisiana. This incident did much to establish the stereotypical characteristics expected of the "clergy abuse" offender, and, in particular, the charge that the abuse arose from an institutional context, rather than merely reflecting individual psychopathology. In the Gauthe case, ecclesiastical authorities admitted having known about incidents of molestation at an early stage of the man's career, but responded merely by transferring him to new parishes where the pattern of abuse soon recurred. Journalistic critics alleged that Church authorities failed to respond adequately, thus aggravating or even acquiescing in the misconduct. Critics charged that this negligence reflected the Catholic church's primary interest in avoiding scandal and protecting its own clergy, rather than assisting victims of molestation.

The Gauthe case also established the precedent that such failure to intervene should result in financial penalties, payment for therapy for the victims and compensatory damages for their families. Following Gauthe's conviction in 1985, a group of concerned clergy and laity submitted a confidential report on abuse to the Catholic hierarchy. This document warned of the need to take urgent action in the face of such scandals, and suggested that legal liability payments could run into billions of dollars (Bennetts 1991; Berry 1992; Burkett and Bruni 1993). It also warned that the Church could no longer rely on the friendship and sympathy of Catholic politicians, judges, and professionals within the criminal justice system, so that exposure and conviction would be far more likely than in the past (Burkett and Bruni 1993:162-65).

Allegations of institutional indifference to abuse gained special credence in scandals involving clergy-run homes and orphanages, where it was difficult to accept that widespread molestation could have failed to come to light over the periods of years or even decades when it had been occurring. In Canada, such a case at the Mount Cashel home in Newfoundland suggested a decades-long pattern of neglect by civil and ecclesiastical authorities (Harris 1991). When the case emerged in the late 1980s, the resulting scandal was perhaps the most damaging in the history of the Catholic church in Canada.

Such cases were increasingly common, or at least were more likely to be reported (Friendly 1986). Between 1985 and 1987, there were at least 40 instances in the United States in which Catholic priests or religious were charged with multiple acts of sexual misconduct ranging from casual molestation to outright rape (Chandler 1990). The proliferation of cases encouraged constructions of the issue as a systematic problem, rather than simply a series of isolated incidents. By mid-decade, a number of experts emerged seeking "ownership" of the problem, the right to have their interpretation accepted as correct and authoritative, and these were without exception strongly critical of the ecclesiastical authorities' tendency to cover-up or "stonewall" in the face of scandal. Among the most quoted experts were Jason Berry, a Louisiana journalist who had covered the Gauthe case, feminist religious writer Marie Fortune, and a few Catholic clergy such as Andrew Greeley and Thomas Doyle (Berry 1992, 1993a,b; Fortune 1986, 1989, 1992; compare Rutter 1989). The press then freely cited these authorities when new abuse cases arose, and the experts' analyses shaped the interpretation of the next "wave" of concern following 1988. In the latter phase, public interest was reflected in the publication of numerous articles and books, as well as an explosion of conferences, seminars, workshops, and "consciousness-raising" events.

By the end of the 1980s, several major scandals contributed to perceptions of a national clergy abuse crisis. The Mount Cashel case in Canada has already been cited. In the United States during 1990, there was a scandal over the management of the New York City-based Covenant House, which provided shelter to teenage runaways, when the priest-director (a prominent advocate for exploited children) was charged with sexually exploiting his charges (Ritter 1988; Sennott 1992). In Minnesota, a jury awarded several million dollars in damages to the victims of a priest with a long record of abuse, who (like Gauthe) had been repeatedly transferred to new parishes. The following year brought the case of Dino Cinel, a New Orleans priest who both collected and manufactured child pornography, as well as the first of several incidents within the archdiocese of Chicago (Hirsley 1991a,b,c; Steinfels 1992a,b). Other cases involved the mass abuse of pupils at seminaries or boarding schools, for example, in California and Wisconsin (Mydans 1993a,b).

Charges reached a crescendo during 1992 and 1993, with several reported incidents involving clergy who had been active in molestation over years or decades (Steinfels 1992c–f, 1993a–j). The most notorious involved a priest named James Porter, who had molested numerous children in his parish in southern Massachusetts during the mid-1960s (Butterfield 1992a–d). When the offenses were originally discovered, Church authorities placed him in a rehabilitative facility for clerical sex offenders, but upon his release he was returned to a parish context where the abuse recommenced. Porter eventually left the priesthood, but continued to be active in the sexual exploitation of minors, and would be convicted of the abuse of a babysitter in his Minnesota home. During the early 1990s, one of his Massachusetts victims eventually recalled the earlier abuse, and began to contact others who might also have been molested. This group then began to pressure authorities to investigate and prosecute the former Father Porter, who was convicted and sentenced in 1993.

The Porter case was widely reported, and firmly established the problem of "pedophile priests" as a newsworthy issue. This encouraged reporting of other cases, both current and drawn from the quite distant past, which culminated in charges made against Cardinal Joseph Bernardin of Chicago, one of the most distinguished and powerful clergy in the American Catholic church (the Bernardin charges were withdrawn some months afterward) (Graham 1993). The intense media coverage naturally generated an impression of crisis, and critics suggested that the issue presented that church with its gravest moral threat in centuries, perhaps since the Reformation. Journalists wrote of an "ecclesiastical Watergate," a "meltdown" (Bennetts 1991). Priest and author Andrew Greeley suggested that "Pedophilia is the S. and L. disaster of the Catholic church," that "You just don't know where it's going to stop" (A&E 1993; Jenkins 1992c).

Since the mid-1980s, clergy abuse has been regularly covered in the news media, including articles in magazines and periodicals of all political and cultural shades, and in reports on television news documentaries and talk shows. Between 1991 and 1993, case studies or lengthy analyses of the problem appeared in periodicals as diverse as *The Nation* (Disch 1992), *National Review* (Buckley 1993), *Playboy* (Petersen 1992; Scheer 1990; Sennott 1993), *Rolling Stone* (Gaboury 1993), the *New Yorker* (Wilkes 1993), and *People Weekly* (1992). Newsmagazines like *Time*, *Newsweek*, and the Canadian *MacLean's* often referred to the theme (see for example Allen, 1989, 1990; Ostling 1991, 1993; Press 1993; Woodward 1993a,b; Woodward and King 1989). To take an admittedly crude index of newsworthiness, it is possible to search under the terms "clergy" and "abuse" in the computerized database of *Newspaper Abstracts*, which covers major metropolitan papers in the United States. Prior to the late 1980s, the use of these two words almost invariably produced stories about clergy active in the fight against drug abuse or child abuse, but this picture changed with a massive upsurge of stories about clergy themselves being active as abusers. For the 3 years from 1989 through 1991, 130 such items appeared, or about 40 each year. In 1992, the total number of stories rose dramatically to about 240, with over 200 more published in 1993. In the secular media, clergy abuse has probably become the most discussed item of religious news since the upheavals in the Catholic church during the 1960s, and already parallel debates are occurring in the many other nations where the American media occupy such an influential role. In addition, hundreds of articles have appeared in virtually every religious and denominational periodical during the last decade, including *Christianity Today, Christian Century* (Clark 1993), *America* (Connors 1992; Loftus 1990), *US Catholic* (Burns 1992; Castelli 1993; Connors 1993; Unsworth 1993), *Commonweal* (Steinfels 1993i), and *Episcopal Life* (Wortman 1991a,b; Wortman and Stannard 1991). Especially active was the *National Catholic Reporter,* one of the first religious papers to concentrate heavily on the Gauthe case and its aftermath, and long the harshest critic of the Catholic hierarchy in these matters (see below). In the religious press, more articles appeared on this theme during 1992 than in the previous 10 years combined.

Most news stories presented extremely high estimates for the scale of the problem. One widely quoted estimate was that perhaps 5 or 6% of Catholic clergy were involved in abuse and sexual exploitation to some degree, suggesting a figure of almost 3000 "pedophile priests" at large and threatening the nation's young (Bennetts 1991; Harris 1991). However, such quantitative claims may well distort the scale and seriousness of the problem. Recent cases involving clergy "abuse" often concerned sexual relationships between priests or ministers and older teenagers or young men, acts that might be regarded as immoral or illegal, but that lack the elements of exploitation and breach of trust that make the abuse of younger children so heinous. In addition, the "clergy abuse" literature sometimes subsumes into this category acts of consensual heterosexual intercourse between clergy members and adult women. With the definition of the problem so apparently vague, it is not surprising that estimates of the frequency of clergy abuse vary so widely.

THE MEDIA AND CLERGY SEX ABUSE

Clergy sex abuse is a model example of a social problem that appears to undergo mushroom growth, receiving virtually no attention from media or policymakers before about 1984, yet becoming a major focus of popular concern within a few years. To explain the rapid growth of interest, we must appreciate changes in the mass media during these years. At mid-century, the mass media exercised considerable restraint in investigating or reporting news stories involving scandals in mainstream churches. As late as 1981, a traditionalist cleric noted that "It was not long ago that the press would file the story of a bishop arrested for drunken driving" (Kelly 1981:315). Before the 1970s, the cinema seldom portrayed a priest in anything other than a heroic or saintly guise (Keyser and Keyser 1984). Partly, this may have reflected concern about criticizing such powerful interests, and films with a religious content went to great lengths to avoid commercially disastrous condemnation by Church authorities. In addition, there were fears about offending public perceptions of good taste.

The recent interest in clergy abuse represents a reversal of this trend, and reflects a fundamental shift in news values during the 1970s and 1980s. There was an unquestionable shift toward sensationalist coverage in the news media, toward "tabloid" television news shows, sensationalistic talk shows, and "true crime" documentaries, which often blurred the lines between fact and fiction. Perhaps the media also found that attacking established churches did not in itself conspicuously offend public taste, and, in fact, appealed to constituencies who actively favored the exposure of abuses. As will be argued below, a variety of interest groups employed the abuse issue as a weapon against ecclesiastical hierarchies, and we can trace activity by feminist and gay groups as well as radical reformers within the churches themselves.

Standards of religious reporting therefore changed substantially during the decade, and it became common to present the churches as pervaded with exploitative sexuality. This was as true of fictional works such as TV movies as of purportedly objective news sources and documentaries. Increasingly, the media tended to draw on ancient imagery of lascivious priests and perverted clerical sexuality, while television investigations of abuse in institutional settings even repeated ancient canards about secret murders of orphans and others in the care of Catholic religious orders.

Many instances might illustrate television's treatment of these themes. The Gauthe case was fictionalized in a made-for-television movie, *Judgment* (1990), which focused on the Church's apparent refusal to place a priority on the needs and interests of the child victims. *Judgment* presented a picture of heroic parents and their lawyer, engaged in a populist struggle against a monolithic, secretive, reactionary Catholic hierarchy with the power to influence the decisions of secular authorities. This movie enjoyed a long afterlife in reruns on the female-oriented "Lifetime" network. *Judgment* established the "heroic" themes that would dominate media coverage during the following years, including the focus on the victims of abuse and their families, and their struggle to achieve justice against a faceless and powerful institution determined to preserve its own image at any cost.

During the peak of media concern during 1992 and 1993, the clergy abuse problem was the subject of several reports on news programs, many in the exposé format pioneered by CBS's *60 Minutes*. These stories described the exposure of a problem or scandal, usually through the heroic efforts of one or more principled individuals, while highly placed perpetrators are interviewed by one of the journalistic team who are presented as the guardians of the public interest. In two July 1992 (July 2 and 23) stories, ABC's *Primetime Live* used this inquisitorial mode of presentation to bring to public attention the case of Father James Porter. Frank Fitzpatrick, the former abuse victim who pursued Porter to his Minnesota home, occupied the heroic role. The program used the familiar *60 Minutes* technique of having the reporter literally pursue the accused individual in the streets, placing him in the position of apparently hiding from the public eye, and implying forcefully that the person had something to hide. *60 Minutes* used the "pursuit" device with no less powerful a cleric than Archbishop Roberto Sanchez of Santa Fe, New Mexico, who was accused of having had sexual relationships with several women (March 21, 1993). This in itself was a remarkable departure from earlier broadcast standards, as reporters interrupted the bishop while he was leading a pilgrimage, an interference with a religious ceremony that would have been inconceivable three or four decades previously. In other cases, journalistic standards so thoroughly rejected traditional restraints as to press perilously close to provocation or entrapment. In 1993, the St. Louis channel KMOV paid the expenses of a male prostitute who arranged a sexual assignation with a priest, placing a hidden camera in the hotel room (Kurtz 1993). This case not only raised ethical questions, but even brought the station under criminal investigation.

By the end of 1993, the clergy abuse problem had been repeatedly discussed on all the major talk shows, including *Geraldo, Sally Jessy Raphael*, and *Donahue*. Two hour-long documentaries adopted a tone of reporting unrelievedly hostile to the position of the church hierarchy. In both an *Investigative Reports* special broadcast on the Arts and Entertainment (A&E) Network (January 29, 1993) and a *CNN Presents* special (November 14, 1993), the preponderance of speakers were from groups very critical of the clergy and the hierarchy. All suggested that the prevalence of abusive behavior was extremely high, and that the Church had for years systematically engaged in cover-ups. Repeated use of the Porter or Gauthe cases as examples implied that such extreme instances were typical of clerical behavior and official responses.

The CNN program *Fall from Grace* illustrates the critical nature of coverage in these years. Although it would be inconceivable to present "a balanced view" of the issue by having an individual defend pederasty, the program effectively presented no speaker who argued that the Church had ever responded correctly or honestly to the problem, and even the quite far-reaching local reforms introduced by some dioceses were described as "a sham." The authorities quoted most extensively

included Father Andrew Greeley, who, though a Catholic p
been among the most trenchant critics of church policies in thi
example, he wrote the introduction to Jason Berry's *Lead U
Temptation*) (Berry 1992; Greeley 1992a,b, 1993). Others quoted included
Jason Berry and Jeanne Miller, the founder of the victims' support group
VOCAL, "Victims of Clergy Abuse Linkup" (for Miller, see Burkett and
Bruni 1993:238–251). The main official spokesman for the church was
Cardinal Bernardin, who responded to confrontational questions. Individual segments offered a series of harrowing vignettes, such as a Chicago family who found themselves countersued when they attempted to
take legal action against a priest, and other grievances were aired at a
meeting of a chapter of VOCAL. The program repeatedly suggested that
the problem resulted from the church hierarchy's secretive attitudes, and
that even the pedophile priests were themselves victims of the excesses of
their institutional superiors. The concluding line suggested that "It is not
just the priests who are falling from grace, it is also the church."

The *Investigative Reports* program "Sins of the Fathers" also focused on
Catholic "priest abuse" rather than the earlier "clergy abuse." Like the
CNN program, it showed a similar range of experts and authorities,
including Jeanne Miller, Andrew Greeley, Jason Berry, and Eugene Kennedy, who had written on the crisis for the radical *National Catholic
Reporter* (Kennedy 1992, 1993). Again the Porter and Gauthe cases
played central roles, and much of the program involved harrowing testimony from "survivors," who were bitterly critical of the Church's structural flaws. Some, like Christine Clark and former Porter victim Dennis
Gaboury, also appeared frequently in other talk shows and media reports (compare Burkett and Bruni 1993; Clark 1992; Gaboury 1993). In
the *Investigative Reports* program, Gaboury suggested that the lack of
sanctions against priestly misconduct meant that the bishops "might as
well be standing behind him and cheering him on" while the priest
abused a child. Andrew Greeley explicitly compared the church's closed
structure to that of the Mafia, with the difference that the Mafia did
enforce internal sanctions against deviants. Jason Berry estimated that
up to a half of Catholic priests might be homosexual in orientation,
while author Malachi Martin suggested that pedophile priests were shel-
tered by "a network of homosexuals within the Church." Following
such damning charges, the program asserted that:

> Victims say the deeper issue is an abuse of power, that Church leaders
> have consistently covered up for the perpetrators, stonewalled the vic-
> tims, and in many cases quietly shuffled the abusers from one diocese to
> another, leaving parishioners in the dark. Critics also say the church has
> been hiding behind its lawyers, and neglecting its moral duty to offer care
> and sympathy.

Though placed in the context of reporting what "victims say," there is no doubt that this is the message viewers were intended to accept.

The same themes emerged from other clergy-oriented news reporting. While many did not directly concern sexual abuse, the programs reinforced related ideas of clerical hypocrisy and duplicity, child neglect, and institutional cover-ups. The ABC network took the lead in this matter, as it had earlier done over the issue of ritual child abuse. In March 1993, ABC's *20/20* suggested that the Catholic church was suffering a widespread crisis in its enforcement of clerical celibacy, and that many priests simply ignored church regulations. The same network's magazine program *Primetime Live* had run exposés of perceived Catholic misdeeds, including early reporting of the Porter case in 1992. In May 1993, the same program recounted the experiences of numerous children who had been placed in clergy-run orphanages in the province of Québec during the mid-century. Among many serious allegations, the program suggested that children had been systematically neglected and falsely diagnosed as mentally retarded, and even that some orphans had died in mysterious circumstances (compare Farnsworth 1993). As with the sexual abuse cases, crucial testimony was provided by "survivors" of their orphanage experiences, who subsequently returned to confront the clergy and nuns who had mistreated them. In January 1994, *Primetime Live* aired a hostile account of abuses in the Catholic church's policy toward marriage annulment, suggesting that a cynical and secretive church bureaucracy harshly treated women and children. Another widely covered story in 1993 concerned the American woman who had clandestinely married an Irish bishop, and borne him a son. Once again, the story implied themes of clerical hypocrisy and covert sexuality (Murphy and DeRosa 1993).

Changes in media attitudes are critically important because they increased the likelihood that individual abuse cases would become widely known, which in turn increased public awareness of the prevalence of the offense, and fostered future reporting. The media also provided a wider arena in which interest groups could present and establish claims about the nature and severity of the problem, usually dramatic and hostile interpretations that placed ecclesiastical conduct in the most sinister context.

PROFESSIONAL INTEREST GROUPS

Apart from the mass media, certain professional interest groups have played an important claimsmaking role in defining and shaping the clergy abuse problem. The legal profession is an obvious example. During the 1980s, numerous law cases established child sexual abuse as a major area of litigation, in which large sums of money could be won from defendants or their insurers. In practical terms, this had the effect of encouraging those who believed they had been victimized to pursue their grievances, and nursery schools had been heavily hit by a series of liability claims. Initially there was doubt that church institutions were vulnerable to comparable litigation, as at least some were covered by the doctrine of charitable immunity, but this changed in 1984 and 1985. This was the time of several innovative actions, including a pioneering suit instituted by feminist attorney Gloria Allred on behalf of an adult woman who had had sexual relations with a number of clergy. The suits failed, but matters changed with the Gauthe settlement (Berry 1992; Goldman 1985).

Successful lawsuits proliferated from 1985 onward. Between 1985 and 1994, between $400 million and one billion dollars is reported to have been paid in settlements and legal costs, and many other actions are pending: by the start of 1993, there were two thousand suits nationwide involving Catholic clergy alone, and the number grew month by month (Berry 1992:371–373). The fiscal damage was so severe that the archdiocese of Santa Fe, New Mexico announced an imminent threat of bankruptcy (Margolick 1993). In 1993, there was even an attempt to prosecute Catholic bishops under the Racketeer Influenced and Corrupt Organizations Act (RICO), a move that, if successful, would vastly increase damage payments in this and successive suits.

The ensuing scandals can be seen as having a snowball effect, encouraging past victims, real or imaginary, to come forward and register their complaints. Moreover, the media criticized church attempts to defend such suits, and the CNN program *Fall from Grace* complained that Sunday donations were finding their way to the defense of pedophile priests (compare Geyelin 1993). Another program described defense efforts as the Church "hiding behind its lawyers" (A&E 1993). In May 1994, *60 Minutes* devoted a segment ("I Solemnly Swear") to attacking the church for "playing hardball" in its legal battles with victims. In such a public mood, it is likely that jurors will be extremely sympathetic to claims of clergy abuse, and will make awards accordingly: the average settlement currently runs at about one million dollars per victim. Perhaps inevitably, there are already a few well-known attorneys who specialize in clergy abuse cases (Shulruff 1993). Attorneys such as Jeffrey Anderson may be sincerely dedicated to obtaining justice for their clients in the face of perceived church hostility, but others are less scrupulous. The Catholic church presents a singularly tempting target for litigation, a multibillion dollar economic enterprise with vast holdings in property and real estate. Taken in the most cynical terms, this in itself may help to explain why the "clergy abuse" issue came to focus on the Catholic church, as opposed to any of the smaller and less centralized organizations whose ministers had been implicated in abuse.

Like lawyers, therapists have a clear vested interest in the promotion of distinctive views of the clergy abuse problem. The earlier recognition of the child sexual abuse phenomenon had greatly enhanced the authority and visibility of therapists and psychologists as experts in dealing with this problem. Throughout the 1980s, a series of court battles and legal controversies established and expanded the expertise of therapists, and it was natural that the therapeutic community would be closely involved in the new clergy abuse problem. Moreover, the common assumptions and interests of therapists helped to determine how the problem would be formulated. For example, it was an article of professional orthodoxy not only that such abuse was extremely widespread, but that victims were likely to deny or conceal the crime, and could be persuaded to admit the behavior only after extensive expert treatment and questioning.

By the end of the decade, this belief in victim denial became linked with the still more controversial question of repressed memory, and the issue of whether therapists could draw forth early memories that a subject had concealed because they were too troubling for the conscious mind to confront. The objective reality of such hidden memories remains unresolved, and many critics regard them as perilously likely to be false rather than merely suppressed recollections. However, repressed memories were central to several of the most celebrated clergy abuse cases, including the James Porter affair in Massachusetts, and the charges against Cardinal Bernardin. The Porter accusations are well substantiated, but in the Bernardin case, the alleged memories involved an incident that occurred when the putative victim was 17 years old, and therefore well outside the normal age range for such memory suppression. (Indeed, the accuser himself later agreed that the charges were too unsafe to be the basis for legal action.)

Therapists and their ideas were important in several ways in propagating certain views of the abuse problem. For purposes of litigation, there is a natural commonality of interest between therapists, child abuse experts, and the lawyers who seek to prove the extent of clergy abuse. Also vital were the victims' self-help groups, which drew on the familiar rhetoric of the "survivors'" movements that had earlier mobilized victims of rape, abuse, or incest. "Survivors" of clergy abuse formed well-organized pressure groups such as VOCAL and SNAP (Survivors' Network of those Abused by Priests) (Thornton 1991; Woodall 1993). Both were extremely successful in keeping the issue in the news by a variety of tactics, such as demonstrating at gatherings of the episcopal hierarchy, and providing articulate spokespersons for news programs and documentaries.

Once the clergy abuse problem had been defined, both media reactions and bureaucratic responses cooperated to sustain the momentum of exposure and investigation. The churches themselves played a critical role in this process, as they developed swifter and more efficient ways of dealing with the newly recognized problem (Stahel 1994). In the Catholic case, this meant introducing streamlined disciplinary procedures for accused priests, and 24-hour telephone hotlines to report allegations. These arrangements contributed to increased reporting of the offense, and increased the probability that the number of known cases would continue to spiral upward. A similar cyclical process ensured that the clergy abuse crisis would increasingly focus on abusers who were Catholic priests. As more notoriety attached to Catholic cases, public stereotypes and expectations developed so that priests, rather than other ministers, were more likely to be suspected and reported for abuse, and in turn juries would be more prepared to find against them. As the media demonstrated their usual tendency to view reports of a behavior as an accurate measure of the behavior itself, the "clergy abuse" problem became synonymous with "priest pedophilia."

THE POLITICAL CONTEXT

Political factors account for the extremely critical picture presented of the churches in general and the Catholic church in particular. The "abuse crisis" would not have erupted so quickly without a preexisting public demand or expectation about the likely truth of such charges. The atmosphere of belief and acceptance was to some extent created by the more general concern over child abuse during the previous decade, but specific concerns about the churches were enhanced by the apparently growing gulf between traditional religious values and changing social patterns. Since the 1960s, changes in American society had resulted in a general weakening of traditional family structures and an increasingly independent role for women. Within the religious communities, some churches accommodated women's demands for greater visibility and power, the "fomenting feminism" so crucial in "reshaping normative religious styles" (Roof 1993:233). However, the Catholic church remained obdurate to calls for changes in attitudes to matters like divorce, abortion, and contraception, as well as to women's ordination and an end to priestly celibacy (Kosmin and Lachman 1993:10–11). This church thus seemed increasingly visible as a bastion of "patriarchal" values, and even of hostility to women's claims to social equality. In addition, the church emerged as a primary opponent of any extension of "gay rights," either within the clergy or in society at large. In the moral and social issues that were central to American politics during the 1980s, the Catholic church had become a prominent and powerful force on the side of conservatism and traditional values. This was all the more important because of the church's status in communities (above all urban ethnic groups), which were likely to be strong supporters of many liberal and Democratic causes.

There was some outright criticism of the church's political positions, but in political and media terms, this was quite risky for the groups involved. For example, from about 1989 onward, homosexual rights groups such as ACT-UP and Queer Nation adopted increasingly militant tactics, promoting direct confrontation with ecclesiastical authorities, holding demonstrations which interrupted Catholic church services, and including salacious parodies of clerical figures in gay rights parades and protests (Goss 1994). Among the most controversial incidents were the ACT-UP protest in St Patrick's Cathedral in New York City during 1989, and the televising of ACT-UP's film *Stop the Church* on some public broadcasting stations during 1991. However, there is much evidence that these tactics were counterproductive, as they attracted criticism from normally sympathetic liberal media. News footage of demonstrations and other incidents was freely used in advertising by moral conservative groups and religious fundamentalists, who sought to raise funds by demonstrating the extremism and antireligious attitudes of gay rights and other radical groups. It seems that such aggressive displays are less acceptable and appealing in an American context than in many European societies, and conservative "traditional values" rhetoric apparently has widespread public appeal in the United States.

However, the abuse issue placed Church critics in a very different position. The rhetorical focus could shift from the individual misdeeds of a few clerics to the apparent structural hypocrisy of the Church and its hierarchy, and consequences could be presented in terms of sharp contrasts and contradictions: while the Church affected to speak for traditional values and sexual restraint, its clergy were heavily involved in sexual excess and exploitation; while the Church denounced homosexuality between consenting adults, its clergy committed homosexual acts against vulnerable children; and while the Church's "pro-life" stance asserted the absolute value of human life and the defense of small children, the institution made strenuous efforts to protect clergy who assaulted and raped the young. To quote Jason Berry, "When the bishops say that life in the womb is sacred and at the same time for years have been playing musical chairs with pedophiles, something doesn't wash,

there is an inconsistency here, there is a tremendous problem of credibil-
ity" (CNN 1993). This rhetoric of hypocrisy and contradiction threatened
to subvert the most successful aspects of the Catholic social position.
More broadly, there was the argument, potentially invaluable for feminists, that the patriarchal social system exemplified by the Catholic
church is founded upon the real or symbolic sexual exploitation of the
powerless, specifically women and children.

The clergy abuse issue had wide appeal in feminist circles, and a
broadly feminist analysis has been very influential in mainstream media
reporting of the problem. It is scarcely coincidental that one of the
phrases most commonly employed in such reports is some variation of
"the sins of the fathers" (for this usage, see, for example, Burns 1992;
Disch 1992; Hechler 1993; Ostling 1991; Sennott 1993; Woodward 1993a).
Since 1990 there have been lengthy and repeated discussions of clergy
abuse in magazines directed chiefly at a women's audience, including
Vanity Fair (Bennetts 1991), *Redbook* (Clark 1992), and *Ms.* (Bonavoglia
1992). All emphasize the same themes: the frequency of the offense, its
roots in patriarchal values and beliefs, and the structural inability of the
church to eradicate the problem without abandoning traditional gender
roles (Armstrong 1991). Generally speaking, such accounts focus on the
"abuse" involved when clergy have sexual relations with women, rather
than the more publicized exploitation of minors, but the articles sub-
sume both into a common pattern of deviance.

There are also frequent complaints of the alleged tendency of both
ecclesiastical and civil authorities to disbelieve and disparage victims,
suggesting the intense hostility to women in mainstream religious systems (Ranke-Heinemann 1990). To quote a 1992 article in *Ms.*, "Reaching
back to their Biblical roots, some Judaeo-Christian clerics blame the
woman" (Bonavoglia 1992). It is also common to link clergy abuse with
other forms of female victimization, including rape, "femicide," and
incest. A 1991 article in *Christian Century* emphasizes the role of unequal
power relations in abuse, drawing an extended parallel between clergy
sex abuse and wife-battering (Cooper-White 1991). Feminist activists
and theologians attempted to incorporate concepts of abuse, battering,
and victimization into their critique of religious patriarchy, and in this
literature child sexual abuse becomes a paradigm of social injustice and
absolute sin. In 1989, an impressive range of leading feminist theologians contributed to a major symposium on "Christianity, Patriarchy,
and Abuse" (Brown and Bohn 1989).

Feminists thus found in the abuse issue potent ideological ammuni-
tion for an attack on the institution of the Catholic church. However, it
would not be correct to see this critique as solely an external assault
upon the institution, as the same feminist arguments also appeared

within radical or dissident sections of the church itself. Clergy abuse thus served as a focus for debates and controversies that had been simmering within the church for decades, battles over the privileged position of the clergy, and the role of women. Among Catholics, since the 1960s there had been demands for a greatly enhanced role for the laity, and a change in the strongly hierarchical nature of the church (Leddy, DeRoo, and Roche 1992; Hastings 1991; Hebblethwaite 1975, 1980, 1986; Kelly 1981; Lernoux 1989; McBrien 1992; Seidler and Meyer 1989). In the 1980s, dissent was manifested in issues such as the right of Catholic clergy and theologians to support moral and political positions contrary to official teaching, and the question of women's ordination (Briggs 1992a; Lernoux 1989). Gender concerns often stood in the forefront of these debates, and there was a large and vocal Catholic feminist movement whose continued affiliation with the church at times seemed tenuous (Carmody 1986; Greeley and Durkin 1984; King 1993:177–197; Steichen 1991; Steinfels 1993c; Weaver 1985). Critics of the policy on celibacy charged that a substantial number of priests might be ignoring the church's regulations by illicitly engaging in sexual relationships with women (Murphy and DeRosa 1993; Rice 1990; Sipe 1990; Sweeney 1992; Sweeney and Sweeney 1993).

Political conflicts within the Church reached a new height in 1984, when the Catholic hierarchy denounced Democratic Vice-Presidential candidate Geraldine Ferraro for her support of abortion rights. Liberal Catholics criticized this apparent interference in secular politics, and a number of nuns and other religious published a petition of protest. The Church took steps to discipline the nuns (the "Vatican 24") and the Vatican began a general investigation of American religious orders (Ferraro, Hussey, and O'Reilly 1990). Hostilities flared again in 1986, with a controversy over granting Church platforms to proabortion politicians, and simultaneous attempts to silence or discipline leading liberals who were outspoken critics of Church regulations concerning sexual or political matters. Theologian Charles Curran lost his license to teach at the Catholic University of America, and Seattle Archbishop Raymond Hunthausen suffered a sharp reduction of his powers over his diocese. Critics alleged that these acts were part of a concerted "Roman Restoration" in the United States, a deliberate scheme to reestablish strict Vatican orthodoxy and hierarchical control over the Church, and protests culminated with the Pope's visit to the United States in 1987 (Lernoux 1989). Particularly contentious were the closed, secretive proceedings in which liberal clerics were apparently denounced, tried, and punished, effectively without representation. 1986–1987 has been described as "the year that shook Catholic America" (Briggs 1992a).

As the clergy abuse issue emerged, then, there was a large constituen-

cy within the Catholic church predisposed to affirm the rights and powers of the laity against those of the clergy, and of the lower clergy against
the Church hierarchy. This also meant criticizing the hierarchy for its
entrenched bureaucratic positions, and its tendency to deal with clerical
failings through secretive internal procedures. This approach was most
clear in the pages of the *National Catholic Reporter* (*NCR*), "the stalwart
evangelist of the Catholic Left" (Briggs 1992a:17; compare Kelly 1981).
NCR was among the leading periodicals both in attacking the "Roman
Restoration" and in reporting the clergy sex abuse problem, emphasizing its scale, and demanding an urgent and proactive response (Briggs
1992b; Fox 1992, 1993; Kennedy 1992, 1993; MacLoughlin 1993; McClory
1992; Unsworth 1992, 1993). As early as 1985, a special issue of the paper
was the first to formulate what would become the standard interpretation of the "priest pedophilia" cases, providing an ample platform for
Jason Berry's groundbreaking coverage of the Gauthe case (*NCR* June 7,
1985). Throughout the next decade, the paper repeatedly charged that
the hierarchy was covering up "the see-no-problem, hear-no-problem,
speak-no-problem" (Kennedy 1993).

Although Catholic papers such as *NCR* and *Commonweal* do not reach
a large audience, their point of view won support because of the ways in
which the mass media were likely to seek Catholic experts on the abuse
issue. The broadcast media have long demonstrated sympathy to feminist and liberal stances on religious issues, as suggested by the overwhelmingly unsympathetic coverage of the Church's reluctance to
ordain women priests. The customary experts sought on such conflicts
had been prominent Catholic reformists, most notably the well-known
and visible Andrew Greeley, and the same individuals and groups were
naturally drawn in when the clergy abuse problem arose. More conservative church spokesmen virtually never appeared, and thus the authorities
employed to present "the Catholic view" of the question almost invariably presented vigorous criticisms of the hierarchy and its procedures.

The significance of the abuse issue for feminist and other dissidents
within the Church can be best appreciated in the context of the remedies
suggested for the problem, as these included essentially all the major
changes advocated by liberal Catholic reformers for decades, though
now with the added force supplied by the pedophile theme. Demands
included an end to mandatory celibacy, the ordination of women to the
priesthood, and limitations on the sanctity of the confessional. Reformers argued that each would in its way contribute to the protection of
the young. Following the exposure of the Mount Cashel affair in Newfoundland, there were many protest meetings by parishioners and other
citizen groups, and a typical statement was that "the only way to purge
the Church was to allow priests to marry and to open the seminary

doors to women. Other radical means were proposed, including the abolition of confession so that fallen priests wouldn't have an easy means of homing in on their victims" (Harris 1991:18).

The A&E program *Sins of the Fathers* favorably quoted church critics who seek "drastic" remedies "shutting down the seminaries or making celibacy an option for priests instead of a demand," while "many" saw a partial solution in ordaining women (compare Kennedy 1992). Jason Berry (1992) advocated an end to both mandatory celibacy and the seminary system. The CNN program *Fall from Grace*, for example, identified celibacy as a primary evil: the celibate priesthood offered "an attractive hiding place for men struggling with deviant sexual urges," "a safe hiding place for men struggling with sexual conflict." Also emphasized in most reporting were the misdeeds of "the hierarchy," and the suggestion that the Church should become less clerical-oriented and more open to the needs of the laity. Dioceses that introduced reforms to combat the pedophile problem usually introduced review panels with substantial or majority lay participation, in contrast to the traditional emphasis on purely clerical solutions.

The clergy abuse crisis therefore led to a sharp focus on precisely those aspects of Catholicism that had previously been most under attack from feminist and liberal critics, both within the church and outside. During 1989, the Canadian hierarchy found itself under intense popular pressure to consider permitting married priests, and surveys indicated that abuse scandals have been the chief factor in motivating support for reforms. In both the United States and Canada, opinion polls consistently suggest that lay support for both women's ordination and clerical marriage has grown dramatically in the last 5 years, and while clergy abuse cannot be adduced as the sole reason for this change, it has certainly contributed (Goldman 1992).

Other ecclesiastically liberal implications were less overt, but nonetheless present. In any television presentation, it is usual to illustrate a theme with related visual footage, and in the case of a clandestine act like clergy pedophilia, it is natural to use church-related footage involving stained glass windows, religious statues, film of a mass or religious processions, together with plainsong or liturgical music. In the context of the program, however, the juxtaposition of specifically Catholic imagery with accounts of pedophilia tends to stigmatize traditional "high" Catholic practice, and this visual association follows the lines of the ancient stereotypes of lascivious, cynical priests.

The political value of the clergy abuse problem can be illustrated by comparing today's debates with those 20 years ago over the issue of reforming the Catholic church. In the 1970s, there were vigorous movements within the Church calling for the ordination of women and the abolition of compulsory clerical celibacy, while liberal activists attacked the church for its stand on moral issues such as abortion and homosexuality. However, the Catholic reformers used the rhetoric of religious and moral justice, of compliance with divine law, and of conformity to contemporary secular standards of fairness and social equality. All were powerful arguments, but none had the immediate force of the contemporary debate, in which it is claimed quite simply that the reforms are imperative to protect children, to prevent ruined lives, and to forestall the new cycles of abuse believed to stem from such exploitation. For secular critics of the church, rhetoric traditionally focused on the confrontation between the supposedly archaic, patriarchal moral standards of the churches and enlightened secular liberalism. This rhetoric of enlightenment might still be effective in many political contexts, but it runs the risk of losing force in eras like the 1980s and 1990s when prevailing social and political values reemphasize tradition and religion to the disparagement of terms like liberalism and progress. However, arguments based on secularism and enlightenment are not as potentially powerful as the rhetoric of hypocrisy, which in effect rejects the whole moral foundation of the Catholic church, its hierarchy, and any of its spokespersons.

CONCLUSION: "WOMEN AND CHILDREN FIRST"

Sexual relations between adults and minors can occur in almost any social or institutional setting, and some individuals are likely to commit such acts on a frequent or habitual basis. The issue is therefore not so much to understand what made an individual like James Porter or Gilbert Gauthe become a "pedophile priest," but how these discrete cases become constructed as part of a generalized social problem, and the moral or political dimensions that such a problem will attain. In typifying the "clergy abuse problem" of the last decade, it is possible to imagine interpretations that might have blamed (for example) the changing sexual standards of the wider society, the prevalence of pornography, or the aberrations of the individual priests involved. It is even possible to suppose a pro-church reaction that would have attacked the excessive litigiousness of contemporary society, and attacked the lawyers and therapists active in exposing the abuse. Of course these alternative interpretations did not occur, and both the emphasis and the stigma have clearly been on the institution of the Catholic church, its closed and hierarchical organizational structure, and the specific disciplinary rules under which its clergy operate. That the problem developed in this direction is richly informative both about the underlying hostility that the Church and its hierarchy had attracted in the previous two decades, and the resulting political agendas that emerge forcefully in media coverage and expert interpretation of the issue.

While the construction of this problem suggests the latent anti-Catholicism of the American media, it also exemplifies shifts in social values that are likely to be apparent in other controversies. In 1981, a conservative cleric complained that the press had lost the respectful restraint traditionally shown toward churches and clergy:

> But lately news for news sake is the compelling moral norm for revelations regardless of the consequences. . . . Magazines like *Newsweek* have a penchant for shocking audiences with stories about irregular priests. . . . In a secularized culture, however, nothing is sacred, especially the sacred. Deflating or dethroning authority figures is fashionable. (Kelly 1981:315)

One may or may not agree with this complaint, especially its emphasis on secularism, but it is accurate in its observation about changing criteria for the groups and individuals who merit respect and reverence.

The clergy abuse affair says much about values, in the sense of those things that are most prized in a given society, and the extent to which these values are now in flux. At least rhetorically, contemporary American society has come to place a very high premium on certain concepts of childhood, and these cultural values must be protected even at the cost of sacrificing what were once considered profoundly important religious and cultural beliefs, such as the sanctity of the priesthood, the secrecy of the confessional, and so on. In addition, the increased social status of women has made suspect any institution that explicitly asserts masculine and patriarchal authority, and the social and legal consequences of this distrust are apparent. Whereas once religious institutions would have been believed worthy to enforce internal standards of behavior and morality, the current trend is to seek external controls from the civil and criminal law, and to impose the value systems of nonreligious groups, especially the therapeutic community. The relative decline of clerical status is well reflected in the increased willingness of the mass media to investigate and criticize perceived ecclesiastical misdeeds. In that sense, it is quite correct to observe that "Deflating or dethroning [male, traditional] authority figures is fashionable" (Kelly 1981:315).

For activists, the clergy abuse issue reinforces valuable lessons about the best means of making and establishing claims, and the best grounds of authority on which a problem can be built. In contrast to earlier centuries, it would be quite unsound today to base an argument on traditional religious criteria ("The Bible says . . . ," "The Church has always believed . . ."), or indeed on traditional authority of any kind.

Far more successful is any approach that links the issue in question either to defending and promoting the status of women, or to any threat that can be postulated against children, a rhetorical development ably pioneered in the early twentieth century by the Temperance movement. To take a current example, pornography is thus depicted as evil not because it violates the Seventh Commandment, but because it leads both to child pornography and sexual violence against women. Drugs appear to represent consensual victimless crime, but drug-taking leads to the innocent suffering of "crack babies," "ice babies," and the rest. A celibate clergy is wrong not because it is antiscriptural, but because it creates a situation in which priests molest boys in the sacristy. The rhetoric of contemporary social problems thus illustrates the fundamental importance of placing the interests of women and children in the forefront of any feasible issue, to take advantage of new sensibilities. In the case of clergy abuse, such a shift of emphasis has already undermined what once appeared impregnable ideological positions.

NOTE

1. In Catholic usage, it is customary to use the word "religious" as a noun denoting a member of a religious order or congregation, whether or not that person is an ordained priest. Monks, friars and nuns are therefore "religious," and they are so termed here.

REFERENCES

A&E *Investigative Report*. 1993. "Sins of the Fathers." Broadcast on January 29.
Allen, G. 1989. "A Church in Crisis." *Maclean's* November 27:66.
———. 1990. "Breaking the Faith." *Maclean's* July 30:16–17.
Armstrong, S. 1991. "Sexual Abuse of Women and Girls by Clergy." *Canadian Women Studies* 114 (Summer).
Bennett, D. H. 1990. *The Party of Fear*. New York: Vintage.
Bennetts, L. 1991. "Unholy Alliances." *Vanity Fair* 54(December):224–229.
Berry, J. 1992. *Lead Us Not Into Temptation*. New York: Doubleday.
———. 1993a. "Investigating Child Sexual Abuse in the Catholic Church." *IRE Journal* January:10–11.
———. 1993b. "Listening to the Survivors: Voices of the People of God." *America* November 13:4–9.
Best, J. (ed.). 1989. *Images of Issues*. Hawthorne, NY: Aldine de Gruyter.
———. 1990. *Threatened Children*. Chicago: University of Chicago Press.
Bonavoglia, A. 1992. "The Sacred Secret." *Ms.* 2(March–April):40–46.

Briggs, K. A. 1992a. *Holy Siege*. San Francisco: Harper.

———. 1992b. "Size of Pedophilia Crisis More Obvious Than Causes." *National Catholic Reporter* October 30:22.

Brown, J. C., and C. R. Bohn. 1989. *Christianity, Patriarchy and Abuse: A Feminist Critique*. New York: Pilgrim.

Bruce, S. 1985. "Puritan Perverts: Notes on Accusation." *Sociological Review* 33:47–63.

Buckley, W. F. 1993. "The Church's Newest Cross." *National Review* 45(April 26):63.

Burkett, E., and F. Bruni. 1993. *Gospel of Shame*. New York: Viking.

Burns, R. E. 1990. "Mind Your Own Celibacy." *US Catholic* 55(12):02.

———. 1992. "Should All Priests Pay for the Sins of the Fathers?" *US Catholic* 57(12):02–05.

Butterfield, F. 1992a. "Silent Decades Ended, Dozens Accuse a Priest." *New York Times* June 9:A18.

———. 1992b. "Priest Accused of Sexual Abuse Is Extradited." *New York Times* September 23:A25.

———. 1992c. "Report Says Ex-Priest Admitted Sex Abuse to Pope." *New York Times* October 25:I20.

———. 1992d. "Diocese Reaches Settlement With 68 Who Accuse Priest of Sexual Abuse." *New York Times* December 4:A22.

Carmody, D. L. 1986. *The Double Cross: Ordination, Abortion and Catholic Feminism*. New York: Crossroad.

Castelli, J. 1993. "Abuse of Faith." *US Catholic* 58(9):6–15.

Chandler, R. 1990. "Sex Abuse Cases Rock the Clergy." *Los Angeles Times* August 3:A1.

Clark, C. 1992. "Broken Vows." *Redbook* 180(November):51–56.

Clark, D. C. 1993. "Sexual Abuse in the Church: The Law Steps In." *Christian Century* 110(April 14):396–398.

CNN. 1993. *Fall from Grace*. News report broadcast on November 14.

Connors, C. 1992. "Priests and Pedophilia: a Silence That Needs Breaking?" *America* 166(May 9):400–401.

———. 1993. "The Search for Answers." *US Catholic* 58(9):08–11.

Cooper-White, P. 1991. "Soul Stealing: Power Relations in Pastoral Sexual Abuse." *Christian Century* 108(February 20):196–199.

Davis, D. B. 1986. "Some Themes of Counter-Subversion: an Analysis of Anti-Masonic, Anti-Catholic, Anti-Mormon Literature." Pp. 137–154 in *From Homicide to Slavery*. New York: Oxford University Press.

Disch, T. M. 1992. "The Sins of the Fathers." *The Nation* 255(November 2):514–516.

Farnsworth, C. H. 1993. "Orphans of the 1950s, Telling of Abuse, Sue Quebec." *New York Times* May 21:A3.

Ferraro, B., P. Hussey, and J. O'Reilly. 1990. *No Turning Back: Two Nuns' Battle with the Vatican over Women's Right to Choose*. New York: Poseidon Press.

Fortune, M. M. 1986. "Confidentiality and Mandatory Reporting: A False Dilemma?" *Christian Century* 103(June 18):582–583.

—————. 1989. *Is Nothing Sacred? When Sex Invades the Pastoral Relationship*. San Francisco: Harper & Row.

—————. 1992. "How the Church Should Imitate the Navy." *Christian Century* 109 (August 26/September 2):765–766.

Fox, T. C. 1992. "Sex and Power Issues Expand Clergy-Lay Rift." *National Catholic Reporter* November 13:17–19.

—————. 1993. "As Nation Discusses Pedophilia, Even Pope Admits It's a Problem." *National Catholic Reporter* July 2:2–3.

Friendly, J. 1986. "Catholic Church Discussing Priests Who Abuse Children." *New York Times* May 4:I26.

Gaboury, D. 1993. "The Secret of St Mary's." *Rolling Stone* November 11:48–54.

Geyelin, M. 1993. "Cross Purposes: The Catholic Church Struggles with Suits Over Sexual Abuse." *Wall Street Journal* November 24:A1.

Goldman, A. L. 1985. "Three Cases Challenge Privacy of Talks with Clergy" *New York Times* August 27:I19.

—————. 1992. "Religion Notes: Sentiment for Married Priests." *New York Times* June 13:I10.

Goss, R. 1994. *Jesus Acted Up: A Gay and Lesbian Manifesto*. San Francisco: Harper.

Graham, M. 1993. "Archbishop of Chicago Is Accused of Sex Abuse." *Philadelphia Inquirer* November 13:A1.

Greeley, A. 1992a. "Priestly Silence on Pedophilia."*New York Times* March 13:A31.

—————. 1992b. "How Serious Is the Problem of Sexual Abuse by Clergy?" *America* 166(March 20):6–10.

—————. 1993. "A View from the Priesthood." *Newsweek* 122(August 16):45.

Greeley, A., and M. G. Durkin. 1984. *Angry Catholic Women*. Chicago, IL: Thomas More Press.

Harris, M. 1991. *Unholy Orders: Tragedy at Mount Cashel*. Toronto: Penguin.

Hastings, A (ed.). 1991. *Modern Catholicism: Vatican II and After*. New York: Oxford University Press.

Hebblethwaite, P. 1975. *The Runaway Church*. London: Collins.

—————. 1980. *The New Inquisition: Schillebeeckx and Kung*. London: Collins/Fount Paperbacks.

—————. 1986. *Synod Extraordinary*. New York: Doubleday.

Hechler, D. 1993. "Sins of the Father." *McCall's* 120(September):113–114.

Hirsley, Michael. 1991a. "Panel to Examine Priests in Sex Cases." *Chicago Tribune*. October 26:2C,3.

—————. 1991b. "Removal of Priests Angers Parishioners." *Chicago Tribune*. November 21:3C,1.

—————. 1991c. "Removal of Priests Leaves Parishes Torn." *Chicago Tribune*. November 26:2C,6.

Jenkins, P. 1992a. *Intimate Enemies: Moral Panics in Contemporary Great Britain*. Hawthorne, NY: Aldine De Gruyter.

—————. 1992b. "G. K. Chesterton and the Anti-Catholic Tradition." *Chesterton Review* 183:345–369.

————. 1992c. "Priests and Pedophiles?: The Attack on the Catholic Church." *Chronicles: a Magazine of American Culture* December:24–27.

————. 1994. *Using Murder: The Social Construction of Serial Homicide*. Hawthorne, NY: Aldine De Gruyter.

Kelly, G. A. 1981. *The Battle for the American Church*. New York: Doubleday Image.

Kennedy, E. 1992. "Seminary System Rates Quick Christian Burial." *National Catholic Reporter* July 17:6.

————. 1993. "The See-no-problem, Hear-no-problem, Speak-no-problem." *National Catholic Reporter* March 19:5.

Keyser, L. J., and B. Keyser. 1984. *Hollywood and the Catholic Church*. Chicago: Loyola University Press.

King, U. 1993. *Women and Spirituality: Voices of Protest and Promise*. University Park, PA: Penn State Press.

Kosmin, B. A., and S. P. Lachman. 1993. *One Nation Under God: Religion in Contemporary American Society*. New York: Harmony Books.

Kurtz, H. 1993. "A TV Station's Dirty Trick." *Washington Post* June 12.

Leddy, M. J., R. J. DeRoo, and D. Roche. 1992. *In the Eye of the Catholic Storm: The Church Since Vatican II*. Toronto: Harper Collins.

Lernoux, P. 1989. *People of God*. New York: Viking.

Loftus, J. A. 1990. "Question of Disillusionment: Sexual Abuse Among the Clergy." *America* 163(December 1):426–429.

MacLoughlin, J. 1993. "Just Following Orders: The Politics of Pedophilia." *National Catholic Reporter* April 16:15.

Margolick, D. 1993. "Facing Costly Abuse Suits, Diocese Turns to Parishioners."*New York Times* December 22:A1.

McBrien, R. P. 1992. *Report on the Church: Catholicism After Vatican II*. San Francisco: Harper.

McClory, R. 1992. "Bernardin Issues Rigorous Pedophile Policy." *National Catholic Reporter* October 2:3.

Murphy, A., and P. de Rosa. 1993. *Forbidden Fruit*. Boston: Little Brown.

Mydans, Seth. 1993a. "Eleven Friars Molested Seminary Students, Church Inquiry Says." *New York Times* December 1:A1.

————. 1993b. "Report on Friars' Abuse Eases a Victim's Burden." *New York Times* December 2:A18.

National Catholic Reporter. 1992. "Chicago Sex-Abuse Policy Thoughtful and Firm." October 2:24.

Ostling, R. N. 1991. "Sins of the Fathers." *Time* 137(August 19):51.

————. 1993. "The Secrets of St Lawrence." *Time* 141(June 7):44.

People Weekly. 1992. "Up Front." July 27.

Petersen, J. R. 1992. "When the Church Sins." *Playboy* December:54–55.

Press, A. 1993. "Priests and Abuse." *Newsweek* 121(August 16):42–44.

Ranke-Heinemann, U. 1990. *Eunuchs for the Kingdom Of God*. New York: Doubleday.

Rice, D. 1990. *Shattered Vows: Priests Who Leave*. London: Michael Joseph.

Ritter, B. 1988. *Sometimes God Has a Kid's Face*. New York: Covenant House.

Roberts, N. 1990. "Have Anti-Catholic Attitudes Gone With the Wind?" *US Catholic* 55(1):33.

Roof, W. C. 1993. *A Generation of Seekers: The Spiritual Journeys of the Baby Boom Generation*. San Francisco: Harper.

Rossetti, S. J. 1990. *Slayer of the Soul: Child Sexual Abuse and the Catholic Church*. Mystic, CT: Twenty-Third.

Rutter, P. 1989. *Sex in the Forbidden Zone: When Men in Power—Therapists, Doctors, Clergy, Teachers and Others—Betray Women's Trust*. Los Angeles: J. P. Tarcher.

Scheer, R. 1990. "Such Unholy Business." *Playboy* 37(June):55,169–170.

Seidler, J., and K. Meyer. 1989. *Conflict and Change in the Catholic Church*. New Brunswick, NJ: Rutgers University Press.

Sennott, C. M. 1992. *Broken Covenant*. New York: Simon & Schuster.

———. 1993. "Sins of the Fathers." *Playboy* 40(July):74–76.

Shulruff, L. I. 1993. "His Specialty: Sex Abuse Suits Against Priests." *New York Times* June 25:B16.

Sipe, A. W. R. 1990. *A Secret World: Sexuality and the Search for Celibacy*. New York: Brunner/Mazel.

Smothers, R. 1988. "Preacher's Journey: Long Trail of Abuse." *New York Times* November 15:I1.

Stahel, T. H. 1994. "A Pastoral Response to Abuse: Interview with Joseph P. Chinnici OFM." *America* 170(January):15–22.

Steichen, D. 1991. *Ungodly Rage: The Hidden Face of Catholic Feminism*. San Francisco: Ignatius.

Steinfels, P. 1992a. "Inquiry in Chicago Breaks Silence on Sex Abuse by Catholic Priests." *New York Times* February 24:A1.

———. 1992b. "New Panel in Chicago to Study Sexual Abuse of Children by Priests." *New York Times* June 16:A17.

———. 1992c. "Church Panel to Investigate Sexual Abuse Charges." *New York Times* September 22:A21.

———. 1992d. "Giving Healing and Hope to Priests Who Molested." *New York Times* October 12:A11.

———. 1992f. "Data in Priest Abuse Case Show Pattern of Treatment." *New York Times*, October 22:A12.

———. 1992e. "Bishops Vow Firm Action on Sexual Abuse by Priests." *New York Times* November 20:A18.

———. 1993a. "Archbishop Concedes He Had Relationships with Three Women." *New York Times* March 10:A12.

———. 1993b. "Archbishop Is Resigning After Accusations of Sex." *New York Times* March 20:I6.

———. 1993c. "Catholic Feminists Ask: Can We Remain Catholic?" *New York Times* April 16:A19.

———. 1993d. "O'Connor Orders Priests to Meetings on Sexual Conduct." *New York Times* May 26:B1.

———. 1993e. "Bishops Struggle Over Sex Abuse by Parish Priests." *New York Times* June 18:A1.

———. 1993f. "Pope Vows to Help US Bishops Oust Priests Who Molest Children." *New York Times* June 22:A1

———. 1993g. "The Church Faces the Trespasses of Priests." *New York Times* June 27:IV1.

———. 1993h. "Policy Is Issued on Investigating Abuse by Priests." *New York Times* July 2:A1.

———. 1993i. "Needed: A Firm Purpose of Amendment." *Commonweal* 120(March 12):16–18.

———. 1993j. "Bishops Assail Press on Sex Charges." *New York Times* November 16:A24.

Sweeney, T. 1992. *A Church Divided*. Buffalo, NY: Prometheus Books.

Sweeney, T. A., and P. S. Sweeney. 1993. *What God Hath Joined*. New York: Ballantine.

Thornton, J. 1991. "Cleric Abuse Group to Share Information." *Chicago Tribune* November 4:2C,3.

Unsworth, T. 1992. "Church, State, Wrangle Over Pedophilia Cases." *National Catholic Reporter* September 25:14.

———. 1993. "How One Diocese Responds." *US Catholic* 58(9):13.

Weaver, M. J. 1985. *New Catholic Women: A Contemporary Challenge to Traditional Religious Authority*. San Francisco: Harper.

Wilkes, P. 1993. "Unholy Acts." *New Yorker* 68(June 7):62–79.

Woodall, M. 1993. "Conference Focussing on Abuse by Priests." *Philadelphia Inquirer* May 22:B1.

Woodward, K. L. 1993a. "The Sins of the Fathers." *Newsweek* 121(July 12):57.

———. 1993b. "Sex and the Church." *Newsweek* 121(August 16):38–41.

Woodward, K. L., and P. King. 1989. "When a Pastor Turns Seducer." *Newsweek* 114 (August 28):48–49.

Wortman, J. A. 1991a. "Pain May Overwhelm Exploited Victims." *Episcopal Life* October:1.

———. 1991b. "Full Disclosure of Abuse Helps Parishes Heal." *Episcopal Life* November:1.

Wortman, J. A., and E. Stannard. 1991. "Exploitation a Major Church Problem." *Episcopal Life* September:1.

7

The Social Construction of Infertility: From Private Matter to Social Concern

SHIRLEY A. SCRITCHFIELD

Not long ago, infertility and reproductive impairments were invisible phenomena. When couples had trouble conceiving children, the dramas were personal ones, not part of a public, social issue. Today, considerable public attention is focused upon the plight of those defined as infertile.

The popular press is replete with articles describing the infertility "epidemic" and the treatments provided by the wonders of modern medical technology. Biomedical interventions to facilitate fertility have exploded in the last two decades; physicians who treat problems in conception proclaim a new medical specialty—"infertility and reproductive endocrinology." By one estimate, the number of women seeking assistance in conceiving a child in the previous year increased by 25% from 1982 to 1988 (Mosher and Pratt 1990; Wilcox and Mosher 1993); Royte (1993) suggests there were more than one and a quarter million such consultations in 1992.

Taken together, these trends suggest a dramatic increase in infertility. Is that the case? Is there more infertility today than there was 20 years ago? Are we in the midst of an epidemic of infertility?

The evidence presented in the next section of this chapter shows that there is *no* indication of increase—dramatic or otherwise—in the incidence of reproductive impairment. If that is the case, what *does* account for the current public attention given to infertility?

I argue here that complex changes in social definitions of and responses to reproduction and reproductive impairments have fostered the *perception* that infertility is increasing—the perception that we face an epidemic requiring immediate attention. Furthermore, the changing definitions and responses not only shape our understanding of the incidence and prevalence of infertility, but they also define how the problem should be resolved. Specifically, current social constructions of infertility

131

problems promote high technology medical treatments as solutions rather than emphasizing prevention of reproductive impairments.

The chapter begins by examining the available data on the incidence and prevalence of infertility. Then, I identify the factors that redefined reproductive capacities and incapacities leading to the perception of an infertility epidemic and its appropriate resolution. The discussion closes by exploring some implications of this social construction of infertility.

ESTIMATING THE PREVALENCE OF INFERTILITY

Assessing the prevalence and nature of infertility in the United States is difficult, in part, because the definition of the term is ambiguous. Contrary to popular conceptions, infertility is not a concrete, objective, definitive trait or state of being. Rather, medical authorities use the term to refer to a relative situation. Specifically, physicians define infertility as failure to conceive during 12 months or longer of unprotected intercourse when neither partner is surgically sterile. In other words, a couple will be diagnosed as infertile if they have been sexually active for a year, have not used contraceptives, and have not conceived during that time.

Because this definition of infertility is relative and time-bound, it "confounds inability ever to conceive with difficulty in conceiving quickly" (Menken, Trussel, and Larson 1986:1391). There is evidence that suggests that a sizable proportion of fecund couples (couples with the capacity to conceive) may take longer than 12 months to conceive (see discussion in Menken et al. 1986). For example, in a study of couples diagnosed as having fertility problems, Collins, Wrixon, Janes, and Wilson (1983) found that while 41% of those whose infertility was treated subsequently conceived, *so did 35% of those couples who were not treated*. In other words, the use of a time-bound definition of infertility results in many nonsterile couples being counted as infertile.

Because some couples deemed infertile eventually conceive, using this definition to measure the prevalence of infertility inevitably exaggerates the extent of the problem. However, assessments using this definition provide the only basis for examining trends in reproductive impairments. Specifically, the most comprehensive data available come from the 1965 National Fertility Study and the National Surveys of Family Growth conducted in 1976, 1982, and 1988 (Mosher and Pratt 1985, 1990). Table 7.1 gives the percentages of married women classified as infertile, surgically sterile, and fecund for these 4 years, with comparisons between whites and blacks for three of those years.

Given the recent attention to infertility, these data are surprising. According to Table 7.1, the proportion of married women classified as

Table 7.1. Infertility Status of Married Women (Aged 15–44) by Race: 1965, 1976, 1982, and 1988[a], with each group equalling 100%

	1965 (%)	1976 (%)	1982 (%)	1988 (%)[b]
ALL WOMEN				
Infertility	11.2	10.3	8.5	7.9
Surgically sterile	15.8	28.2	38.9	42.4
Fecund	73.0	61.5	52.6	49.7
WHITES				
Infertile	10.5	9.4	8.1	n.a.
Surgically Sterile	15.9	29.0	38.9	n.a.
Fecund	73.6	61.6	53.0	n.a.
BLACKS				
Infertility	16.3	18.1	13.1	n.a.
Surgically sterile	14.2	21.6	36.3	n.a.
Fecund	69.5	60.3	50.6	n.a.

[a] Source: Mosher and Pratt (1985, 1990).
[b] Data on infertility were not available by racial grouping for 1988.

infertile actually declined from 11.2% in 1965 to 7.9% in 1988 (Mosher and Pratt 1985, 1990). However, this decline may be more apparent than real; Mosher and Pratt (1985) suggest that the decline reflects a substantial increase in the use of surgical sterilization as a means of contraception. Specifically, they argue that "the increasing use of contraceptive sterilizations reduced the proportions of women who would otherwise find themselves infertile at age 30 and older" (Mosher and Pratt 1985:4). Thus, to better depict the extent of infertility, Table 7.2 presents the

Table 7.2. Infertility Status of Married Women (Aged 15–44) by Race: 1965, 1976, 1982, and 1988, (each group equalling 100%)[a] Excluding Surgically Sterilized, in Percentage

	1965	1976	1982	1988[b]
ALL WOMEN				
Infertile	13.3	14.3	13.9	13.7
Fecund	86.7	85.7	86.1	86.3
WHITES				
Infertile	12.5	13.3	13.3	n.a.
Fecund	87.5	86.7	86.7	n.a.
BLACKS				
Infertile	19.0	23.1	20.6	n.a.
Fecund	81.0	76.9	79.4	n.a.

[a] Source: Mosher and Pratt (1985, 1990).
[b] Data on infertility were not available by racial grouping for 1988.

numbers and percentages of married women classified as infertile when we exclude those who are surgically sterile. Once surgical sterilizations are excluded, it becomes apparent that the rate of infertility has remained remarkably stable.

Tables 7.1 and 7.2 also present some data by race. These data reveal that the rate of infertility was considerably higher among black women than among white women for the first 3 survey years. Unfortunately, racial comparisons were not available for 1988. However, it is likely that patterns of racial difference found in earlier years would persist over time.

What conclusion can be drawn from these data? Clearly, there is little evidence of an infertility epidemic. Indeed, the rate of infertility has been amazingly stable over almost 25 years. Thus, the increased attention to infertility reflects something other than the extent of infertility.

CHANGING DEFINITIONS OF REPRODUCTIVE CAPACITY

If there has been no dramatic increase in infertility, why all the recent medical and public attention centered on the issue? I suggest that the increased concern about infertility reveals a social redefinition of reproductive capacities and impairments. It is not that there has been a dramatic increase in couples unable to conceive; rather, expectations and definitions of "normal" patterns of reproduction have changed so that contemporary couples are quicker to suspect reproductive problems, quicker to seek assistance, and more likely to expect solutions than previous generations. Moreover, the plight of those seeking medical and other forms of assistance is more apparent than in previous eras; the nature of their treatment, tribulations, and triumphs is more visible to the general public.

Several social changes facilitated this transformation in normative expectations and social visibility. Specifically, there are at least four interrelated factors contributing to the redefinition of infertility: (1) advances in contraceptive methods fostering a greater sense of control over reproduction, (2) the marked increase in couples postponing childbearing until their late 20s or early 30s, (3) the declining and differential nature of fertility rates, and (4) the development of and attention paid to technological innovations in diagnostic and treatment procedures.

Contraception and the Illusion of Control

Of all the factors contributing to the growing social concern over infertility, one of the most important—and most ironic—is our improved knowledge about contraception. Birth control is not new; throughout history women in most cultures have practiced some form of contraception (ranging from contraceptive or abortifacient herbs to barrier methods to infanticide). However, until recently, the reproductive lives of women were largely matters of chance, not choice. Only during the last century have contraceptive methods become sufficiently effective and available that large numbers of women have gained considerable control over the patterns of their reproductive lives.

These advances in contraceptive knowledge and technology have transformed Americans' attitudes toward their reproductive capacities. Where once couples could not "decide" if and when to have children, today's couples perceive that they can choose *whether* to have children, *when* to have children, and *how many* children to have. And, to an extent, their perceptions are correct; they have more control, and, hence, more choice than previous generations. However, this control is not complete.

The control over reproduction provided by effective contraceptive methods has fostered a "naive view that reproduction is a simple, natural process—deciding to conceive leads to conception leads to pregnancy leads to the birth of a baby" (Reinharz 1988: 85). People think and speak in terms of the choice to have or not have children (Fabe and Wikler 1979; Daniels and Weingarten 1980). However, biology is not always, or even usually so amenable to human control and intent. Not all couples who plan their families according to this perception are successful. Even among the highly fecund, the average time to conception is more than 8 months (Bongaarts 1975).

Reproduction always involves uncertainty. True, choice plays an increasing role in reproduction because of technological advances in contraceptive methods and improved access for many women to safe abortion. However, *reproduction is not entirely a matter of choice*, regardless of the technological management of the process. Biological processes continue to interfere with complete individual control. Bodies are not machines (despite medical metaphors to the contrary); they cannot be ordered to become pregnant and produce children on demand.

Yet, particularly among the socially and economically advantaged, the notion of choice and total control over reproduction persists. For example, in a study of infertile, middle-class couples, Griel (1991) found that the vast majority of both husbands and wives clearly assumed that having children was essentially a matter of deciding to have children. When "Mother Nature" did not cooperate with their decisions, they were shocked and experienced a marked sense of loss of control. Would they have reacted so intensely 30 years ago, when there was not the same sense of personal control over reproduction? After several years without a conception, they probably would have concluded there was a problem. But, today, they are likely to reach that conclusion much

sooner, in part, because they perceive that they should be able to "reproduce on demand."

The Trend of Postponing Parenthood

Most American couples expect to become parents at some point in
their married lives. However, in the last two decades, it has become
clear that a significant portion of these couples are delaying parenthood,
not just for 1 or 2 years after marriage, but for 5–10 years. Indeed,
national surveys conducted by the Bureau of the Census indicate a clear
and persistent pattern for many women to postpone their childbearing
until their late 20s or early 30s (Ventura 1982; O'Connell 1991). Just over
36% of women who had a child in 1992 were 30–44 years of age, and
one-fourth of those were first births (Bachu 1993).

Those postponing tend to be white, relatively affluent couples in
which the wife is highly educated and employed, most typically in a
profession. In 1992, approximately 32% of all first births to employed
women were among those 30–44, over 51% of first births to women with
family incomes over $50,000 were among those 30–44, over 42% of first
births among women who had completed 4 years of college were among
those 30–44, and 73% of first births to women who had completed some
graduate school were to those 30–44 (Bachu 1993).

This profile is consistent with other evidence that suggests that postponing couples delay parenthood for "as long as it takes to accomplish
intricate 'preparental' agendas of personal, marital, or career development" (Daniels and Weingarten 1980). Indeed, research indicates that
the desire of many women to complete their education and become
established in a career is one of the most important reasons for postponing childbearing.

What happens when these people finally decide that it is time to
become parents? Their relatively advantaged position in society gives
them a strong sense of personal control over all parts of their lives.
These are high achievers, planners used to controlling their schedules
and lives. Reports indicate that female executives tend to plan their
pregnancies carefully, scrupulously identifying the ebb and flow of
workplace demands so as to minimize the impact of having a child on
their work performance (Heneson 1986). College professors and teachers plan to have their babies early in the summer to accommodate their
teaching schedules. "many women blithely schedule their babies to arrive before or after the bar exam; others debate whether they should
wait until 2 months after they get their MBA or whether they should
plan their heaviest months for the cooler months of the year" (Heneson

1986:59). These are persons who expect to have complete control of their reproductive fates.

Yet biology does not always cooperate with neatly designed time-tables. And postponing parenthood into the 30s makes it less likely that "Mother Nature" will cooperate on schedule. While age alone does not cause fertility problems (Daniels and Weingarten 1979), human reproductive capacity appears to peak for both sexes in the mid-20s, and then gradually declines. In addition, older people have had more exposure to environmental and behavioral hazards associated with reproductive impairments (Aral and Cates 1983). While this does not mean that most couples will be unable to conceive, it may take them longer to do so. Evidence suggests that the average "waiting time" to conception is longer for women over age 30 than for those in their 20s (Hendershot 1983).

So, what happens when pregnancy does not occur on schedule? How are believers in personal efficacy, planning, and the achievement ethic likely to respond? *These* persons are likely to experience immense frustration and anxiety. One woman described her feelings this way (Caminiti 1994: 99): "For the first time in my life, it didn't matter how hard I worked or how much I tried. Getting pregnant was beyond my control." Her remarks are consistent with the report that highly achievement-oriented couples who had difficulty conceiving were more strongly affected than less directive couples (Menning 1982). Achievement-oriented couples often react strongly to a diagnosis of infertility and, because of their socioeconomic status and their desire for control, they are likely to aggressively pursue treatment at all costs.

The Decline and Differential Distribution of Fertility

The total fertility rate (number of births women have over their reproductive lives) in the United States declined sharply from an all-time high of 3.6 in 1957 to an all-time low in 1976. Since 1976, it has remained relatively low, fluctuating between 1.7 and 2.1 (O'Connell 1991). This substantial change in fertility reflects increased age at first marriage, delays in the initiation of child-bearing, more time between births, and the smaller desired family size. For example, in 1990, 65% of women aged 20–24 remained childless, compared to 50% for the previous generation. Even more remarkably, 42% of women aged 25–29 in 1990 were childless compared to 19% of their 1950s counterparts (Thornton and Freedman 1983; O'Connell 1991).

This demographic shift contributed to societal definitions of reproductive capacities and impairments. Specifically, the decline in fertility affected the current attention directed to infertility by (1) fostering greater medical attention to those experiencing reproductive difficulties, and (2) raising concerns about race and class differentials in birth rates.

First, the declining birth rate affected social definitions and responses toward infertility by cutting the demand for traditional obstetrical services. Particularly among middle-class, white couples, the need for the childbirth services of an obstetrician diminished considerably as the average number of children declined. This "shrinking" of the market, coupled with increased demand for infertility services from postponing couples, led to (1) increased visibility for infertility concerns, as those with reproductive problems formed a greater proportion of those seeking services (Aral and Cates 1983; Menken et al. 1986), and (2) a substantial proportion of obstetricians shifting their specialty to endocrinology/infertility as technological knowledge expanded and innovations in diagnostic and treatment procedures emerged (American College of Obstetricians and Gynecologists 1982; Aral and Cates 1983).

Second, while the birth rate declined in all groups, there are substantial class and race differences in fertility patterns. In general, the fertility rates of the more highly educated and financially secure are lowest, while less advantaged couples have more children (Weller and Bouvier 1983). There are also substantial differences by race, with people of color having considerably higher birth rates than whites; in 1988, the total fertility rate among people of color was 2.5, compared to 1.9 for the general population (U.S. Bureau of the Census 1991).

These class and race differentials in fertility suggest that current concern about infertility problems focuses primarily on affluent white couples—those whose birth rate has fallen below replacement (*Contemporary Ob/Gyn*, 1985). Indeed, concern about the fertility patterns of those from lower classes and minorities tends to focus on the need for effective family planning, that is contraception and sterilization (Shapiro 1985), rather than on infertility issues.

Considered together, these two aspects of the decline of fertility help explain both the increased medical attention directed to infertility problems *and* the nature of the populations receiving these services. The increase in medical attention reflects the perception of many physicians that infertility is increasing and that there is a growing market for their services. Further, despite the fact that people of color have higher rates of infertility than whites, the concern about infertility is not directed to people of color with their higher birth rates. Rather, the concern for infertility is class and race biased; it is upper-middle class white couples who are most likely to see assistance with fertility problems, most likely to be encouraged to seek treatment, and for whom treatment is most available and affordable.

Innovations in Diagnostic and Treatment Procedures

One of the serendipitous outcomes of contraceptive research and de- velopment is that biomedical science has learned a great deal about human reproductive systems. This new knowledge provided the base for developing diagnostic and treatment procedures for those who have (or perceive) difficulties conceiving. Indeed, biomedical interventions to facilitate fertility have exploded in recent decades, with fertility drugs, laparoscopies, *in vitro* fertilization, embryo transfer with donated eggs, and microinjection of sperm among the newly available means for diag- nosing and treating infertility.

The mere existence of these techniques and their associated medical specialists helps center attention on infertility. Furthermore, these new methods of diagnosis and treatment have received considerable publici- ty. The popular press presents detailed stories about the frustrations and agonies of the infertile and the wondrous resolutions "available" with medical intervention (e.g., *Newsweek* 1982; Dranov 1993). While the utility and success of many of these techniques are exaggerated[1] and their disadvantages understated by the media, people's attention has been drawn to the issue of infertility and its possible resolution.

All this attention has made infertility problems more salient for both the public at large and couples planning to have children. As the public becomes convinced that infertility is on the increase, couples seeking to become parents become more anxious about their potential infertility. This stimulates additional demand for infertility services, further rein- forcing the growth of these services and the perception of increased prevalence of infertility.

The focus on new diagnostic and treatment protocols appears to sig- nal a redefinition of the infertility experience. Persons now perceive that not only can the source of infertility be diagnosed, but it can be *treated*. Where once a couple that could not conceive was at the mercy of fate, now the medical community is seen as capable of helping. While that help is neither so miraculous nor so easy as the media would lead one to believe, nor available to those without the independent means to afford it, persons with fertility problems no longer perceive the situation as hopeless. Again, they have a sense of personal control; they can exercise their options. But, again, their sense of control is more exaggerated than real. Perceiving that there are options and treatments not only increases the probability that couples will seek assistance when conception does not occur as planned, but it increases the likelihood that couples will persist in their quest for a child of their own. Indeed, Greil (1991) and Lasker and Borg (1987) found that the ever-growing set of possible medi- cal treatments pressures couples to keep trying. In so doing, they further reinforce the growth and development of infertility services and the visibility of the infertility "epidemic."

New medical technologies, coupled with the increased demand for assistance, fosters a growing business in infertility services. Getting pregnant has become a "big business." Diagnostic (not treatment) costs have been estimated at $3,000–8,000 per couple; treatment costs begin at $1000 for some of the simpler, less technologically or chemically complex procedures and escalate upward for the more "high-tech" procedures (DeWitt 1993; Royte 1993). For example, the bill for a single IVF attempt easily can exceed $8,000, a sperm injection runs in the range of $10,000, and, egg-donor procedures can cost over $14,000 per attempt (DeWitt, 1993; Royte, 1993). One estimate suggests that over 1 million couples seek assistance every year (Royte, 1993). The resulting infertility industry generates revenues exceeding $2 billion per year. Clearly, the development and diffusion of technological diagnostic and treatment procedures have important economic and social consequences, and the future may hold still more.

TO WHAT END?

When one considers the various factors shaping social definitions of reproductive capacities and impairments, it becomes clear why there is such concern about infertility. As Menken et al. (1986:1389) suggest, "the changes in patterns of childbearing and fertility control that took place during the last quarter century make it predictable and almost inevitable that infertility . . . would be perceived as a problem requiring attention." Add recent advances in reproductive technology, and the issue looms even larger.

But, what of the future? Where does this increased concern and expansion of services lead? What are the implications of this distorted construction of biological and social reality? Let me suggest two emerging outcomes.

A Stable Incidence of Infertility

One of the ironies of the current emphasis on infertility is that the incidence of fertility problems is unlikely to change. Current constructions of the problem center on treatment rather than on working toward prevention of fertility impairment. However, treatment is not always—or even usually—effective. For example, even when IVF is undertaken in situations deemed most favorable to its success (i.e., where the woman is under 40 and her partner has no problems with sperm count or movement), 84% of those admitted to an IVF program will not achieve a live birth. While other, less dramatic treatments are relatively more successful (U.S. Congress, Office of Technology Assessment 1988), only about one-half of those seeking assistance are likely to become parents (Hammond and Talbert 1985; U.S. Congress, Office of Technology Assessment 1988).

By attacking such widespread causes of infertility as sexually transmitted diseases and environmental, pharmaceutical, and workplace hazards, preventive efforts would have a greater impact upon the rate and incidence of infertility. However, there is little chance that the medical and business establishments will reconstruct both the problem and its solutions to emphasize prevention. The structure and organization of our current health care system mitigate against such a change of course. As Fisher (1986) points out, the U.S. medical care system is controlled by the private sector, which has a disproportionate investment in revenue-generating technology and illness-oriented treatment. An emphasis on and commitment to prevention could threaten the expanding market for infertility services.

Moreover, the health care system features an individualistic ideology that emphasizes what individuals do wrong and then treats the outcomes of such self-destructive behavior (Fisher 1986). In other words, patients are defined as responsible for the behavior that resulted in their malady; they should have taken better care of themselves or done things differently. Health care is then directed to changing the behavior that "causes" such maladies and treating the illness that results.

Prevention of infertility does not mesh well with such an approach. The majority of reproductive impairments are not easily traced to individual choices and behaviors; the primary causes of infertility are pollution and other environmental hazards, workplace hazards, iatrogenic outcomes (caused by doctors treating other illnesses), and sexually transmitted diseases (Andrews 1984; U.S. Congress, Office of Technology Assessment 1988). Thus, an emphasis on preventing rather than treating infertility would shift much of the blame and efforts at solving the problem toward environmental and occupational hazards. Attacking environmental and workplace hazards means questioning the operation of industrial and corporate organizations, ultimately endangering corporate profit margins.

Thus, the structure of infertility services, like other medical services, is neither ideologically nor organizationally oriented toward major prevention efforts. Yet without such a reorientation, it is unlikely that major declines in infertility will occur.

Implications for Women

Infertility is usually defined as a woman's problem (Rothman 1982; Corea 1985). That being the case, the current attention to infertility and its treatment affects women most directly. Not only do women's bodies sustain the most invasive treatment procedures (Corea 1985; Spallone 1989; Raymond 1993), but the ideology of the health care system, coupled with the changing role of women in the labor force, ensures that women will bear the brunt of the current social construction of infertility. Let me explain.

For some time now, young women have been following a pattern of postponing childbearing until they complete educational, professional, and other important personal agendas. In so doing, they have followed the career patterns typical of men's achievement. Then, when the "time was right," they sought to have their children and, in some cases, found it difficult to do so.

Given that pattern of behavior, coupled with the individualistic ideology of the health care system, the response of medical practitioners to the "rise in infertility" has been to blame women. The tone of this blaming has been subdued, but the theme is nevertheless clear: Women should change the timing of their reproduction, have their babies earlier, and then return to work and move toward career advancement (DeCherney and Berkowitz 1982; *Contemporary Ob/Gyn* 1985). This response is consistent with the ideology and organization not only of the medical establishment, but of our society in general. Yet, such a "solution" not only puts the burden upon women's shoulders, but it also overlooks several important facts.

First, such advice builds upon the current treatment construction of infertility, while ignoring the sizable proportion of infertility associated with workplace and environmental hazards. Further, by focusing on postponers as the group most likely to experience reproductive impairments, it does not acknowledge the fact that the only group for whom infertility seems to be on the rise is 20–24 year olds—a group little affected by decisions to delay childbearing.

Second, by viewing infertility as a women's problem, this typification ignores the fact that men are subject to at least as many threats to their fertility as women. Indeed, there is some evidence that men are especially affected by the workplace and environmental hazards of the modern world (Andrews 1984). Among couples experiencing reproductive impairments, the proportion associated with the man's system is roughly equal to that associated with the woman's (Isaacs and Holt 1987).

Lastly, such advice does not acknowledge that the world of work is still organized around the "clockwork of male careers" (Hochschild

1975). Typically, most professional occupations require continuous participation and considerable time and energy commitments during the early years—the same years that most couples have their children. Such dedication of time and energy to one's work does not mesh well with the demands of bearing and caring for small children. This is particularly true for women because they still have the primary responsibilities for child rearing as well as childbearing.

So long as the world of work remains structured around traditional conceptions of "correct" (male-oriented) career patterns and traditional divisions of family responsibilities, women who aspire to professional achievements are likely to risk infertility problems. True, there is little doubt that optimum fecundity for females, and possibly males, is in their 20s; thus, from a biological standpoint, postponing childbearing does increase the likelihood of difficulties and delays in conceiving and bearing children. However, there is little evidence of a major restructuring in the worlds of work or family life to accommodate these needs, despite the growing numbers of women of reproductive age in professional positions.

Thus, women who seek advancement in the world of work are caught in a Catch 22—they may postpone childbearing to advance professionally, risking diminished reproductive capacity, or they may postpone career agendas for childbearing and substantially detract from career advancements. Either way, women are likely to be held accountable for their choices—either they will be responsible for any fertility problems that may arise or they will be defined as less committed and less capable professionals because they must turn their attention to the needs of their children.

CONCLUDING REMARKS

Throughout this chapter, I argued that recent attention to infertility reflects new social constructions more than an epidemic in biological subfecundity. In so doing, I was not suggesting that the incidence and prevalence of infertility are insignificant; that is by no means the case.

Infertility is a very real problem in the modern world, and it is a problem that warrants public attention, concern, and appropriate policy development. However, current perceptions of both the extent and resolution of fertility problems do not foster the type of attention that is needed if the problems of infertility are to be addressed effectively. Indeed, the current social construction of infertility is unlikely to result in any major decreases in the incidence of such impairments; it actually may contribute to an increase.

Because infertility is perceived as an individual (or couple) phenomenon, attention is diverted from the larger structural and situational factors that increase the probability of subfecundity problems—the
capitalist emphasis on profit margins rather than workplace safety or
protection of the environment, the mismatch between the structure of
professional work and family life—the various structural arrangements
that foster workplace hazards, environmental toxins, iatrogenic factors,
sexually transmitted diseases, and less than optimal timing in childbearing. These are the factors that pose the greatest threat to fertility, by
giving rise to hazards, toxins, and constrained choices injurious to
men's and women's reproductive capacities.

Furthermore, current construction of infertility centers on high-tech
treatment as the solution to the problem of infertility. This commitment
to high-tech treatment diverts the resources—money, research, staff
commitment—needed to bring the many causes of infertility under control. Thus, prevention of future reproductive impairment receives very
little attention.

In sum, the current construction of infertility not only distorts the
present state and resolution of reproductive impairments, it may negate
future progress on the problem. Indeed, unless current definitions of
infertility are reconstructed so as to focus upon the larger context contributing to the incidence and solutions of fertility problems, it is possible that future generations may face an actual infertility epidemic.
Certainly, the prognosis for the future is uncertain.

NOTE

1.   According to Soules (1985), the most accurate assessment of general success rates for *in vitro* fertilization (IVF) is that based upon the pooled results for
all IVF clinics. In 1991, 24,671 cycles of IVF were initiated in the 212 programs in
the United States, resulting in 3,125 deliveries—30% of which were multiple
births (Society for Assisted Reproductive Technology 1993). Thus, in 1991, the
probability of achieving a live birth upon initiation of IVF was 0.13. Data from
other industrialized countries are comparable (e.g., FIVNAT 1993).

REFERENCES

American College of Obstetricians and Gynecologists. 1982. *Manpower Planning
    in Obstetrics and Gynecology*. Washington, DC: American College of Obstetri-
    cians and Gynecologists.

Andrews, L. 1984. *New Conceptions: A Consumer's Guide to the Newest Infertility Treatments*. New York: St. Martin's Press.

Aral, S. O., and W. Cates. 1983. "The Increasing Concern with Infertility: Why Now?" *Journal of the American Medical Association* 250:2327–2331.

Bachu, A. 1993. *Fertility of American Women: June 1992, U. S. Bureau of the Census. Current Population Reports, P20-470*. Washington, DC: U. S. Government Printing Office.

Bongaarts, J. 1975. "A Method for the Estimation of Fecundability." *Demography* 12:645–660.

Caminiti, S. 1994. "The Ordeal of Infertility." *Fortune* 130 (August 8):98–100, 102–103.

Collins, J. A., W. Wrixon, L. B. Janes, and E. H. Wilson. 1983. "Treatment-independent Pregnancy among Infertile Couples." *New England Journal of Medicine* 309:1201–1206.

Contemporary Ob/Gyn. 1985. "Broad Impact of Deferred Childbearing." 20 (June):232.

Corea, G. 1985. *The Mother Machine: Reproductive Technologies from Artificial Insemination to Artificial Wombs*. New York: Harper & Row.

Daniels, P., and K. Weingarten. 1979. "A New Look at the Medical Risks in Late Childbearing." *Women and Health* 4:5–36.

———. 1980. "Postponing Parenthood: The Myth of the Perfect Time." *Savvy Magazine* 1 (May):55–60.

De Witt, P. M. 1993. "In Pursuit of Pregnancy." *American Demographics* 15(5):48–54.

DeCherney, A. H., and G. S. Berkowitz. 1982. "Female Fecundity and Age." *New England Journal of Medicine* 307:424–426.

Dranov, P. 1993. "New Hope for Couples Who Can't Conceive: More and More Cases of Infertility Are Now Being Treated." *Redbook* 181 (August 1):67–68, 70.

Fabe, M., and N. J. Wikler. 1979. *Up Against the Clock: Career Women Speak Out on the New Choice of Motherhood*. New York: Random House.

FIVNAT (French In Vitro National). 1993. "French National IVF Registry: Analysis of 1986 to 1990 Data." *Fertility and Sterility* 59 (3):587–595.

Fisher, S. 1986. *In the Patient's Best Interest: Women and the Politics of Medical Decisions*. New Brunswick, NJ: Rutgers University Press.

Greil, A. L. 1991. *Not Yet Pregnant: Infertile Couples in Contemporary America*. New Brunswick, NJ: Rutgers University Press.

Hammond, M. G., and L. M. Talbert (eds.). 1985. *Infertility: A Practical Guide for the Physician*. Oradell, NJ: Medical Economics Books.

Hendershot, G. E. 1983. "Maternal Age and Overdue Conceptions." *American Journal of Public Health* 74:35–38.

Heneson, N. 1986. "Clockwork Babies." *Savvy Magazine* 7 (August):54–59.

Hochschild, A. R. 1975. "Inside the Clockwork of Male Careers." Pp. 47–80 in *Women and the Power to Change*, edited by F. Howe. New York: McGraw-Hill.

Isaacs, S. L., and R. J. Holt. 1987. "Redefining Procreation: Facing the Issues" *Population Bulletin* 42(3). Washington: Population Reference Bureau.

Lasker, J. N., and S. Borg. 1987. *In Search of Parenthood: Coping with Infertility and High-Tech Conception*. Boston: Beacon.

Menken, J., J. Trussell, and U. Larsen. 1986. "Age and Infertility." *Science* 233:1389–1394.

Menning, B. E. 1982. "The Psychological Impact of Infertility." *Nursing Clinics of North America* 17:155–163.

Mosher, W. D., and W. F. Pratt. 1985. "Fecundity and Infertility in the United States, 1965–1982." *National Center for Health Statistics, Advance Data 104.* Hyattsville, MD: Public Health Service.

————. 1990. "Fecundity and Infertility in the United States, 1965–88." *Advance Data from Vital and Health Statistics, No. 192*, December 4. Hyattsville, MD: National Center for Health Statistics.

Newsweek. 1982. "Infertility: New Cures, New Hopes." 55 (December 6):102–110.

O'Connell, M. 1991. "Late Expectations: Childbearing Patterns of American Women for the 1990s." *Studies in American Fertility. Current Population Reports, Series P-23, No. 176.* Washington, DC: U.S. Government Printing Office.

Raymond, J. G. 1993. *Women as Wombs: Reproductive Technologies and the Battle over Women's Freedom.* New York: Harper Collins.

Reinharz, S. 1988. "What's Missing in Miscarriage?" *Journal of Community Psychology* 16:84–103.

Rothman, B. K. 1982. *In Labor.* New York: W. W. Norton.

Royte, E. 1993. "The Stork Market." *Lear's* 6 (10):52–57.

Shapiro, T. M. 1985. *Population Control Politics: Women, Sterilization, and Reproductive Choice.* Philadelphia: Temple University Press.

Society for Assisted Reproductive Technology, The American Fertility Society. 1993. "Assisted Reproductive Technology in the United States and Canada: 1991 Results from the Society for Assisted Reproductive Technology Generated from The American Fertility Society Registry." *Fertility and Sterility* 59:956–962.

Soules, M. R. 1985. "The In Vitro Pregnancy Rate: Let's Be Honest with One Another." *Fertility and Sterility* 43:511–513.

Spallone, P. 1989. *Beyond Conception: The New Politics of Reproduction.* Grandby, MA: Bergin & Garvey.

Thornton, A., and D. Freedman. 1983. "The Changing American Family." *Population Bulletin* 38. Washington, DC: Population Reference Bureau.

U. S. Bureau of the Census. 1991. *Statistical Abstract of the United States—1991*, 111th Edition. Washington, DC.

U. S. Congress, Office of Technology Assessment. 1988. *Infertility: Medical and Social Choices.* Washington, DC: U.S. Government Printing Office.

Ventura, S. J. 1982. "Trends in First Births to Older Mothers, 1970–1979." *Monthly Vital Statistics Report* 31 (2), Supplement 2.

Weller, R. H., and L. F. Bouvier. 1983. *Population: Demography and Policy.* New York: St. Martin's Press.

Wilcox, L. S., and W. D. Mosher. 1993. "Use of Infertility Services in the United States." *Obstetrics & Gynecology* 82(1):122–127.

8

The Crack Attack: America's Latest Drug Scare, 1986–1992

CRAIG REINARMAN and HARRY G. LEVINE

"America discovered crack and overdosed on oratory."
editorial, *New York Times* (1988)

In the spring of 1986, American politicians and news media began an extraordinary antidrug frenzy that ran until about 1992. During this period, newspapers, magazines, and network television regularly carried lurid stories about a new "epidemic" or "plague" of drug use, especially of crack cocaine. They said this "epidemic" was spreading rapidly from cities to the suburbs and was literally destroying American society. Politicians from both parties made increasingly strident calls for a "War on Drugs." They even challenged each other to take urine tests to provide chemical proof of their moral purity and fitness for high office. In one of the most bizarre episodes, the President and Vice-President of the United States had their own urine tested for evidence of cocaine, marijuana, and heroin use. It is certainly true that the United States has real health and social problems that result from illegal and legal drug use. But it is also certainly true that the period from 1986 through 1992 was characterized by antidrug extremism.

"Drug scares" are periods when antidrug crusades achieve great prominence and legitimacy. Drug scares are phenomena in their own right, quite apart from drug use and drug problems. Drug scares have recurred throughout U.S. history independent of actual increases in drug use or drug problems. During "red scares," like the McCarthy period in the 1950s, leftists were said to be seriously threatening to destroy the American way of life. Similarly, during drug scares all kinds of social problems have been blamed on one chemical substance or another. Drug scares typically link a scapegoated drug to a troubling subordinate group—working-class immigrants, racial or ethnic minorities, rebellious youth.[1]

The period from 1986 to 1992 was in many ways the most intense drug scare of the twentieth century. With few dissenting voices, politicians and the media embraced the Reagan administration's metaphor "The War on Drugs" and pronounced the "drug war" to be good social policy. At dead center of all the hysteria was "crack." Crack appeared in 1984 and 1985, primarily in impoverished African-American and Latino inner-city neighborhoods, especially in New York, Miami, and Los Angeles. Crack is smokeable cocaine. It gained its named from the "crackling" sound it makes when heated. It is easily produced in a pot on a kitchen stove by "cooking down" a mixture of powdered cocaine, water, and baking soda. Crack is typically sold in tiny vials or envelopes that cost between 5 and 20 dollars. Crack was not a new drug, for its active ingredient is entirely cocaine. Nor was it a new way of using cocaine; smoking cocaine freebase had been practiced since the mid-1970s.

Crack was a marketing innovation. It was a way of packaging a relatively expensive and upscale commodity (powdered cocaine) in small, inexpensive units. So packaged, this form of smokable cocaine (crack) was then sold, usually on the street by young Latinos and African-Americans, to a whole new class of customers: residents of poverty neighborhoods. The marketing innovation was successful for at least two reasons. First, there was a huge workforce of unemployed young people ready to take jobs in the new, neighborhood-based business of crack preparation and sales. Working in the crack business offered these people better jobs, working conditions, and pay than any straight job they could get (and arguably better than most entry-level criminal jobs such as burglary or stealing car radios and batteries).[2] Second, the marketing innovation succeeded because turning powdered cocaine into smokeable "crack" changed the way cocaine was consumed and thereby dramatically strengthened the character of cocaine intoxication. Smoking crack offered an intense but very brief intoxication. This inexpensive and dramatic "high" was much better suited to the inner-city poor's finances and needs for "instant escape" than was the more subtle and expensive effect provided by powdered cocaine.

Cocaine in any form is a stimulant, much like amphetamine or even caffeine. When powdered cocaine is sniffed in small doses (as it usually is), it makes one moderately alert and energized. Thus the typical psychotropic effects of sniffing powdered cocaine are subtle. Users report having to learn to recognize it (Waldorf, Reinarman, and Murphy 1991). In the 1930s, Cole Porter wrote the line "I get no kick from cocaine" about powdered cocaine.

Cole Porter would have gotten a kick from crack, but he probably would not have liked the experience very much. When cocaine is smoked, it enters the bloodstream quickly, providing a powerful rush. Crack is a strong, even harsh, drug. One experienced cocaine user from Liverpool, who bought some crack in New York City, said that after smoking 10 dollars worth of it: "I was so high I was frightened—and I don't frighten easily. . . . I wouldn't bother with it again" (quoted in McDermott, O'Hare, and Reinarman 1995). Most of the people who have tried crack or smoked cocaine have not continued to use it. From its first appearance, crack has always been used heavily by the same population that has always used heroin heavily: the urban poor. Daily crack smoking, like daily heroin injecting, occurs mainly among the poorest, most marginalized people in American society—and only among a tiny minority of them. In its most popular year, crack was used heavily (or abused) by only a small percentage of those people who had used cocaine. Crack never became a popular or commonly used drug in the United States, or anywhere else in the world.

This, however, is not the way the mass media and politicians talked about crack from 1986 to 1992. Rather, they portrayed crack as the most contagious, addicting, and destructive substance in what *Newsweek* called "a whole pharmacopeia of poisons." Politicians and the media depicted the use of crack and other illicit drugs as virulent diseases that were destroying American society. Consider some of the news stories from the spring and summer of 1986, the first year of the crack scare. *Newsweek*'s March 17th cover story, "Kids and Cocaine," quoted, without skepticism, a drug expert who announced that "crack is the most addictive drug known to man" (Morganthau 1986:58–59). He also said that smoking crack produces "instantaneous addiction." As a result, *Newsweek* asserted, crack "has transformed the ghetto" and "is rapidly spreading into the suburbs." On March 20th, the *New York Times*'s front page explained that crack was spreading from the inner-city to "the wealthiest suburbs of Westchester county;" "It's all over the place' said John French" from the New Jersey Health Department (Kerr 1986a:A.1). A month later, another *Times* story reported that crack was spreading from the city to suburbs. "If we don't stop crack now, it will destroy our young people" said a politician from Westchester (Melvin 1986:11.1). On June 8th, the headline of a third front page *Times* story announced that "Crack Addiction Spreads Among The Middle Class" (Kerr 1986b). On the same day, the *Times* also reported that in suburban Long Island "the use of crack has reached epidemic proportions" (Domash 1986:11.5).

On June 16th, *Newsweek* (1986a:18) published a full-page editorial about drugs titled "The Plague Among Us" that began: "An epidemic is abroad in America, as pervasive and dangerous in its way as the plagues of medieval times. [The epidemic] has taken lives, wrecked careers,

broken homes, invaded schools, incited crimes, tainted businesses, toppled heroes, corrupted policemen and politicians." A week later, the
New York Times reported the "growing use of crack" in three suburban
and rural counties in New York. With neither evidence nor skepticism,
the *Times* reported that in Westchester, Rockland, and Sullivan counties
[the latter is part of the Catskills] the "per capita use of cocaine is the
heaviest in the state" (Feron 1986:11.1). On July 28th, *U.S. News and
World Report* told readers that "illicit drugs pervade American life . . . a
situation that experts compare to medieval plagues—'the No. 1 problem
we face'" (Lang 1986:49). Two weeks later, *Newsweek* reported that
"nearly everyone now concedes that the plague is all but universal"
(Martz 1986:19).

On occasion, a newspaper, magazine, or TV show did a follow-up
story that contradicted its earlier accounts. For example, in 1990, after
years of reporting that crack is instantly addicting, *Newsweek* wrote:

> Don't tell the kids, but there's a dirty little secret about crack; as with most
> other drugs, a lot of people use it without getting addicted. In their zeal to
> shield young people from the plague of drugs, the media and many drug
> educators have hyped instant and total addiction. (Martz 1990:74–75)

Newsweek did not also tell readers that it had been among the first to
have "hyped instant and total addiction" and to have quoted, without
questioning, the "drug educators" who also did so. Similarly, in 1989,
after being a crucial source for the news that in New York suburbs crack
was an "epidemic" and "all over the place," the *New York Times* quietly
noted that just the opposite was true. The *Times* reported that except for
a few "urban pockets" in suburban counties, "educators, law enforcement officials, and young people say crack and most other narcotics are
rarely seen in the suburbs, whether modest or wealthy." Crack, the
Times now said, "is confined mainly to poor urban neighborhoods"
(Foderaro 1989:26).

By and large, the media and politicians' pronouncements about drugs
spread exaggerations, misinformation, and simplistic theories of cause
and effect. During this time, some writers, journalists, commentators,
TV and radio reports, news articles, and some whole publications provided thoughtful and accurate information about drugs. But such good
reports were vastly outnumbered by the misleading and false ones.

First, in this chapter, we trace the media coverage of the "crack crisis"
and summarize the core claims made about the destructiveness of the
cocaine and crack "plague." Second, we contrast these claims with the
primary U.S. government data on which they were purportedly based.
We show that a gap existed between the official statistical evidence[3] and
the prevalence claims of the media and politicians. We maintain that the

media and politicians misrepresented or ignored the evidenc
stead provided propaganda for the drug war. The crack scare
words, was not merely a rational response to a new threat to pu~~
health and public order. It possessed its own causes and logic.

Third, we locate the crack scare's causes and logic in the conservative
political and economic context of the Reagan and Bush eras. In this
conservative ideological environment, supporting the drug war became
extremely useful politically for Democrats as well as Republicans. The
drug war was not effective or wise policy, but politicians promoted it
nonetheless because, among other reasons, it provided a convenient
explanation—a scapegoat—for enduring and ever growing urban poverty.

THE FRENZY: COCAINE AND CRACK IN THE PUBLIC EYE

The use of powdered cocaine by affluent people in music, film, and
sports had been common since the 1970s. The National Institute on
Drug Abuse (NIDA) found that by 1985 more than 22 million Americans
in all social classes and occupations had reported at least trying cocaine.
Cocaine smoking originated with "freebasing," which began increasing
by the late 1970s (Inciardi 1987; Siegel 1982). Then (as now) most cocaine
users bought cocaine hydrochloride (powder) for intranasal use (snorting). Some users had begun to "cook" powdered cocaine down to crys-
talline or "base" form for smoking. All phases of freebasing, from selling
to smoking, tended to take place in the privacy of homes and offices of
middle class or well-to-do users. They typically purchased cocaine in
units of a gram or more costing $80 to $100 a gram. These relatively
affluent "basers" discovered the intense rush and risks of smoking cocaine years before the term crack was coined. But most such users had a
stake in conventional life; they had valuable things to lose if they got
into trouble with cocaine. Therefore, when they felt their cocaine use
was too heavy or out of control, they had the incentives and resources to
cut down, quit, or get private treatment (Waldorf, Reinarman, and Murphy 1991).

There was no orgy of media and political attention in the late 1970s
when the prevalence of cocaine use jumped sharply, or after middle-
class and upper-class users began to use heavily, especially when freebasing. Many basers found that this mode of ingesting cocaine produced
a significantly more intense and shorter "high" than snorting. Like the
crack users that followed them, basers had found that the intense, bru-
tally brief rush, combined with the painful "low" or "down" that immediately followed, produced a powerful desire to immediately repeat

use—to binge. This pattern of an intense, brief high, quickly followed by a painful low, is the pharmacological source of the short-term binging characteristic of much freebase and crack use (Waldorf, Reinarman, and Murphy 1991).

Crack's pharmacological power alone does not explain the attention it received. In 1986, politicians and the media focused on crack—and the drug scare began—when cocaine smoking became visible among a "dangerous" group. Crack attracted the attention of politicians and the media because of its downward mobility to and increased visibility in ghettos and barrios (Duster 1970; Washton and Gold 1987). Crack was sold in small, cheap, units, on ghetto streets, to poor, young buyers who were already seen as a threat (Kerr 1987b; Miller 1987). Crack spread cocaine smoking into poor neighborhoods already beset with troubles. These primarily Latino and African-American young people tended to have fewer bonds to conventional society, less to lose, and far fewer resources to cope with, or shield themselves from, drug-related problems (Wilson 1987).

The earliest mass media reference to the new form of cocaine may have been a *Los Angeles Times* article in late 1984 (11/25/84:cc 1) on the use of cocaine "rocks" in ghettos and barrios in Los Angeles. By late 1985, the *New York Times* made the national media's first specific reference to "crack" in a story about three teenagers seeking treatment for cocaine abuse (Boundy 1985:B.12). At the start of 1986, crack was known only in a few impoverished neighborhoods in Los Angeles, New York, Miami, and perhaps a few other large cities.

When two celebrity athletes died in what news stories called "crack-related deaths" in the spring of 1986, the media seemed to sense a potential bonanza. Coverage skyrocketed and crack became widely known. "Dramatic footage" of Black and Latino men being carted off in chains, or of police breaking down crack house doors, became a near nightly news event. In July 1986 alone, the three major TV networks offered 74 evening news segments on drugs, half of these about crack (Diamond, Accosta, and Thornton 1987; Reeves and Campbell 1994). In the months leading up to the November elections, a handful of national newspapers and magazines produced roughly 1,000 stories discussing crack (Inciardi 1987:481; Trebach 1987:6–16). Like the TV networks, leading news magazines like *Time* and *Newsweek* seemed determined not to be out-done; each devoted five cover stories to crack and the "drug crisis" in 1986 alone.

In the fall of 1986, the CBS News show *48 Hours* aired a heavily promoted documentary called "48 Hours on Crack Street," which Dan Rather previewed on his *Evening News*: "Tonight, CBS News takes you to the streets, to the war zone, for an unusual two hours of hands-on horror." Among many shots from hidden cameras was one of New York Senator Alphonse D'Amato and then-U.S. Attorney Rudolf Guiliani, *in cognito*, purchasing crack to dramatize the brazenness of streetcorner sales in the ghetto. All this was good business for CBS: the program earned the highest Nielsen rating of any similar news show in the previous 5 years—15 million viewers (Diamond, Accosta, and Thornton 1987:10). Three years later, after poor ratings nearly killed *48 Hours*, the show kicked off its 1989 season with a 3-hour special, "Return to Crack Street."

The intense media competition for audience shares and advertising dollars spawned many similar shows. Three days after "48 Hours on Crack Street," NBC ran its own prime-time special, "Cocaine Country," which suggested that cocaine and crack use had become pandemic. This was one of over 400 separate stories on crack and cocaine produced by NBC alone—an unprecedented 15 hours of air time—in the 7 months leading up to the 1986 elections (Diamond, Accosta, and Thornton 1987; Hoffman 1987). By mid-1986, *Newsweek* (1986b:15) claimed that crack was the biggest story since Vietnam and Watergate, and *Time* soon followed by calling crack "the Issue of the Year" (Lamar 1986:25). The words "plague," "epidemic," and "crisis" had become routine. The crack scare began in 1986 but it waned somewhat in 1987 (a nonelection year). In 1988 drugs returned to the national stage as stories about the "crack epidemic" again appeared regularly on front pages and TV screens (Reeves and Campbell 1994). One politician after another reenlisted in the War on Drugs. In that election year, as in 1986, overwhelming majorities of both houses of Congress voted for new antidrug laws with long mandatory prison terms, death sentences, and large increases in funding for police and prisons. The annual federal budget for antidrug efforts surged from less than $2 billion in 1981 to more than $12 billion in 1993. The budget for the Drug Enforcement Administration (DEA) quadrupled between 1981 and 1992 (Massing 1993; Murphy 1994). The Bush administration alone spent $45 billion—more than all other Presidents since Nixon combined—mostly for law enforcement (Horgan 1993; Office of National Drug Control Policy 1992).[4]

An April 1988, ABC News "Special Report" termed crack "a plague" that was "eating away at the fabric of America." According to this documentary: Americans spend "twenty billion a year on cocaine"; American businesses lose "sixty billion" dollars a year in productivity because their workers use drugs; "the educational system is being undermined" by student drug use; and "the family" is "disintegrating" in the face of this "epidemic." This program did not give its millions of viewers any evidence to support such dramatic claims, but it did give them a powerful *vocabulary of attribution*: "drugs," especially crack, threatened all the central institutions in American life: families, communities, schools, businesses, law enforcement, and even national sovereignty.

The media frenzy continued into 1989. Between October 1988 and October 1989, for example, the *Washington Post* alone ran 1565 stories— 28,476 column inches—about the drug crisis. Even Richard Harwood (1989), the *Post*'s own ombudsman, editorialized against what he called the loss of "a proper sense of perspective" due to such a "hyperbole epidemic." He said that "politicians are doing a number on people's heads." The drug war heated up again in the fall of 1989, when another major new federal antidrug bill to further increase drug war funding (S-1233) began winding its way through Congress.

In September 1989, President Bush's "Drug Czar," William Bennett, unveiled his comprehensive battle plan, the *National Drug Control Strategy*. His Introduction asks, "What . . . accounts for the intensifying drug-related chaos that we see every day in our newspapers and on television? One word explains much of it. That word is *crack*. . . . Crack is responsible for the fact that vast patches of the American urban landscape are rapidly deteriorating" (The White House 1989:3 original emphasis). Bennett's plan proposed yet another $2.2 billion increase in drug war spending, 70% to be allocated to police and prisons, a percentage unchanged since the Nixon administration (Weinraub 1989:A.1). The funds would be used to nearly double prison capacity so that even casual users as well as dealers could be incarcerated. The plan also proposed the sale of drug war bonds (reminiscent of World War II) as a means of financing the $7.9 billion first-year costs. President Bush returned to Washington early from summer vacation at his estate on the Maine coast to rehearse with his media advisors the presentation of the plan.

On September 5, 1989, President Bush made his first major prime-time address to the nation; it was broadcast on all three national television networks. He spoke from the presidential desk in the Oval Office and announced his plan for achieving "victory over drugs." We want to focus on this incident as an example of the way politicians and the media intentionally misinformed the public to promote the War on Drugs.

During the address, Bush held up to the cameras a clear plastic bag of crack labeled "EVIDENCE." He announced that it was "seized a few days ago in a park across the street from the White House" (Isikoff 1989:A.1). Its contents, Bush said, were "turning our cities into battle zones and murdering our children." The President proclaimed that, because of crack and other drugs, he would "more than double Federal assistance to state and local law enforcement" (Weinraub 1989:A.1). The next morning, the picture of the President holding a bag of crack was on the front pages of newspapers across America.

About 2 weeks later, the *Washington Post*, and then National Public Radio and other newspapers, discovered how the President of the United States had obtained his bag of crack. "The idea of the President holding up crack was [first] included in some drafts" of his speech by advisors. Bush enthusiastically approved. A White House aid told the *Post* that the President "liked the prop. . . . It drove the point home." Bush and his advisors also decided that the crack should be seized in Lafayette Park across from the White House or nearby so that the President could say that crack had become so pervasive that men were "selling drugs in front of the White House" (Isikoff 1989:A1).

This decision set up a complex chain of events. White House Communications Director David Demarst asked Cabinet Affairs Secretary David Bates to instruct the Justice Department "to find some crack that fit the description in the speech." Bates called Richard Weatherbee, special assistant to Attorney General Dick Thornburgh, who then called James Millford, executive assistant to the DEA Chief. Finally, Milford phoned William McMullen, Special Agent in charge of the DEA's Washington office, and told him to arrange an undercover crack buy near the White House because "evidently, the President wants to show it could be bought anywhere" (Isikoff 1989:A1).

Despite their best efforts, the top Federal drug agents were not able to find anyone selling crack (or any other drug) in Lafayette Park, or anywhere else in the vicinity of the White House. Therefore, to carry out their assignment, DEA agents had to entice someone to come to the Park to make the sale. Apparently, the only person the DEA could convince was Keith Jackson, an 18-year-old African-American high school senior. McMullan reported that this was difficult because Jackson "did not even know where the White House was." The DEA's secret tape recording of the conversation revealed that the teenager seemed baffled by the request: "Where the [expletive deleted] is the White House?" he asked. McMullan told the *Post*, "we had to manipulate him to get him down there. It wasn't easy" (Isikoff 1989:A1).

The undesirability of selling crack in Layafette Park was confirmed by men from Washington D.C. imprisoned for drug selling, and interviewed by National Public Radio's "All Things Considered" news show. They agreed that nobody would sell crack in Layafette Park because there would be no customers; the crack-using population was in Washington's poor African-American neighborhoods some distance from the White House. The *Washington Post* and other papers also reported that the undercover DEA agent had not, after all, actually seized the crack, as Bush had claimed in his speech. Rather, the DEA agents purchased it from Jackson for $2,400 dollars and then let him go.[5]

This entire incident is a perfect example of the way a drug scare distorts and perverts public knowledge and policy. The idea of claiming that crack was threatening every home in America, including the White House, first appeared in the minds and speech drafts of Bush's advisers. When they sought to purchase their own crack, they found that reality did not match the script. Instead of changing the speech to reflect reality, a series of high-level officials instructed federal drug agents to create a reality that would fit the script: they manufactured an event so the President could talk about it. Finally the President of the United States told about the "seizure" and displayed the procured prop on national television. Yet, when all of this was revealed, it did not seem to cause politicians or the media to question either the President's policies or his claims about crack's pervasiveness.

As a result of Bush's performance and all the other antidrug publicity and propaganda, in 1988 and 1989, the drug war commanded more public attention than any other issue. The media and political antidrug crusade succeeded in making many Americans even more fearful of crack and other illicit drugs. A *New York Times/CBS News* Poll has periodically asked Americans to identify "the most important problem facing this country today." In January 1985, 23% answered war or nuclear war; less than 1% believed the most important problem was drugs (*New York Times* 1989). In September 1989, shortly after the President's speech and the blizzard of media stories about drugs that followed, 64% of those polled believed that drugs were now the most important problem and only 1% thought that war or nuclear war was most important. Even the *New York Times* (1989:A.26) declared in a lead editorial that this reversal was "incredible" and gently suggested that problems like war, "homelessness and the need to give poor children a chance in life" should perhaps be given more attention.

A year later, during a lull in antidrug speeches and coverage, the percentage citing "drugs" as the nation's top problem dropped to 10%. Noting this "precipitous fall from a remarkable height," the *Times* observed that an "alliance of Presidents and news directors" shaped public opinion about drugs. Indeed, once the White House let it be known that the President would be giving a prime-time address on the subject, all three networks had tripled their coverage of drugs in the 2 weeks prior to his speech and quadrupled it for a week afterward (Oreskes 1990:A22; see also, Reeves and Campbell 1994). As we will show in the next section, all this occurred while nearly every index of drug use was dropping.

Figures 8.1–8.3 summarize data from national household surveys of drug use. Three patterns in these data are noteworthy. First, use of all drugs tends to be higher among young adults (aged 18–25), than among adolescents or older adults. Second, among all age groups, cocaine use is less common than marijuana use, which in turn is used much less

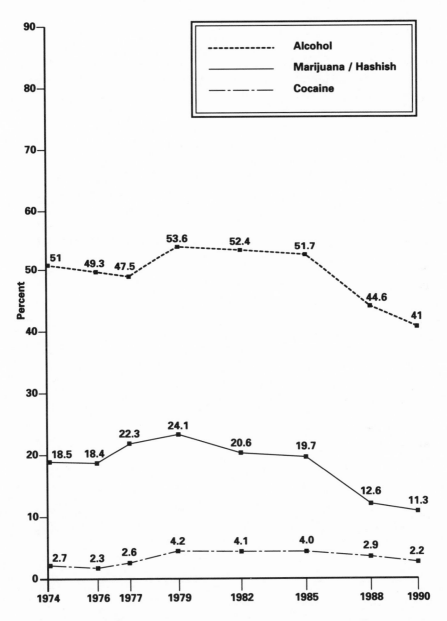

Figure 8.1.   Percentage of 12 to 17 year olds using marijuana/hashish, cocaine, and alcohol once or more in the last year, selected years, 1974–1990. From Maguire, Pastore, and Flanagan (1992:337).

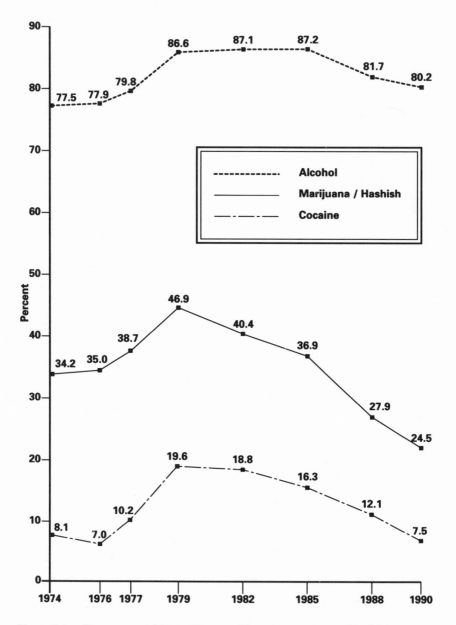

Figure 8.2. Percentage of 18 to 25 year olds using marijuana/hashish, cocaine, and alcohol once or more in the last year, selected years, 1974–1990. From Maguire, Pastore, and Flanagan (1992:337).

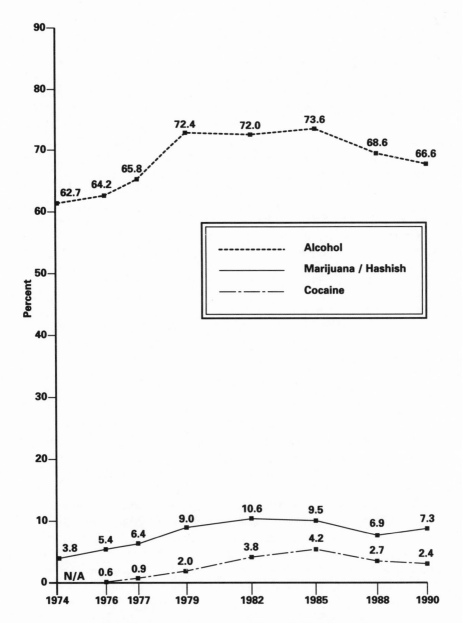

Figure 8.3. Percentage of those 26 years and older using marijuana/hashish, cocaine, and alcohol once or more in the last year, selected years, 1974–1990. From Maguire, Pastore, and Flanagan (1992:337).

often than alcohol. Third, the use of all drugs by all age groups fell during the 1980s.

The crack scare continued in 1990 and 1991, although with somewhat less media and political attention. By the beginning of 1992—the last year of the Bush administration—the War on Drugs in general, and the crack scare in particular, had begun to decline significantly in prominence and importance. However, even as the drug war received less notice from politicians and the media, it remained institutionalized, bureaucratically powerful, and extremely well funded (especially police, military, and education/propaganda activities).

From the opening shots in 1986 to President Bush's national address in 1989, and through all the stories about "crack babies" in 1990 and 1991, politicians and the media depicted crack as supremely evil—the most important cause of America's problems (on crack babies, see Litt and McNeil 1994). As recently as February 1994, a prominent *New York Times* journalist repeated the claim that "An entire generation is being sacrificed to [crack]" (Staples 1994). As in all drug scares since the nineteenth century crusade against alcohol, a core feature of drug war discourse is what we call the *routinization of caricature*—worst cases framed as typical cases, the episodic rhetorically recrafted into the epidemic.

OFFICIAL GOVERNMENT EVIDENCE

On those rare occasions when politicians and journalists cited statistical evidence to support their claims about the prevalence of crack and other drug use, they usually relied on two basic sources, both funded by the National Institute on Drug Abuse (NIDA). One was the Drug Abuse Warning Network (DAWN), a monitoring project set up to survey a sample of hospitals, crisis and treatment centers, and coroners across the country about drug-related emergencies and deaths. The other was NIDA's national surveys on drug use among general population households and among young people.[6] Because they are still considered by experts and claimsmakers to be the most reliable evidence available, we review what these two NIDA data sources had to say about crack.[7]

The Drug Abuse Warning Network

DAWN collects data on a whole series of drugs—from amphetamine to aspirin—that might be present in emergencies or fatalities. These data take the form of "mentions." A drug "mention" is produced when someone tells attending medical personnel that the patient recently used the drug, or, less often, if a blood test shows the presence of the drug. These data provided perhaps the only piece of statistical support for the crack scare. Cocaine was "mentioned" in an increasing number of emergency room episodes in the 1980s. During 1986, as the scare moved into full swing, there were an estimated 51,600 emergency room episodes in which cocaine was "mentioned" (NIDA 1993a). In subsequent years, the estimated number of such "mentions" continued to rise, providing clear cause for concern. By 1989, for example, the estimated number of emergency room episodes in which cocaine was "mentioned" had more than doubled to 110,000. Although the estimate dropped sharply in 1990 to 80,400, by 1992 it had risen again to 119,800 (NIDA 1993a).

Unfortunately, the meaning of a "mention" is ambiguous. In many of these cases cocaine was probably incidental to the emergency room visit. Such episodes included routine cases in which people went to emergency rooms, for example, after being injured as passengers in auto accidents or in home accidents. Moreover, in most cases, cocaine was only one of the drugs in the person's system; most people had also been drinking alcohol. Finally, the DAWN data do not include information about preexisting medical or mental health conditions that make any form of drug use riskier. For all these reasons one cannot properly infer direct cause from the estimates of "emergency room mentions." Cocaine did play a causal role in many of these emergency cases, but no one knows how many or what proportion of the total they were.

The DAWN data on deaths in which cocaine was "mentioned" by medical examiners also must be examined closely. When the crack scare got underway in 1986, coroners coded 1,092 deaths as "cocaine-related" (NIDA 1986b), and as crack spread this number, too, increased substantially. In 1989 the Secretary of Health and Human Services reported a 20% decline in both deaths and emergency room episodes in which cocaine was mentioned, but both indices rose again in 1991 and 1992 (*New York Times* 1990; Shenon 1990; Treaster 1990). The 1992 DAWN figures showed 3,020 deaths in which cocaine was "mentioned" (NIDA 1992).

But cocaine was "mentioned" as the *only* drug in a fraction of these deaths; in 1986, for example, in less than one in five (NIDA 1986b). In most cases, cocaine had been used with other drugs, again, most often alcohol. Although any death is tragic, cocaine's role in such fatalities remains ambiguous. "Cocaine-related" is not the same as "cocaine-caused," and "cocaine-related deaths" does not mean "deaths *due to* cocaine." There is little doubt that cocaine contributes to some significant (but unknown) percentage of such deaths. But journalists, politicians, and most of the experts on whom they relied never acknowledged the ambiguities in the data. Nor did they commonly provide any comparative perspective. For example, for *every one* cocaine-related death in the United States, there have been approximately 200 tobacco-related deaths and 50 alcohol-related deaths. Seen in this light, cocaine's role in mortality and morbidity was substantially less than media accounts and political rhetoric implied.

Interpretive and empirical difficulties increased when the DAWN data were used to support claims about crack. Despite all the attention paid to the crack "plague," the DAWN data for 1986 contained *no specific information on crack* as distinct from cocaine. In fact, the DAWN data show that, in the vast majority of both emergencies and deaths in which cocaine received a "mention," the mode of ingestion of cocaine was *not* "smoking" and therefore these incidents could not have been caused by crack. Thus, while it is likely that crack played a role in some of the emergencies and deaths in which cocaine was "mentioned," the data necessary to accurately assess crack's impact did not exist.

NIDA Surveys

The NIDA surveys of drug use produce the data that are the statistical basis of all estimates of the prevalence of cocaine *use*. One of the core claims in the crack scare was that drug use among teenagers and young adults was already high, and that it was growing at an alarming rate. While politicians and the media often referred to teen drug use as an "epidemic" or "plague," the best official evidence available at the time did not support such claims.

NIDA's national surveys of over 8,000 randomly selected households showed that the number of Americans who had used any illegal drug in the previous month began to decline in 1979, and in the early years of the crack scare drug use continued to plunge, cocaine most sharply of all (Berke 1989; Martz 1990). Lifetime prevalence of cocaine use among young people (the percentage of those 12–25 years old who had "ever" tried it) peaked in 1982, *four years before the scare began,* and continued to decline after that (NIDA 1990:14). The sharpest rise in lifetime prevalence among young adults had taken place between 1972 and 1979; it produced no claims of an "epidemic" or "plague" by politicians and journalists (NIDA 1986a; cf. Johnston, O'Malley and Bachman 1988; see Figures 8.1–8.3).

NIDA researchers reported and commented on their findings in prominent publications. In 1986, two leading NIDA scholars reported the results of the household survey in *Science* magazine and wrote that "both annual prevalence and current prevalence [of all drug use] among college students and the total sample up to four years after high school has been relatively stable between 1980 and 1985" (Kozel and Adams 1986:973). The director of NIDA's high school surveys, Dr. Lloyd Johnston, made a similar point in 1987: "To some degree the fad quality of drugs has worn off" (Kerr 1987a:A.21). When the findings of the high school senior survey for 1987 were released, the survey's director reported that "the most important" finding was that cocaine had again "showed a significant drop in use." He even reported a decline in the use of crack (Johnston, O'Malley, and Bachman 1988).

These reported declines were in keeping with the general downward trend in drug use. In the early 1980s, according to the NIDA surveys, about one in six young Americans had tried powdered cocaine. But between 1986 and 1987 the proportion of both high school seniors and young adults who had used cocaine in any form in the previous year dropped by 20% (Johnston, O'Malley, and Bachman 1988). Further, two-thirds of those who had ever tried cocaine had not used it in the previous month. Although a significant minority of young people had tried powdered cocaine at some point, the great majority of them did not continue to use it.

It is important to note that there had been a few signs of increasing cocaine use. The proportion of youngsters who reported using cocaine at least once in the previous month had increased slightly over the years, although it never exceeded 2% of all teens in the seven national household surveys between 1972 and 1985. The 1988 NIDA household survey found an increase in the number of adult daily users of cocaine, presumably the group that included crack addicts. But this group constituted only about 1.3% of those adults who had ever used any cocaine. NIDA also estimated that about 0.5% of the total U.S. adult population had used cocaine in the last week (NIDA 1988).

But aside from these few slight increases, in almost every category of drug use, the trends in official drug use statistics had been down even before the scare began. The figures for cocaine use in particular were dropping sharply just as crisis claims were reaching a crescendo, and had dropped still further precisely when the Bush/Bennett battle plan was being announced with such fanfare in 1989. Indeed, as White House officials anonymously admitted a few weeks after the President's "bag of crack" speech, the new plan's "true goals" were far more modest than its rhetoric: the Bush plan was "simply to move the nation 'a little bit' beyond where current trends would put it anyway" (Berke 1989:A.1).

NIDA Survey Data on Crack

Tom Brokaw reported on *NBC Nightly News* in 1986 (May 23) that crack was "flooding America," that it had become "America's drug of choice." His colleagues at the other networks and in the print media had made similar claims. An ordinarily competent news consumer might well have gathered the impression that crack could be found in the lockers of most high school students. Yet, at the time of these press reports, *there were no prevalence statistics at all on crack*, and no evidence of any sort showing that smoking crack had become even the preferred mode of cocaine use, much less of drug use.

When NIDA released the first official data on crack a few months later, they still did not support claims about widespread crack use. On the contrary, the NIDA survey found that the preferred mode of use for 90% of cocaine users was "sniffing" rather than smoking (NIDA 1986b; Inciardi 1987). An all-but-ignored Drug Enforcement Administration press release issued in August 1986, during the first hysterical summer of the crack scare sought to correct the misperception that crack use was now the major drug problem in America. "Crack is currently the subject of considerable media attention" observed the DEA. "The result has been a distortion of the public perception of the extent of crack use as compared to the use of other drugs. . . . [Crack] presently appears to be a secondary rather than primary problem in most areas" (quoted in Diamond, Accosta, and Thornton 1987:10; and in Inciardi 1987:482).[8]

The first official measures of the prevalence of teenage crack began with NIDA's 1986 high school survey. It found that 4.1% of high school seniors reported having *tried* crack (at least once) in the previous year. This figure dropped to 3.9% in 1987, and to 3.1% in 1988, a 25% decline (*National Report on Substance Abuse* 1994:3; Johnston, O'Malley, and Bachman 1988). This means that at the peak of crack use, 96% of America's high school seniors had never tried crack, much less gone on to more regular use, abuse, or addiction. Any drug use among the young is certainly worrisome, particularly when in such an intense form as crack. However, at the start of the crusade to save "a whole generation" of children from death-by-crack in the Spring of 1986, the latest official data showed a national total of eight "cocaine-related" deaths of young people 18 and under for the preceding year (Trebach 1987:11). There was no way to determine whether any of these deaths involved crack use, or even if cocaine was in fact the direct cause.

In general, the NIDA surveys indicate that a substantial minority of teenagers and young adults experiment with illicit drugs. But as with other forms of youthful deviance, most tend to abandon such behavior as they assume adult roles. Politicians, the media, and antidrug advertisements said that cocaine is inevitably addicting, but that crack is still worse because it is "instantaneously addicting." However, according to the NIDA surveys, two-thirds of Americans in all age groups who had ever tried cocaine had not used it in the past 30 days. It is clear that the vast majority of the more than 22 million Americans who have tried cocaine do not use it in crack form, do not escalate to regular use, and do not end up addicted.

The 1992 household survey found that even among the age groups in which crack is most widely used (18–34 years old), only about 3% of them had "ever used" it (NIDA 1993b:37). Moreover, only about one-third of those who had ever used crack reported having used it in the previous year (0.9–1.1%), and only about one-third of these (0.4%) said they had used it in the past month. In short, NIDA's general household surveys indicated that the lifetime prevalence of crack use began low and declined thereafter. And, despite all the claims that it is "instan-taneously addicting," a clear majority of those who did try it did not continue to use it.

The high school surveys similarly showed that the annual prevalence of crack use had declined steadily to 1.5% for 1991, 1992, and 1993. Indeed, when the findings from the 1993 survey of 50,000 students were announced (2/1/94), the six pages of text in the press release did not even *mention* cocaine or crack (University of Michigan 1994). An ap-pended graph showed that there had been no significant change in the low prevalence of cocaine use, but the prevalence of crack use was apparently too small to register on the graph. Yet, rather than note that the crack "plague" had not materialized after all, the researchers began their report by exclaiming that "Drug use among American young people has been making a clear comeback" (p. 1). They were referring primarily to a "three or four percentage point" rise (p. 2) in the number of high school seniors who had used *marijuana* at least once in the previous year.

In sum, the official evidence on cocaine and crack available during the crack scare gave a rather different picture than Americans received from the media and politicians. The sharp rise in "mentions" of cocaine in emergency room episodes and coroners' reports did offer cause for con-cern. But the best official evidence of drug use never supported the claims about an "epidemic" or "plague" throughout America, or about "instantaneous addiction." Moreover, as media attention to crack was burgeoning, the actual extent of crack use was virtually unknown and most other official measures of cocaine use were actually decreasing. Once actually measured, the prevalence of crack use turned out to be low to start with and declining throughout the scare (*National Report on Substance Abuse* 1994:3).

Crack as an "Epidemic" and "Plague"

The empirical evidence on crack use suggests that politicians and journalists routinely used the words "epidemic" and "plague" imprecisely and rhetorically. Like most other drug researchers and epidemiologists, we have concluded that crack addiction has never been anything but relatively rare across the great middle strata of the U.S. population. If the word "epidemic" is used to mean a disease or disease-like condition that is "widespread" or "prevalent," then there has never been an epidemic of crack addiction (or even crack use) among the vast majority of Americans. Among the urban poor, however, especially African-American and Latino youth, heavy crack use has been more common. An "epidemic" of crack *use* might arguably be used to describe what happened among a distinct minority of teenagers and young adults from impoverished urban neighborhoods in the mid to late 1980s. However, many more people use tobacco and alcohol heavily than use cocaine in any form. Alcohol drinking and tobacco smoking each kills far more people than all forms of cocaine and heroin use combined. Therefore "epidemic" would be more appropriate to describe tobacco and alcohol use. But politicians and the media have not talked about tobacco and alcohol use as epidemics or plagues. The word "epidemic" also can mean a rapidly spreading disease. In this precise sense as well, in inner-city neighborhoods crack use (and problems) may have been epidemic (spreading rapidly) for two or three years among poverty-stricken African-American and Latino teenagers and young adults. However, crack use was never spreading fast or far enough among the general population to be termed an epidemic there.

"Plague" is even a stronger word than epidemic. Plague can mean a "deadly contagious disease," an epidemic "with great mortality." Continuous heavy use of crack often does substantial psychological and physical harm, but even extremely heavy and daily crack use rarely directly kills the users. In this sense crack use is not a plague.

It is instructive to compare claims about the crack epidemic with the treatment of other drug use patterns. For example, an unusually balanced *New York Times* story compared crack and alcohol use among suburban teenagers and focused on the middle-class (Foderaro 1989). The *Times* reported that except for a few "urban pockets" in suburban counties, "crack and other narcotics are rarely seen in the suburbs, whether modest or wealthy." As the *Times* explained:

> Unlike crack, which is confined mainly to poor urban neighborhoods, alcohol seems to cut across Westchester's socio-economic lines. . . . Westchester is not unusual. Across the United States, alcohol eclipses all other drugs tried by high school students. According to a survey by the Institute for Social Research at the University of Michigan, 64 percent of 16,300 high school seniors surveyed in 1988 had drunk alcohol in the last month, compared with 18 percent who had smoked marijuana and 1.6 percent who had smoked crack.

The *Times* also reported that high school seniors drink more than the general adult population. Furthermore, teenagers have been outdrinking adults since at least 1972 when the surveys began. Even more significant is the *kind* of drinking teenagers do—what the *Times* called "excessive 'binge' drinking": "More than a third of the high school seniors had said that in the last two weeks they had had five or more drinks in a row." Drinking is, of course, the most widespread form of illicit drug use among high school students. As the *Times* explained, on the weekend, "practically every town has at least one underage party, indoors or out" and that "fake identification cards, older siblings, friends, and even parents all help teenagers obtain" alcohol.

The point we wish to emphasize is that even though illicit alcohol use was far more prevalent than cocaine or crack use, and even though it held substantial risk for alcohol dependence, addiction, drinking–driving deaths, and other alcohol-related problems, the media and politicians did not campaign against teen drunkenness. If "epidemic" means "prevalent," the word fits teenage drinking far better than it does teenage crack use. Although many organizations have campaigned against drinking and driving by teenagers, the politicians and media have not used terms like "epidemic" or "plague" to call attention to illicit teenage drinking and drunkenness. Unlike the *Times'*s articles on crack, which frequently made the front page, this article on teen drunkenness appeared in the second section on a Saturday.

It is also worth noting the unintentionally ironic mixing of metaphors when advocates for the War on Drugs described crack use as an "epidemic" or "plague" and then urge arresting and imprisoning more users. If crack use is primarily a crime problem, then terms like "wave" (as in crime wave) would be more fitting. But if this truly is an "epidemic"—a widespread disease—then prisons are the wrong remedy and the victims of the epidemic should be offered treatment, public health programs, and social services.

Finally, we wish to call attention to an influential generalization made about the crack "epidemic"—and a good example of the careless journalism about drugs. As we noted earlier, the editor-in-chief of *Newsweek*, Richard M. Smith, began a full-page 1986 editorial with the assertion that "An epidemic [of illicit drugs] is abroad in America, as pervasive and dangerous in its way as the plagues of medieval times" (Newsweek 1986a:18). This is not true. The medieval plague was (and still is) a deadly bacterial disease that often kills very quickly. The bubonic plague killed roughly 100 million people in the Middle East, Europe, and Asia during the sixth century. In the fourteenth century, the so-called "Black Death" killed one-fourth to one-half the entire population of Europe, about 75 million people, *in a few years*. On the other hand, in the United

States, perhaps 7,000 to 10,000 deaths a year are "related" to all forms of illicit drug use combined. It is simply untrue that in America the effects of illicit drug use are "as pervasive and dangerous" as medieval plagues. The *Newsweek* editorial offered falsehoods as news. However, it was a high profile, well thought out statement—a model, by one of the top news magazine editors, of the way reporters should write about drug issues. And reporters and editors certainly seemed to pick up the message. For example, a month later, *U.S. News and World Report* noted that "illicit drugs pervade American life . . . a situation that experts compare to medieval plagues—the No. 1 problem we face" (Lang 1989:49). After *Newsweek* and *U.S. News and World Report* had both confirmed that crack was equivalent to medieval plagues, countless politicians repeated it as well. It was now a certified "fact."

THE POLITICAL CONTEXT OF THE "CRACK CRISIS"

If the many claims about an "epidemic" or "plague" endangering "a whole generation" of youth were at odds with the best official data, then what else animated the new War on Drugs?[9] In fact, even if all the exaggerated claims about crack had been true, it would not explain all the attention crack received. Poverty, homelessness, auto accidents, handgun deaths, and environmental hazards are also widespread, costly, even deadly, but most politicians and journalists never speak of them in terms of "crisis" or "plague." Indeed, far more people were (and still are) injured and killed every year by "domestic violence" than by illicit drugs, but one would never know this from media reports or political speeches. The existence of government studies suggesting that crack contributed to the deaths of a small proportion of its users, that an unknown but somewhat larger minority of users became addicted to it, that its use was "related" to some forms of crime, and so on, was neither a necessary nor sufficient condition for all the attention crack received (see Spector and Kitsuse 1977).

Like other sociologists, historians, and students of drug law and public policy, we suggest that understanding antidrug campaigns requires more than evidence of drug abuse and drug-related problems; such evidence can be found in almost any period. It requires analyzing these crusades and scares as phenomena in their own right, and understanding the broader social, political, and economic circumstances under which they occur (Bakalar and Grinspoon 1987; Brecher 1972; Duster 1970; Gusfield 1963, 1981; Lindesmith 1965; Morgan 1978; Musto 1973; Rumbarger 1989). The crack scare also must be understood in terms of its political context and its appeal to important groups within American society. The mass media and politicians, however, did not talk about drugs this way. Rather, they decontextualized the drama, making it appear as if the story had no authors aside from dealers and addicts. Their writing on the crack drama kept abusers, dealers, crimes, and casualties under spotlights while hiding other important factors in the shadows. We suggest that over and above the very real problems some users suffered with crack, the rise of the New Right and the competition between political parties in a conservative context contributed significantly to the making of the current drug scare.

The New Right and Its Moral Ideology

During the post-Watergate rebuilding of the Republican Party, far right-wing political organizations and fundamentalist Christian groups set about to impose what they called "traditional family values" on public policy. This self-proclaimed "New Right" felt increasingly threatened by the diffusion of modernist values, behaviors, and cultural practices—particularly by what they saw as the interconnected forms of 1960s hedonism involved in sex outside (heterosexual) marriage and consciousness alteration with (illicit) drugs. The New Right formed a core constituency for Ronald Reagan, an extreme conservative who had come to prominence as governor of California in part by taking a hard line against the new political movements and cultural practices of the 1960s.

Once he became President in 1981, Reagan and his appointees attempted to restructure public policy according to a radically conservative ideology. Through the lens of this ideology, most social problems appeared to be simply the consequences of *individual moral choices* (Ryan 1976). Programs and research that had for many years been directed at the social and structural sources of social problems were systematically defunded in budgets and delegitimated in discourse. Unemployment, poverty, urban decay, school crises, crime, and all their attendant forms of human troubles were spoken of and acted upon as if they were the result of *individual* deviance, immorality, or weakness. The most basic premise of social science—that individual choices are influenced by social circumstances—was rejected as left-wing ideology. Reagan and the New Right constricted the aperture of attribution for America's ills so that only the lone deviant came into focus. They conceptualized people *in* trouble as people who *make* trouble (Gusfield 1985); they made social control rather than social welfare the organizing axis of public policy (Reinarman 1988).

Drug problems fit neatly into this ideological agenda and allowed conservatives to engage in sociological denial—to scapegoat drugs for many social and economic problems. For Reagan-style conservatives and the New Right, people did not so much abuse drugs because they were jobless, homeless, poor, depressed, or alienated; they were jobless, homeless, poor, depressed, or alienated because they were weak, immoral, or foolish enough to use illicit drugs. For the right-wing, American business productivity was not lagging because investors spent their capital on mergers and stock speculation instead of new plants and equipment, or for any number of other economic reasons routinely mentioned in the *Wall Street Journal* or *Business Week*. Rather, conservatives claimed that businesses had difficulty competing partly because many workers were using drugs. In this view, U.S. education was in trouble not because it had suffered demoralizing budget cuts, but because a "generation" of students were "on drugs" and their teachers did not "get tough" with them. The new drug warriors did not see crime plaguing the ghettos and barrios for all the reasons it always has, but because of the influence of a new chemical bogeyman.

Crack was a godsend to the Right. They used it and the drug issue as an ideological fig leaf to place over the unsightly urban ills that had increased markedly under Reagan administration social and economic policies. "The drug problem" served conservative politicians as an all-purpose scapegoat. They could blame an array of problems on the deviant individuals, and then expand the nets of social control to imprison those people for causing the problems.

The crack crisis had other, more specific political uses. Nancy Reagan was a highly visible antidrug crusader, crisscrossing the nation to urge school children to "Just Say No" to drugs. Mrs. Reagan's crusade began in 1983 (before crack came into existence) when her "p.r.-conscious operatives," as *Time* magazine called them, convinced her that "serious-minded displays" of "social consciousness" would "make her appear more caring and less frivolous." Such a public relations strategy was important to Mrs. Reagan because the press had often criticized her for spending hundreds of thousands of dollars on new china for the White House, lavish galas for wealthy friends, and high-fashion evening gowns at a time when her husband's economic policies had induced a sharp recession, raised joblessness to Depression-era levels, and cut funding for virtually all programs for the poor. *Time* explained that "the timing and destinations of her anti-drug excursions last year were coordinated with the Reagan-Bush campaign officials to satisfy their particular political needs" (Andersen 1985:30).

For the Reagan administration and others on the right, America's drug problems functioned as opportunities for the imposition of an old moral agenda and the appearance of a new social concern. Moreover, the remedies that followed from this view were in perfect harmony with "traditional family values"—individual moral discipline and abstinence, combined with police and prisons for those who indulged. Such remedies avoided all questions about the economic and political sources of and solutions to America's social problems. The Reagan administration preached this ideology from the highest platforms in the land, and transformed public policy in its image. It made a most hospitable context for a new drug scare.

Political Party Competition

The primary political task facing liberals in the 1980s was to recapture some of the electorate that had gone over to the Right. Reagan's shrewdness in symbolically colonizing "middle American" fears put Democrats on the defensive. Most Democrats responded by moving to the right and pouncing upon the drug issue. Part of the early energy for the drug scare in the spring and summer of 1986 came from Democratic candidates trading charges with their Republican opponents about being "soft on drugs." Candidates challenged each other to take urine tests as a symbol of their commitment to a "drug-free America." One Southern politician even proposed that candidates' spouses be tested. A California senatorial candidate charged his opponent with being "a noncombatant in the war on drugs" (Balzar 1986:1.3). By the fall of 1986, increasingly strident calls for a drug war became so much a part of candidates' standard stump speeches that even conservative columnist William Safire (1986) complained of antidrug "hysteria" and "narcomania." Politicians demanded everything from death penalties in North America to bombing raids in South America.

Crack could not have appeared at a more opportune political moment. After years of dull debates on budget balancing, a "hot" issue had arrived just in time for a crucial election. In an age of fiscal constraint, when most problems were seen as intractable and most solutions costly, the crack crisis was the one "safe" issue on which all politicians could take "tough stands" without losing a single vote or campaign contribution. The legislative results of the competition to "get tough" included a two-billion dollar law in 1986, the so-called "Drug-Free America Act," which whizzed through the House (392 to 16) just in time for members of Congress to go home and tell their constituents about it. In the heat of the preelection, antidrug hysteria, the symbolic value of such spending seemed to dwarf the deficit worries that had hamstrung other legislation. According to *Newsweek*, what occurred was "a can-you-top-this competition" among "election-bound members of both parties" seeking tough antidrug amendments. The 1986 drug bill, as Representative David McCurdy (D—Oklahoma) put it, was "out of control," adding through a wry smile, "but of course I'm for it" (Morganthau 1986b:39).

The prominence of the drug issue dropped sharply in both political speeches and media coverage after the 1986 election, but returned during the 1988 primaries. Once again the crack issue had political utility. One common observation about the 1988 Presidential election campaigns was that there were no domestic or foreign policy crises looming on which the two parties could differentiate themselves. As a *New York Times* headline put it: "Drugs as 1988 Issue: Filling a Vacuum" (Dionne 1988). In the 1988 primary season, candidates of both parties moved to fill this vacuum in part by drug-baiting their opponents, attacking them as "soft on drugs." In the fall, both Democrats Dukakis and Bentsen, and Republicans Bush and Quayle, claimed that their opponents' antidrug commitment was weak while asserting that their side would wage a *"real* War on Drugs." And, just as they did before the 1986 election, members of Congress from both parties overwhelmingly passed a new, even stricter and more costly antidrug bill.

The antidrug speeches favoring such expenditures became increasingly transparent as posturing, even to many of the speakers. For example, Senator Christopher Dodd (D—Connecticut) called the flurry of antidrug amendments a "feeding frenzy" (Roberts 1988:4.4). An aide to another Senator admitted that "everybody was scrambling to get a piece of the action" (Dionne 1988:A.14). Even President Reagan's spokesperson, Marlin Fitzwater, told the White House press corps that "everybody wants to out-drug each other in terms of political rhetoric." But however transparent, such election-year posturing—magnified by a media hungry for the readers and ratings that dramatic drug stories bring— enhanced the viability of claims about the menace of crack far more than any available empirical evidence could. In the fall of 1989 Congress finalized yet another major antidrug bill costing more than the other two combined. According to research by the Government Accounting Office, the federal government spent more than $23 billion on the drug war during the Reagan era, three-fourths of which was for law enforcement (*Alcoholism and Drug Abuse Week* 1989:3).

As we mentioned earlier, in opinion polls in 1986, 1988, and 1989 more people picked "drugs" as the "most important problem facing the country" than any other public issue. Politicians and the press frequently cited such poll results as the reason for their speeches and stories. For example, the *New York Times* titled one story, "The People's Concern: Illegal Drugs Are an Issue No Politician Can Resist" (Roberts 1988). That title got it half right; politicians could not resist playing the drug issue, but the drug issue was not so much "the People's Concern" until they did. The reporter rightly noted that the 1988 election campaign would "resemble a shoving match" over "who can take a tougher line on drugs," and that "those who counsel reason are vulnerable to accusations of being 'soft'." But then he falsely attributed this phenomenon to the citizenry: "The politicians were reflecting the concerns of their constituents." He also quoted an aide to then-Vice President Bush saying the same thing: "Voters have made this an issue."

Politicians and the media were *forging*, not following, public opinion. The speeches and stories *led* the oft-cited poll results, not the other way around. In 1987, between elections—when drug problems persisted in the ghettos and barrios but when the drug scare was not so inflamed by election rhetoric and media coverage—only 3 to 5% of those surveyed picked drugs as our most important problem (Dionne 1988). But then again in 1989, immediately following President Bush's speech escalating the drug war, nearly two-thirds of the people polled identified drugs as America's most important problem. When the media and politicians invoked "public opinion" as the driving force behind their actions against crack, they inverted the actual causal sequence (Edelman 1964:172).

We argued in the previous section that the New Right and other conservatives found ideological utility in the crack scare. In this section we have suggested that conservatives were not the only political group in America to help foment the scare and benefit from it. Liberals and Democrats, too, found in crack and "drugs" a means of recapturing Democratic defectors by appearing more conservative. And they too found "drugs" to be a convenient scapegoat for the worsening conditions in the inner cities. All this happened at a historical moment when conservatives successfully stigmatized liberals' traditional solutions to the problems of the poor as ineffective and costly. Thus, in addition to the political capital to be gained by waging the war, the new chemical bogeyman afforded politicians across the ideological spectrum both an explanation for pressing public problems and an excuse for not proposing the unpopular taxing, spending, or redistributing needed to do something about them.

The End of the Crack Scare

In the 1980s, the conservative drive to reduce social spending exacerbated the enduring problems of impoverished African-American and Latino city residents. Partly in response, a minority of the young urban poor turned either to crack sales as their best shot at the American Dream, and/or to the crack high as their best shot at a fleeting moment of pleasure. Inner-city churches, community organizations, and parent groups then tried to defend their children and neighborhoods from drug dealing and use on the one hand, and to lobby for services and jobs on the other hand. But the crack scare did not inspire politicians of either party to address the worsening conditions and growing needs of the inner-city poor and working class, or to launch a "Marshall Plan for cities." In the meantime, the white middle-class majority viewed with alarm the growing numbers, visibility, and desperation of the urban poor. And for years many Americans believed the central fiction of the crack scare: that drug use was not a symptom of urban decay but one of its most important causes.

All this gave federal and local authorities justification for widening the nets of social control. Of course, the new drug squads did not reduce the dangerousness of impoverished urban neighborhoods. But the crack scare did increase criminal justice system supervision of the underclass. By 1992, one in four young African-American males were in jail or prison, or on probation or parole—more than were in higher education (Duster, 1995). During the crack scare, the prison population more than doubled, largely because of the arrests of drug users and small dealers. This gave the United States the highest incarceration rate in the world (Currie 1985; Irwin and Austin 1994).

By the end of 1992, however, the crack scare seemed spent. There are a number of overlapping reasons for this. Most important was the failure of the War on Drugs itself. Democrats as well as Republicans supported the War on Drugs, but the Reagan and Bush administrations initiated and led it, and the drug war required support from the White House. George Bush appointed William Bennett to be a "tough" and extremely high profile "Drug Czar" to lead the campaign against drugs. But Bennett, criticized for his bombastic style, quit after only 18 months (some press accounts referred to it as the "Czar's abdication"). After that, the Bush Administration downplayed the drug war, and it hardly figured during the Presidential primaries or campaign in 1992. Bill Clinton said during the campaign that there were no easy solutions to drug problems, and that programs that work only on reducing supply were doomed to fail. The Clinton administration eschewed the phrase "War on Drugs," and Lee Brown, Clinton's top drug official, explicitly rejected the title of Drug Czar (Reinarman 1994). After billions of tax dollars had been spent and millions of young Americans had been imprisoned, our hard-core drug problems remained. Moreover, with both parties firmly in favor of the get tough approach, being a drug warrior no longer offered a political advantage. Politicians had discovered the limits of the drug issue as a political weapon.

The news media probably would have written dramatic stories about the appearance of smokable cocaine in poverty neighborhoods at any time. Television producers have found that drug stories, especially timely, well-advertised, dramatic ones often receive high ratings. But the context of the Reagan-lead drug war encouraged the media to write such pieces. Conservatives had long complained that the media had a liberal bias; in the mid-1980s, drug coverage allowed the media to rebut such criticism and to establish conservative creditials (Reeves and Campbell 1994). As we have suggested, news coverage of drugs rose and fell with political initiatives, especially those coming from the President. Therefore, as the White House withdrew from the drug issue, so did the press.

After about 1989, it became increasingly difficult to sustain the exaggerated claims of the beginning of the crack scare. The mainstream media began to publish stories critical of earlier news coverage (though usually not their own). It became increasingly clear, even to the most obtuse observers, that heavy crack use was not spreading beyond the same poverty context that had long given rise to hard core heroin addiction. Moreover, because of the obvious destructive effects of heavy crack use, people in ghettoes and barrios had come to view "crackheads" as even lower in status than winos or heroin junkies. Even crack dealers preferred powdered cocaine and routinely disparaged crackheads (Williams 1989). All of this meant that drugs in general, and crack in particular, declined in newsworthiness. Media competition had fueled the crack scare in its early years, and the same scramble for dramatic stories guaranteed that the media would move on to other stories. By 1992, the crack scare had faded beyond the media's horizon of hot new issues.

Finally, the crack scare could recede into the background partly because it had been *institutionalized*. Between 1986 and 1992 Congress passed and two Presidents signed a series of increasingly harsh antidrug laws. Federal antidrug funding increased for seven successive years and an array of prison and law enforcement programs were established or expanded. All levels of government, from local schools to cities, counties, and states, established agencies to warn about crack and other drug problems. And multimillion dollar, corporate-sponsored private organizations such as the Partnership for a Drug-Free America had been established to continue the crusade.

CONCLUSION

Crack *is* an especially dangerous way to use an already risky drug. Despite all the exaggerations, heavy use of it *has* made life more difficult

for many people—most of them from impoverished, urban neighborhoods. If we agree that too many families have been touched by drug-
related tragedies, why have we bothered criticizing the crack scare and
the War on Drugs? If even a few people are saved from crack addiction,
why should anyone care if this latest drug scare was in some measure
concocted by the press, politicians, and moral entrepreneurs to serve
their other agendas? Given the damage that drug abuse can do, what's
the harm in a little hysteria?

First, drug scares do not work very well to reduce drug problems and
they may well promote the behavior they claim to be preventing. For all
the repression successive drug wars have wrought (primarily upon the
poor and the powerless), they have yet to make a measurable dent in
our drug *problems*. For example, prompted by the crack crisis and inspired by the success of patriotic propaganda in World War II, the Partnership for a Drug-Free America ran a massive advertising campaign to
"unsell drugs." From 1987 to 1993 the Partnership placed over a billion
dollars worth of advertising donated by corporations and the advertising industry. The Partnership claims to have had a "measurable impact"
by "accelerating intolerance" to drugs and drug users. The Partnership
claims it "can legitimately take some of the credit for the 25% decline in
illicit drug usage since our program was launched" (Hedrick 1990).
However, the association between the Partnership's antidrug advertising and the declines in drug use appears to be spurious. Drug use was
declining well before the Partnership's founding (see Figures 8.1–8.3).
More important, drug *problems* continued throughout their campaign.
Furthermore, Partnership ads scrupulously avoided any mention of the
two forms of drug use most prevalent among youth: smoking and drinking. This probably had much to do with the fact that the alcohol and
tobacco industries spend billions each year on advertising in the media
and were major financial contributors to the Partnership's campaign
against illicit drugs. Surely public health education is important, but
there is no evidence that selective antidrug propaganda and scare tactics
have reduced drug use.

Indeed, hysterical and exaggerated antidrug campaigns may have increased drug-related harm in the United States. There is the risk that
all of the exaggerated claims made to mobilize the population for war
actually arouse interest in drug use. The *New England Journal of Medicine*
reported that the frequency of teenage suicides increases after lurid
news reports and TV shows about them (Gould and Shaffer 1986; Phillips and Carstensen 1986). Reports about drugs, especially new and
exotic drugs like crack, may work the same way. In his classic chapter,
"How to Launch a Nation Wide Drug Menace," Brecher (1972) shows
how exaggerated newspaper reports of dramatic police raids in 1960

functioned as advertising for glue sniffing. The arrests of a handful of sniffers led to antiglue sniffing hysteria that actually spread this hitherto unknown practice across the United States. In 1986, the media's desire for dramatic drug stories interacted with politicians' desire for partisan advantage and safe election-year issues so that news about crack spread to every nook and cranny of the nation far faster than dealers could have spread word on the street. When the media and politicians claimed that crack is "the most addictive substance known to man," there was some common sense obligation to explain why. Therefore, alongside all the statements about "instant addiction" the media also reported some very intriguing things about crack: "whole body orgasm," "better than sex," and "cheaper than cocaine." For TV-raised young people in the inner city, faced with a dismal social environment and little economic opportunity, news about such a substance in their neighborhoods may well have functioned as a massive advertising campaign for crack.[10]

Further, advocates of the war on drugs and the crack scare explicitly rejected public health approaches to drug problems that conflicted with their ideology. The most striking and devastating example of this was the total rejection of syringe distribution and exchange programs by the Reagan and Bush administrations and by drug warriors such as Congressman Charles Rangel. Drug addiction is rarely fatal; AIDS always is. People can and often do recover from drug addiction, but no one recovers from AIDS. By the end of the 1980s, the fastest growing AIDS population was intravenous drug users, primarily heroin addicts. Because syringes were hard to get, or their possession criminalized, heroin injectors shared their syringes and infected each other and their sexual partners with AIDS. In the early 1980s, activists in a number of other Western countries had developed syringe distribution and exchange programs, first to deal with an outbreak of hepatitis, and then with the far more deadly AIDS. Major cities in the Netherlands, England, Australia, Switzerland, Germany, and other Western countries adopted and subsidized needle exchange programs. There has been mounting evidence from all these places that such programs work to reduce the spread of AIDS. But the U.S. government rejected such "harm reduction" programs on the grounds that they conflicted with the policy of "zero tolerance" for drug use. Needle exchange programs, it was said, "sent the wrong message." As a result, cities such as Amsterdam, Liverpool, and Sydney that have needle exchange programs have very low or almost no transmission of AIDS by intravenous drug users. In New York City, on the other hand, half of the hundreds of thousands of intravenous drug users are HIV positive or already have AIDS. In short, drug war policies, and the fears created during the crack scare, will directly kill by AIDS hundreds of thousands of people including the families, children, and sexual partners of the infected drug users.

Another important harm resulting from American drugs scares is they have routinely blamed individual immorality and personal behavior for endemic social and structural problems. In so doing, they diverted attention and resources away from the underlying sources of drug abuse and the array of other social ills of which it is a part. One necessary condition for the emergence of the crack scare (as in previous drug scares) was the linking of drug use with the problems faced by racial minorities, the poor, and youth. In the logic of the scare, whatever economic and social troubles these people have suffered was due largely to their drug use. Obscured or forgotten during the crack scare were all the social and economic problems that underlie crack abuse—and that are much more widespread—especially poverty, unemployment, racism, and the prospects of life in the permanent underclass.

Democrats denounced the Reagan and Bush administrations' hypocrisy in proclaiming "War on Drugs" while at the same time cutting the budgets for drug treatment, prevention, and research. However, the Democrats usually neglected a more important development: the "Just Say No To Drugs" administrations had, with the help of many Democrats in Congress, also "just said no" to virtually every social program aimed at creating alternatives for and improving the lawful life chances of inner-city youth. These Black and Latino young people were (and still are) the group with the highest rate of crack abuse. Although most inner city youth have always steered clear of drug abuse, they could not "just say no" to poverty and unemployment. Dealing drugs, after all, was (and still is) accurately perceived by many poor city kids as the highest-paying job—straight or criminal—that they are likely to get.

The crack scare, like previous drug scares and antidrug campaigns, promoted misunderstandings of drug use and abuse, blinded people to the social sources of many social problems (including drug problems), and constrained the social policies that might reduce those problems. The crack scare routinely featured inflated, misleading rhetoric and blatant falsehoods such as Bush's televised account of how he came into possession of a bag of crack. At best, the crack scare was not good for public health; at worst, by so manipulating and misinforming citizens about drug use and effects, it perverted social policy and political democracy.[11]

ACKNOWLEDGMENTS

Parts of this chapter were presented at the 37th Annual Meeting of the Society for the Study of Social Problems, Chicago, 1987. Earlier versions of it were published as "The Crack Attack: Politics and Media in America's Latest Drug Scare," in J. Best (ed.), *Images of Issues: Typifying Contemporary Social Problems* (Aldine de Gruyter, 1989) and "Crack in Context," in *Contemporary Drug Problems* 16 (1989). Our work has been inspired by the courageous research of Alfred Lindesmith, Howard Becker, Edward Brecher, Norman Zinberg, Troy Duster, Arnold Trebach, Lester Grinspoon, James Bakalar, Dan Waldorf, and Andrew Weil. We thank John Brown Childs, Sheigla Murphy, Ethan Nadelmann, Marsha Rosenbaum, and Dan Waldorf for helpful comments on earlier versions.

NOTES

1. The first modern antidrug campaign was the temperance movement of the nineteenth and early twentieth century. It culminated in the passage of the Eighteenth Amendment to the Constitution in 1919 banning the production and sale of alcoholic drink (Levine 1984, 1985, 1986; Rumbarger 1989). Other antidrug campaigns and scares include the antiopium crusade in California at the end of the nineteenth century that was part of anti-Chinese racism (Morgan 1978; Musto 1973; Sandmeyer 1939), the anticocaine scare at the beginning of the twentieth century that expressed white fears of black rebellion, the antimarijuana scare of the 1930s (Becker 1963, Dickson 1968, Grinspoon and Bakalar 1933), and the antidrug campaign of the 1960s and early 1970s that focused on marijuana and psychedelic drugs (Himmelstein 1983; National Commission on Marijuana and Drug Abuse 1972; National Research Council 1982).

One reason for examining scares as phenomena in their own right is that they have not been limited to drugs and communists. For example, in 1920, there was a ouija board scare of several months duration that shared some characteristics with the crack scare. Newspapers spoke of "a wave of insanity" caused by ouija boards that had grown to "national prominence." A typical front-page article in the *San Francisco Chronicle* (1920a) read, "Breaking into a house at El Cerrito, . . . police officers yesterday took into custody several persons who had become insane from playing with ouija boards." It seems a 15-year-old girl had used the board to "induce unknown power" over the others. Two days later in another raid, other "victims," including a policeman, were found to have been transformed "from a state of normality to that of madness" under the parlor game's influence. In a fit of what appeared to be superhuman strength usually attributed to a drug, the policeman had "knocked down two guards," escaped, hijacked a car, and "dashed into the Central National Bank in a nude condition" (*San Francisco Chronicle* 1920b). Before the ouija board scare had run its course, many others had been arrested and jailed or committed to asylums, and "experts" held serious discussions about "abolishing 'seances'" (*San Francisco Examiner* 1920).

2. See Fagan (1992) for a strong empirical study showing that the youth drawn into crack and other drug sales in distressed neighborhoods were not drawn away from legal employment into the crack economy. Rather, most were unemployed and lacked the human capital necessary to break into the legal labor

market. For these youth, the drug world provided economic opportunity as well as recreation.

3.   We use the word "official" here because (1) we are referring to data produced by federal government agencies whose task is to define and document a particular form of deviance (Kitsuse and Circourel 1963), (2) they are data considered by experts to provide the "best" (i.e., systematically collected from representative national samples) estimates of the prevalence of drug use, and (3) they are explicitly gathered to provide policymakers with a society-wide database as a foundation for policymaking.

Also, by analyzing the scare on its own terms, we do *not* wish to deny the fact that crack use had terrible medical, psychological, social, and economic consequences for some users and in some inner-city neighborhoods. And we believe it is very important to understand the social conditions underlying most heavy crack use. But in this chapter we focus on the claims about crack and other drugs, especially the wrong and exaggerated ones, and on why so many of them achieved such prominence.

4.   These successive increases in drug war funding were so great that the money could not be effectively spent. Even the "Drug Czar" admitted in 1990 that less than half of the fund earmarked for police and prisons from 1987 to 1990 had been spent (*Washington Post* 1991).

5.   Keith Jackson was soon arrested, but his trial for selling drugs to an undercover DEA agent in Lafayette Park ended in a hung jury. A few months later he was convicted and sentenced to 10 in years in prison.

6.   Other data sources besides NIDA and DAWN existed, but these usually were either anecdotal, specific to a particular location, or based on a skewed sample.

There are several reasons why local police statistics are problematic for assessing the pervasiveness of crack use. Most obviously, they deal with only those users who are apprehended. Police statistics in several major U.S. cities clearly show that cocaine and crack use are pervasive among arrestees. It is also true that crack users now comprise a growing share of those seeking treatment. But just as treatment samples, by definition, tell us little about the much larger population of users who do not seek treatment, arrest figures cannot tell us much about the central question of societal prevalence, even though claimsmakers routinely use them that way.

Perhaps more important, police statistics often *reflect* crisis claims (Kitsuse and Cicourel 1963). In New York City, for example, then-Mayor Koch, Harlem Congressman Charles Rangel, and the editors of the *New York Times* played leading roles as moral entrepreneurs in drawing attention to crack use. As a consequence, a variety of New York City agencies were politically mobilized, and the number of police assigned to special crack units *tripled*. This mobilization and vastly expanded law enforcement capacity focused specifically on crack users helps explain why crack users loomed so large in arrest statistics.

Similarly, crack arrestees were treated far more harshly by the city's criminal justice system than comparable cocaine arrestees, according to studies by the New York City Criminal Justice Agency. In their comparative analysis of 4,321 crack arrestees and 9,975 earlier cocaine arrestees, the agency found that crack users were twice as likely to be charged with felonies, four times more likely to be detained for arraignment, less likely to be released on recognizance or fined, and more likely to be sentenced to jail terms—even though the crack arrestees had a lower mean number of prior arrests than the cocaine arrestees. The authors concluded "that crack arrests are being treated more seriously than other comparable drug cases," and that this was "apparently [due to] more stringent charging decisions."

7.   A variety of questions might be raised about this evidence. It is, for example, the product of organizations whose job it is to define and document deviance, and is thus as likely to reflect this organizational mandate as it is to describe accurately some "objective" empirical reality (see Kitsuse and Cicourel [1963], on the important distinction between "rate-producing processes" and "behavior-producing processes"). Both DAWN and the NIDA surveys were explicitly set up to allow policymakers to make claims about the prevalence of— and the dangers presumed to follow from—"illicit drug abuse." Mere "yes" responses regarding *use* in the past year or even in one's lifetime are typically taken as indices of *abuse*. On the other hand, some critics claim that the NIDA high school surveys miss the very dropouts who are most prone to drug abuse, or that the household surveys sample only one household member. We focus only on the inferences that have been made on the basis of this "best" "official" evidence. We will assume for the sake of argument that these data are reasonable measures of something "real" and ask (1) how well they support the many claims of mass destruction purportedly based on them, and (2) irrespective of evidence, why such claims have achieved such prominence.

8.   The DEA later took a very different view, regularly reporting that crack use had spread far and wide with terrible consequences. Our point in citing this early memo is to show that the crack scare has had a momentum of its own, racing ahead of DEA experts and other official evidence upon which it was purportedly based.

9.   Even if we accept hyperbole as a "normal" means of attracting readers, viewers, and voters, it is still not possible to explain the character of the crack scare in terms of simple exaggerations of official evidence. Journalists consistently caricatured crack use and users and routinely employed rhetoric that is rare in other types of news stories. They also did not hesitate to make claims for which there was no evidence to "stretch."

10.   This advertising effect was probably strongest in 1986, the first year of the crack scare, when crack was new. Antidrug campaigns probably also have different effects on different populations: they may frighten away some middle-class experimenters, while increasing interest among those most prone to abuse. In 1986 one student told Arnold Trebach that when he heard that crack was "better than sex and that it was cheaper than cocaine and that it was an epidemic, I wondered what I was missing. I questioned why I seemed to be the only one not doing the drug. The next day I asked some friends if they knew where to get some" (Trebach 1987:7).

11.   This drug scare has produced a growing number of drug research, treat-

ment, and policy professionals appalled at the gap between realities and rhetoric, between what works and what is being done, between what the United States does and what other comparable industrial democracies do. Led by Baltimore Mayor Kurt Schmoke, there has been a growing chorus of voices advocating a national debate on alternatives to the war on drugs, including decriminalization. Prominent conservatives like William F. Buckley, Jr., former Reagan Administration Secretary of State George Schultz, and Nobel Prize-winning economist Milton Freedom have urged Republicans to consider drug decriminalization. An increasing number of judges and police officials have also said that the drug war should be stopped and decriminalization considered. To be fair to the media, we note that ABC's *Nightline* and National Public Radio's *All Things Considered* and *Business Update* have given decriminalization advocates a chance to present their views. Although the *New York Times* news department has generally ignored all such opposition voices, *Times* columnists Russell Baker and Anthony Lewis have written positively about alternatives, and some space in the op-ed and letters pages has been given to drug war critics. In short, largely in response to the failures and negative consequences of the War on Drugs, there has been a growing antidrug prohibition movement and sentiment. The institutional center for such activities in the United States is the Drug Policy Foundation in Washington, D.C.

REFERENCES

Alcoholism and Drug Abuse Week. 1989. "$23 Billion Spent on Federal Drug Effort Since 1981." July 5:3–4.

Andersen, K. 1985. "Co-Starring at the White House." *Time* 125 (January 14):24–30.

Bakalar, J. B., and L. Grinspoon. 1987. *Drug Control in a Free Society*. Cambridge: Cambridge University Press.

Balzar, J. 1986. "Zachau Braves Tenderloin District in S.F. to Rap Foe." *Los Angeles Times* (August 12):1.3.

Becker, H. S. 1963. *Outsiders*. New York: Free Press.

Berke, R. L. 1989. "President's 'Victory Over Drugs' Is Decades Away, Officials Say." *New York Times* (September 24):A.1).

Boundy, D. 1985. "Programs for Cocaine-Abuse Under Way." *New York Times* (November 17):B.12.

Brecher, E. M. 1972. *Licit and Illicit Drugs*. Boston: Little Brown.

Currie, E. 1985. *Confronting Crime*. New York: Pantheon.

Diamond, E., F. Accosta, and L.-J. Thornton. 1987. "Is TV News Hyping America's Cocaine Problem?" *TV Guide* (February 7):4–10.

Dickson, D. 1968. "Bureaucracy and Morality." *Social Problems* 16: 143–156.

Dionne, E. J., Jr. 1988. "Drugs as 1988 Issue." *New York Times* (May 24):D.26.

Domash, S. F., 1986. "Use of Drug 'Crack' Growing on L.I." *New York Times* (June 8):11.5.

Duster, T. 1970. *The Legislation of Morality*. New York: Free Press.

————. 1995. "Pattern, Purpose, and Race in the Drug War." In *Demon Drugs and Social Justice: Crack Cocaine in Context*, edited by C. Reinarman and H. G. Levine. Berkeley: University of California Press. In press.

Edelman, M. 1964. *The Symbolic Uses of Politics*. Urbana: University of Illinois Press.

Fagan, J. 1992. "Drug Selling and Illicit Income in Distressed Neighborhoods." Pp. 99–146 in *Drugs, Crimes, and Social Isolation*, edited by A. V. Harrell and G. E. Peterson. Washington, DC: Urban Institute Press.

Feron, J. 1986. "New Training Program for Police Bolsters Efforts Against Cocaine." *New York Times* (June 29):11.1.

Foderaro, L. W. 1989. "Drinking Keeps Its Grip on Suburban Teen-Agers." *New York Times* (October 7):26.

Gould, M. S., and D. Shaffer. 1986. "The Impact of Suicide in Television Movies: Evidence of Imitation." *New England Journal of Medicine* 315:690–694.

Grinspoon, L., and J. B. Bakalar. 1976. *Cocaine: A Drug and Its Social Evolution*. New York: Basic Books.

Gusfield, J. 1963. *Symbolic Crusade*. Urbana: University of Illinois Press.

————. 1981. *The Culture of Public Problems*. Chicago: University of Chicago Press.

————. 1985. "Alcohol Problems—An Interactionist View." Pp. 71–81 in *Currents in Alcohol Research and the Prevention of Alcohol Problems*, edited by J. P. von Wartburg, P. Magnenat, R. Muller, and S. Wyss. Berne, Switzerland: Hans Huber.

Harwood, R. 1989. "Hyperbole Epidemic." *Washington Post* (October 1): D6.

Hedrick, T. A., Jr. 1990. "Pro Bono Anti-Drug Ad Campaign Is Working." *Advertising Age* 61 (June 25):22.

Himmelstein, J. 1983. *The Strange Career of Marijuana*. Westport, CT: Greenwood Press.

Hoffman, A. 1987. *Steal This Urine Test: Fighting Drug Hysteria in America*. New York: Penguin Books.

Horgan, J. 1993. "A Kinder War." *Scientific American* 25(July):6.

Inciardi, J. 1987. "Beyond Cocaine: Basuco, Crack, and Other Coca Products." *Contemporary Drug Problems* 14:461–492.

Irwin, J., and J. Austin. 1994. *It's About Time: America's Imprisonment Binge*. Belmont, CA: Wadsworth.

Isikoff, M. 1989. "Drug Buy Set Up for Bush Speech." *Washington Post* (September 22):A.1.

Johnston, L. D., P. M. O'Malley, and J. G. Bachman. 1988. *Illicit Drug Use, Smoking, and Drinking by America's High School Students, College Students, and Young Adults, 1975–1987*. Washington, DC: National Institute on Drug Abuse.

Kerr, P. 1986a. "Extra-Potent Cocaine." *New York Times* (March 20):A.1.

————. 1986b. "Crack Addiction Spreads Among the Middle Class." *New York Times* (June 8):A.1.

————. 1987a. "High-School Marijuana Use Still Declining, U.S. Survey Shows." *New York Times* (February 24):A.1.

————. 1987b. "Rich vs. Poor: Drug Patterns Are Diverging." *New York Times* (August 30).

Kitsuse, J. I., and A. V. Cicourel. 1963. "A Note on the Use of Official Statistics." *Social Problems* 11:131–139.

Kozel, N., and E. Adams. 1986. "Epidemiology of Drug Abuse: An Overview." *Science* 234:970–974.

Lamar, J. V., Jr. 1986. "Rolling Out the Big Guns." *Time* 128 (September 22):25–26.

Lang, J. S. 1986. "America on Drugs." *U.S. News and World Report* 101 (July 28):48–55.

Levine, H. G. 1984. "The Alcohol Problem in America: From Temperance to Alcoholism." *British Journal of Addiction* 79:109–119.

————. 1985. "The Birth of American Alcohol Control: Prohibition, Repeal and the Power Elite." *Contemporary Drug Problems* 12:63–115.

————. 1986. "Prohibition, Alcohol Control, and the Problem of Lawlessness." Pp. 151–160 in *Culture and Politics of Drugs*, edited by P. Park and W. Matverychuk. Debuque, IA: Kendall Hunt.

Lindesmith, A. R. 1965. *The Addict and the Law*. Bloomington: Indiana University Press.

Litt, J., and M. McNeil. 1994. "'Crack Babies' and the Politics of Reproduction and Nurturance." Pp. 93–113 in *Troubling Children*, edited by J. Best. Hawthorne, NY: Aldine de Gruyter.

Martz, L. 1986. "Trying to Say 'No'." *Newsweek* 108 (August 11):14–20.

————. 1990. "A Dirty Drug Secret." *Newsweek* 115 (February 19):74–77.

Massing, M. 1993. "Delusions of the Drug Cops." *New York Review of Books* 40 (July 15):30–33.

McDermott, P., P. O'Hare, and C. Reinarman. 1995. "Crack in Britain: Hard Times and Harm Reduction in Liverpool." In *Demon Drugs and Social Justice: Crack Cocaine in Context*, edited by C. Reinarman and H. G. Levine. Berkeley: University of California Press. In press.

Melvin, T. 1986. "Hearing Called to Explore Use of 'Crack' by Teen-Agers." *New York Times* (April 27):11.1.

Miller, M. 1987. "Drug Use: Down, But Not in the Ghetto." *Newsweek* 110 (November 23):33.

Morgan, P. 1978. "The Legislation of Drug Law: Economic Crisis and Social Control." *Journal of Drug Issues* 8:53–62.

Morganthau, T. 1986a. "Kids and Cocaine." *Newsweek* 107 (March 17):58–65.

————. 1986b. "Drug Fever in Washington." *Newsweek* 108 (September 22):39.

Murphy, P. 1994. "Keeping Score" The Frailties of the Federal Drug Budget." *DPRC Issue Paper*. Santa Monica, CA: The Rand Drug Policy Research Center, January.

Musto, D. 1973. *The American Disease: Origins of Narcotic Control*. New Haven, CT: Yale University Press.

National Commission on Marijuana and Drug Abuse. 1972. *Marihuana: Signal of Misunderstanding*. First Report. Washington, DC: U.S. Government Printing Office.

National Institute on Drug Abuse. 1986a. *National Household Survey on Drug Abuse, 1985*. Washington, DC: Division of Epidemiology and Statistical Analysis, National Institute on Drug Abuse.

———. 1986b. *Data From the Drug Abuse Warning Network: Annual Data 1985*. Statistical Series I, #5. Washington, DC: National Institute on Drug Abuse.

———. 1988. *National Household Survey on Drug Abuse: 1988 Population Estimates*. Washington, DC: Division of Epidemiology and Prevention Research, National Institute on Drug Abuse.

———. 1990. *National Household Survey on Drug Abuse: Main Findings 1990*. Washington, DC: Epidemiology and Prevention Research, National Institute on Drug Abuse.

———. 1992. *Annual Medical Examiner Data, 1991: Data from the Drug Abuse Warning Network*. Washington, DC: Division of Epidemiology and Prevention Research, National Institute on Drug Abuse.

———. 1993a. *Estimates from the Drug Abuse Warning Network: 1992 Estimates of Drug-Related Emergency Room Episodes*. Washington, DC: Substance Abuse and Mental Health Services Administration, U.S. Dept. of Health and Human Services.

———. 1993b. *National Household Survey on Drug Abuse: Population Estimates 1992*. Washington, DC: Substance Abuse and Mental Health Services Administration, U.S. Dept. of Health and Human Services.

National Report on Substance Abuse. 1994. "Federal Officials Express Alarm at Youth's Rising Illicit Drug Use." February 11:2.

National Research Council. 1982. *Analysis of Marijuana Policy: Report of the Committee on Substance Abuse and Habitual Behavior on Drug Policy*. Washington, DC: National Academy of Sciences.

Newsweek. 1986a. "The Plague Among Us" (editorial). 107 (June 16):18.

———. 1986b. "The Drug Crisis: Crack and Crime." 107 (June 16):15.

New York Times. 1988. "New Drug Law" (editorial). (October 4):A.30

———. 1989. "War: 1 Percent. Drugs: 54 Percent" (editorial). (September 28):A.26.

———. 1990. "Medical Emergencies for Addicts Are Said to Have Dropped by 20%." (May 15):A.13.

Office of National Drug Control Policy. 1992. *National Drug Control Strategy: Budget Summary*. Washington, DC: U.S. Government Printing Office.

Oreskes, M. 1990. "Drug War Underlines Fickleness of Public." *New York Times*(September 6):A.22.

Phillips, D. P., and L. L. Carstensen. 1986. "Clustering of Teenage Suicides after Television News Stories about Suicide." *New England Journal of Medicine* 315:685–689.

Reeves, J. L., and R. Campbell. 1994. *Cracked Coverage: Television News, the Anti-Cocaine Crusade, and the Reagan Legacy*. Durham, NC: Duke University Press.

Reinarman, C. 1988. "The Social Construction of an Alcohol Problem: The Case of Mothers Against Drunk Drivers and Social Control in the 1980s." *Theory and Society* 17:91–119.

————. 1994. "Glasnost in U. S. Drug Policy?: Clinton Constrained." *International Journal of Drug Policy* 5:42–49.

Roberts, S. V. 1988. "Illegal Drugs Are an Issue No Politician Can Resist." *New York Times* (May 22):4.4.

Rumbarger, J. 1989. *Profits, Power, and Prohibition*. Albany: State University of New York Press.

Ryan, W. 1976. *Blaming the Victim*. New York: Vintage.

Safire, W. 1986. "The Drug Bandwagon." *New York Times* (September 11):A.27

Sandmeyer, E.C. 1939. *The Anti-Chinese Movement in California*. Urbana: University of Illinois Press.

San Francisco Chronicle. 1920a. "Ouija Board Denounced by Prominent Psychologists." (March 1):1.

————. 1920b. "Ouija Board Drives Two More Insane." (March 6):1.

San Francisco Examiner. 1920. "Ouija Board Drives Policeman to Street Naked." (March 6):1.

Shenon, P. 1990. "U.S. Says Hospital Statistics Show Use of Cocaine May Have Peaked." *New York Times* (September 1):L.5.

Siegel, R. 1982. "Cocaine Smoking." *Journal of Psychoactive Drugs* 14:271–359.

Spector, M., and J. Kitsuse. 1977. *Constructing Social Problems*. Menlo Park, CA: Cummings.

Staples, B. 1994. "Coke Wars." *New York Times Book Review* (February 6):11.

Treaster, J. B. 1990. "U.S. Cocaine Epidemic Shows Signs of Waning." *New York Times* (July 1):A.14.

Trebach, A. 1987. *The Great Drug War*. New York: Macmillan.

University of Michigan. 1994. "Drug Use Rises Among American Teen-Agers." News and Information Services (January 27).

Waldorf, D., C. Reinarman, and S. Murphy. 1991. *Cocaine Changes*. Philadelphia: Temple University Press.

Washington Post 1991. "States Seen Failing to Spend Millions in Anti-Drug Grants." January 2:A.13.

Washton, A., and M. Gold. 1987. "Recent Trends in Cocaine Abuse." *Advances in Alcohol and Substance Abuse* 6:31–47.

The White House. 1989. *National Drug Control Strategy*. Washington, DC: U.S. Government Printing Office.

Weinraub, B. 1989. "President Offers Strategy for U.S. on Drug Control." *New York Times* (September 6):A.1.

Williams, T. 1989. *The Cocaine Kids*. Reading, MA: Addison Wesley.

Wilson, W. J. 1987. *The Truly Disadvantaged*. Chicago: University of Chicago Press.

PART III

Connections

Research on the construction of social problems consists largely of case studies, in which sociologists examine how and why particular claims emerged about particular issues. Case studies draw their data from—and draw our attention to—the special features of the substantive case at hand. As a consequence, many case studies downplay, even ignore, connections among claimsmaking campaigns.

Yet it is obvious that there are ties linking many claimsmaking campaigns. In particular, one campaign's visible success often inspires other claimsmakers to borrow what seems to work for their own campaigns. Claimsmakers may adapt others' rhetoric, tactics, or organizational forms for their own purposes. For example, the successful 1953 bus boycott in Baton Rouge, Louisiana served as a model for later boycotts in Montgomery, Alabama and elsewhere; similarly, throughout the civil rights movement's history, local activists used what had worked elsewhere to press their own claims (McAdam 1983; Morris 1984). And, of course, the civil rights movement served as a model for the antiwar movement, the women's movement, and so on.

It seems likely that connections are especially common among claimsmakers who see themselves as somehow allied. For example, those active in one "progressive" movement, such as the peace movement, probably know something about and favor other progressive causes (e.g., campaigns for racial equality and women's rights). Information flows relatively freely among such allies, and they exchange rhetoric, ideologies, tactics, personnel, mailing lists, and other resources. But it is important to realize that connections can exist among claimsmakers who have far less in common. Thus, pro-life demonstrations at abortion clinics use tactics of civil disobedience developed by the civil rights movement. Similarly, in Chapter 9, Gwyneth I. Williams and Rhys H. Williams argue that the fathers' rights movement has borrowed much of its rhetoric about gender equality from the women's movement.

One key connection among campaigns occurs when claimsmakers seek to expand a social problem's domain (Best 1990). Typically, early claimsmaking tends to typify a social problem in the most dramatic terms. For example, early claims about child abuse tended to focus on severe beatings of very young children; these were powerful claims because virtually everyone found these cases troubling. Once the claimsmakers had succeeded in drawing attention to child abuse and instituting new child abuse policies, such as laws requiring physicians to report suspected cases of abuse, they began to expand the problem's domain by arguing that other troubling behaviors also needed to be recognized as abusive. Thus, later claims characterized neglect, psychological abuse, and sexual abuse as forms of child abuse. Such domain expansion has advantages for claimsmakers, who find it easier to raise concern for a new aspect of an already established social problem than it would be to construct a completely new problem. In Chapter 10, Valerie Jenness examines efforts to expand the domain of hate crimes, including both the successful campaign by gay and lesbian claimsmakers to include attacks on homosexuals, and the more recent claimsmaking by women's advocates to add rape and other crimes against women to the category of hate crimes.

In Chapter 11, Karl R. Kunkel describes another sort of connection—what he calls rationale expansion. Here, claimsmakers who find that their rhetoric is not sufficiently persuasive expand the list of reasons or rationales they offer for supporting their claims. Kunkel's example concerns FARM, an animal rights organization dedicated to reducing the suffering of farm animals. This is not a cause with broad appeal; most people feel little concern for the living conditions of the cows, pigs, and chickens being raised for food. As a result, FARM has begun emphasizing additional reasons—unrelated to animal rights—for opposing widespread farming methods. These broader appeals should mobilize more support for the claimsmakers' cause.

REFERENCES

Best, J. 1990. *Threatened Children*. Chicago: University of Chicago Press.
McAdam, D. 1983. "Tactical Innovation and the Pace of Insurgency." *American Sociological Review* 48:735–753.
Morris, A. 1984. *The Origins of the Civil Rights Movement*. New York: Free Press.

9

"All We Want Is Equality": Rhetorical Framing in the Fathers' Rights Movement

GWYNETH I. WILLIAMS and RHYS H. WILLIAMS

Since the 1960s, enough changes have taken place in gender relations in American society to almost qualify for the much-heralded status as a "revolution." Debates over gender roles have become public and political. The "women's movement," animated by an ideology of "feminism," has been a crucial player in these changes. As with many large scale-social movements, however, a significant countermovement has developed in response. This "men's movement" has tackled a wide variety of issues; in particular, one segment has had a significant impact on family law.

In the past 15 years, a wave of reforms has washed over family law. Among the most notable changes are statutes that make joint custody of children the preferred option in divorce settlements. One major group promoting joint custody has been the "Fathers' Rights Movement," a collection of organizations dedicated to ending what they view as gender bias in divorce and custody proceedings.

This chapter examines the rhetoric of the Fathers' Rights Movement (FRM). We contend that the FRM uses a particular interpretation of the "liberal feminist" rhetoric (Williams 1993) of *gender neutrality* to construct a "movement frame" (Snow, Rochford, Worden, and Benford 1986) that has the ironic consequence of *privileging* fathers' claims to child custody.

We use the term "frame" to mean a device that "simplifies and condenses the 'world out there' by selectively punctuating and encoding objects, situations, events, experiences, and sequences of actions within one's present or past environment" (Snow and Benford 1992:137). In other words, a "frame" interprets the world for the individual. In addition to interpretation, a "movement frame" (or "collective action frame") provides a group of individuals with both prescriptions for changing a particular social condition and motivations for taking action. It links a social movement to its members and then to the imperfect state of the

191

world. "Master frames" do what collective action frames do, but on a larger scale. They elaborate and articulate certain aspects of the world in a way common to a number of different social movements. Thus movement frames are often derivative of master frames. But one can find these master frames only through hindsight—by finding framing elements used in common by a variety of movements.

The FRM has constructed a collective action frame using elements of the ideological "master frame" of "equal rights" that entered current American political discourse through the civil rights movement of the 1950s and 1960s. This master frame was used by the liberal feminist movement of the 1960s and 1970s. Feminist activists employed the concept of "equal rights" and added the rhetoric of "gender neutrality" to combat sex discrimination in the political, economic, and social arenas. The FRM has adapted an "equal rights/gender-neutral" frame to legitimate its agenda and proposed solutions as well as to combat charges that its goals are patriarchal.

Thus the FRM is a classic "countermovement" (Lo 1982; Mottl 1980). It arose in response to the women's movement and the changes that movement helped bring to American society. Moreover, the FRM has adopted rhetorical frames first used by the women's movement and turned them to what are often antithetical ends. We analyze this framing, place it in the context of the political struggles over family law specifically and gender relations generally, and conclude with considerations on countermovements, rhetoric, and contemporary American political culture.

THE MEN'S MOVEMENT: AN OVERVIEW

The FRM is but one faction of a larger "men's movement." Gross, Smith, and Wallston (1983) maintain that the men's rights movement has its roots in feminism. In the early 1970s, men who sought to break out of traditional male roles and experience personal growth began to form local groups. Informally, these men discussed the problems of males caught between societal expectations and the desire to become more caring, expressive individuals. Some groups included feminist women who supported men's attempts to restructure male/female relationships. These early organizations usually consisted of young, college-educated, heterosexual whites—the same demographics that characterized the women who formed early liberal feminist organizations.

By the late 1970s, the pro-feminist men's movement held national conferences. Simultaneously, however, a different type of men's group was forming at the grass roots level. These organizations had a different agenda and a different constituency than the groups described above. They were composed largely of men who had gone through bitter divorces and custody disputes; they gathered to offer each other support and promote custody reform. Their remedy for men's problems was more straightforwardly political and involved legal change rather than the cultural–psychological focus of the earlier groups. A specific concern with *fathers'* rights dominated their developing agenda. In 1981, the "National Congress for Men" formed in Houston; it was a national organization that local, independent fathers' rights organizations could join.[1]

Like many social movements, the FRM is a coalition of small social movement organizations held together by a few particularly salient symbols and rhetorical frames. Within the movement there are many different understandings of men's primary problems, the best solutions to those problems, and the best strategies—both political and rhetorical—for attaining those goals.

Thus, the movement overall is marked by "frame disputes" (Benford 1993) in its rhetoric. As a matter of analytic convenience, the FRM can be viewed as having both "liberal" and "conservative" wings. A slightly different version of the dominant fathers' rights ideology animates each wing. The differences usually involve matters of emphasis as much as different substantive goals or strategies. We shall examine these differences below. For both wings, though, the symbols of "gender discrimination" and the importance of the father to the child's "best interests" are the primary mobilizing and justificatory symbols. Importantly, these symbols borrow from liberal feminist framing of familial gender roles. Thus, we turn to the "master frame" animating the liberal feminist and Fathers' Rights movements.

THE MASTER FRAME OF EQUAL RIGHTS

Several scholars posit a "cycle of protest" involving social movement activity (see Snow and Benford 1992; Tarrow 1988, 1993). The idea is that certain social structural conditions, including political opportunities, foster the genesis of various social movements and social movement organizations. At the beginning of a cycle, movements launch an innovative "master frame" that offers the diagnosis of current social ills, prescriptions for social change, and motivations for mobilizing movement constituents. Subsequent movement organizations adopt and adapt this innovative master frame (Snow and Benford 1992). Using a recognized and resonant frame to motivate new constituencies can facilitate mobilization, but it can also constrain movements later in the cycle because the frame defines the political and social terrain in particular ways.

Movement frames, and the broader master frames, vary in their elaboration. Some are specified and particularistic, or "restricted" (Snow and Benford 1992). These "restricted" master frames "organize a narrow band of ideas in a tightly interconnected fashion" (Snow and Benford 1992:140). They allow for little deviance in the interpretation of events and offer clear prescriptions for action. An example of a "restricted" master frame is that used by the pro-life/right-to-life movement. "Pro-life" refers almost exclusively to the life of a fetus; abortion is simply defined as murder; the action indicated is to stop all abortions. Groups trying to adapt the "pro-life" frame for other types of action (e.g., opposing capital punishment) have found themselves unsuccessful in mobilizing the same constituencies.

"Elaborated" master frames, however, are more flexible and universal. They use language that is open to interpretation, can be used to address a large variety of social ills, and allows for a variety of collective action. An elaborated frame "allows for numerous aggrieved groups to tap it and elaborate their grievances in terms of its basic problem-solving schema" (Snow and Benford 1992:140). Its flexible language makes it resistant to being made irrelevant by the course of events, and thus can be adopted by differing groups over a period of decades. Particularly for social movements that are coalitions of separate, loosely overlapping organizations, elaborated master frames hold the coalitions together even when there is not complete ideological agreement. In Kertzer's words (1988:69) they can "create solidarity without consensus."

"Equal rights" is such an elaborated master frame. It has the advantages of a favorable emotional response (few Americans would say they disapprove of the concept) and a fair amount of ambiguity in terms of content (e.g., the concept is invoked by both proponents and opponents of affirmative action). It is a frame many movements can use with some effectiveness, even when those movements work at cross-purposes to each other. The general understanding of equal rights in contemporary American rhetoric comes out of the assumptions of political liberalism.

Classical liberalism begins with the premise that social relationships are like "contracts"; that is, they are the products of persons entering into equal, voluntary exchange relationships. A voluntarily chosen "fair deal" is the basis of social justice. Importantly, this notion of justice is "procedural." That is, if persons of formally equal status enter into the contract relationship freely, with full knowledge, then justice has been served. The content of the contract, or the outcome of its terms, is not a matter for collective arbitration. Fairness resides in process and procedure: if those treat all individuals equally, justice is assured.

Rodgers (1987:45–79) illustrates how the concept of "natural rights" has evolved in American political culture since Independence. He notes that interpretations of natural rights by marginalized populations have been a powerful wedge into American political society. That the extensions of the concept have far outstripped the founders' intentions has not made the concept any less useful in the political arena. Particularly since the end of World War II, formerly disenfranchised populations have used the concepts of natural rights or equal rights as potent weapons in the fight against legal discrimination. The paradigmatic example, of course, was the early civil rights movement, when African-Americans in the South, with white Northern allies, fought to dismantle the legal apartheid of Jim Crow. Bus boycotts, lunch counter sit-ins, and similar actions typified a movement that argued for a "color-blind" society where individuals would be judged "for the content of their character rather than the color of their skin" (Martin Luther King, Jr. quoted in Burns 1990; Goldberg 1991). Individuals deserved the freedom to develop themselves fully, based on their own merit and willingness to work, without external coercion.

Importantly, the major rhetorical messages of the civil rights movement equated "freedom" with formal legal opportunity,[2] that is, the movement was committed to the notion that individuals unfettered by laws based on irrelevant personal characteristics (such as skin color) would achieve according to their individual wills and abilities. The outcome of such individual liberty and political equality would be a just society. The national legislative victories credited to the civil rights movement, the Civil Rights and Voting Rights Acts of 1964 and 1965, were designed to dismantle discriminatory laws and create a level political playing field.

Significantly, over the course of the social movement cycle being considered here, there was an important shift in the concept of "rights." The early movement saw rights as liberties—areas in which the individual was free from government or societal coercion. This was the basis of the argument that ended legal segregation. However, in subsequent phases of the civil rights movement—and movements following it—the conception of rights began to be understood as "claims," a just and equal claim any citizen could make to things available to other citizens. The latter formulation moved beyond the call just to end government-sanctioned discrimination to the demand that government foster conditions of political, economic, and social equality. The idea of "affirmative action" arises from this second notion of rights as legitimate claims on the body politic.

As McAdam (1988) points out, the involvement of white, middle-class young people in the civil rights movement, particularly in the "Freedom Summer" project of 1964, had an important impact on other political and cultural movements that cumulatively became the hallmark of "the Sixties." Motivations, ideologies, and tactics for social change were diffused through a substantial portion of an entire generation, and formed the new movement cycle. An important element in this diffusion was the rhetorical "master frame" of "equal rights." Its application moved from African-Americans to Hispanics, Native Americans, farmworkers, gays and lesbians, the disabled, and many other people who were disproportionately underrepresented in the spheres of public power, including, of course, women.

Indeed the "master frame" of equal rights has become so pervasive—in both its "rights as liberties" and its "rights as claims" forms—that its rhetoric has spread beyond human society (e.g., "animal rights" campaigns by vegetarian and antivivisectionist groups), and to movements whose basic positions advocate the restrictions of individual choice (e.g., the "Right-to-Life" movement). Equal rights has become a master frame for an entire generation—a cycle—of social movements.

LIBERAL FEMINISM AND THE GENDER-NEUTRAL FRAME

Just as the early civil rights movement drew upon liberalism's individualist premises and sponsored a rhetorical frame that emphasized "colorblindness" as a way of achieving a just society, liberal feminism sponsored a "gender-neutral" frame in its early years. The early "women's liberation" movement was the product of the dissatisfactions of white, middle-class, career-oriented women. They had many of the same ambitions as men, in many cases were similarly educated, yet found their careers blocked by job discrimination, pay inequality, and gender stereotypes. The National Organization for Women (NOW), responding to these frustrations, chose to work within establishment channels for change, lobbying legislatures and major institutions. NOW's initial goal was to "bring women into the mainstream of American society . . . in fully equal partnership with men" (Goldberg 1991:200).

Many activists in the early women's movement were women who had been active in the civil rights and student movements and who experienced sexism and second-class status there. According to an early feminist manifesto: "Assumptions of male superiority are as wide-spread and deeply rooted and every much [sic] as crippling to the woman as the assumptions of white superiority are to the Negro" (quoted in Goldberg 1991:203). Thus the early rhetoric of the mainstream women's movement made an easy transition from a "color blind" to a "gender-neutral" frame. Lower legal barriers to participation seemed the best way to ensure an equality of opportunity; women's equal rights would be best served by gender-neutral application of many laws. The women's movement was not striving to turn women into men; rather, they were pushing for a more "androgynous" model of human life where both men and women had domestic responsibilities and equal career opportunities.

Jaggar (1983) emphasizes the extent to which liberal feminism considered gender an "irrelevant" status to the full development of individuals' human potential. The universalism characteristic of liberalism understands human nature as basically uniform and thus influenced by—but not dependent upon—statuses such as race, gender, or culture. The essence of human nature is the capacity for reason. Combined with the goal of individual freedom, this faith in reason had an egalitarian slant, granting individuals the latitude to make their own decisions, uncoerced by social arrangements. Beginning from such individualistic assumptions, liberal feminism valued liberty, equality, and justice, and posited "equality of opportunity" as the surest method of achieving the good society (Jaggar 1983:173–175).

Of course, while the accents on political liberty and procedural equality resonate with classical liberalism, liberal feminism was not a "pure" type, and continues to develop as an ideological position. Jaggar (1983:178) notes that rights are relatively meaningless without the access to resources with which to exercise them. Consequently, liberal feminists make some assumptions of substantive equality, yet recognize that the state must pay some attention to differences to truly produce the famed "level playing field." Thus, issues of daycare and maternity leave have been important to liberal feminism and its proposals for social change.

Reflecting its origins in the assumptions, life-styles, and problems of the white middle-class, liberal feminism has dealt primarily with reform of the public sphere of political and economic opportunities. However, the reasoning behind liberal feminism could be translated into the private sphere of domestic relations. Liberal feminism has expressed "its critique of contemporary sexual norms only in terms of such 'political' concepts of liberty and equality" (Jaggar 1983:179). But that has implications for domestic work and child care. Clearly women are not biologically predisposed to carry this burden. Men's nurturing sides can be developed as easily as women's achievement orientations could be. Feminists have argued, plausibly, that families would be better served by expanding women's opportunities. Not only would children benefit from having a more fulfilled and personally developed woman as a mother, but they would also benefit from having more direct parenting from fathers.[3]

Despite the hopes that gender equality rested primarily on the removal of legal barriers, feminists have admitted that public remedies such as affirmative action are necessary to combat phenomena such as institutional discrimination and the entrenchment of gender stereotypes in social customs. These caused liberal feminists to abandon "their original requirement of 'sex-blindness': the requirement that laws should be written in sex-neutral language and applied without regard to sex" (Jagger 1983:182). Genuine equality of opportunity, feminists now believe, requires the state to take positive, compensatory steps in behalf of women. This is consistent with the expansion of the notion of rights from "liberties" to "claims."

It is this expansion of the equal rights frame beyond gender-neutral individualism that is contested by the FRM. To gain an analytic foothold on the FRM's equal rights frame, we offer a summary of the equal rights frame emerging from liberal feminism. We have drawn on some primary sources, such as Friedan's (1963) classic book, as well as secondary accounts (Burns 1990; Goldberg 1991; Jaggar 1983) for the frame's elements.

Key elements of the "liberal feminist" frame are as follows:

1. *Women are victims* of systematic discrimination and institutional arrangements that disadvantage them.

2. Human happiness and dignity depend on individual self-fulfillment and thus *external constraints on individual choice constitute discrimination*. Individuals should be judged not as members of social groups but as unique persons that have as complete freedom as possible to compete and succeed in the endeavors of their choosing.

3. The *differences between men and women are primarily cultural* rather than biological. While there is a sexual division of labor in reproduction, the "public man" of worldly achievement and the "private woman" of domestic nurturance are cultural constructions, not biological givens. Both men and women can be career-oriented and child care-givers.

4. *Liberating women is in the best interests of everyone*, including children. Task sharing in the household leads to better relationships between children and both parents, and gives children healthier environments and role models.

5. While ideally, civil society should experience a minimum of state

interference into its relationships, it is occasionally *necessary for the state to proactively prohibit discrimination*. That is, along with fostering a legal and political climate free of discriminatory rules, the state must also intercede to stop discrimination within society. Further, the failure to enforce laws without regard to sex is a form of discrimination.

THE FATHERS' RIGHTS MOVEMENT'S FRAMES

The FRM has taken these elements from liberal feminism and, with significant changes, incorporated them into their frame of the joint custody issue. (An exception is Claim 5—although affirmative action is a tenet of liberal feminism, it is rejected by the FRM as a violation of the equal rights/gender-neutral frame.) Claim 1 (with "women" changed to "men") and Claim 2 are embraced by virtually all fathers' rights activists. Claims 3 and 4 are disputed within the FRM, with the "liberal" wing cleaving tightly to them and the "conservative" wing challenging their validity at every turn.

Framing the Issues

Before we discuss the FRM's framing of joint custody, we need to clarify the term itself. Joint custody basically has two meanings: joint legal custody in which the parents' share responsibility for the major decisions in a child's life, and joint physical custody in which the child actually lives with both parents in two different locations. Further, the legal changes in custody law fall into three basic categories: laws making joint custody an option, those making joint custody a preference, and those making joint custody the presumption. Though various individuals and groups who say they support joint custody may be supporting any one of the above variations, fathers' groups overwhelmingly demand from courts and state legislatures a presumption in favor of both joint physical and joint legal custody. In pursuit of presumptive joint custody, father's rights groups have revised the liberal feminist frame. This revision of liberal feminism involves the following claims:

Claim 1: *Men* Are Victims

The central theme in FRM rhetoric is the claim that men are victims of systematic discrimination in family law and the courts. Men are saddled with alimony and child support payments, and there is a maternal preference in custody decisions regarding children. The FRM claims that although the women's movement argues that gender should be largely irrelevant in the domestic division of labor, the courts continue to systematically favor mothers at the expense of fathers' rights.

Thus the FRM argues that a strict gender neutrality in child custody proceedings is necessary for equality between the sexes; it frames maternal preference in child custody as sexist and discriminatory against men. The FRM applies the language of formal political equality to child custody decisions (Coltrane and Hickman 1992). However, this ignores how social conditions continue to disadvantage women in child custody cases (Williams 1990).

Men's groups maintain that sole custody of children after divorce is a denial of equal rights. This is apparent in the names of many Fathers' Rights organizations: Dads Against Discrimination, Texas Fathers for Equal Rights, and Fathers United for Equal Rights in New Jersey. They believe that family law, and custody law in particular, is an area that routinely discriminates against men, depriving men of equal rights at virtually every stage of divorce proceedings. Women usually receive custody, men must pay unfair amounts of child support and alimony, while visitation rights are seldom enforced.

One of the grounds (Best 1987) for this argument is a statistic often cited by FRM activists: that in divorces involving children, the mother receives custody 90% of the time.[4] Men's activists charge that women receive "excessive alimony, with little consideration for the ex-wife's real ability to earn money in today's modern society" (Silver and Silver 1987). Men must pay child support that they often believe is burdensome, and federal legislation has greatly strengthened the enforcement of support orders. However, as activists point out, there is no corresponding legislation that enforces visitation: a man's legal right to see his child is frequently denied by a vengeful wife and nothing is done about it. Laws may exist to protect fathers' rights, but they are not enforced:

> In California, it is a felony to conceal a child with the intent to deprive a person of custody or visitation, but the law is enforced quite selectively. It almost invariably is applied to men who have kidnapped their children from their ex-wives. Rarely is a woman prosecuted for denying visitation rights to the child's father. (Silver and Silver 1981)
>
> Judicial bias prevails . . . despite laws in Virgina and almost every other state that prohibit custody awards on the basis of gender. (Middleman 1993)

Activists argue that family law systematically treats men worse than women: "[t]he findings of the [Texas Gender Bias] task forces uniformly have ignored or glossed over the deep, enduring and universal discrimination against men in our justice system" (Nations 1992). And the most flagrant example of this discrimination is custody. Giving sole custody to the mother, men's groups say, denies the father his equal right to parent.

Claim 2: External Constraints Against Individual Choice Constitute Discrimination

FRM supporters often make their claim of victimhood in specific constitutional terms. For example, the FRM often refers to sole custody as a denial of the constitutional right to due process. Since the 1920s, the U.S. Supreme Court has recognized that parents have a "liberty," guaranteed by the due process clause of the 14th Amendment, to "establish a home and bring up children" (in the language of *Meyer* v. *Nebraska*, 1923) and "to be free from unreasonable state interference in raising their children" (in *Pierce* v. *Society of Sisters*, 1925). Some joint custody advocates point out that if each parent has this fundamental liberty prior to divorce, each should retain it after divorce. And the only way in which both parents can retain their rights is through joint custody. Pushing one parent off to the sidelines with "noncustodial" status means denying that parent the fundamental, "due process" right to rear his or her children (Joint Custody Association 1982).

The FRM has also argued that current custody practices violate fathers' equal protection rights. It is through the application of the 14th Amendment's Equal Protection clause that minorities and women have gained equality in many areas. If judges favor women in custody disputes for no reason other than their gender, then this denies men equal protection of the laws, according to men's rights activists. The chairman of the Constitutional Rights committee of the National Congress of Men has helped individuals file suits in federal courts, alleging the denial of equal protection and due process by state judges (Denman 1985).

Similarly, when FRM activists discuss visitation arrangements, and their violation by mothers, some men argue that there is a First Amendment issue at stake: "Should someone be rewarded for violating our First Amendment right of freedom of association? When that has been court ordered" (Williams 1994)? While this argument is not widespread among movement activists concerned with legal issues, it resonates with the central contention of the FRM—that men, as holders of immutable natural rights, are being discriminated against by the judicial system.

More frequently than not, however, men's rights advocates simply make an ambiguous appeal for "equal rights" rather than spelling out the specific constitutional guarantees they believe have been violated. They perceive a basic unfairness, a general tendency of the legal system to discriminate against men during divorce proceedings by failing to apply laws in a gender-neutral way. In expressing their frustrations, the FRM employs language usually associated with liberal feminism. For example, the following quotations use equal rights as synonymous with "simple gender neutrality." Deviation from such procedural and formal equality is "gender discrimination," or "sexism," and a civil rights issue:

> The plight of American fathers and their children is an example of de facto discrimination. Most divorce laws have had the sexually prejudiced wording removed, but attorneys will tell you that your sex is still the bottom line when seeking child custody. Be female and you'll win 90% of the time. Be male and you'll lose 90% of the time. (Hyde 1984:3)

> In this area [family law], the women have been very successful in affecting laws and court rulings that strongly favor the female in sometimes a sexist and discriminating manner. (Caldwell 1985:5)

> We're out to balance the scale, to get it equal so that fathers can have a fair shake in court. (Liebler 1985:5)

In using this language, FRM activists, to an extent, yoke themselves to the rhetorical framing, and the political legitimacy, of the women's movement. They equate what they want with what many liberal feminists want: a society in which the law treats individuals the same, regardless of sex. Men should be allowed to be custodial parents after a divorce in the same way women are.

Claim 3: Differences between Men and Women Are
Primarily Cultural

Claim 4: Liberating Women Is in the Best Interests
of Everyone

It is here that some fathers' rights advocates part company with liberal feminist rhetoric. In fact it is in presenting a vision of the ideal family that the differences in the rhetoric between the "liberal" and "conservative" wings of the FRM become apparent. The two wings differ most clearly in their descriptions of appropriate gender roles and familial relationships. Claims 3 and 4 of our ideal-typical description of liberal feminism carry serious implications for the organization of the family; the FRM displays a potential schism in this area.

These claims are, of course, closely linked. If one believes that gender roles are a product of nurture and not nature, then liberating women from restrictive social roles is both possible and desirable. Furthermore, such liberation will allow men to escape their own sex-role straightjackets. Conversely, if men's and women's biological differences are the cause of the different social and familial roles played by each sex, then any attempt to change these roles is foolhardy and destined to create problems for all.

The liberal wing of the FRM sympathizes with the liberal feminist ideal of absolute equality with regard to gender. They say they seek to share roles with women and to redefine what it means to be a man or a woman. Many of these men claim to have supported the Equal Rights Amendment and believe that gender does not determine what an individual's capabilities or potential might be. Therefore, they maintain that they have remained true to the original vision of feminism. They continue to want to free men and women from their stereotypical roles and from any type of legal discrimination. But because many feminists do not support joint custody, these men claim that the women's movement has become merely another special interest group, seeking advantages for its members alone:

> I as an individual was doing all that I could possibly do through organization and personally to implement the ERA. But, after November 16, 1983 [the date the U.S. House of Representatives passed the child support enforcement bill] and with the effective steamrolling of the women's/traditionalists' movement on the enforcement of child support, I am no longer in favor of the ERA nor will I do anything to help toward its passage. (Barbier 1984:3)

> Whatever it once may have been in theory, the women's movement today is nothing more than a lobby, single-mindedly promoting the interests of one group at the expense of another, without regard to logic, principle, or justice. . . . Despite its protestations of sexual egalitarianism, when the National Organization of [sic] Women argues against (as it does) efforts to redress the traditional anti-male bias of child-custody settlements, it is not merely working for women, as it will tell you it is; it is also working against men. (Gordon 1985:67–68)

The FRM recognizes, at least implicitly, that the women's movement has changed its fundamental argument from rights as liberties to that of rights as claims; liberal feminism has gone beyond ending legal discrimination to fostering conditions of substantive equality. In the FRM rhetoric, however, this constitutes hypocrisy. The women's movement has betrayed its original principles by abandoning the ideal of gender neutrality. Those who advocate treating the sexes differently, particularly in custody issues, may be termed "female chauvinists"—again, reversing the language of early feminism:

> "Equal rights": This is a euFEMism [writer's neologism] for "WOMEN'S rights." It is used when ever the speaker wants to avoid the fact that the

most sexist entity on the American scene is the entity which claims its mission is anti-sexism. (Hayward 1984:10)

There is a *real* woman's movement that wants equality, equal jobs, equal responsibility. Then there's the extreme feminists that don't want equality, they just want more and more and more. (Williams 1994)

Many feminists do oppose joint custody as a legal presumption; rather, they advocate awarding custody to the parent who has been the primary care-giver within the marriage. But according to the FRM, such a position reinforces the stereotype that women are innately superior nurturers and should not venture outside the home and thus sets the women's movement back. Joint custody, on the other hand, reaffirms the original feminist notion of both sexes being nurturers and breadwinners. To deny a man the opportunity to be a care-giver undermines the basic premises of the women's movement:

[I]t's pure hypocrisy . . . [Feminists] will say that a child should be raised by the primary nurturer. . . . Well, if we *really* believe that, a husband should be able to go to court and get a temporary restraining order to stop his wife from going out and working. Or a woman should not be able to give up custody of her child. . . . In *MS.* magazine they said the reason they were focusing on [joint custody] was that children are an effective bargaining chip in a divorce, and that women should not give up this bargaining chip. To me, that's a terrible thing to say about a mother's relationship to her children. A second reason for opposing joint custody was that it allows a father to "interfere" with the way a mother wants to raise her children, which to me is a really chauvinistic idea. (Hayward 1984)

So some of the anger directed at feminists comes from those men who originally considered themselves sympathetic to the women's movement. Now they see that movement as having betrayed its original goals and lapsed into a "get what's best for women" mentality. This interpretation translates the master frame of equal rights into legal procedures that are gender neutral: if gender is irrelevant to parenting then custody decisions must be made without regard to gender. "Rights" involve the liberty to be free from coercion.

The conservative wing of the FRM uses a rhetoric that basically favors a "return to patriarchy." It is much more virulent in attacking women, especially feminists. These men decry the breakdown of the "traditional" family and clearly distinguishable sex roles. They hold feminists responsible for the destruction of patriarchy and the "emasculation of men." Feminists are wrong not because they have betrayed their ideals, but because their initial ideals were wrong. This faction of the FRM's anger goes beyond the issue of child custody to the entire range of

male/female interactions. They often have little good to say about feminism at all, irrespective of the women's movement call for equality.

> The feminist assault on the family has wide-reaching effects on children
> that most Americans probably never think to tie in with feminism. . . .
> [T]hose who've made careers of denouncing poverty as the cause of the
> nations' crime wave could do society a tremendous favor by turning their
> accusatory fingers instead at the family-destroying feminists whose cru-
> sade most of them so faithfully support. (Freedman 1985:38–39)

> [Feminists] are often would-be castrators with a knee-jerk, obsessive aver-
> sion to anything male. . . . [The women's lib philosophy] distorts the true
> perspective of male/female relationships and upsets the laws of nature
> with undesirable consequences. The incidence-of-divorce curve follows
> the-sexual-liberation-of-women curve. (Doyle 1976:118)

Despite these differences, the movement's two wings do have a significant agenda in common. Along with portraying men as the victims of
systemic discrimination, both wings of the FRM argue that joint custody
is important for the "best interests" of the child. While this claim is
important for both wings of the movement, they offer different rationales for making the claim. Again, the liberal branch of the FRM replicates
much of the reasoning used by liberal feminism, that both men and
women can be and should be care-givers to their children. Like liberal
feminists, liberal members of the FRM see the ideal family as one that
excludes traditional gender roles.

The conservative faction premises its call for joint custody on the
cultural tradition of two-parent families. These activists use rhetoric familiar to many "pro-family" positions in contemporary politics—that is,
"men and women are not interchangeable" (Williams 1994) and "the
two-parent family has remained the preferred environment for raising
children" (*Family Matters* 1982). The blurring of gender lines, and the
disintegration of strong males as family leaders, has hurt children and
society:

> The current situation of sole custody is destroying the children of Massa-
> chusetts with evidence of increased violence, lack of financial and emo-
> tional support, abuse, rape, and murder. These destructive influences lead
> to the destruction of the basic family unit as we know it. (Concerned
> Fathers 1985)

> Practically everything that is wrong with the country: crime, drugs, teen-
> age pregnancy, you name it, is a direct result of the Women's Revolution.
> Why? . . . [T]he primary cause for crime is broken families. And the pri-
> mary cause of broken families is the women's movement. (Gregory
> 1994:24)

The liberal perspective on joint custody among FRM organizations claims that the problem with sole custody is that it has not kept pace with current social reality. The maternal preference perhaps made sense when most women were not employed and were the primary care-givers. But with the majority of mothers working outside the home, there is no longer that justification:

> Here's Mom, she will be a nurturer. Dad, he will be a provider. And there will be no blending of these roles in any way. . . . It's a 1930s version of a divorce. . . . [S]ociety has changed quite a bit, and the system has not really caught up with some of these changes. (Kelly 1985)

This argument, using liberal feminism's understanding of human na-ture, attributes nurturing to cultural roles rather than biological destiny. It recognizes the "new" nurturing father and women's expanded oppor-tunities outside the home. It assumes that two-parent families are pref-erable, but primarily because the best interests of the child are served by two nurturing adults:

> Love and caring are non-gender issues. Men have a right and a respon-sibility to be involved in the lives of their children. Men can be loving, nurturing, and caring parents. . . . There is no evidence to substantiate the fact that a female is better able to be a parent than a male. (Lebow 1985)

The idea of "men's rights" and policy positions favoring joint custody holds the two wings together. The rhetorical theme expressing the com-mon ground is the idea of men as victims of discrimination.

In sum, the Fathers' Rights Movement has used, in one form or anoth-er, most of the key elements contained in the feminists' master frame of equal rights and gender. Certainly FRM activists turn arguments gleaned from liberal feminism back on the women's movement with more than a little glee, and often a great deal of anger. And their interpretation of the equal rights frames and the claims of liberal feminism often pays little attention to the intellectual or socio-political context in which they were first made. But the rhetoric of equal rights before the law, and a gender-neutral application of law in order to end systemic discrimination, is a power rhetorical tool in their political arsenal.

RHETORIC AND CLAIMSMAKING IN
SOCIAL MOVEMENTS

The politics surrounding joint custody reform are confusing because they do not fall along standard or easily recognizable fault lines. The issue can be interpreted as both "liberal" and "conservative;" both feminists and men's activists are split over the issue and its ramifications. Further, the rapidity with which joint custody became an issue in state legislatures left politicians without many of their normal guideposts, justifying rationales, or predetermined ideological slots (Williams 1989).

Because normal constituency coalitions have not formed predictably around joint custody, legislators are left without the "cuing" that interest groups and lobbyists usually provide. In the absence of reliable interest group cues, the rhetoric and symbols of the joint custody issue are particularly important. The lack of hard data—gathered by independent sources—on the problems surrounding custody arrangements makes it difficult for any side of the joint custody debate to dominate discussion with statistics. Under these conditions, the "rhetoric of rationality" (Best 1987) justifying policy positions is less common and effective than the "rhetoric of rectitude." The moral high ground becomes the most important turf. Therefore, individualized examples, anecdotes, and emotional symbols dominate many of the claims made in joint custody rhetoric. Legislators' personal experiences with divorce and custody may explain more of the politics of joint custody than standard political divisions (Williams 1989).

Best's (1987) analysis of the rhetoric in claimsmaking divides claims into three parts: "grounds" (the basic statements about what the problem is and illustrations of its severity), "conclusions" (calls for changes in public awareness and policy necessary to deal with the problem), and "warrants" (the statements that justify drawing the conclusions from the grounds).

The FRM's grounds are twofold: the existence of systematic gender discrimination against men in family law and the concern with the best interests of the child after divorce. The FRM's conclusions are basically unified: the establishment of joint custody as a legal presumption. The warrants tying the grounds to the conclusions, as we have demonstrated, can have either a liberal or a conservative cast. We have focused primarily on the ways in which the FRM uses the language of "rights" as a warrant in their claims (see Best 1987:112). However, there is also a warrant connecting sole custody to the breakdown of the "traditional" family and a host of subsequent social problems. The movement has been able to hold its coalition together, we argue, through the strength and salience of "rights" in American political discourse, and the unity in the practical political outcome of policies favoring joint custody.

Claims help to form a social movement even as the movement's claimsmaking helps construct a social problem. Equal rights resonates in the cultural field of American politics and shaped the dominant frame of the early women's movement. Even as feminism has developed and fragmented, the dominant frame of gender-neutral equality continues to "stick" to the movement and its claims. The FRM, by drawing on traditional liberal notions of equal rights, is able to accuse the women's movement of betraying its initial laudable principles. Further, any straying from gender-neutral liberal individualism can be portrayed as a capitulation to "special interests."

THE FATHERS' RIGHTS MOVEMENT AS A COUNTERMOVEMENT

The FRM is a "countermovement" (Lo 1982; Mottl 1980). It arose to undo the changes effected by the women's movement. Countermovements often adopt the strategies of the movements they seek to counter (Burnstein 1991); we demonstrate that they may adopt and adapt the rhetorical frames as well.

Many activists in the FRM see themselves as participating in a countermovement, even if they would not use that term. Often their rhetoric portrays the men as picking up the abandoned mantle of the women's movement and carrying the cause of true gender equality into the future: "This is the civil rights issue of the '80s" (Lebow 1985). At both the first and second annual meetings of the International Education Forum, organized by the Missouri Center for Men's Studies, speakers proclaimed the significance of the gathering by calling it the "Seneca Falls of the Men's Movement" (Williams 1994). By explicitly tying itself to the women's movement, the FRM seeks liberal feminism's political legitimacy, as well as its rhetorical frames.

The chief irony of the adoption of the same master frame used by liberal feminism, of course, is that the FRM uses it not only to oppose political positions many women's groups have taken, but often to attack feminists, and women generally. The language of equal rights is used by the FRM in a limited way, as support for a set of political arrangements that would promote men's interests at the expense of women's. By focusing on custody arrangements, and treating all other institutional statuses and social resources outside of the custody decision itself as irrelevant, the FRM's procedural equality would often give men an advantage in situations where custody is contested.

Many opponents of presumptive joint custody (particularly feminists) believe that men are advantaged under this arrangement because they become part-time primary caregivers of their children, even though they usually are not primary caregivers within intact marriages. Women are much more likely to have interrupted careers and/or taken low-paying jobs to give birth and rear children. Under presumptive joint custody, the caregiving roles within marriage have little standing when determining caregiving status in the postdivorce family. Further, sex discrimination in the marketplace means employed women are less likely to have the disposable income available to provide a middle-class lifestyle for a child. And these employed women are more likely to arouse suspicion as to their fitness as parents than are working fathers (almost a redundancy)—particularly when the decision is in the hands of middle-aged, male judges who are not inclined to assume that they were poor fathers because of their career involvement. Thus, if one considers gender roles and gender discrimination occurring outside the custody case as irrelevant to the decision, and yet uses earning capacity as an important criterion for deciding the best interests of the child, women are systematically disadvantaged.[5] Therefore we see that the rhetoric of the women's movement has been a major ideological weapon of the men's rights countermovement in pursuing policies that may be antithetical to women's interests.

We have analyzed the Father's Rights Movement's ideological frames and demonstrated their roots in the master frame of "equal rights." The master frame has become a *lingua franca* of American political discourse through the efforts of the women's, feminist, and civil rights movements. Thus our research has implications for the study of social movements generally and for understanding the nature of political culture and discourse. Processes of ideological interpretation, adaptation, and cooptation in social movements and countermovements illuminate the paradoxes of moralized political discourse in American culture and reveal the extent to which movements and countermovements are rhetorically linked even when they are politically opposed.

NOTES

1. Recently, yet a third branch of the men's movement has emerged. Known generically as the "mythopoetic" movement (Clatterbaugh 1990), it contains middle-class men, typically professionals, interested in developing the expressive, caring aspects of their personalities and trying to produce a new model of the appropriate male role. In that sense, they are like the early pro-feminist men's groups. However, the mythopoetic movement insists that this can be done by men only in isolation from women. Mythopoetic adherents think men have lost something in contemporary society, and it can be retrieved only by bonding with other men. While it does not have the instrumental, political focus of the FRM, the mythopoetic faction is nonfeminist and, in fact, considers women something of a threat to the development of healthy men.

2. Of course, the black liberation movement was not ideologically unified, as the "black power" debate demonstrated (Burns 1990). Neither were King's major

speeches so flat-footedly "liberal." However, the message American society was able to hear most comfortably was this version of liberal individualism, and thus it came to typify the movement's agenda. Certainly these liberal assumptions are embodied in the civil rights movement's major legal victories.

3.   For two-career families in the middle class and above, one practical solution has been to pass the burden down the class ladder—women with fulfilling careers are able and willing to hire help, usually lower-class women, to meet domestic demands.

4.   This statistic is generally agreed on when referring to *all* divorces. However, the frequency with which mothers receive custody when fathers have also sought custody through litigation is a matter of dispute.

5.   It is also interesting to note that one area in which women are generally advantaged—the maternal preference for custody—is also an area in which "equal rights" claims from aggrieved men have met with rapid political success.

REFERENCES

Barbier, J. A. 1984. *Balance the Scales*. (newsletter) July:3.

Benford, R. D. 1993. "Frame Disputes within the Nuclear Disarmament Movement." *Social Forces* 71:677–701.

Best, J. 1987. "Rhetoric in Claims-Making: Constructing the Missing Children Problem." *Social Problems* 34(2):101–121.

Burns, S. 1990. *Social Movements of the 1960s*. Boston: Twayne Publishers.

Burnstein, P. 1991. "'Reverse Discrimination' Cases in the Federal Courts: Legal Mobilization by a Countermovement." *Sociological Quarterly* 32:511–528.

Caldwell, R. C. 1985. "The Emasculation of Man." *Legal Beagle: A Family Reform Newsletter* April:5.

Clatterbaugh, K. 1990. *Contemporary Perspectives on Masculinity: Men, Women, and Politics in Modern Society*. Boulder, CO: Westview Press.

Coltrane, S., and N. Hickman. 1992. "The Rhetoric of Rights and Needs: Moral Discourse in the Reform of Child Custody and Child Support Laws." *Social Problems* 39:400–420.

"Concerned Fathers" (fathers' rights organization). 1985. Testimony before Massachusetts Senate Judiciary Committee March 7.

Denman, N. 1985. "Justice, Pro Se." *Legal Beagle: A Family Reform Newsletter*. November:19–20.

Doyle, R. F. 1976. *The Rape of the Male*. St. Paul, MN: Poor Richards.

Family Matters (newsletter of Texas Fathers for Equal Rights). 1982. "The Child's Right of Access to Both Parents." November–December.

Freedman, C. H. 1985. *Manhood Redux*. Brooklyn, NY: Samson.

Friedan, B. 1963. *The Feminine Mystique*. New York: W.W. Norton.

Goldberg, R. A. 1991. *Grassroots Resistance*. Belmont, CA: Wadsworth.

Gordon, J. 1985. "What Else Do Women Want?" *Playboy* March:67–68.

Gregory, H. 1994. "Wolfgang's Secret." *The Liberator* (newsletter) Aug:24.

Gross, A. E., R. Smith, and B. S. Wallston. 1983. "The Men's Movement: Personal Versus Political." Pp. 71–81 in *Social Movements of the Sixties and Seventies*, edited by J. Freeman. New York: Longman.

Hayward, F. 1984. "euFEMisms." *Legal Beagle: A Family Reform Newsletter* December:10.

———. 1985. Personal interview, September 9.

Hyde, Kurt. 1984. "Kurt's Column." *Legal Beagle: A Family Reform Newsletter*. June:3.

Jaggar, A. M. 1983. *Feminist Politics and Human Nature*. Totowa, NJ: Rowan and Allanheld.

Joint Custody Association. 1982. "Joint Custody is a Fundamental Right," leaflet, June 11.

Kelly, G. 1985. Personal interview, April 15.

Kertzer, D. I. 1988. *Ritual, Politics, and Power*. New Haven: Yale University Press.

Lebow, A. 1985. Quoted in Steward, D. L. "A Losing Battle." *The Journal Herald* (Dayton, OH) April 2.

———. 1985. Quoted in Anessi, T. "Men: Fathers Have Rights, Too." *Catholic Telegraph* (Cincinnati) April 19.

Liebler, R. 1985. *Legal Beagle: A Family Reform Newsletter* July:5.

Lo, C. Y. H. 1982. "Countermovements and Conservative Movements in the Contemporary U. S." *Annual Review of Sociology* 8:107–134.

McAdam, D. 1988. *Freedom Summer*. New York: Oxford University Press.

Middleman, D. 1993. "Virginia Study Discloses Bias Against Dads." *The Liberator* (newsletter) May:3.

Mottl, T. 1980. "The Analysis of Countermovements." *Social Problems* 27:620–635.

Nations, H. 1992. Remarks delivered before the Texas Gender Bias Task Force, October 15. Reprinted in *The Liberator* May 1993:3.

Rodgers, D. T. 1987. *Contested Truths*. New York: Basic Books.

Seidman, S. 1983. *Liberalism and the Origins of European Social Theory*. Berkeley: University of California Press.

Silver, G. A., and M. L. Silver. 1981. "What's a Father Worth, Beyond Making Money?" *Los Angeles Times* June 17.

———. 1987. "The Second Timers." *Legal Beagle: A Family Reform Newsletter*: 8.

Snow, D. A., and R. D. Benford. 1992. "Master Frames and Cycles of Protest." Pp. 133–155 in *Frontiers in Social Movement Theory*, edited by A. Morris and C. M. Mueller. New Haven: Yale University Press.

Snow, D. A., E. B. Rochford, Jr., S. K. Worden, R. D. Benford. 1986. "Frame Alignment Processes, Micromobilization, and Movement Participation." *American Sociological Review* 51:464–481.

Tarrow, S. 1988. "Old Movements in New Cycles of Protest." *International Social Movement Research* 1:281–304.

———. 1993. "Cycles of Collective Action: Between Moments of Madness and the Repertoire of Contention." *Social Science History* 17(2):281–307.

Williams, G. I. 1989. "The Politics of Joint Custody." Ph.D. dissertation, Princeton University.

————. 1990. "The Politics of Joint Custody: The Father's Rights Movement."
Paper presented to the American Political Science Association, San
Francisco.
————. 1993. "Joint Custody and the Women's Movement." Unpublished
manuscript.
————. 1994. Field notes, Second Annual International Men's Educational Forum, Kansas City, MO, February 9–12.

10

Hate Crimes in the United States: The Transformation of Injured Persons into Victims and the Extension of Victim Status to Multiple Constituencies

VALERIE JENNESS

Consider four events. First, in Raleigh, North Carolina, two white men beat to death a 24-year-old Chinese-American man, Jim Loo, with the butt of a gun and a broken bottle. Afterward, the men explained that they attacked Mr. Loo because they did not like "orientals" (Fernandez 1991). Second, just after midnight on the most sacred Sabbath of the Jewish new year, two teenagers desecrated a synagogue in Brooklyn, New York. The boys spray-painted swastikas on the walls, set fires around the building, and ripped up and burned six Torah scrolls. Jewish tradition considers such desecration equivalent to murder (Fernandez 1991). Third, in Concord, California, a local AIDS activist received repeated telephone threats, including a bomb threat, at his home and at the store where he worked. One caller told the activist "We don't want any faggots in Concord" and that he should leave town "if you care about your friends." To protect his friends and fellow employees, the activist left his job and moved to another community (National Gay and Lesbian Task Force 1991). Fourth, two young women were playing tennis on a university campus in Nebraska when three men attacked them and used the women's clothing to tie them up. Both women were then raped. The women reported that their attackers later bragged to them that they had been stalking them and had similarly attacked other women (Majority Staff of the Senate Judiciary Committee 1992:iii). The examples are endless, but the point remains: activities such as these, as well as many others, are increasingly defined as "hate crimes" in the United States.

Throughout the 1980s and into the 1990s, "hate crimes" emerged to secure a place in the social problems marketplace (Best 1990; Hilgartner and Bosk 1988). In his 1990 State of the Union Message, President Bush acknowledged and addressed the problem: "Everyone of us must confront and condemn racism. Anti-Semitism. Bigotry and hate. Not next week, not tomorrow, but right now" (Bush 1990). This declaration was later underscored by John Conyers, Jr., member of the U.S. House of Representatives: "whether based on sexual orientation, race, religion, or ethnicity, bigotry and the violence it inspires poses a grave threat to the peace and harmony of our communities. The need to alert Americans to this threat is great" (Conyers 1992:xv).

Over the last decade and a half, hate crimes became the subject of highly politicized public debates, mandates that "something must be done," and proposals for reform. Increased public discussion of hate crimes has taken many forms, including editorials in many of the nation's most prestigious papers, official hearings before both houses of Congress, and an increasing number of publications attesting to the urgency and scope of the problem of hate-motivated violence in the United States. Journalists, activists, politicians, educators, law enforcement officials, and, more recently, social scientists have written volumes on the causes, manifestations, consequences, and control of hate crimes (Kelly 1993; Levin and McDevitt 1993). Combined, these activities ensured that select types of conduct—hate crimes—became identifiable as a social problem, one that has transformed private injuries into a public issue that identifies select constituencies as victims.

THEORETICAL CONSIDERATIONS

As in the construction of most social problems, claimsmaking about hate crimes renders victims apparent. We routinely label persons who have been unjustly harmed or damaged by forces beyond their control as victims; we attach the relevant sign to the appropriate (i.e., deserving) referent. In an effort to identify victims of bias- or hate-motivated violence, claimsmakers recently have pointed to Asian-Americans and other members of racial minorities harmed by racially motivated violence, Jews harmed by anti-Semitism, gays and lesbians harmed by homophobic violence, and women harmed simply because they are female. These types, or categories, of people have come to epitomize victims of hate-motivated violence.

It is very difficult, if not impossible, to think of a social problem that does not have attendant victims; indeed, Loseke (1993) and Holstein and

Miller (1990) suggest that a social problem is not fully constructed until its victims are made apparent. A social constructionist approach to victimization examines the social processes through which persons become recognizable, known, and understood as "victims." This approach assumes that the meaning of objects—including people—is not inherent, but is conferred upon them as they are interpreted, organized, and represented through social interaction and public policy (Blumer 1969; Holstein and Miller 1989, 1990; Loseke 1993). Accordingly, social constructionists study the definitional processes that result in assigning victim status to some individuals and groups, but not to others. These processes are critical; the label "victim" implies that certain social relations surround the individual, as well as his or her relationship to a larger social problem. Among other things, the "victim" label identifies the individual as an injured person harmed by forces beyond his or her control, dramatizes the person's essential innocence, renders her or him worthy of others' concern and assistance, and makes it easier to label the implicated social condition(s) as a social problem (Holstein and Miller 1990).

Constructionists view social problems as projections of collective sentiments rather than simple mirrors of objective conditions (Best 1989; Holstein and Miller 1989, 1990; Mauss 1975; Miller and Holstein 1993; J. Schneider 1985; Spector and Kitsuse 1977). Therefore, understanding victimization requires that we focus less on objective harm(s) and more on the categorization processes that bestow victim status upon select groups and individuals at particular points in time (cf, Collins 1989). Loseke (1993:207) argues that "there are 'putative people' as well as 'putative conditions;'" accordingly, assigning victim status to particular individuals depends upon situated evaluations of conditions and people. It is only through a process of recognition, identification, and labeling that select people get social recognition as victims. This approach to understanding victimization "departs radically from conventional formulations of the victimization process, for it allows us to reconceptualize victimization in terms of interactional and discourse practices. In particular, it directs our attention to the interpretive and descriptive work through which assignments of victim status are made" (Holstein and Miller 1990:104).

This chapter examines one element of the construction of hate crimes as a social problem: the process whereby select constituencies are defined as victims. Specifically, it asks: why has bias-motivated violence and its attendant categories of victimization only recently come to the fore as an identifiable social problem in the United States? Related, who gets categorized as a legitimate victim of hate-motivated violence and why have some (minority) constituencies been conceived as victims of hate crimes while others have not?[1] Addressing these questions points to two interrelated social processes, one wherein "social problems-in-the-making" can be seen as "social conditions-in-need of-victims," and one through which victim status can be extended to innumerable constituencies overtime.

ANALYSIS

In the following sections, I identify some of the actors and social processes that have contributed to the construction of hate crimes as a social problem in the United States. Specifically, I demonstrate how the concept of hate-motivated violence has been extended first to racial, ethnic, and religious constituencies, then to sexual minorities, and most recently to girls and women. I begin by describing how various watchdog organizations and their attendant claimsmakers have brought new attention to old forms of violence by documenting incidents of violence and pointing to the law as a source of remedy. Then, I describe the law as an institution with considerable "defining power," one that has used public policy to bestow victim status upon select individuals and groups and not others. Finally, to underscore how the designation of victims is a matter of collective definition and "domain expansion" (Best 1990),[2] I examine contemporary efforts to define violence against women as a hate crime. This "case in point" makes clear that the definitional processes, much more so than objective conditions, are the key to understanding the construction of both social problems and their attendant victims.

The Emergence of Watchdog Organizations: "New" Attention to "Old" Violence

What is now commonly called "bias-" or "hate-motivated violence" is not a new phenomena; rather, it is a theme throughout American history (Bensinger 1992; Bullard 1988; Herek 1992; Lutz 1987; Sheffield 1987, 1992). In *Racial and Religious Violence in America: A Chronology,* Newton and Newton (1991:ix) document "a time line of atrocity, acts of mayhem, murder, and intimidation perpetrated on the grounds of racial or religious prejudice, from the discovery of North America to modern times." They conclude that "bloodshed based on race or creed is interwoven with the fabric of our culture from the first arrival of explorers to the present day . . . our modern spate of ethnic mayhem is by no means new, unprecedented, or unique" (Newton and Newton 1991:ix). Similarly, *Gay American History* (Katz 1976), a book that covers a period of over 400 years, documents a history of violence directed at individuals because of their sexual orientation, identity, or (same sex) behavior. Historically, violence directed at gays and lesbians, as well as people of color, often represented official state policies and was committed by officials as well as private citizens (Katz 1976; Newton and Newton 1991). Finally, feminist historians, activists, and scholars have documented literally thousands of acts of violence against women (Caputi 1992; Radford and Russell 1992). This violence, which includes everything from rape to wife burning to genital mutilation, spans history and is not bound by culture or region (Radford and Russell 1992; Sheffield 1987, 1992). In short, violence directed at individuals because of their real or imagined social characteristics and group membership has a long history.

What is new, however, is the proliferation of organizations whose *raison d'être* is to monitor and publicize specific types of conduct as "bias-" or "hate-motivated" violence and to attach attributions of psychological and physical harm to them. At the national, regional, state, and local levels, various watchdog organizations have played a key role in documenting instances of bias-motivated violence, identifying and publicizing harm associated with such violence, submitting proposals for reform, and calling on the law to intervene on behalf of affected constituencies. In the process, these groups have collectively redefined historically familiar conduct and constructed new portraits of victimization. While there are many of these organizations, brief descriptions of five of the larger, more established, and pivotal antiviolence organizations reveal how these organizations engage in activism that both "discovers" hate-motivated violence and promotes the interests of select constituencies by demanding changes in public policy, especially law.

The most established antiviolence organization in the United States, the Anti-Defamation League of B'nai B'rith (ADL), was founded in 1969. While concerned with many types of bias crimes, its primary focus is anti-Semitic violence. Since 1979 the ADL has tracked anti-Semitic violence and published an annual "Audit of Anti-Semitic Incidents." Based on data reported to ADL regional offices around the nation, these reports describe various "acts of harassment, threat and assault against individuals, their property and their institutions" (Anti-Defamation League 1990:1). Moreover, these reports consistently reveal a substantial increase in anti-Semitic vandalism and violence from year to year (Anti-Defamation League 1988). In addition to the "Audit of Anti-Semitic Incidents," the ADL produces and disseminates other publications on bias-motivated violence. For example, in 1982 it released the first edition of *Hate Groups in America* (Center for Democratic Renewal 1992). In response to the findings documented in these publications, the ADL's counteraction program seeks to increase media exposure, establish and sustain education programs, demand more effective law enforcement, and actively support new legislation designed to combat anti-Semitic and racist violence. In 1981 the ADLs Legal Affairs Department drafted a model hate *crimes* bill to be introduced in state legislatures (see next section); implicit in this legislation are new definitions of the activity and conduct that (now) fall under the rubric of hate crimes. Like other lesser known organizations, including many civil rights groups, the ADL's work continually underscores the victim status of those harmed by violence *because of* their race and/or religion. In effect, they have created a new type of crime (i.e., hate crimes) and attendant victims (i.e., of racial bias).

Like the ADL, the National Institute Against Prejudice & Violence (NIAPV) in Baltimore, Maryland has focused on what they term "ethnoviolence": violent acts motivated by racial, religious, or ethnic prejudice, including physical assaults, verbal harassment, attacks on people's homes, and vandalism (Ephross, Barnes, Ehrlich, Sandnes, and Weiss 1986). A letter to NIAPV members states:

> While other organizations deal with select aspects of prejudice and violence, the Institute is unique in its comprehensive approach. We act as a clearinghouse of information on reported incidents of intergroup conflict; study the effects of victimization; track the quantity and quality of news media activity; publish reports and educational materials; provide training, education, and consultation within communities; and work with law makers advising on appropriate state and federal legislative remedies.

Since its founding in 1984, the NIAPV has published over 15 public documents, including *Striking Back at Bigotry: Remedies Under Federal and State Law for Violence Motivated by Racial, Religious, or Ethnic Prejudice* (National Institute Against Prejudice and Violence 1991). This report inventories the criminal and civil remedies available under federal and state law for violence motivated by racial, religious, and ethnic hatred. The report's goal is to enable attorneys and their clients to arrive at the most effective combination of legal remedies to fully vindicate the "victim's" rights by informing aggrieved persons and their attorneys of avenues of recourse against offenders of bias crime. An NIAPV membership letter declares: "central to all of our work is our own motivation to help people break free of the norms of denial and the culture of silence that has characterized intergroup relations in the United States through its history."

Founded in 1979, the Center for Democratic Renewal (CDR), formerly known as the National Anti-Klan Network, is an Atlanta-based antiracist organization with offices in Kansas City and Seattle. According to their bimonthly newsletter, the CDR is "leading the fight against bigoted violence and hate group activity in America today. The CDR is a multi-racial, multi-ethnic, interfaith, non-profit organization dedicated to promoting constructive, non-violent responses to hate violence and the white supremacist movement" (*The Monitor* 1991:23). Like the ADL and the NIAPV, the CDR acts as a national clearinghouse for efforts to counter hate group activity and bigoted violence through public education, community response, leadership training, and research. The CDR has been primarily concerned with monitoring and addressing antiracist violence associated with the Ku Klux Klan (KKK). In addition to tracking the organization and activities of the KKK, the CDR collects data on bias-motivated violence and seeks legal redress in light of previously documented and publicized reports of bias-motivated violence. Although the CDR's original focus was on racist violence, over the years it has developed a much broader agenda. Like the ADL and the NIAPV, the CDR's purview currently includes violence motivated by bigotry and directed at homosexuals. By broadening their agenda over the years, these organizations have expanded the domain of victim status to include gays and lesbians.

As a nonprofit foundation supported by private donations, the Southern Poverty Law Center (SPLC) in Montgomery, Alabama was founded in 1971. The SPLC's Klanwatch Project was established in 1980 to address racist violence through litigation, education, and monitoring. The SPLC's Klanwatch Project continues to operate as a private intelligence agency; it collects data on the KKK and other white supremacist groups and sustains one of the most complete lists of hate groups and hate leaders in the United States (Klanwatch 1989), compiles perpetration and victimization data based on police and news sources, and pursues legal redress by bringing lawsuits against members of the Klan's Invisible Empire in Alabama, Texas, North Carolina, and Georgia. While the Klanwatch Project primarily focuses on racist violence, it nonetheless acknowledges the importance of devoting attention to antigay and lesbian violence. Indeed, the Klanwatch Project uses the term "hate violence" to refer to "crimes committed by whites against minorities, Jews, and gays where there is evidence of bias motivation" (Klanwatch 1989:28).

Finally, the National Gay and Lesbian Task Force (NGLTF) was founded in Washington, D.C. in 1973 to promote the interests of gays and lesbians in the United States. A civil rights organization representing gays and lesbians, the NGLTF has over 17,000 members and houses various projects, including the privacy/civil rights project, the lesbian and gay families project, the campus organizing project, and the anti-violence project. Established in 1982, the NGLTF's Anti-Violence Project

focuses on promoting appropriate officials' responses to antigay violence, improving the criminal justice system's treatment of lesbians and
gay men, and assisting local communities in organizing against prejudice and violence. Using a combination of incident reports and survey
research, the NGLTF's Anti-Violence Project has collected data since
1984. These data are reported in annual publications like *Anti-
Gay/Lesbian Violence, Victimization, and Defamation in 1990* (National Gay
and Lesbian Task Force 1987, 1991). Consistent with the epidemic of
violence that is revealed in these reports, the NGLTF seeks legal reform
on behalf of gays and lesbians across the United States.

The efforts of the ADL, the NIAPV, the CDR, the SPLC, the NGLTF,
and many other civil rights organizations across the United States have
resulted in unprecedented attention devoted to violence motivated by
bigotry in this country. These organizations, as well as many state and
local organizations sharing similar tactics and goals, have generated
local, state, and national attention. They have done so by documenting
and monitoring bias-motivated violence, providing information to attorneys committed to prosecuting perpetrators of bias-motivated violence,
producing reports for the general public, sponsoring public education
campaigns, and developing model hate crime statutes. Combined, these
activities point to multiple and multiplying types of violence motivated
by hate or bias, while also defining them as criminal conduct. Not surprisingly then, these organizations disseminate claims that point to the
law as a source of intervention in what has historically been an invisible,
unnamed, and unpunished form of violence with heretofore unrecognized victims.

Changes in the Legal Arena: Transforming
Bias-Motivated Incidents into Hate Crimes
and Injured Persons into Victims

The 1980s and 1990s saw the introduction and institutionalization of
legislation that criminalized violence and intimidation motivated by bigotry. Sponsored by groups such as the ones described above, the proliferation of hate crime legislation made select forms of bias-motivated
violence visibly distinct from other forms of violent crime. In effect,
these laws generated a new category of violent personal crime in the
United States, as well as new categories of victims associated with violent crime. This occurred at both the federal and state levels.

As early as 1983, the U.S. Civil Rights Commission recommended that
the federal government develop a reporting system to produce an accurate and comprehensive portrait of "criminal activity that is clearly based

on racial and/or religious motivation" (Anti-Defamation League 1988:3). However, it was not until April 1990 that President Bush signed into law the Hate Crimes Statistics Act at a public ceremony. The Act specified:

> the Attorney General shall acquire data, for the calendar year 1990 and each of the succeeding 4 calendar years, about crimes that manifest evidence of prejudice based on race, religion, sexual orientation, or ethnicity, including where appropriate the crimes of murder, non-negligent manslaughter; forcible rape; aggravated assault, simple assault, intimidation; arson; and destruction, damage or vandalism of property. . . . The Attorney General shall publish an annual summary of the data acquired under this section. (U.S. Congress 1990)

The Hate Crimes Statistic Act of 1990 was supported by "The Coalition on Hate Crimes," comprised of civil rights, religious, peace, gay and lesbian, and ethnic groups, as well as a diverse array of professional organizations and civil rights groups, including: the American Psychological Association, the American Civil Liberties Union, the American Jewish Congress, People for the American Way, the National Organization of Black Law Enforcement Executives, the U.S. Civil Rights Commission, the Police Executives Research Forum, the Criminal Justice Statistics Administration, and the International Association of Police Chiefs (Anti-Defamation League 1991; Fernandez 1991). By the time it passed both houses of Congress, the Act had gained bipartisan support from 62 co-sponsors in the U.S. Senate.

The Hate Crimes Statistics Act of 1990 is a data collection law; it merely requires the Attorney General to gather and make available to the public data on bias-motivated crime. It does not, in any way, stipulate new penalties for bias-motivated crimes, nor does it provide legal recourse for victims of bias-motivated crime. The rationale for the Hate Crimes Statistics Act was to provide a legally mandated mechanism through which the empirical data necessary to develop effective policy could be gathered. Those supporting the Act argued that involving police in identifying and counting hate crimes could help law enforcement officials measure trends, fashion effective responses, design prevention strategies, and develop sensitivity to the particular needs of victims of hate crimes (Fernandez 1991). When the first report required by the Hate Crimes Statistics Act was released in January 1993, FBI Director William S. Sessions noted: "While these initial data are limited, they nonetheless give us our first assessment of the nature of crimes motivated by bias in our society" (U.S. Department of Justice 1993:1). For most of those supporting the Hate Crimes Statistics Act of 1990, however, the ultimate goal is not precise reporting, but the eventual development of a meaningful governmental response to hate crimes.

The Hate Crimes Statistics Act, as well as the 1993 report resulting from its passage, constitutes the federal government's most visible effort to recognize and define hate crimes. It brings national attention to the problem of hate crimes, underscores the need for official response, and creates a new category of crime to be counted as part of larger efforts to keep track of crime in the United States. And "the Hate Crimes Statistics Act is groundbreaking because it requires the federal government to collect specific data on hate crimes and because it recognizes violence against gays and lesbians as a hate crime" (Fernandez 1991:264). After the Hate Crimes Statistics bill was introduced in 1985 and before it was passed in 1990, the "sexual orientation" clause was added to its list of provisions. This addition did not go uncontested, instead it "prompted an assault on the bill by conservatives in the House and Senate" (Fernandez 1991:272). Opposition to the inclusion of the "sexual orientation" provision was based on the grounds that including "sexual orientation" along with "race," "religion," and "ethnicity" would make the data collection effort too broad and expensive, provide gays and lesbians with special rights that are undeserved, and render violence against gays and lesbians equivalent to violence against racial, ethnic, and religious minorities.

Representative William Dannemeyer (R—California), for example, objected to the inclusion of crimes motivated by prejudice on the basis of sexual orientation on the grounds that the bill "will adopt as a matter of public policy sexual orientation on a par with what we have traditionally brought within the protected classes of the 1964 Civil Rights Act, namely, race, religion, and ethnicity" (quoted in Fernandez 1991:281) and this, in turn, would "change the basic definition of the 1964 Civil Rights Act to include a new status that would have the dignity of being within the proscription [sic] of that Act" (quoted in Fernandez 1991:276). Senator Jesse Helms (R—North Carolina) also opposed including sexual orientation in the Act; he claimed that Congress was being "hoodwinked" into passing the "flagship of the homosexual and lesbian legislative agenda" (quoted in Congressional Quarterly Weekly 1990:530). In the end, the status of gays and lesbians as "victims" of hate crimes was contested to a greater degree than was the status of racial, ethnic, and religious minorities, but ultimately it was recognized. Yet, once race, religion, and ethnicity were established as legitimate grounds upon which to speak about bias-motivated violence, the stage was effectively set for discussions of sexual orientation. And, in the end, the domain was expanded to include violence against gays and lesbians as a new category of hate crime.

Several states preceded the federal government in acknowledging and addressing the problem of bias violence. Although federal civil rights statutes historically have protected a limited range of activities from racial, ethnic, and religious bias, federal legislation has not been used to respond to bias-motivated violence (Fernandez 1991; Mazur-Hart 1982; Padgett 1984). As a result, in the early 1980s, states began to enact legislation criminalizing all sorts of bias-motivated violence. Since then, many state officials have taken measures to define, monitor, and control bias-motivated violence through "hate crime legislation." With the exception of Utah, every state in the United States has adopted a criminal or civil statute that addresses the problem.

However, states have yet to reach consensus on how to best use the law to address bias-motivated violence; they have adopted a variety of approaches (Jenness and Grattet 1993; National Institute Against Prejudice and Violence 1991). Most often, state officials rely on laws that are already on the books to legitimate "enhanced penalties" if prosecutors can prove that a crime was motivated by hatred or bias. For example, under Oregon, New York, Vermont, and Wisconsin law, prosecutors can prosecute perpetrators of bias-motivated violence under existing criminal statutes, such as those prohibiting vandalism, trespass, and assault. In these cases, prosecutors can seek a higher penalty for a criminal who "intentionally selects" his or her victim because of their race, religion, sexual orientation, etc. (Savage 1992). By 1992, over half the states had passed "penalty enhancement" laws, which call for longer prison terms for crimes motivated by bigotry (Jenness and Grattet 1993).

In addition to "penalty enhancement" laws, many states have relied upon the ADL's model legislation to shape their legislative efforts. The ADL's model legislation contains two component parts: the first, the Institutional Vandalism Statute, prohibits an individual from vandalizing, defacing, or damaging places of worship, cemeteries, schools, or community centers; and the second, the Intimidation Statute, provides for enhanced penalties for crimes when they are committed because of the victim's actual or perceived race, color, religion, sexual orientation, or national origin. As of 1990, 21 states had adopted statutes based on or similar to the ADL's model legislation (Anti-Defamation League 1991). In Illinois, for example, the "Freedom From Violence and Enjoyment of Legal Rights Act" took effect on January 1, 1991. According to the Act:

A person commits hate crime when, by reason of the race, color, creed, religion, ancestry, sexual orientation, physical or mental disability, or national origin of another individual or group of individuals, he commits assault, battery, aggravated assault, misdemeanor theft, criminal trespass to residence, misdemeanor criminal damage to property, criminal trespass to vehicle, criminal trespass to real property or mob action as these crimes are defined in the criminal code. (Illinois Revised Statutes 1992)

The Act further gives victims of hate crimes the right to pursue civil lawsuits regardless of criminal prosecution. In essence, the ADL's model legislation has provided an institutionalized definition of hate crimes, one available for activists and watchdog organizations to use in efforts to promote legal redress.

Although the ADL's model legislation fosters some consistency in legal reform, state legislation varies immensely. States continue to run the gamut from broad to scant coverage by offering expansive or (comparatively) restrictive definitions of what counts as a bias crime and who counts as a victim of hate (Jenness and Grattet 1993). Some states, such as California and Iowa, have adopted comprehensive statutes designed to protect the civil rights of a range of constituencies. In contrast, states such as Delaware and Hawaii have adopted more limited legislation by prohibiting only one among many forms of bias-motivated violence (i.e., Institutional Vandalism/Desecration or Defacement of Religious Objects or Property), and by legally protecting only select minority groups. At present, there are no less than 16 general types of hate crimes legislation found in the United States, including specific civil rights statutes, specific intimidation/harassment statutes, enhanced penalties, protection for sexual orientation, data collection, law enforcement training, institutional vandalism/desecration or defacement of religious objects or property, interference with/disturbance of religious worship, cross (or other religious symbol) burning, wearing of masks/hoods/disguises, secret societies, paramilitary training, harassment through publications/advertisements/group libel, parental liability, and victim compensation (Jenness and Grattet 1993; *The Monitor* 1991; National Institute Against Prejudice and Violence 1991). Despite substantive differences, all this legislation shares an underlying rationale: the presumption that harassment, assault, and property destruction assume a particularly dangerous and socially disruptive character when motivated by bigotry (Anti-Defamation League 1988, 1991; Mazur-Hart 1982; Padgett 1984).

Although brief, this overview of legislative responses to the problem of hate-motivated violence demonstrates that the law has played a major role in defining hate crimes as a social problem. Indeed, it is only through the adoption of legislation that hate crimes became a meaningful term and the victimization associated with the problem of hate crimes was rendered apparent and clearly defined. In large part because of the claimsmaking activities undertaken by groups like the ones described in the previous section, laws emerged to delineate hate crimes from other forms of bias-motivated violence, as well as other forms of criminal and noncriminal activity that could be seen as inhumane, deviant, and/or malicious (cf, Mullins 1993). Hate crime legislation demarcates specific forms of bias-motivated intimidation and assault as hate crimes, thereby creating new categories of violent crime and new categories of crime victims. In the process of codifying legal remedies designed to address the control of bias-motivated violence, the law—a highly visible form of public policy—has articulated what will and will not "count" as a hate crime, and by extension who does and does not qualify as a victim of hate crime.

The volume of hate crimes legislation adopted throughout the United States since Maryland passed the first data collection law in 1980, coupled with the immense substantive variation in the statutes, ensures that what constitutes a hate crime and who qualifies as a victim of a hate crime varies by jurisdiction and remains open to political contest. Most states have passed laws that recognize race, ethnicity, and religion as protected statuses, while fewer than 15 states have adopted provisions for sexual orientation and only 10 states have passed legislation that recognizes gender as a source of bias-motivated conduct (Jenness and Grattet 1993; The National Institute Against Prejudice and Violence 1991). More recently, the rhetoric of bias crime victimization has expanded to include discussions of personal appearance/physical appearance, age, mental and physical handicap, and political affiliation. This type of legislative activity points to a trend: more and more constituencies are being defined as (potential) victims of bias-motivated violence.

Since the law formally defines what is a crime, as changes in society produce changes in the law, new crimes necessarily emerge (Hagan 1980; Hollinger and Lanza-Kaduce 1988; Rafter 1992). Thus, who officially constitutes a victim remains an open-ended question; and contests over victim status continue to unfold. Nowhere is this more apparent that in current efforts to define violence against women as a hate crime and survivors of sexual assault as victims of bias-motivated violence.

An Ongoing "Descriptive Contest": Transforming Violence Against Women into a Hate Crime

Over the last 25 years, feminist scholars and activists drew attention to the scope and consequences of violence against girls and women (Caputi 1992; E. Schneider 1992). Wife assault and domestic violence, rape, prostitution, sexual harassment, and other forms of violence against women increasingly became recognized as a social problem. In a review article, Caputi (1992:340) observes that "one of the most significant achievements of the Women's Liberation Movement has been the naming of sexual violence as a systematic form of patriarchal oppression." Feminists have documented cases of violence against girls and women, drawn attention to the range of violence against women and girls, developed crisis intervention and assistance programs, founded and sustained shelters and networks of "safe homes," established and maintained telephone hotlines, sponsored public education campaigns and public protests, challenged law enforcement practices that fail to effectively assist injured women, and drafted new legislation to protect women from violence (Caputi 1992; E. Schneider 1992). Taken together, this activity has ensured that battery, rape, sexual harassment, forced prostitution, and other forms of violence are no longer seen as simply personal injuries to be addressed within the private sphere of the family and home (Caufield and Wonders 1993; Wolfe 1991). Instead, such conduct is now recognized as the social problem of institutionalized "violence against women."

For over two decades, feminist activism around violence against women has focused on the law. Feminist antiviolence campaigns treat the law as part of the problem, as well as a venue through which the problem of violence against women can be addressed (Caufield and Wonders 1993; Rhode 1992; Smart 1989). There have been many efforts to change the legal system to develop policies that recognize and ultimately reduce violence against women (Bock and James 1992; Call, Nice, and Talarico 1991; Frug 1992; Rhode 1992; West 1991). Lawsuits, legal advocacy work, and changes in statutes have improved police and court practices. Given this, activists, advocates, and scholars continue to formulate new legal approaches to respond to violence against women (MacKinnon 1993; E. Schneider 1992; Smart 1989).

However, the movement to recognize hate crimes as a social problem generally has not recognized gender as a source of bias-motivated crime; that is, girls and women have not been seen as victims of bias violence because of their gender. Only 10 states have adopted hate crimes statutes with gender provisions, and the ADL's model legislation does not include a provision for gender. Nor does the Hate Crimes Statistics Act of 1990 include a provision for gender. This is not surprising given that key women's rights groups, such as the National Organization for Women (NOW) and the National Coalition Against Domestic Violence (NCADV) were not a part of the Coalition on Hate Crimes (Sheffield 1992), thus there was no direct and sustained pressure to include gender in the Act. The Coalition on Hate Crimes did contemplate including gender as a protected status in the Hate Crimes Statistics Act, but eventually decided against it for a variety of reasons: some members of the Coalition believed that the inclusion of gender would delay, if not completely impede, the (timely) passage of the Act; some members of the Coalition argued that the inclusion of gender in the Act would open the door for age, disability, position in a labor dispute, party affiliation, and/or membership in the armed forces provisions; some believed that including gender would make the enactment of the Hate Crimes Statistics Act too cumbersome—if not entirely impossible—since violent crimes against women are so pervasive, while others argued that not all acts of violence against women fit the definition of a hate crime; and some members of the Coalition argued that expanding the categories of officially recognized hate crimes to include gender would not improve current efforts to collect official data on rape and domestic violence.

The failure to include gender in the Hate Crimes Statistics of 1990 has not gone unrecognized. For example, Sheffield (1992:395–396) recently observed:

> This law [the Hate Crimes Statistics Act], noteworthy in that it represents a far-ranging consensus about the need to address hate-violence in America, and historic in that it recognizes that violence against gay and lesbian people is a crime of hatred and bigotry, is seriously flawed by its omission of sexual violence. Counting hate crimes against women would reveal that 52 percent of the population is in serious jeopardy. The exclusion of sex-hate as a form of hate-violence is not only a profound denial of the most pervasive form of violence in the United States but an attempt to deny the reality of patriarchal/sexist oppression and its interaction with other structures of power and privilege such as race, class, and sexuality. It is an attempt to have it both ways: that is, to rage against such hate-violence when the victims are males (and occasionally females) and yet to protect male superiority over women. The denial of sexual violence as a hate crime is purposeful for the status quo, for it would be detrimental to the social order to define men's violence against women as a serious, hateful crime.

Such analyses have led to proposals for new legislation that includes violence against women within the concept of "hate crime." At a more abstract level, such proposals initiate a process wherein a set of claims that provides new candidates for victimization (i.e., women and girls) is put forth for public consideration.

The recently proposed Violence Against Women Act of 1994 (VAWA), which requires 2.3 billion dollars in federal funding, recognizes, defines, and tries to combat violence against women. The VAWA is organized around numerous categories of concern: "Safe Streets for Women," "Safe Homes for Women," "Civil Rights for Women," "Safe Campuses for Women," "Equal Rights for Women," and "Violence Against Women Improvements." One of the most debatable provisions in the bill, Title III, would make gender-based assaults a violation of federal civil-rights laws and allow victims of all felonies motivated by an animus against the victim's gender to bring civil rights suits against their assailants. If passed, the bill would, for the first time, "permit women to bring civil rights suits for attacks committed simply *because* of their gender, just like existing law provides civil rights remedies for attacks motivated by racial or religious discrimination" (Majority Staff of the Senate Judiciary Committee 1992:vi, emphasis in the original).

The VAWA rejects the notion that acts of violence against women (e.g., domestic violence, battery, rape, and harassment) merely constitute private injuries to individuals. The general rationale underlying the VAWA is that harassment, intimidation, and assault directed at women assumes a particularly offensive, dangerous, and socially disruptive character when motivated by "animus based on gender." Sponsors of the VAWA assert that there is a "public dimension of harm" (E. Schneider 1992) inherent in violence against women, best characterized as systematic gender discrimination (Majority Staff of the Senate Judiciary Committee 1992; E. Schneider 1992; Wolfe 1992). The public harm includes not only the direct and obvious injury of individual girls and women, but the indirect and often overlooked victimization of an entire class of people who are affected by the bias that motivates acts of violence. As a representative for the Center for Women Policy Studies (CWPS) explained:

> We seek to show that acts of violence based on gender—like acts of violence based on race, ethnicity, national origin, religion, and sexual identity—are not random, isolated crimes against persons who happen to be female. Rather, these are crimes against individuals that are meant to terrorize the larger group or class of people—women. (Wolfe 1991:Preface)

Similarly, *Violence Against Women: A Week in the Life of America*, a report prepared by the chief sponsor of the VAWA and the Majority Staff of the Senate Judiciary Committee at the request of Senator Joseph R. Biden, Jr. (D—Delaware), makes the case for redefining violence against women as a hate crime:

> Title III [of the Violence Against Women Act] seeks to put gender-motivated bias crimes against women on the same footing as other bias crimes. Whether the attack is motivated by racial bias or ethnic bias or gender bias, the results are often the same. The violence not only wounds physically, it degrades and terrorizes, instilling fear and inhibiting the lives of those similarly situated. As Illinois Attorney General Roland Burris testified before the committee: "Until women as a class have the same protection offered others who are the object of irrational, hate-motivated abuse and assault, we as a society should feel humiliated and ashamed." (Majority Staff of the Senate Judiciary Committee 1992:46)

This definition of victimization is not confined to legislative hearings and policy position papers. It also has caught the attention of the national press, including: the *New York Times* (1993a, 1993b, 1994; Terry 1993), the *New Republic* (1992, 1993a, 1993b), *U.S. News and World Report* (Leo 1990, 1993), the *National Review* (Gutmann 1993), the *Wall Street Journal* (1993a, 1993b, 1994), the *Los Angeles Times* (1993, Sengupita 1993), and the *Washington Post* (Hentoff 1993, Young 1994). For example, the *New Republic* (1993a:14) reported:

Title 3, called "Civil Rights for Women" would make sexual violence a violation of federal civil rights law. "This is the beginning, middle and end of the legislation," says Biden. In reclassifying rape, wife-beating, and other gender-based felonies as bias crimes, the provision would write into law the view of rape as a socially embedded institution. "Rape as an expression of male dominance has been tolerated because of our society's sexist attitudes," says Sally Goldfarb of the National Organization for Women's Legal Defense Fund. "One of the advantages of the bill is that it codifies the true nature of rape."

Clearly, the development of the VAWA and public discussions surrounding it represent a step toward placing violence against women in the context of recently institutionalized definitions of bias-motivated hate crimes; it also constitutes evidence of further domain expansion. Like the Hate Crimes Statistics Act of 1990, the VAWA represents the federal government's most visible effort to recognize and define violence against women as a hate crime and victims of rape, battery, and sexual harassment as victims of gender bias. With over 62 bipartisan co-sponsors in the U.S. Congress and an array of feminist organizations supporting it, the VAWA brings public attention to the injuries associated with violence against women, underscores the need for official response, and articulates a new category of violent crime. As a Senator Orrin Hatch (R—Utah) explained, "the purpose of this bill is to let people know what is offensive conduct and inoffensive conduct. The existing criminal laws don't send that message" (quoted in Gutmann 1993:45). Senator Joseph Biden (D—Delaware) concurred when he told the Associated Press (AP) that the point of the Violence Against Women Act is to "raise the consciousness of the American public" (quoted in Gutmann 1993:45).

Whether violence against women will ultimately be redefined in terms of bias-motivated victimization remains an open-ended question. First introduced in Congress in 1990, the VAWA recently passed the U.S. House and faces a vote in the U.S. Senate. While some have predicted that the bill will eventually be written into law (E. Schneider 1992), it has not gone uncontested. Detractors in both Congress and the public arena have begun to express concern about the bill, arguing that individual instances of violence against women are not a form of discrimination. For example, a *U.S. News and World Report* (Leo 1990:25) editorial called "Rape is Not an Act of Bias" reasons:

To bring rape and wife beating under the umbrella of civil-rights protection it is necessary to argue that these are acts of prejudice and discrimination, like denying someone a job on the basis of race or sex. But they clearly aren't. . . . Heterosexual rapists attack women (as opposed to a nondiscriminatory target of 50 percent males and 50 females) because of their sexual orientation, not because they arbitrarily decide to single out just one our two leading genders. And husbands beat wives because they are locked into self-defeating, emotional relationships and try, stupidly, to settle matters or gain dominance with their fists. We are a long way here from the original model of civil-rights legislation. . . . This is a perfect example of the now-reflexive American habit of reducing all social problems to ones of bias.

Similarly, in "Are All Men Rapists? The New Violence Against Women Act is Sexual Politics with a Vengeance," the *National Review* (Gutmann 1993:46) surmises:

Most of the VAWA is mere largesse-strewing—much of it to programs that are not needed and potentially destructive. There's $65 million for "rape education" (what would this look like exactly?) in junior highs; millions more for colleges to "fund rape education and prevention programs. . . ." The point is, the view of rape as systemic is leap-frogging from the feminist fringe into more and more areas of our lives.

Finally, opposition to the VAWA claims that the bill constitutes legalized gender discrimination, rather than a response to institutionalized gender discrimination. According to a *Wall Street Journal* (1994:A13) editorial called "The Sexist Violence Against Women Act":

One little-known section of the crime bill is winding its way through Congress is less about fighting crime than it is about waging gender warfare. . . . The Violence Against Women Act has many appealing provisions [but] also mandates "gender sensitivity" training for judges and, in a key section, extends federal civil rights protections to "crimes motivated by gender." Senator Biden and his supporters claim that the Violence Against Women Act, despite its title, is "gender neutral." Clearly, it is not. It is biased against men, who are the primary victims of violent crime. Compared with women, federal statistics show that men face four times the risk of aggravated assault by strangers, twice the risk of aggravated assault by acquaintances, and three times the risk of homicide. . . . Mainstream and conservative support for the Violence Against Women act stems from a vague desire to be "good" on women's issues as well as an old-fashioned paternalism that finds violence toward women uniquely abhorrent. In part, it is a sincere effort to address real problems. But that goal could be accomplished by straightforward legislation on sex crimes and family violence that does not trivialize assaults on men and boys or give an official seal of approval to a radical ideology that sees American women as victims of systematic gender terrorism.

The debate surrounding the passage of the Violence Against Women Act, and, by extension, the status of persons injured by violence against women, constitutes a "descriptive contest." An array of claimsmak~ including legislators, activists, and journalists, are vying for ownership of the problem of violence against women. At issue is the nature of the injuries and the social relations that surround violence directed at women. Hanging in the balance is whether violence against women will be accepted as a source of injury reflecting systematic gender discrimination, and, by extension, whether it will be accepted as a hate crime.

DISCUSSION

Over the past 15 years, hate crimes have been successfully promoted as a social problem that always results in injury and often results in death. However, whose injuries count as bona fide victimization caused by (systematic) bias depends upon how the injury has been defined in the activist and legal claims that construct hate crimes. As with any social construction, what is included in the victimization implied by "hate crimes" can first and foremost be seen as a outgrowth of the recent interplay between key claimsmakers, the law, and the meanings they engender.

Social problems theorists working within the constructionist framework consistently demonstrate that social problems are products of practical and political activity. The construction of social problems often includes a rhetoric of victimization that shapes public and legal definitions of who is and is not harmed unjustly. As ethnomethodologists assert, the orderly and recognizable features of social life are "talked into being" (Heritage 1984:29) as victims are designated and dramatized. In the case of hate crime, the standing of certain individuals and groups as victims is not merely a reflection of an objective state of affairs. Rather, such standings are products of collective definitions developed by watchdog organizations and then institutionalized in law.

The emergence and proliferation of watchdog organizations, coupled with proposed and enacted legal changes, have ensured that selected individuals and groups have been transformed from injured persons into official victims of bias crime. Collective definitions bestow victim status upon those harmed because of their real or imagined membership in a recognizable social group. Attributions of victim status for those harmed because of their race, religion, or ethnicity have been the most 230institutionalized and the least contested in the United States, while those harmed because of their sexual orientation only recently have been awarded the status of victim. As Comstock recently proclaimed, antigay and lesbian violence has finally "taken its place among such societal concerns as violence against women, children and ethnic and racial groups" (1991:1). At least in part, this is because within lesbian and gay communities across the United States there has been an unprecedented level of organizing against violence over the last decade (Jenness 1995; Jenness and Broad 1994; National Gay and Lesbian Task Force 1987, 1991) and because the definitions of race-, religion-, and ethnicity-based bias crime had already been established in legal discourse. Finally, while violence against women as a social problem has a well-established history in this country and abroad (Caputi 1992; Radford and Russell 1992), it is only since the late 1980s that the victimization associated with such violence has been defined as type of "bias-motivated crime." This represents a new generation of definitions for the victims of violence against women, as well as a new stage in the history of the social construction of hate crimes in the United States.

In the end, the evolution of hate crimes as a social problem, complete with attendant victims, demonstrates how domains can be expanded to include more and more types of people as victims. These "victim assignments" (Holstein and Miller 1990:113) described throughout this chapter are not cast in stone. The configuration of meanings that surround them is an ongoing, sometimes problematic, accomplishment. As such, they will continue to be determined by an ongoing political contest that is necessarily fraught with novelty and change.

NOTES

1. In this chapter, I do not devote analytic attention to assessing the factual characteristics of the injuries associated with hate crimes or the "real" nature of persons defined as victims in the social problem of hate crimes. Moreover, I am not concerned with determining which types of harm *should* or *should not* constitute a hate crime and thus qualify as bias-motivated victimization. These omissions are not meant to deny the psychological and physical harm born of violence; rather, they are intended to remain consistent with the constructionist approach to social problems (Best 1989; Holstein and Miller 1989, 1990; Mauss 1975; Miller and Holstein 1993; J. Schneider 1985; Spector and Kitsuse 1977).

2. Domain expansion occurs when claimsmakers offer new definitions for and thus extend the boundaries of the phenomena being deemed problematic. For example, in his work on threats to children as a social problem, Best (1990) examined the evolving definitions of and typifications for child abuse. He found that "by 1976, the issue encompassed a much broader array of conditions threatening children. The more general term 'child abuse' had replaced the earlier, narrower concept of the 'battered child,' and the even broader expression 'child abuse and neglect' had gained currency among professionals" (Best 1990:67). At the same time, the law expanded the official domain of child abuse by requiring

more categories of professionals to report suspected abuse, while also adopting broader definitions of what constitutes abuse and neglect (Best 1990). Similar analyses have been devoted to other forms of violence, including elder abuse (Baumann 1989; Eastman 1991), wife abuse (Loseke 1989), and violence against gays and lesbians (Jenness 1995). Regardless of the specific issue at hand, domain expansion ultimately involves rendering more and more conduct and/or social conditions "at issue."

REFERENCES

Anti-Defamation League. 1988. *Hate Crimes Statutes: A Response to Anti-Semitism, Vandalism and Violent Bigotry*. New York: The Anti-Defamation League of B'nai B'rith.

―――. 1990. *1989 Audit of Anti-Semitic Incidents*. New York: The Anti-Defamation League of B'nai B'rith.

Anti-Defamation League. 1991. *Hate Crimes Statutes: A Response to Anti-Semitism, Vandalism and Violent Bigotry*. New York: The Anti-Defamation League of B'nai B'rith.

Baumann, E. A. 1989. "Research Rhetoric and the Social Construction of Elder Abuse." Pp. 55–74 in *Images and Issues: Typifying Contemporary Social Problems*, edited by J. Best. Hawthorne, NY: Aldine de Gruyter.

Bensinger, G. 1992. "Hate Crimes: A New/Old Problem." *International Journal of Comparative and Applied Criminal Justice* 16:115–123.

Best, J. (ed.). 1989. *Images and Issues: Typifying Contemporary Social Problems*, edition. Hawthorne, NY: Aldine de Gruyter.

―――. 1990. *Threatened Children: Rhetoric and Concern About Child Victims*. Chicago: University of Chicago Press.

Blumer, H. 1969. *Symbolic Interactionism*. Berkeley, CA: University of California Press.

Bock, G., and S. James. 1992. "Introduction: Contextualizing Equality and Difference." Pp. 1–13 in *Beyond Equality and Difference: Citizenship, Feminist Politics, and Feminist Subjectivity*, edited by G. Bock and S. James. New York: Routledge.

Bullard, S. (ed.). 1988. *The Ku Klux Klan: A History of Racism and Violence*. Montgomery, AL: The Southern Poverty Law Center.

Bush, G. 1990. *New York Times* February 1:D22 [President's State of the Union Message].

Call, J. E., D. Nice, and S. M. Talarico. 1991. "An Analysis of Rape Shield Laws." *Social Science Quarterly* 72:774–788.

Caputi, J. 1992. "To Acknowledge and Heal: 20 Years of Feminist Thought and Activism on Sexual Violence." Pp. 340–352 in *The Knowledge Explosion: Generations of Feminist Scholarship*, edited by C. Kramarae and D. Spender. New York: Teachers College Press.

Caufield, S., and N. Wonders. 1993. "Personal and Political Violence Against

Women and the Role of the State." Pp. 79–100 in *Political Crime in Contemporary America*, edited by K. D. Tunnell. New York: Garland.

Center for Democratic Renewal. 1992. *When Hate Groups Come to Town*. Montgomery, AL: The Black Belt Press.

Collins, P. H. 1989. "The Social Construction of Invisibility: Black Women's Poverty in Social Problems Discourse." *Perspectives on Social Problems* 1:77–93.

Comstock, G. 1991. *Violence Against Lesbians and Gay Men*. New York: Columbia University Press.

Congressional Quarterly Weekly. 1990. "Hate-Crimes Measure Passed by Senate." February 10:529–530.

Conyers, J., Jr. 1992. "Foreword." Pp. xiii–xv in *Hate Crimes: Confronting Violence Against Lesbians and Gay Men*, edited by G. Herek and K. Berrill. Newbury Park, CA: Sage Publications.

Eastman, P. 1991. "Elders Under Siege." Pp. 235–237 in *Social Problems*, edited by J. Stimson, A. Stimson, and V. Parrillo. Itasca, IL: F. E. Peacock.

Ephross, P. H., A. Barnes, H. J. Ehrlich, K. R. Sandnes, and J. C. Weiss. 1986. *The Ethnoviolence Project—Pilot Study* Institute Report No. 1. Baltimore: The National Institute Against Prejudice and Violence.

Fernandez, J. 1991. "Bringing Hate Crimes into Focus." *Harvard Civil Rights-Civil Liberties Law Review* 26:261–292.

Frug, M. J. 1992. *Postmodern Legal Feminism*. London: Routledge.

Gutmann, S. 1993. "Are All Men Rapists? The New Violence Against Women Act Is Sexual Politics with a Vengence." *The National Review* August 23:44–47.

Hagan, J. 1980. "The Legislation of Crime and Delinquency: A Review of Theory, Method, and Research." *Law & Society Review* 14:603–628.

Hentoff, N. 1993. "Beware Stiffer Sentences for Thought Crimes." *Washington Post* June 19:A21.

Herek, G. M. 1992. "The Social Context of Hate Crimes: Notes on Cultural Heterosexism." Pp. 89–104 in *Hate Crimes: Confronting Violence Against Lesbians and Gay Men*, edited by G. Herek and K. Berrill. Newbury Park, CA: Sage.

Heritage, J. 1984. *Garfinkel and Ethnomethodology*. Cambridge: Polity Press.

Hilgartner, S., and C. L. Bosk. 1988. "The Rise and Fall of Social Problems: A Public Arenas Model." *American Journal of Sociology* 94:53–78.

Hollinger, R. C., and L. Lanza-Kaduce. 1988. "The Process of Criminalization: The Case of Computer Crime Laws." *Criminology* 26:101–126.

Holstein, J. A., and G. Miller (eds.). 1989. *Perspectives on Social Problems*. Greenwich, CT: JAI Press.

———. 1990. "Rethinking Victimization: An Interactional Approach to Victimology." *Symbolic Interaction* 13:103–122.

Illinois Revised Statutes. 1991. Ch. 38, pars. 12-7.1, sec. a.

Jenness, V. 1995. "Social Movement Growth, Domain Expansion, and Framing Processes: The Gay/Lesbian Movement and Violence Against Gays and Lesbians as a Social Problem." *Social Problems*: 42:145–170.

Jenness, V., and K. Broad. 1994. "Anti-Violence Activism and the (In)Visibility of Gender in the Gay/Lesbian Movement and the Women's Movement." *Gender and Society* 8:402–423.

Jenness, V., and R. Grattet. 1993. "The Criminalization of Hate: The Social Context of Hate Crimes in the United States." Presented at the annual meeting of the American Sociological Association in Miami, Florida.

Katz, J. 1976. *Gay American History: Lesbians and Gay Men in the U.S.A.* New York: Thomas Y. Crowell.

Kelly, R. J. (ed.). 1993. *Bias Crime: American Law Enforcement and Legal Responses.* Chicago: Office of International Criminal Justice/The University of Illinois.

Klanwatch. 1989. *Hate Violence and White Supremacy: A Decade Review, 1980–1990.* Klanwatch Intelligence Report #47. Montgomery, AL: The Southern Poverty Law Center.

Leo, J. 1990. "Rape Is Not an Act of Bias." *U.S. News and World Report* October 8:25.

———. 1993. "Radical Feminism in the Senate." *U.S. News and World Report* July 29:19.

Levin, J., and J. McDevitt. 1993. *Hate Crimes: The Rising Tide of Bigotry and Bloodshed.* New York: Plenum Press.

Loseke, D. R. 1989. "Creating Clients: Social Problems Work in a Shelter for Battered Women." *Perspectives on Social Problems* 1:173–193.

———. 1993. "Constructing Conditions, People, Morality, and Emotion: Expanding the Agenda of Constructionism." Pp. 207–216 in *Constructionist Controversies,* edited by G. Miller and J. A. Holstein. Hawthorne, NY: Aldine de Gruyter.

Los Angeles Times. 1993. "Mere Talk Won't Make Life Any Safer for Women." August 16:B7.

Lutz, C. 1987. *They Don't All Wear Sheets: A Chronology of Racist and Far Right Violence: 1980–1986.* Atlanta, GA: Center for Democratic Renewal.

MacKinnon, C. A. 1993. *Only Words.* Cambridge, MA: Harvard University Press.

Majority Staff of the Senate Judiciary Committee. 1992. *Violence Against Women: A Week in the Life of America.* Washington, DC: U.S. Senate.

Mauss, A. 1975. *Social Problems as Social Movements.* New York: J. B. Lippincott.

Mazur-Hart. 1982. "Racial and Religious Intimidation: An Analysis of Oregon's 1981 Law." *Willamette Law Review* 18:197–218.

Miller, G., and J. A. Holstein (eds.). 1993. *Constructionist Controversies: Issues in Social Problems Theory.* Hawthorne NY: Aldine de Gruyter.

Monitor. 1991. "Hate Crimes Laws: How Are They Doing?" December (24):15–18.

Mullins, W. C. 1993. "Hate Crime and the Far Right: Unconventional Terrorism." Pp. 121–169 in *Political Crime in Contemporary America,* edited by K. D. Tunnell. New York: Garland.

National Gay and Lesbian Task Force. 1987. *Anti-Gay/Lesbian Violence, Victimization, and Defamation in 1987.* Washington, DC: National Gay and Lesbian Task Force Policy Institute.

———. 1991. *Anti-Gay/Lesbian Violence, Victimization, and Defamation in 1990.* Washington, DC: National Gay and Lesbian Task Force Policy Institute.

National Institute Against Violence and Prejudice. 1991. *Striking Back at Bigotry: Remedies Under Federal and State Law for Violence Motivated by Racial, Religious, or Ethnic Prejudice*. Baltimore, MD.

New Republic. 1992. "Crime and Punishment." October 12:7.

———. 1993a. "Caught in the Act." July 12:13–16.

———. 1993b. "Rape and Denial." November 22:14–15.

New York Times. 1993a. "Florio Signs Anti-Bias Law." June 11:8.

———. 1993b. "Excerpts From Court's Decision to Permit Hate-Crime Penalties." June 12:8.

———. 1994. "A Million Mrs. Bobbits." January 28:A26.

Newton, M., and J. A. Newton. 1991. *Racial and Religious Violence in America: A Chronology*. New York: Garland.

Padgett, G. L. 1984. "Racially-Motivated Violence and Intimidation: Inadequate State Enforcement and Federal Civil Rights Remedies." *Journal of Criminal Law and Criminology* 75:103–138.

Radford, J., and D. E. H. Russell (eds.). 1992. *Femicide: The Politics of Women Killing*. New York: Twayne Publishers.

Rafter, N. H. 1992. "The Social Construction of Crime and Crime Control." *Journal of Research in Crime and Delinquency* 27:377–389.

Rhode, D. L. 1992. "The Politics of Paradigms: Gender Difference and Gender Disadvantage." Pp. 149–192 in *Beyond Equality and Difference: Citizenship, Feminist Politics, and Feminist Subjectivity*, edited by G. Bock and S. James. New York: Routledge.

Savage, D. 1992. "Shaky Future for Statutes on Hate Crimes." *Los Angeles Times* (December 8):C1.

Schneider, E. M. 1992. "Particularity and Generality: Challenges of Feminist Theory and Practice in Work on Woman-Abuse." *New York University Law Review* 67:520–568.

Schneider, J. 1985. "Social Problems Theory: The Constructionist View." *Annual Review of Sociology* 11:209–229.

Sengupita, S. 1993. "Hate Crimes Hit Record High in 1992." *Los Angeles Times* March 23:B1, B8.

Sheffield, C. J. 1987. "Sexual Terrorism." Pp. 3–19 in *Women: A Feminist Perspective*, edited by J. Freeman. Palo Alto, CA: Sage.

———. 1992. "Hate Violence." Pp. 388–397 in *Race, Class, and Gender in the United States*, edited by P. Rothenberg. New York: St. Martin's Press.

Smart, C. 1989. *Feminism and the Power of Law*. New York: Routledge.

Spector, M., and J. Kitsuse. 1977. *Constructing Social Problems* Menlo Park, CA: Cummings.

Terry, D. 1993. "In Crackdown on Bias: A New Tool." *New York Times* June 12:8.

U.S. Congress. 1990. H. R. 1048. 101st Congress, 1st session.

U.S. Department of Justice. 1993. *Report on Hate Crimes in the United States*. Washington, DC: Federal Bureau of Investigation.

Wall Street Journal. 1993a. "Congressional Democrats." January 15:A1.

———. 1993b. "High Court Ruling Expected to Increase Hate-Crime Sentences in More States." June 14:B5.

————. 1994. "The Sexist Violence Against Women Act." March 23:A13.

West, R. L. 1991. "The Difference in Women's Hedonic Lives: A Phenome-nological Critique of Feminist Legal Theory." Pp. 115–167 in *At the Boundaries of the Law: Feminism and Legal Theory*, edited by M. A. Fineman and N. S. Thomadsen. New York: Routledge.

Wolfe, L. R. 1991. *Violence Against Women as Bias-Motivated Crime: Defining the Issues*. Washington, DC: Center for Women Policy Studies.

Young, C. 1994. "Gender Poisoning." *Washington Post* January 16:C5.

11

Down on the Farm: Rationale Expansion in the Construction of Factory Farming as a Social Problem

KARL R. KUNKEL

Formed in 1981, the Farm Animal Reform Movement (FARM) claims that modern, rational, intensive farming techniques, referred to as "factory farming," are cruel to animals raised for human consumption. FARM began as a grass roots organization and today has over 10,000 names on its national mailing list. FARM spokespeople say that 60% of those on the mailing list make financial contributions; the group's 1993 annual operating budget was nearly $102,000. FARM's ultimate goal is to eliminate the use of cows, pigs, and chickens as food for humans, but its short-term objective is to end factory farming because this would stop suffering for billions of animals. Throughout the 1980s, FARM experienced trouble generating mass public sympathy for the plight of farm animals. In response, the group expanded the domain of the factory farming problem beyond animal suffering to include threats to human health and the environment. This "rationale expansion" seeks to improve the chances of achieving FARM's short-term objective: eliminating mass animal suffering by abolishing factory farming as method of animal agriculture.

Rationale expansion is one way claimsmakers can increase support for a desired outcome. Thus, FARM hopes to ally those who care about farm animal suffering with those who may not be concerned with the treatment of these animals but are interested in the quality of their own health or the environment. A larger coalition of factory farm opponents has a greater chance of stopping factory farming. But realizing FARM's ultimate objective—ending the suffering of cows, pigs, and chickens—may depend on expanding the issue's domain to include threats to humans.

239

DOMAIN EXPANSION IN THE CONSTRUCTION
OF SOCIAL PROBLEMS

Domain expansion is a process whereby established social problems form the basis for related claimsmaking to construct new problems. Best (1990) noticed that once physical child abuse gained acceptance as a social problem, claimants began to reconstruct the problem, making new claims about related forms of abuse. Typically, claimsmakers attempted to extend the boundary or domain of child abuse to cover additional situations. Thus, neglect, sexual abuse, and emotional abuse became recognized as forms of child abuse; later claims included child-snatching by estranged parents, illicit drug use, inadequate social services, explicit rock lyrics, and even traditional sex-role socialization as additional forms of child abuse. "These new claims can be linked to the established problem: claimsmakers present new, peripheral issues as 'another form of,' 'essentially the same as,' 'the moral equivalent of,' or 'equally damaging as' the original, core problem" (Best 1990:80).

Jenness (1995) discusses gay and lesbian activists' domain expansion of the category of hate crimes to include attacks on homosexuals. Claimsmakers argued that violent crimes against gays resembled attacks on members of religious and ethnic minorities, in that the violence was motivated by hate or bias. Once violent attacks against gays became established as a form of hate crime, activists sought to expand the domain further, claiming that other activities, such as verbal harassment of gays, domestic violence in gay intimate relationships, and the multiple discrimination suffered by African-American or Jewish gays, were also forms of sexual terrorism, because they too involved a predator–prey relationship. Each expanded claim inspired new policies (i.e., hot lines and educational strategies) to deal with these additional problems.

Best (1990) presents a natural history for domain expansion. The first stage involves initial claimsmaking, attempts to attract public attention, and then persuade both the public and policymakers to define some condition as a problem needing solution. Often, these claims are dramatic in order to capture the desired attention (Orcutt and Turner 1993). New claimants are at a disadvantage compared to those who already have public attention, and it helps if the new claim fits a standard frame (Snow and Benford 1988, 1992; Gamson, Croteau, Hoynes, and Sasson 1992) already used in the classification of social problems.

The second stage is validation of the problem by others, especially those viewed as experts in a given area. Nelson (1984) referred to "valence issues" as those accepted, validated, and established on the policymaking agenda. The third and final stage in this natural history of social problems involves domain expansion, where established valence issues become the foundation for additional claims, both by those already involved with the issue and by new "outside" claimsmakers. Insiders seek to expand the problem to gain additional resources and recognition, while outsiders strive to place what they see as salient issues on the public agenda. "Piggybacking new claims upon established social problems increases the chances that the new claims will receive validation" (Best 1990:82). Domain expansion has not received much attention from scholars examining rhetoric in social problems construction. The theoretical propositions put forth by Best and Jenness concerning domain expansion need to be examined in light of claims made by other groups about other issues. FARM offers one such case.

The form of domain expansion found in FARM's rhetoric differs from those discussed in Best's analysis of the construction of child abuse or Jenness's examination of hate crimes against gays. In those studies, claimsmakers sought to add new phenomena to the domain of established problems. In contrast, FARM's rhetoric remains focused on factory farming as a social problem. What FARM's rhetoric expands is the list of reasons—the rationales—for ending factory farming. Initially, FARM's rhetoric focused on cruelty to farm animals. But this did not attract enough sympathy because many individuals did not accept this rationale, and so FARM expanded its rationales by claiming factory farming also posed threats to both human health and environmental quality. This chapter illustrates rationale expansion as another form of domain expansion in the construction of social problems.

STUDYING ANIMAL RIGHTS

The animal rights issue is just beginning to receive attention from social scientists. A few studies examine animal rights as a broad social movement (Jasper and Nelkin 1992; Sperling 1988; Tester 1991; Sutherland and Nash 1994; Finsen and Finsen 1994). Wenzel (1991) looks at the movement's economic and cultural implications for indigenous peoples. Jasper and Poulsen (1993) examine reasons for success or failure in animal rights groups' attempts to change policy on the use of animals in scientific research. A few scholars address the implications of animal rights activities and thought for feminism and ecofeminism (Adams 1990; Donovan 1990; George 1994). Even though the *Social Science Index* (SSI) lists nearly 200 articles published since 1986 dealing with animal rights, most are opinion statements found in natural science periodicals discussing either the virtues or downfalls of the movement or how practitioners in a given field (i.e., medical or veterinary research, psychology) or industry (i.e., agriculture, medicine) can deal with animal rights advocates. Overall, SSI identifies very few sociological attempts to analyze the animal rights issue and controversy. Furthermore, *Sociological Abstracts* cites just 47 such articles since 1974. Again, most are not empirical sociological examinations of the movement and its activities but philosophical or political discussions of movement implications.

Given the political nature of the animal rights movement and the surrounding controversy, this movement is ripe for constructionist analyses of rhetoric. Various interest groups, both in favor of and opposed to the use of animals for human concerns, attempt to convince the public and policymakers that their ideology should form the basis for public policy. With the exception of recent work by Jasper and Poulsen (1993) on social movement success and failure, Phillips' (1994) analysis of the construction of biography among workers in an animal research laboratory, and Maurer's (1995) content analysis of vegetarian rhetoric, constructionists have ignored animal rights issues as a source of data for studies of social problems rhetoric.

To examine domain expansion by animal rights groups, I chose to study FARM rhetoric. As a social issue, factory farming is particularly interesting because the claimsmakers seek to change a dominant cultural pattern in United States society—the ideological preponderance toward meat consumption (Rifkin 1992). During "Decade of the Animals," a 1992 conference organized to commemorate the tenth anniversary of the animal rights movement in the United States, Alex Hershaft, founder and president of FARM, claimed farm animal suffering accounts for 95% of animal suffering in the world. He stated that eight billion animals a year are "tortured and murdered" on farms.

Data for this study were derived from a content analysis of rhetoric as presented in FARM newsletters and other mailings collected from June 1990 through August 1994, and in books advocated by FARM as articulations of their position and arguments on factory farming. These books include John Robbins (1987), *Diet for A New America*, Jim Mason and Peter Singer (1990), *Animal Factories*, Peter Singer (1975), *Animal Liberation*, and C. David Coats (1989), *Old MacDonald's Factory Farm*. In addition, I was a nonparticipant observer at two animal rights conferences in June 1990 and November 1991, in which numerous speakers and seminars provided insights on FARM's rhetoric and strategy in advancing the rights of farm animals.

THE PUTATIVE CONDITION: MODERN INTENSIVE FARMING

The Industrial Revolution brought an emphasis on efficiency and profit maximization, in which the objective is to produce while consuming the least amount of resources, minimizing all costs, and yielding the most profit. FARM and other animal rights activists speak of modern agriculture in industrial terms, calling the method used in contemporary meat production "factory farming" (Singer 1975; Mason and Singer 1990; Rifkin 1992; Coats 1989). Johnson (1991) claims that the shift from labor-intensive to capital-intensive farming developed over the past 200 years. This trend accelerated after 1920, when adequate transportation methods fostered processing and selling meat products. Over the past 70 years, farming in the United States changed significantly. Today, as in most corporate strategy, efficiency and profit are central objectives in farming.

FARM's rhetoric, along with that of other factory-farming critics, depicts modern factory farms as raising the most animals in the least amount of space while consuming minimal resources. Large numbers of animals are kept in controlled-environment warehouses with automatic waste-removal systems. These animals are mechanically fed and have little contact with humans.The slaughter process is also mechanized. Coats (1989) states that almost 90% of the 80 million hogs slaughtered annually in the United States are raised on factory farms. Another 100 million beef cows are slaughtered every year in the United States through mass-production techniques.

> Western countries, since World War II, now want more traditionally expensive meats and easily prepared processed foods. . . . The belief that high meat consumption is an essential ingredient of "the good life" has encouraged farmers and agribusinessmen to raise more, while still keeping it affordable to millions enjoying the prosperity of the postwar period . . . the increased demand over the last forty years has been met by the development of a new style of farming; the mechanized, concentrated mass production of food animals in the factory farm. (Coats 1989:19)

The modern intensive factory farm is the status quo in contemporary United States food production. To use Spector and Kitsuse's (1977:76) terminology, this form of animal agriculture constitutes a "putative condition." FARM, along with other animal rights groups, claims that this mode of production creates cruel circumstances for farm animals and is thus a problem in need of solution and change.

FARM RHETORIC, CLAIMSMAKING, AND RATIONALE EXPANSION

The animal rights movement in the United States formed in the early 1980s. Peter Singer's (1975) book, *Animal Liberation*, provided a philosophical framework for rethinking treatment of animals (Jasper and Nelkin 1992; Finsen and Finsen 1994). The response generated by this book led to the 1981 "Action for Life" conference, credited by Alex Hershaft, founder of FARM, as the occasion when the United States grass roots animal rights movement organized. According to Hershaft, FARM, People for the Ethical Treatment of Animals (PETA), and other animal rights groups, formed with participants from this conference.

The primary concern of FARM—and the reason it formed—is the alleged animal suffering on the factory farm that was vividly described in Singer's book. Singer advocated vegetarianism, not because it was good for health or the environment, but because it was the morally correct choice. His book made no mention of personal health benefits or saving the larger physical environment. His rhetoric claims vegetarianism is the best way to get humans off the backs of animals and end the pain, suffering, and murder of these thinking, feeling creatures.

FARM's Original Rhetoric: Cruelty to Farm Animals

> Animals raised for food account for 95% of the six billion warm-blooded, feeling animals that are abused and killed in the U.S. each year. That works out to 75 animals annually for the average family. For most farm animals, slaughter brings welcome relief from the unceasing agony of crowding, deprivation, manhandling, and mutilation that governs life on today's factory farms. Veal calves are torn from their mothers immediately upon birth, chained by the neck, without bedding, in wood crates that encase their bodies, and fed a liquid diet deficient in iron and fiber for 14–16 weeks. Breeding sows are forced to give birth and to nurse their piglets under similar conditions. (*FARM REPORT* 1992:3)

FARM originated as an animal rights group. The organization's primary concern is ending what they see as pain, suffering, and murder of animals that are raised for food. Slogans appearing on bumper stickers, t-shirts, and posters distributed by FARM promote this position: "Meat is Murder," "I Don't Eat My Friends," "Farm Animals Never Have a Nice Day," "Farm Animals are Live *Not* Stock," and "Breakfast of Cruelty" (bacon and eggs). The organization recommends people read the descriptions of factory farm conditions in books by Singer (1975), Robbins (1987), Mason and Singer (1990), and Coats (1989). These books provide dismal and vivid descriptions of conditions under which cows, pigs, and chickens live on the modern factory farm. For example, this rhetoric claims veal calves are chained in crates that prevent movement because any form of exercise toughens and develops muscles, making the meat less tender. These animals allegedly are kept in the dark and fed a milk-based solution containing antibiotics to prevent disease, which is common under these conditions. Producers prevent the ingestion of any iron because of adverse effects on the meat product.

Pigs, according to FARM rhetoric, live in small cages with concrete floors for easy waste removal. Their lives are spent in environmentally regulated warehouses; the animals are not allowed to see sunlight or graze in fields. Critics of this farming method claim sows are viewed solely as pork producing machines, forced to copulate with boars, and after giving birth are tethered on their sides so that piglets can nurse anytime. As soon as possible, these young pigs are taken from their mothers and placed in cages of their own. Layer hens allegedly are kept three to a cage, unable to spread their wings and forced to always stand on wire cage floors. According to FARM rhetoric, broiler chickens are housed in regulated warehouses that may contain hundreds of thousands of birds. Their beaks are burned off soon after hatching so that they will not peck each other to death in this chaotic living condition. All animals are fed large amounts of growth-enhancing drugs for quicker and larger development as well as huge doses of antibiotics to prevent disease in these overcrowded conditions.

Factory farming and the treatment of animals in these environments are focal points of FARM claimsmakers. Various demonstrations sponsored by FARM and performed by its members and sympathizers have occurred since the group's inception in 1981. In 1985, FARM picketed the United States Department of Agriculture (USDA), protesting factory farming. This protest march was led by "Bobby," a veal calf "rescued" by FARM members and housed at a FARM sanctuary. Since 1982, FARM has held a veal ban campaign with "Veal Ban Action" held every year on Mother's Day. These actions include "informational" advertising in mass media, picketing restaurants serving veal, and advocating legislation that prohibits techniques used in veal raising. Hershaft once fasted for 24 hours in a veal crate in front of the White House to bring attention to the plight of these animals.

FARM engages in acts of civil disobedience such as impeding truck entrances to slaughterhouses (in 1989, Hershaft sat in the way of a livestock truck holding a sign that read "STOP THE AGONY"), obstructing the path of livestock trucks at auction yards, blocking the entrance to the USDA headquarters, and occupying the office of the Secretary of Agriculture. All of these events featured signs with various slogans and were designed to bring media attention to animal suffering on factory farms. FARM advocates legislation, such as the proposed Veal Protection Act in 1991 and laws currently proposed to ban transporting "downed" or injured livestock to auctions and slaughterhouses, and encourages consumers to choose to consume less, and preferably no, animal-food products. Becoming a vegetarian provides the best attack on factory farms because diminishing demand for meat will mean there is no profit in mass production.

Since 1985, FARM sponsors an annual "Great American Meatout" on the first day of spring. FARM members are encouraged to persuade friends, neighbors, and others to sign a pledge that they will not eat meat on that day and spend the time exploring a meat-free diet. In recent years the Meatout was recognized with over 1000 events in all 50 states, many featuring celebrities and lawmakers. Vegan dinners and demonstrations, such as groups picketing fast food restaurants, are common. In 1994 FARM had 42 regional coordinators throughout North America helping to organize these events.

Another annual FARM event, which began in 1983, is "World Farm Animals Day," scheduled for October 2, Gandhi's birthday. FARM claims that a number of public officials proclaim October 2 to be "World Farm Animals Day" in their communities.

> The purpose is to memorialize the suffering and death of billions of inno-
> cent, sentient animals in factory farms and slaughterhouses. Observances
> are held in 100 U.S. cities, as well as Canada and several European coun-
> tries. They include funeral processions, memorial services, exhibits, vigils,
> picketing, and increasingly, civil disobedience. ("A Decade of Progress for
> Farm Animals" n.d.:2)

In its mailings, newsletters, and other rhetoric, FARM's original and primary concern is cruelty to farm animals. However, despite these activities and campaigns, the movement has not received enough support to implement policy changes. Maurer (1995) categorized vegetarian claims using Ibarra and Kitsuse's (1993) notion of claims of entitlement and endangerment. In vegetarian rhetoric, some claims involve entitlement where nonhuman animals are presumed to have a right to equal consideration and treatment as human animals. FARM's rhetoric also focuses on entitlement: farm animals do not deserve the cruel treatment experienced under modern farming conditions. But Maurer convincingly argues that, in United States culture, claims of entitlement do not offer solid reasons to change dietary behavior. She suggests that claims of endangerment—arguments that meat is a threat to health—offer a more concrete basis for change and action. Endangerment claims imply that behavioral changes in diet can bring a longer, higher quality life. Merely arguing that modern farming techniques are cruel and deprive pigs, chickens, and cows of inherent rights does not generate enough support to launch full-scale boycotts of animal-food products or enough pressure for legislators to regulate conditions on farms. Even when people are sympathetic to issues of animal welfare and rights, it is easier to mobilize concern and action for mistreatment and welfare of dogs, cats, monkeys, even rabbits, in scientific research or the testing of cosmetics, than it is to generate sympathy for cows, pigs, and chickens. These animals typically are thought of as food in our culture, reflecting deep-seeded cultural and personal dietary habits. Because claims that the treatment of animals on modern farms constitutes a social problem attract little support, groups such as FARM search for other arguments that might get the attention of consumers and policymakers. Simply asking people to feel sorry for cows, pigs, and chickens will not convince people that the factory farm is a social problem needing remedy.

Expanded FARM Rhetoric: Health Consequences

Nearly 1.5 million Americans are crippled and killed each year by heart failure, stroke, cancer, and other chronic diseases associated with excessive consumption of meat and animal fat. The elements held principally accountable include saturated fat, cholesterol, hormones, pesticides, nitrates. The nutritional value of meat has been greatly exaggerated by the meat industry. Its highly touted protein level ranks alongside that of soybeans, lentils, nuts, and seeds, but it comes heavily laced with saturated fat. Moreover, meat is totally lacking in carbohydrates—the most readily usable source of energy, contains very little calcium needed to build healthy bones, and its vitamin content is spotty at best. (*FARM REPORT* 1992:3)

During the early 1990s, FARM began to advocate and adopt endangerment arguments designed for appeal to individuals' rationality and interest in personal survival. The group started to claim that meat and other animal product consumption causes such fatal or debilitating diseases as heart attacks, strokes, certain cancers, and even osteoporosis. Much of the rhetoric came from John Robbins' (1987) book *Diet for A New America*.

Robbins, heir to the Baskin-Robbins ice cream chain, became an "advisor" to FARM in 1989. As a child he suffered from a form of polio and became interested in ways of regaining health. He studied the link between diet and health and came to believe that moving away from an animal-based diet was central to being both morally and physically healthy. His book contains a section on the relationship between diet and health, as well as cross-cultural comparisons for rates of disease that suggest that countries where consumption of animal-food products is low have lower rates of breast cancer, prostate cancer, colon cancer, heart disease, and strokes than countries where animal product consumption is high. He argues that osteoporosis depends more on the amount of animal protein consumed than a lack of calcium derived from dairy products, that high animal protein intake causes calcium loss through urine, and that the body replenishes lost calcium by taking it out of bones, thereby causing the bones to weaken.

Robbins' book is widely discussed and advocated among FARM members. They refer to and quote from it at their conventions and seminars. FARM uses Robbins to claim that people should stop consuming animal products and switch to a vegetarian-based diet. Clearly his argument neatly fits the group's objective. FARM also points to Dr. Michael Klapper, an anesthesiologist, who is listed as an "advisor" for FARM, to demonstrate the unhealthy nature of an animal-based diet. Klapper attends FARM conferences and conducts seminars on the health consequences of consuming animal-food products, discussing medical phenomena in lay terms. FARM supplies its members with rhetoric and symbols to use in clarifying their claim. The organization sends numerous small "warning" stickers to its members featuring a drawing of a physician with the word "WARNING" written in large red letters; the sticker reads, "The Surgeon General has found that this product is hazardous to your health." Members are encouraged to place these stickers on animal-food products in grocery stores. FARM also distributes a drawing of a steak with various parts labeled "heart failure and stroke," "cancer," "hormones," "antibiotics," "premature sexual development," "vulnerability to infectious diseases," "fat and cholesterol," "kidney failure," "nitrites and benzopyrene," "pesticides and heavy metals," and "excess protein." This image is entitled "Here's the Beef."

Further Expansion of FARM Rhetoric:
Environmental Devastation

> While 800 million people around the world face agonizing starvation, we continue feeding animals the grains and legumes that could save these lives. Production of these foodstuffs uses up 90 percent of our agricultural resources, drastically depletes our vital topsoil and groundwater. . . . Millions of acres of forestland are devastated through conversion to grazing land and cropland to feed farm animals, both in the U.S. and abroad. Runoff from these lands carries suspended and dissolved solids, organic matter, nutrients, and pesticides into our lakes and streams. (*FARM REPORT* 1992:3)

The final section of Robbins' (1987) book deals with the environmental consequences of mass animal production for any society, such as the

United States, that makes meat central to diet. Robbins discusses the large amount of physical space necessary for animal production, arguing that 12 pounds of grain are necessary to produce one pound of beef. Thus, large amounts of acreage are devoted to growing grain to feed these animals. This leads to deforestation, massive use of herbicides and pesticides necessary to grow mass amounts of grain, and depletion of fresh water for irrigation of crops in areas normally too dry to sustain these fields. Numerous environmental perils are claimed.

Massive deforestation allegedly contributes to lower levels of oxygen in the atmosphere, global warming, and changing weather patterns. Dangerous agricultural chemicals contaminate water tables, rivers, and streams. Water that could be used for people in cities is allocated for growing grain in semiarid deserts. Robbins claims that the Ogallala Aquifer, the world's largest underground supply of fresh water located under the middle states in the United States, the richest farming land in the nation, could be dry in less than 30 years. He argues that factory farming is rapidly liquidating this precious resource. In addition, Robbins claims that large factory farms produce an enormous amount of manure; since no modern sewer system exists to deal with these stockpiles, mounds of manure grow month after month, wind blows the residues into dairy products, and nitrates contaminate drinking water. These are just a few of the environmental problems claimed by Robbins. He concludes that drastically lowering demand for animal-food products, and hence the need for factory farming techniques, will reduce these threats to the environment.

Robbin's book, along with Michael W. Fox's (1986) *Agricide*, examines environmental threats caused by the industrialization of American agriculture. FARM sells these books, and its mailings encourage sympathizers to read and use their arguments. In addition to mailed announcements and newsletters, during meetings and seminars, FARM now stresses the environmental threat posed by factory farming as an additional rationale for abolishing factory farming.

DISCUSSION AND ANALYSIS

Since FARM's origin in 1981, its claimsmaking strategy evolved from emphasizing the single issue of animal suffering on factory farms to expanding the rationales for its claims. FARM's early stance reflected Singer's emphasis on cruelty to farm animals; the group sought agricultural reform through ending factory farming and returning to smaller scale operations that allegedly involve more humane living and dying conditions for the animals. Early FARM activities reveal this focus: its vigils, marches, pickets, civil disobedience, and demonstrations all centered around ill treatment of farm animals on the factory farm.

The Limits of Cruelty Rhetoric

Given our long history of carnivorous dietary habits (Rifkin 1992), it is difficult for many people in a meat-consuming culture to feel enough sympathy for the plight and treatment of farm animals to make them take action to change the situation. For such sympathy to be meaningful, demand for animal-food products must decrease; people must reduce significantly the amount of meat, eggs, and dairy products they consume. As Maurer (1995) observes, this action involves a radical change in lifestyle. Because emotional claims of entitlement, centered upon sympathy for the cruel and unreasonable treatment of farm animals, are not effective in changing food choices, other, more rational claims are needed to rally opposition to factory farming. To gain additional support, claims of endangerment, based on personal health and longevity (Maurer 1995), and environmental well-being, became part of FARM's claimsmaking rhetoric. These expanded claims might have broader appeal. FARM needed to increase antifactory farm sentiment and attempted to do so through rational arguments supplementing the emotional and moral issue of cruelty to farm animals. Unlike the domain expansion occurring in the social construction of child abuse (Best 1990) or hate crimes (Jenness 1995) as social problems, the tactic utilized by FARM involves expanding rationales for a particular solution to a claimed problem. Over the past 5 years, at the bottom of its mailings and stationary, FARM has presented a brief mission statement that summarizes both its original rhetoric and the rationale expansion: "To Moderate and Eliminate Animal Suffering and Other Adverse Impacts of Animal Agriculture."

A content analysis of FARM REPORT, a newsletter sent to members and contributors, provides further evidence of this rationale expansion. This newsletter originated in 1989 and is published on an irregular basis. Some years the newsletter appears three times, other years twice, and in 1993 it did not appear at all. Even though FARM REPORT does not appear regularly, it provides some information on FARM-sponsored events both completed and upcoming, as well as updates on legislative activities of interest to those concerned with factory farming or the plight of farm animals. Examples of legislative updates include progress of the Downed Animal Protection Act (S 367, HR 559), the Veal Calf Protection Act (HR 1455), and the Humane Methods of Poultry and

Slaughter Act (HR 649), all dealing with cruelty issues. Similarly, *FARM REPORT* discusses the progress of legislation dealing with health and environmental consequences of factory farming, such as the Bovine Growth Hormone Milk Labeling Act (S 735, HR 1906) and proposed amendments to the Clean Water Act of 1972 that would require control of agricultural runoff and wetland protection. This newsletter can be used as a source for analyzing FARM's rhetoric. Figure 11.1 illustrates the number of column inches in editions of *FARM REPORT* devoted to discussion of three alleged problems resulting from factory farming: cruelty to animals, threats to humans' health, and environmental threats.

Even as late as 1989, FARM's rhetoric remained narrowly focused on issues of cruelty. Threats to human health began receiving some attention in 1990, and environmental threats began receiving coverage in 1992. Personal health and environmental issues receive much more newsletter space, and have become commonplace, major themes in

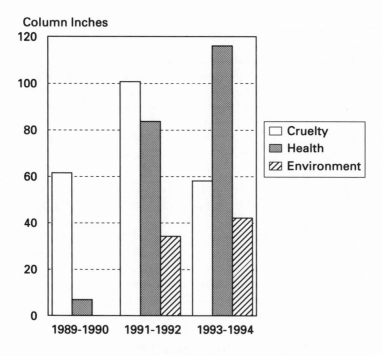

Figure 11.1. Column inches in *FARM REPORT* devoted to cruelty, health, and environmental issues.

FARM REPORT's rhetoric. From 1992 to 1994 entire pages of the newsletter are devoted to health and environmental issues. In 1994, *FARM REPORT* began printing excerpts from scientific studies linking a meat-based diet to human disease. The Spring/Summer 1994 edition printed excerpts from 19 such studies subdivided into the categories "General Diseases," "Cardiovascular Diseases," "Cancer," and "Infectious Diseases." In 1992, "What's Wrong with Meat," first appeared. This statement, found in various FARM mailings and several editions of *FARM REPORT*, briefly describes the animal suffering, human health consequences, and environmental implications of factory farming. In the Fall 1992 issue FARM printed the "Farm Animal Action Pledge," asking its constituents to sign and return the pledge indicating they will devote a certain number of hours per week over the next 12 months to alleviating and ending factory farming practices by becoming involved in one or more activities from a list provided on the pledge sheet. Included are several items related to "educating" the public about animal suffering, threats to human health, and dire environmental consequences of factory farming.

Rationale Expansion in Social Problems Development

The initial studies of domain expansion focused on how claims about new problems built upon established social problems. FARM's rhetoric reveals a different sort of domain expansion—rationale expansion—in which claimsmakers expand their list of reasons for addressing a particular problem. Instead of arguing that their issue was the moral equivalent of some already established problem, FARM remained focused on a particular goal, the abolition of factory farming, but when its initial claims about animal cruelty on factory farms did not achieve the desired results, FARM offered new rationales for eliminating this mode of farming, expanding its rationales to include issues of personal health and environmental destruction.

Thus, even if consumers are not concerned with emotional entitlement claims about living and dying conditions for farm animals, FARM believes they will respond to rational endangerment claims of threats to personal health and the environment. No matter which rationale elicits a response and behavioral change, FARM's objective, the abolition of factory farms, is achieved. The strategy is one of linking people concerned with different issues. In this case, those concerned with farm animal rights, join with others who have either a self-interest in health or a larger concern with the environment, in hopes of mounting a collective effort for a single policy, the eventual elimination the factory farm.

FARM's goal of ending animal suffering will be met if factory farming ends, even if many of those demanding this change care little about animal rights.

This rationale expansion involves an indirect approach to changing social policy not yet documented in the constructionist literature. Rationale expansion is fundamentally different from other domain expansion. Domain expansion occurs when an established problem becomes the foundation for related claims. Claimsmakers argue that the related issue is essentially part of the same problem. Best (1990) provides three reasons claimants attempt to expand the domain of existing problems. First, they delay controversy until there is consensus on part of the issue. Second, media coverage declines as a problem becomes more familiar and new claims keep the issue fresh for media sources. Third, the established problem forms the foundation on which a new claim can build. Furthermore, both claimsmakers already associated with the established problem and new claimants desiring to link their concern to a valence issue can engage in domain expansion. Domain expansion lets both types of claimsmakers obtain additional resources, personnel, or policies dealing with problems, as well as possible professional or personal recognition. In contrast, rationale expansion involves a different theoretical principle: concentrating on a policy solution for a perceived problem and then expanding the reasons or rationales for advocating that policy. In the case of FARM's rhetoric, the objective was alleviating alleged suffering of farm animals on factory farms by ending factory farming. To gain more support for this policy, FARM offered additional reasons for opposing factory farming in its rhetoric, including the health threat of an animal-based diet and the environmental destructiveness of this agricultural practice.

The case study of FARM rhetoric suggests conditions under which rationale expansion may occur. When certain putative conditions are deeply embedded cultural practices, claimsmakers are unlikely to generate widespread agreement that the condition constitutes a problem. Therefore, groups perceiving these practices as problems need to concentrate on anticipated solutions while deriving other, more culturally accepted reasons for favoring the same policy outcome. Rhetoric centered upon a culturally unpopular theme may never be persuasive or successful in problem construction. Rationale expansion thus provides an indirect attempt to solve the original problem. People who accept one of these added rationales, and take action for the cause, become advocates for the policy that solves the original problem. Even though they may not view the original condition as a problem, their activities do contribute indirectly to the solution. Rationale expansion requires that claimsmakers be flexible, willing to make new, indirectly related claims

advocating the same policy outcome. In the case of FARM these conditions are present. Viewing cows, chickens, and pigs as having rights and
being capable of suffering is contrary to dominant cultural dietary cus-
tom. Obviously claims along these lines will not convince enough
people of the need to change their behavior to lead to the end of factory
farming. But FARM found rhetoric calling for the same outcome and
incorporated this rhetoric in an attempt to persuade those convinced by
endangerment concerns to resist embedded dietary habits. This action
implies the same outcome, ending factory farming. Taking action for
these related reasons indirectly ends the suffering of farm animals. This
study of FARM rhetoric reveals an attempt to use other, indirectly related claims to gain backdoor support for an outcome. When striving for
solutions to perceived social problems, outcomes are more important
than the rationales used in claimsmaking.

CONCLUSION

In the case of FARM's rhetoric, rationale expansion cannot yet be
judged as a successful or unsuccessful strategy. The expanded rationales
are relatively new, and it will be several years before FARM's strategy
can be assessed. Will many people convert to a vegetarian lifestyle during the 1990s? If so, what will account for their conversion? Will the
number and size of factory farm operations increase or decline over the
next 10 years? An increase will imply more demand, or at least a steady
demand, for animal-food products, while a decrease will indicate less
demand for these products. In addition, passage or rejection of laws
regulating factory farm techniques also will indicate the strategy's
success.

Rationale expansion, a newly recognized form of linking problems,
can provide an analytical tool for examining other claimsmaking. Other
studies of this process will not only present more examples and possibly
additional forms of this phenomenon, but they may either reaffirm or
revise our understanding of the conditions under which rationale expansion occurs. More importantly, additional case studies may evaluate
the effectiveness of rationale expansion as a claimsmaking strategy. Examining campaigns that attempt to link various problems, either through
domain or rationale expansion, provides fertile ground for theory building as scholars seek better understanding of the construction of social
problems.

ACKNOWLEDGMENTS

Partial support for this research came from a National Endowment for the Humanities Summer Seminar for College Teachers. The author thanks John Harms for comments on an earlier draft.

REFERENCES

"A Decade of Progress for Farm Animals." n.d. Promotional brochure published by the Farm Animal Reform Movement: Washington, D.C.

Adams, C. J. 1990. *The Sexual Politics of Meat: A Feminist-Vegetarian Critical Theory*. New York: Continuum.

Best, J. 1990. *Threatened Children: Rhetoric and Concern about Child-Victims*. Chicago: University of Chicago Press.

Coats, C. D. 1989. *Old MacDonald's Factory Farm*. New York: Continuum.

Donovan, J. 1990. "Animal Rights and Feminist Theory." *Signs* 15:350–375.

FARM REPORT. 1992. "What's Wrong with Meat." Winter:3.

Finsen, L., and S. Finsen. 1994. *The Animal Rights Movement in America: From Compassion to Respect*. New York: Twayne

Fox, M. W. 1986. *Agricide: The Hidden Crisis that Affects Us All*. New York: Schoken Books.

Gamson, W. A., D. Croteau, W. Hoynes, and T. Sasson. 1992. "Media Images and the Social Construction of Reality." *Annual Review of Sociology* 18:373–393.

George, K. P. 1994. "Should Feminists Be Vegetarians?" *Signs* 19:405–434.

Ibarra, P. R., and J. I. Kitsuse. 1993. "Vernacular Constituents of Moral Discourse: An Interactionist Proposal for the Study of Social Problems." Pp. 21–54 in *Constructionist Controversies: Issues in Social Problems Theory*, edited by G. Miller and J. A. Holstein. Hawthorne, NY: Aldine de Gruyter.

Jasper, J. M., and D. Nelkin. 1992. *The Animal Rights Crusade: The Growth of a Moral Protest*. New York: The Free Press.

Jasper, J. M., and J. Poulsen. 1993. "Fighting Back: Vulnerabilities, Blunders, and Countermobilization by the Targets of Three Animal Rights Campaigns." *Sociological Forum* 8:639–657.

Jenness, V. 1995. "Social Movement Growth, Domain Expansion, and Framing Processes: The Gay/Lesbian Movement and Violence Against Gays and Lesbians as a Social Problem." *Social Problems* 42:145–170.

Johnson, A. 1991. *Factory Farming*. Cambridge, MA: Blackwell.

Mason, J., and P. Singer. 1990. *Animal Factories* (revised and updated). New York: Harmony Books.

Maurer, D. 1995. "Meat as a Social Problem: Rhetorical Strategies in the Contemporary Vegetarian Literature." Pp. 143–163 in *Eating Agendas: Food and Nutrition as Social Issues*, edited by D. Maurer and J. Sobal. Hawthorne, NY: Aldine de Gruyter.

Nelson, B. J. 1984. *Making an Issue of Child Abuse*. Chicago: University of Chicago Press.

Orcutt, J., and J. B. Turner. 1993. "Shocking Numbers and Graphic Accounts: Quantified Images of Drug Problems in the Print Media." *Social Problems* 40:190–206.

Phillips, M. T. 1994. "Proper Names and the Social Construction of Biography: The Negative Case of Laboratory Animals." *Qualitative Sociology* 17:119–142.

Rifkin, J. 1992. *Beyond Beef: The Rise and Fall of the Cattle Culture*. New York: Dutton.

Robbins, J. 1987. *Diet for a New America*. Walpole, NH: Stillpoint.

Singer, P. 1975. *Animal Liberation: A New Ethics for Our Treatment of Animals*. New York: Avon Books.

Snow, D. A., and R. D. Benford. 1988. "Ideology, Frame Resonance, and Participant Mobilization." *International Social Movements Research* 1:197–217.

———. 1992. "Master Frames and Cycles of Protest." Pp. 133–155 in *Frontiers in Social Movement Theory*, edited by A.C. Morris and C.M. Mueller. New Haven: Yale University Press.

Spector, M., and J. I. Kitsuse. 1977. *Constructing Social Problems*. Hawthorne, NY: Aldine de Gruyter.

Sperling, S. 1988. *Animal Liberators*. Berkeley: University of California Press.

Sutherland, A., and J. E. Nash. 1994. "Animal Rights as New Environmental Cosmology." *Qualitative Sociology* 17:171–186.

Tester, K. 1991. *Animals and Society: The Humanity of Animal Rights*. New York: Routledge.

Wenzel, G. 1991. *Animal Rights, Human Rights, Ecology, Economy, and Ideology in the Canadian Arctic*. Toronto: University of Toronto Press.

PART IV

Policies

It is significant that Americans speak of "social problems," rather than "social issues" or "social conditions." A "social issue" implies a debate in which there are two or more competing opinions—something unresolved, perhaps unresolvable, about which people may agree to disagree. Similarly, the term "social condition" seems to suggest permanence, that little or nothing can be done to change matters. In contrast, the term "social problem" presents a very different message. Problems have solutions. The label "social problem" implies that something can be done, that the matter can be solved. People might have to learn to live with "social issues" and "social conditions," but they are likely to believe that they can solve "social problems."

Most claimsmakers seek solutions in social policies—new laws, new programs, and the like. Claimsmaking shapes policy in at least two ways. Most obviously, claimsmakers often promote an agenda of new policies; they present lists of demands, identify what sorts of policies are needed, or in some cases develop draft policies, such as model legislation. But claims influence policy in another, subtler way. Claimsmaking inevitably typifies social problems, suggesting that X is a social problem, and that it is a problem of a particular sort. Policymakers respond to these typifications when developing social policies. Among social scientists, political scientists pay the most attention to policymaking, and a number of recent works by political scientists share the constructionists' interest in the ways claims can shape policy choices (Edelman 1988; Kingdon 1984; Rochefort and Cobb 1994; Schneider and Ingram 1993; Stone 1988).

The relationship between claims and policy can be ironic. Policies can backfire, making things worse. In Chapter 12, Donileen R. Loseke examines the debate over what should be done for the homeless mentally ill. Claimsmaking campaigns during the 1950s and 1960s criticized mental hospitals and, particularly, compulsory commitment policies. These campaigns led to deinstitutionalization; hospitals closed and many patients were released. Some of these patients became homeless and, when homelessness began to attract more attention during the 1980s, some claimsmakers blamed deinstitutionalization for the problem. Loseke's analysis shows how competing constructions of the homeless mentally ill emerged, and how those different constructions had very different implications for social policy.

Of course, not all claimsmaking succeeds. In Chapter 13, David F. Luckenbill contrasts two claimsmaking campaigns mounted by the film industry in response to the spread of videocassette recorders. By giving millions of people the technology to reproduce films, VCRs threatened the film industry's control over movie profits. The industry turned to Congress for relief, asking for federal laws to (1) require the VCR industry to compensate the film industry for its losses, and to (2) increase the criminal penalties for video piracy. The latter campaign succeeded, but the former failed. Luckenbill asks what these different outcomes reveal about the conditions under which claimsmakers can influence policy.

Finally, Chapter 14, by Lawrence T. Nichols, addresses international relations—particularly changes in how key U.S. claimsmakers constructed the economic consequences of Japanese trading practices. This is an unusual topic for constructionist research; most constructionist studies concern social policy, rather than economic or foreign policy. However, this chapter suggests that claimsmaking shapes these other sorts of policies, and that it is important to understand how the international context shapes the claims that emerge, as well as the responses those claims receive.

REFERENCES

Edelman, M. 1988. *Constructing the Political Spectacle*. Chicago: University of Chicago Press.

Kingdon, J. W. 1984. *Agendas, Alternatives, and Public Policies*. New York: Harper Collins.

Rochefort, D. A., and R. W. Cobb. 1994. *The Politics of Problem Definition*. Lawrence: University of Kansas Press.

Schneider, A., and H. Ingram. 1993. "Social Construction of Target Populations." *American Political Science Review* 87:334–347.

Stone, D. A. 1988. *Policy Paradox and Political Reason*. New York: Harper Collins.

12

Writing Rights: The "Homeless Mentally Ill" and Involuntary Hospitalization

DONILEEN R. LOSEKE

What should the public do about a person who wants to live on the streets? What is the public's responsibility for this type of person? What can the public demand from such a person? These practical questions became central to controversies surrounding a policy of removing the "homeless mentally ill" from New York City's streets in the 1980s. I want to explore the roots of these controversies and examine how the *New York Times* constructed the morality of the resolution to them.

This examination is located within the social constructionist perspective on social problems. This perspective can examine how socially constructed images of conditions (such as "homelessness") and persons (such as the "homeless mentally ill") serve as justifications for public policies (e.g., Best 1989, 1990; Loseke 1992, 1993; Margolin 1994). This focus on imagery complements more traditional approaches understanding policy in terms of motives (White 1992), social power (Castle 1988), or material conditions such as a government fiscal crisis (Ilchman and Rosenblatt 1987). Regardless of power, motives, or material conditions, social policies must be *morally* justified and this can be accomplished by constructing images of types of persons in types of conditions.

This chapter addresses two specific issues. First, I want to explore how social policy can be examined as a package of claims in which images of *types* of conditions and persons serve as moral justifications for particular types of public responses. Using the debates concerning what to do about persons who wanted to live on the streets of New York City in the 1980s as an example, my concern is with relationships between constructions of such persons and policies: Some claims constructed persons living on the streets as rational actors and hence promoted their right to remain on the streets; other constructions characterized such persons as "mad" and promoted policies of sending such persons to mental hospitals, whether they wanted to go or not. Further-

261

more, because resolutions of controversies in one era can set the stage for controversies in the next era, I will place this 1980s debate in its immediate historical context: The post-World War II era policies of "community mental health" that can be read as setting both the rhetorical and the practical stage for the controversies of the 1980s.

Second, I want to explore rhetorical relationships between constructions of types of people and the meaning of the cultural values of freedom and rights. In particular, I will argue that some constructions of persons living on the streets are consistent with images of freedom as a right to self-determination; other constructions lead to images of self-determination as slavery, and confinement in mental hospitals as freedom. Hence, my title, "Writing Rights."

Three general social constructionist understandings about *all* social policy inform my analysis. First, central to my argument is the belief that socially constructed images of *types* of conditions and *types* of persons underlie social policies of all types and that these images are important. Consider how even the *labels* we assign to categories evoke images. For example, the label of mental illness suggests that this condition is an illness, that there are similarities between those who are physically ill and those who are mentally ill, and that medical authorities should be in charge of resolving this condition. Likewise, the label of "homelessness" draws attention to a lack of housing; it implies that housing is the solution.

As social constructions, labels—and the specific contents of categories— are constantly changing. Persons in the past were not "mentally ill," they were "mad," "crazy," or "insane"; persons in the past were not "homeless," they were "tramps," "winos," "bums," or "derelicts." Yet current constructions have not simply replaced prior ones; new constructions contain seeds of previous images, and while one or another image might become dominant in any given era, images can compete. Images of "madness" have not disappeared from the social scene, and the public and researchers alike still want to know *why* persons are without homes, and sometimes answers include images of persons without homes *because* they are "tramps," "winos," and so on.

A second general understanding informing this examination again applies to *all* public efforts to do something about conditions defined as troublesome and in need of repair. Any level of government in the United States can intervene in private lives for only two reasons: intervention must be justified as either necessary to protect the public by *controlling* those who violate social rules, or as *helping* persons requiring assistance.[1] These constructions of the purpose of policy often are confusing. At times, one group of claimsmakers may argue that a particular policy helps individuals, while another group may claim its purpose is social control. At times, there can be contrasting constructions of why social control is or is not necessary; there often are different constructions of what constitutes help, and so on. My point is general: Any justifications for policy depend, at least in part, upon imagery. For example, when constructions of "madness" reigned, most policy focused on controlling the mad to protect the public from the contagion and social disruption of lunacy. Places then called asylums made few claims about their powers to help or cure; they explicitly were about social control (Bassuk and Gerson 1985; Rothman 1971). In the same way, when individual pathologies were constructed as the cause of persons being without homes, social policies were justified first and foremost in terms of punishment and, hence, social control (Rothman 1971). While more contemporary images of "mental illness" and "homelessness" encourage justifying policy in terms of how it will help persons in such conditions, there remain issues of what constitutes help, and there remain issues of social control: How should the good of individuals be balanced with the good of a larger public?

This leads to a third and final point about social policy: Social policies raise questions about the limits of individual freedom and rights. Such questions are obvious when the issue is involuntary confinement in a jail, prison, or hospital. More typically, questions about individual freedom and rights are subtle. Since the advent of modern charity, individuals who need social services have been required to follow the instructions of social service providers; to receive services, the client "must show readiness to take advice" (Glazer 1968:113). While often justified in terms of how such advice or client monitoring helps, these methods nonetheless control individual behavior and, hence, reduce individual freedom.

This is an underlying constructionist framework for studying contemporary debates about a type of person called the "homeless mentally ill." Examining controversies surrounding *any* social policy requires attending to the socially constructed nature of images, to the dual nature of policy to help and control, and to relationships between policies and individual freedom.

I turn now to a brief history that sets the stage for controversies in the 1980s concerning what to do about persons who wanted to live on the streets of New York City. My historical examination is biased in two important ways. First, while a history of this controversy could reasonably focus on a history of "homelessness," I shall rather look primarily at a history of "mental illness." In doing so, I am *not* claiming that this is a correct framing of the issue. Rather, I focus on "mental illness" for the very practical reason that the controversy in New York City was resolved by enacting policies of involuntary hospitalization in *mental* institutions, and this can be justified only for a type of person constructed as "mentally ill." Second, rather than examining a long history of how "mental illness" became medicalized (i.e., Conrad and Schneider 1985), I will concentrate on the era between the late 1940s and the late 1970s in the United States because it sets an immediate historical stage for controversies in the 1980s. This short history of "mental illness" is organized around the theme of how claims can be read as offering justifications for a policy called "community mental health." Some claimsmakers in the 1980s would construct this policy as an important cause for a new type of person called the "homeless mentally ill."

COMMUNITY MENTAL HEALTH AND IMAGES OF SANITY

In the United States, since the beginning of the 1800s, the first and primary social response to the condition now called mental illness was the mental hospital. Although there were criticisms of such places as early as the 1870s (Rothman 1971), the practice of relying on them did not change until 1947 when patients started spending less time in hospitals; it was not until 1956 that decreasing numbers of people were admitted to them (Ilchman and Rosenblatt 1987). This was the beginning of a new policy called "community mental health." Defined by observers as a "momentous shift in the ideology of treatment for mental illness" (Bassuk and Gerson 1985), this new policy changed both the *setting* of social interventions and the definitions of the *rights* of those classified as mentally ill:

> We have moved from a system in which patients spent long periods of time in segregated settings with few of the legal protections afforded to other citizens to one in which a variety of more integrated treatment settings afford patients the same legal protections they would enjoy as citizens in any setting. (Wagenaar and Lewis 1989:503)

I want to examine rhetorical justifications for this new policy that reduced the population of state mental hospitals by 75% between 1955 and 1980 (Bassuk and Gerson 1985), and accorded the "mentally ill" person the rights enjoyed by "citizens in any setting."

Although there is continuing debate about which claimsmakers and which agendas were the most important in this policy shift, there is general agreement that psychiatrists, social workers, academic social scientists, politicians, past and current mental patients, social movement advocates for the "mentally ill," and civil rights lawyers converged on constructing this change as beneficial for all and detrimental to none.

How did such an "amazing coalition of advocates" (Coates 1990:156) come together? Here I shall take a broad view to place the community mental health movement into a larger perspective. In particular, the retreat from mental hospitals and the increasing rights of the "mentally ill" can be seen as part of a larger social trend from the 1950s through the 1970s promoting the morality of decreased institutionalization of—and increasing rights for—many types of people such as the "elderly," the "mentally retarded," and "criminals" (Ilchman and Rosenblatt 1987). I will emphasize how policy changes in general can be understood as reflecting three prominent cultural themes of the era: The loss of faith in institutions and institutional representatives, the construction of individual troubles as environmentally created, and the fragmentation of moral consensus. These threads of rhetoric came together to normalize "mental illness" and to promote the belief that treatment outside hospitals was beneficial, easy, and morally required.

First, the postwar era was characterized by a loss of faith in *all* institutions (Ilchman and Rosenblatt 1987). In the 1950s, for example, Americans worried that the Soviet Union was winning the "space race," and there were claims that American schools were failing to educate future scientists. In the 1960s, the Vietnam War challenged the legitimacy of government, as did the Watergate crisis in the 1970s. Likewise, prisons were criticized for their failure to reform; the previously hallowed institution of the family was criticized for its oppression of women, church attendance declined, and so on.[2] Not surprisingly, mental hospitals also came under attack. Research repeatedly claimed that these places were worse than ineffective in curing illness: Mental hospitals were criticized for actually creating such illness; they were constructed as places actually encouraging patients to remain in them rather than to return to independent lives (e.g., Mechanic and Rochefort 1992). Such claims even came from psychiatrists, the formal authorities in mental hospitals: By the 1950s there were claims that this professional group was "embarrassed and ashamed" about the treatment of patients (Ilchman and Rosenblatt 1987); psychiatrists increasingly refused to work in mental hospitals (Grob 1987). Whether told in academic prose such as Erving Goffman's *Asylums*, or in such popular novels as Ken Kesey's *One Flew Over the Cuckoo's Nest*, the story was the same: Claimsmakers constructed mental hospitals as "great warehouses of abandoned souls; they were hard to defend" (Isaac and Armat 1990).

Accompanying the theme of a loss of faith in institutions was the loss of faith in institutional representatives. Within this climate, children challenged the authority of their parents, students challenged the wisdom of their teachers, medical patients were advised to solicit second opinions, and so on. It is not surprising that psychiatrists' competence also was challenged. Claimsmakers such as Thomas Szasz and R. D. Laing constructed psychiatry as merely a "pseudo-scientific explanation" for personal troubles (Brown 1981); there were claims that the process of dividing humans into those who were "normal" and those who were "mentally ill" had more to do with patients' social class than with any scientific indicator of illness (Brown 1981; Siegel, Kahn, Pollack, and Fink 1962). Such claims constructed no good reason for the public to trust psychiatrists. Combined with a loss of faith in the institutional structure, a package of claims emerged that did far more than make it seem sensible to stop believing in the value of mental hospitals and psychiatrists. The depth of criticisms could be read as constructing a *moral* necessity for doing so.

A second cultural theme justifying a retreat from mental hospitals were claims constructing the *social order* as the principal cause of individual differences and individual problems. To take only the most obvious example, prior to the 1950s, it was most common to see those we now call African-Americans constructed as a type of person who was not as intelligent, not as motivated, and not as hardworking as European-type persons. Within such constructions, economic and social disadvantages were due to individuals' failures. In stark contrast, the postwar period constructed African-Americans—and many other types of persons—as socially or economically disadvantaged because of one or more characteristics of the social order. In the same way, previously individualized constructions of "mental illness" competed with constructions of this condition as a "product of structural, not individual, breakdown" (Stern 1984). "Mental illness" could be constructed as a "normal reaction to oppressive social conditions" (Brown 1981).

This definition of the social environment as the cause of individual troubles is important for two reasons. First, postwar constructions increasingly defined persons as *victims* of the social order. Within folk reasoning, victims deserve compassion, sympathy, and help (Clark 1987; Loseke 1993). Certainly, a sympathetic response to "mental illness" would *not* be to send persons to despicable mental hospitals with their questionable personnel. Second, within folk reasoning of that era, this construction of environmental causes of individual troubles led to optimism that if something was environmentally created it could be environmentally resolved. Indeed, the era was characterized by an "enthusiastic optimism" (Bassuk and Gerson 1985), a sense that "everything is possible" (Fuller 1988:97). Reflecting such optimism, for example, then-President Johnson declared that America would *win* the "war on poverty." In the case of "mental illness" there was optimism on three fronts. First, the community mental health movement was a program first and foremost to *prevent* "mental illness," and there was great confidence that this could be accomplished (Bassuk and Gerson 1985; Fuller 1988; Morrissey and Goldman 1987; White 1992). Second, while mental hospitals were constructed as antitherapeutic, the "gospel of social treatment" defined home and community life as having positive therapeutic value (Ilchman and Rosenblatt 1987:15–16). Third, newly emerging psychotropic drugs were promoted as offering easy relief from disruptive symptoms (Morrissey and Goldman 1987). When combined, these constructions lead to a belief that transferring care of the "mentally ill" from hospitals to local communities would be easy (Mechanic and Rochefort 1992:147). As stated by then-President John F. Kennedy, new knowledge and new drugs "make it possible for most of the mentally ill to be successfully and quickly treated in their own communities and returned to a useful place in society" (*New York Times* 2-6-63). The shift to community mental health, in brief, was not only a retreat *from* mental hospitals, it was constructed as an advance *to* something defined as an easier, better, and more humane response to persons experiencing reactions to an oppressive social environment.

Third and finally, consistent with a loss of faith in institutions, the postwar era was a time of moral fragmentation as one group after another advanced claims about the undemocratic and unfair character of cultural expectations for individual behavior. From women challenging the oppressive nature of gender expectations, to male students who grew their hair long and wore earrings, to increasing social tolerance of such previously stigmatized behaviors as "divorce," "homosexuality," or "births out of wedlock," the trend was the same: Claims constructed institutionalized versions of "normality" as oppressive and promoted the value of a "loosely bounded" culture (Merelman 1984) where individual reasoning, rather than institutional expectations, were the judge of "normality" and "morality."

In the case of "mental illness," this social trend had three, interrelated consequences. First, because there was no institutionalized standard of "normality," lines between "mental illness" and "normality" became blurred (Fuller 1988): "Mental illness" could be constructed as a mere "exaggeration of normal adaptations" (Mechanic and Rochefort 1992:130). Such claims made it difficult to label specific behaviors as those of "mental illness." Second, given negative constructions of institutionalized expectations for behavior, individual self-determination and individual differences were constructed as positive values. This made it morally difficult to assign specific individuals to a category called "mentally ill" because seemingly bizarre behaviors and characteristics might alternatively be categorized in a socially valued category called "lifestyle choice." Third, and also related, when disruptive behaviors associated with "mental illness" are normalized, they become definable as merely "bothersome" (Morse 1982:81). While others might not appreciate persons who are "bothersome," such an image does *not* justify public intervention.

In summary, claims came together after World War II in ways that *rhetorically* normalized many behaviors and characteristics, including those of "mental illness." This interrelated package of claims justified very *practical* changes in the social order. First and most simply, claims justified releasing tens of thousands of persons from mental hospitals. As the patient population fell, hospitals closed or remained open with far fewer workers. So, while hospitals in earlier eras had been the option of *first* choice, they increasingly were *not* an option at all. In the same way, there were changes in *laws* regarding many types of persons. In the case of the "mentally ill," given constructions of hospitals as mere warehouses, new laws gave patients a right to treatment if confined to such places. Because treatment costs money, hospitals became more expensive than in the past. Also, given constructions of "mental illness" as "normality," new legal standards gave the "mentally ill" the right to be deemed legally competent even if residing in a mental hospital. In turn, given a legal standing of competence, it made sense that patients should have the right to refuse treatment if they did not want it (Coates 1990: Appendix 1; McLeod and Milstein 1993). While such legal changes occurred sporadically on federal, state, and local levels, virtually all were in the same direction of reducing the power of police, psychiatrists, and other institutional representatives and increasing the right to individual self-determination for many types of persons, including the "mentally ill."

By the late 1970s, claims about the condition of "mental illness" and the "mentally ill" person had been enshrined into practice. The social order had changed in very real ways. And this was as it should be, for the policy of community mental health had been constructed as beneficial for all and detrimental to none.

By the late 1970s, the social order was changing in another way. Particulary in large cities, there was increasing concern about persons without homes. The first question asked was *why* there seemed to be an increasing number of such persons? The social problem called homelessness arose when previous constructions of "vagrants" and "winos" as persons who had chosen to be without homes were challenged by new constructions of the "homeless" as people "disenfranchised or marginalized or scared off by processes beyond their control" (Marin 1987:40). Within this construction, claimsmakers blamed a range of *social* conditions (e.g., the demolition of low-cost hotels, the declining wages for low-skilled workers, reduced welfare benefits) for the increasing number of persons who simply could not afford housing.

There were counterclaims to this newly emerging construction of the "homeless" as victims of the institutional order.[3] In particular, by the early 1980s there was *popular* consensus linking the newly constructed problem of "homelessness" with the consequences of community mental health policies. Academic observers *still* disagree about the extent— or even the existence—of a relationship between "homelessness" and the practical consequences of community mental health policies. But these could be linked in the popular imagination: The press constructed the "homeless" as the "remnants of the grand and noble experiment" of deinstitutionalization (*Time* 12-2-85); persons without homes were called the "walking wounded of that largely discredited policy" (*New York Times* 11-22-85).[4] Within this construction, persons who lived on the streets in the 1980s would have been in mental hospitals in earlier eras. These two competing images of the "homeless" as either victims of institutional failure or as "mentally ill" inform answers to a very practical question facing New York City residents in the 1980s: What should the public do about persons who live on the streets? My argument is that answers to this question depend on images of both the problem and the person. Using data from 132 articles in the *New York Times* (*NYT*) between 1981 and 1992, I turn now to how answers were constructed on the pages of this one newspaper.[5] First, I will examine how these articles constructed claimsmakers and the characteristics of social policy. Then I will turn to exploring moral justifications for policies toward the type of person who lived on the streets of the city.

CLAIMSMAKERS AND PUBLIC POLICY

The pages of the *NYT* contain the voices of many claimsmakers debating what to do about persons who wanted to live on the streets of New York City. In historical retrospect, the victors in these debates were those promoting the policy of involuntary hospitalization. One person, then-Mayor Edward Koch, was identified by the *NYT* as the primary person advocating this policy. The *NYT*, for example, repeatedly identified the policy as "Koch's plan" (2-19-82); the newspaper reported that "Koch wants to change the law," and so on.[6] Yet while the Mayor was the original—and the most vocal—spokesperson for policies of involuntary hospitalization, the pages of the *NYT* also can be read as containing a choir of supporting voices. For example, policies of involuntarily hospitalization were supported by *NYT* editorials as early as 1982 (2-19-82). The paper regularly commended the Mayor for his efforts (11-15-85), and eventually complained that the policy was a only a "token response" that should be *expanded* (11-14-87). In addition, policies of involuntary hospitalization were supported by such powerful claimsmakers as a state senator (2-3-85), the president of the American Psychological Association, and city and state health officials (9-6-87). There also were supportive opinion editorials (9-4-87), letters to the editor (2-13-88), and reports that the plan won praise in "man-on-the street" polls (9-8-87).

The other side of this controversy, as constructed through the pages of the *NYT*, was twofold. First, the *practical* consequences of community mental health policies were that few hospital beds were available for the "mentally ill," and there were laws making hospital commitment time-consuming, difficult, and expensive. Therefore, many counterclaims constructed practical, procedural, legal, or monetary problems associated with involuntary hospitalization policies. To take only a few examples, one article was titled "Resources Said to be Lacking for Koch Plan on Homeless" (9-2-87b); another claimed the Hospital Union opposed the policy because these workers did not have sufficient resources to implement it (9-5-87b). Originally, the city had problems hiring psychiatrists to work at night (12-4-85), and so on. Claims about the illegality of the plans given then-current laws were a constant theme. In 1981, for example, Mayor Koch proposed "rounding up the homeless" to give them food, baths, and medical care. Yet he dropped the plan the next day because everyone agreed it was illegal—vagrancy laws had been struck down by the courts and there were no laws dictating minimum standards of cleanliness in public life (3-27-81). In brief, many counterclaims were about practical problems posed by existing laws and the lack of material resources. Such claims were about *how* the policy could or should be implemented; they illustrate how the resolution of controversies in one era sets the practical stage for controversies in the next era.

My primary concern is claims constructing the morality of policy: *Should* policies promoting involuntary hospitalization be implemented? Although Mayor Koch often identified social workers, homeless advocates and civil libertarians as his *moral* opposition (9-1-87), this construction is both too broad and too narrow. First, it is misleading to claim that some groups always opposed policies of involuntary confinement or that they opposed these policies on moral grounds. For example, Robert Hayes, representing the Coalition for the Homeless, said that his group had "absolutely no objection" to proposals advocating involuntarily confinement when the weather was very cold. This advocacy group was not concerned with the morality of such policies; their concern was that such policies would reduce attention to the social causes of homelessness (1-23-85). In the same way, another advocacy group, "Partnership for the Homeless," endorsed policies of involuntary hospitalization as long as they were "compassionately implemented" (8-29-87). And, social workers could agree that involuntary commitment should be easier. Their spokespersons could oppose suggested policies only on the grounds that existing laws made it illegal to do what policy promoted (2-8-82). Hence, it is too broad to claim that *moral* objection from organized groups was consistent. Conversely, the formation of organized groups as the moral opposition is too narrow because their moral objections were supported by explicit questions of morality raised in articles written by *NYT* reporters (11-11-87), opinion editorials (2-16-82), and court rulings printed in the newspaper (11-13-87). Hence, while the *NYT* could explicitly construct the two sides to the controversy as "Mayor Koch" versus "homeless advocates, civil libertarians, and social workers," the cast of claimsmakers was much larger and, critically, the sides were not clearly drawn.

The policy itself also was constructed in the *NYT*. Most certainly, what could be done was greatly influenced by legal codes. Indeed, although the problem facing city residents in 1981 could easily have been constructed as one of persons who—for *whatever* reason—wanted to live on the street, nothing could be legally done about the "street homeless" until the weather was so cold that the city could step in to help because the cold "automatically creates the necessary presumption that, to us, that person is in danger of dying" (1-23-85). Therefore, policies quickly became focused on persons living on the street *because* they were "mentally ill."

In retrospect, a history of these policies for the "homeless mentally ill" can be read as one of domain expansion (Best 1990). First, policies expanded the amount of *time* persons could be kept in mental hospitals against their will. In the early 1980s, persons taken involuntarily to such places could leave in 3 days unless a court hearing found legal cause to keep them confined (1-27-82). In 1987, the law allowed 15 days of involuntary confinement without such a court order. Second, policy expanded the *grounds* for taking persons off the street. In the early 1980s, involuntary commitment required a judgment of "substantial and imminent risk of death or serious physical harm to self or others" (3-28-81). In November 1985, the criteria of "imminent danger" was extended in two ways. First, "danger" previously had been constructed in terms of what people were *doing* (e.g., walking through traffic). Now it could include "neglect," or things people were *not* doing (e.g., dressing warmly in winter, eating properly). Second, the requirement of "imminent" danger was replaced by the more vaguely defined and far-reaching criterion of the "reasonably foreseeable future" (11-14-85). The third expansion was controversial enough to attract national attention: As of October 29, 1987, city representatives were ordered to use the *broadest interpretation possible* of the existing law. It was not clear what this meant in practice, but the *NYT* told readers that this change "vastly expands" the grounds for involuntary commitment (11-14-86).

Clearly, such policies promoting hospitalization reversed those of community treatment; policies making involuntary commitment increasingly easier reversed the prior trend of making commitment increasingly more difficult. Such changes did not come quickly or easily: Mental hospitals needed to be reopened and laws needed to be changed. Yet as in the past, practical changes could be justified by images of types of conditions and persons. I turn now to these constructions.

CONSTRUCTING IMAGES OF INSANITY
AND INVOLUNTARY CONFINEMENT

New constructions of types of conditions and persons must compete with others already present in the social order. For the case in point, persons who *opposed* policies of involuntary hospitalization constructed the problem as first and foremost one of a lack of housing; they constructed "mental illness" as a normal condition; they constructed the "mentally ill" person as a rational actor capable of self-determination. In other words, the types of constructions that had been the positive support for community mental health policies became defensive claims criticizing proposed new policies of involuntary hospitalization.

As in earlier times, some claims criticized the social order and constructed environmental explanations for the condition of persons living on the streets. Within this construction, the problem was the lack of low-income housing creating "homelessness" in the first place (3-12-86), or the lack of "safe and decent" places for people to sleep once they were without homes (12-8-85). Claims constructed the city's shelter system as "big, barracks like quarters" (11-14-85) that were "depressing" and sometimes "dangerous" (1-24-85). According to these claims, persons were on the street because they could not afford homes; they remained on the street because the city shelter system was despicable. Within this construction, persons on the street would go to shelters willingly *if* shelters were better (12-7-85).

Constructing the social order as the problem yields an image of persons on the street as *rational* actors no different from persons who have homes. After all, the majority of Americans would not like the "long lines and regimentation" in shelters (3-25-83); most people might choose to live on the streets if their only alternative was despicable, regimented, and downright dangerous shelters (11-14-85). Within this construction, the decision to remain on the streets rather than enter a city shelter becomes a sign of mental *health* rather than of mental illness (12-8-85).

While such constructions implied the *absolute* normality of persons refusing to leave the streets, others constructed such a person as "mentally ill" yet nonetheless *rational*. Within such constructions, the problem was not that such persons refused treatment for their condition, it was that the "city and state are not providing the hospital space to treat them" (11-14-85). Because it was the "scarcity of beds" that kept people out of mental hospitals (9-2-87a); the "real obstacle" to mental health care for persons living on the streets was the shortage of beds in mental hospitals (9-17-87). Within such images, the "homeless mentally ill" is a type of person who would rationally choose to enter treatment *if* the city had "more inviting outpatient care" (11-22-85).

In addition, and again as in earlier eras, claims could produce indications of "mental illness" as normal reactions to oppressive environments. Such claims warned readers to not confuse behavior realistically resulting from the experience of street living with "actual" psychiatric disorder (10-10-84). Even seemingly bizarre behaviors could be normalized. For example, while common-sense reasoning might judge "burning money" as an indication of "mental illness," if money is burned only when it is rudely thrown by passersby, then this might be an act of self-respect. Or, if money is burned only when it is not needed for that particular day, then the act might be constructed as indicating a rational understanding that it *is* dangerous to have money and live on the street (11-2-87). Likewise, while urinating or defecating on a public sidewalk might be judged a sign of "mental illness," such behaviors also can be constructed as merely unfortunate consequences of a lack of publicly available toilets. Similarly, while "cursing" and "chasing" city workers attempting to help might be taken as a sign of "mental illness," such behaviors might also indicate a good memory if such workers had been responsible for previous periods of involuntary confinement (11-6-87).

Constructions promoting the normality of such behaviors simultaneously promote the right to self-determination. Indeed, persons who live on the street could be constructed as exemplary Americans who have a "fiercely independent lifestyle" (1-16-88). Hence, one homeless man claimed he was a free man in a free society and, because he had violated no laws, his wishes to remain on the street must be respected (11-27-85). Likewise, another woman living on the street argued "I like the streets, and I am entitled to live the way I want to live" (11-2-87); another woman turned down an offer for transportation to a shelter because "I want to be independent" (3-25-83). These can be read as comments of rational actors exemplifying the highly valued American love of freedom.

In brief, the earlier constructions of "mental illness" and the "mentally ill" person associated with the community mental health policy did not simply disappear. They remained a part of the social scene in the 1980s

and promoted the absolute normality of persons living on the streets or
at least the rationality of those who were both "homeless" and "mentally
ill." These defensive claims challenged newly emerging policies of involuntary hospitalization for the "homeless mentally ill." If the problem
was in city services, as spokespersons for various advocacy groups argued, then policies directed to hospitalizing individuals diverted attention away from "failed city policy" (12-7-85); they diverted attention
from the "real issues" such as the need for low-income housing (3-12-86).
Similarly, if the behaviors of persons living on the street were rational,
then such persons were citizens whose right to self-determination was
legally protected: If people are rational actors neither violating the law
nor harming others then you "can't make them do anything against
their will" (11-14-87).

And this was as it *should* be. Within common-sense reasoning, it
should be very difficult to take away the right to self-determination for
rational actors who are not harming others. Hence, the morality of laws
making involuntary commitment very difficult is accomplished by constructing the rationality of persons living on the streets.

Yet if persons living on the streets are *not* rational, then laws making
commitment difficult can be challenged. I turn now to a second construction of persons living on the streets that supports policies promoting the
morality of suspending their individual rights to self-determination.
Within this construction, persons choosing to live on the streets are not
rational, so laws making it difficult to hospitalize them are morally wrong.
Or, in the often-quoted opinion of Mayor Koch, "the law is an ass"
(3-25-83) and needs to be changed.

Claims challenging the rationality of persons living on the streets were
made on the grounds of *common sense* (1-24-85). As a background image,
the condition repeatedly was linked with "deinstitutionalization of the
mentally ill" by simple assertion rather than by logic, evidence, or argument. For example, readers were simply told that new policies were
needed to "reverse the worst failures of deinstitutionalization" (11-22-85),
editorials could begin by simply asserting that present problems were
due to deinstitutionalization (12-17-85), a psychologist agreed with the
Mayor that deinstitutionalization had created the condition, and so on.
By rhetorically linking the consequences of community mental health
policies with the condition of persons living on the streets, these constructions implied that persons on the street would have been in mental
hospitals in previous eras. Such constructions also imply that if "deinstitutionalization" caused the problem then "reinstitutionalization" could
resolve it.

Claims also constructed the common sense *content* of the problem.
According to these claims, normalizing mental illness and promoting

unlimited rights to self-determination might lead to stimulating dinner party conversation and Philosophy I discussions (11-14-87), but common sense dictated that persons living on the streets were not "normal." Within this construction, the "homeless mentally ill" was a person whose decisions and behaviors could *not* be normalized by practical reasoning.

First, claims promoting the need for involuntary hospitalization formed the condition as one residing in the *practical experience* of *NYT* readers. There were articles about the large number of persons living on the streets (10-10-84), and editorials claimed the number of such persons was sharply increasing (9-2-87). Because four out of five city residents said they saw such persons every day (6-29-89), the "homeless mentally ill" was constructed as one of the city's most visible problems (11-14-85). The paper advised its few readers who did not daily encounter such persons that the condition would be "perfectly obvious" by simply taking a walk through Times Square or the Grand Central Terminal (1-28-89). Readers were instructed to "trust the reality of your senses"; if they simply looked, they would see "craziness" (1-26-89).

While claims forming the rationality of persons living on the streets constructed behaviors in terms of their *causes* or *meanings*, craziness was constructed by purely *behavioral* descriptions. For example, Rebecca Smith was a woman who froze to death in a cardboard box rather than accept a ride to a shelter (1-27-82); Judy was a woman who sat docile all day but arose each and every night at 11:00 P.M. and spent the next several hours screaming obscenities and intimate details about her life into the night (12-17-84). The "homeless mentally ill" were constructed as persons who "stumble about addressing strangers . . . or unseen deities . . . , sometimes shouting obscenities or urinating against buildings" (10-10-84). They were "dirty, disheveled, and malodorous" (11-2-87), and they committed "filthy nuisances on streets and gutters" (8-24-84). Such descriptions of appearance and behavior cannot easily be read as forming a normal citizen. The type of person known as the "homeless mentally ill" was rather constructed as a "wild presence" on the streets of New York City (8-24-84).

Common-sense logic continues: How do we know that a person living on the street is "mentally ill?" We know because the person is on the street. Within middle-class folk reasoning, problems with the city shelter system might lead rational persons to live on the streets during summer months. But a person who continues to live on the streets in subzero temperatures when *any* choices are available is, by definition, not rational. Therefore, in response to claimsmakers who argued that persons made rational choices to remain on the streets in the winter, Mayor Koch replied: "baloney, baloney" (11-14-85). According to the

Mayor, persons remained on the street because they were "deranged" (3-25-83).

By common-sense logic, a deranged person is not normal. Such persons "don't have their wits about them" (1-29-82); they suffer from "disorientation and impaired judgment" (12-17-85). Given this, such a person is "incapable of logical thinking" (9-5-87a), "incapable of taking care of themselves" (8-29-87), "incompetent" (10-25-85). Indeed, the act of being on the street is a sufficient sign of incompetence: "Anyone who chooses to be on the streets in the cold when we offer that person . . . a shelter, that person is not competent" (11-14-85).[7] "Incompetence" is doubly constructed. First, this type of person is not competent at *self-diagnosis*. They are "too sick to know they are sick" (11-27-87), "so sick they imagine they need no care" (1-22-88). It follows that such a person also is incapable of making *rational decisions*. A person who is "seriously mentally ill often doesn't realize that he's sick. He will deny that he is ill and refuse to be treated" (2-3-85). Such a person "often resists treatment precisely because he [is] mentally ill" (11-22-85). Therefore, it goes without saying that others must make decisions because such persons "can not be held competent to choose beds of stone and to resist help" (8-24-84).

This construction of the "homeless mentally ill" as a mad person who is, by definition, incompetent, challenges the value of the right to self-determination. Within middle-class logic, "the freedom to sleep in doorways is no freedom at all" (8-24-84). The right to self-determination for persons living on the streets becomes the "freedom to die in the streets" (10-29-87), the freedom to "remain wrapped in their agonies of illness of the mind" (9-4-87), the "freedom to be left enslaved to madness" (1-26-89). Freedom was slavery.

What, then, constitutes freedom for this type of person? According to claimsmakers, this was the "freedom from the prison of mental illness" (10-29-87). Involuntary commitment was a "rescue" (1-28-89) that allowed people to "regain rationality" (1-22-88). Involuntary commitment could "save the homeless from themselves" (12-7-85). So, although the United States Supreme Court ruled that involuntary incarceration in a mental institution was a "massive deprivation of liberty" (9-17-87), for the "homeless mentally ill" such hospitalization was freedom.

These obviously are moral constructions; they justify hospitalization as the only conceivable policy toward a type of person who, if allowed self-determination, would die. Because policy was justified in terms of how it literally saved lives, it follows that failure to support this policy was *immoral*: Government cannot be forgiven for "letting them just lie there" (8-24-84); a "civilized society" has an obligation to help those "so deranged that they are likely to die if left alone on the streets" (11-27-87).

Failure to treat "mental illness" is a cruel neglect on the part of society" (11-11-87). This was not simply a *civil* obligation—it was a *"human* obligation to intervene" (11-26-87: emphasis added). Hence, the humanity of the policy was "beyond challenge" (1-24-85).

Such constructions of the morality of involuntary commitment policies did more than silence criticisms—they transformed them into nonsense. Asked rhetorically: "Is caring for people too sick to know they need care truly a violation of their freedom?" (11-23-90). Indeed, criticisms were pure folly: Persons who argued against intervention were "the crazies" (9-1-87); persons who argued against the policy were "turning away from madness" and this was "true madness" (9-4-87).

As in earlier eras, claimsmaking justified practical changes in the social environment. As compared with the early 1980s, by the end of the decade it was procedurally easier to involuntarily commit persons to mental hospitals, and there were now many more facilities. But claimsmakers constructed such change as insufficient. Persons living on the streets had become an "unmanageable presence" (11-28-91). When the public expressed sympathy for a man who had killed an aggressive homeless person, the *NYT* claimed such sympathy reflected the "community's disgust, and fear, about a continuing assault on public decency" posed by persons living on the streets (1-28-89). The "homeless mentally ill" now was constructed as a type of person who befouled private and public property (11-23-90), a type of person whose very presence devalued "everything" in the city (11-15-92). Citizens were described as increasingly irritated (8-14-89); neighborhoods were "living in absolute terror" (8-26-92). Again, behavioral descriptions predominated. One editorial author wrote of walking past a woman who "raised her dress, bared herself, and defecated in the gutter" (11-23-90); one reader wrote "I don't want to be stepping over people. I don't want them approaching me all over the place" (6-22-91). While claims in the early- and mid-1980s emphasized *helping* persons living on the streets, by the late 1980s, the *NYT* claimed that the public mood had "soured," and that compassion from earlier years had been replaced with a simple desire to "get them out of here" (11-18-89). The condition was constructed as "madness in the streets" (11-23-90), and "madness is not an acceptable alternative lifestyle to sanity" (1-26-89).

The scales of tolerance had tipped, and so, too, had the scales balancing the rights of a public with the rights of individuals. Stated bluntly by a radio talk show host: "What about the rights of people like me who walk past the people who urinate on the sidewalk? I'm a taxpayer. What about my rights?" (2-13-88). An editorial bemoaned: "when and why did this country accept madness in the streets as a part of the city scenery?" (11-23-90) With public opinion polls indicating that residents wanted city police to get tougher on homeless persons who made a "nuisance" of themselves (1-18-89), there were claims about the necessity of making it more difficult to live on the streets (6-22-91), and reports about efforts to once again "expand the criteria" for involuntary commitment to mental hospitals (10-28-91).

Concern about the rights of the public—defined implicitly as persons who have homes—now became central. Rhetoric shifted to justifying policy in terms of social control: Involuntary commitment was necessary to protect the public from the contagion of madness. According to a New York City Council member: "You do not have the right to occupy the sidewalks or the street. Otherwise we have a total breakdown of law and order" (11-9-87). But shifting from a rhetoric of help to one of social control did not pose a moral dilemma: By the late 1980s it was simply taken for granted that involuntary confinement was good for the "homeless mentally ill." If policies also were constructed as good for the public then all was at it should be—the policy was beneficial for all and detrimental to none.

SOCIAL CONSTRUCTION AND PUBLIC POLICIES

What should the public do about persons who want to live on the streets? What is the public's responsibility for such a person? What can the public demand from such a person? While this chapter certainly has not answered questions about what *should* be done, exploring how moral justifications are constructed has practical implications. I will focus my concluding comments on what often is missing from public debates and on what a social constructionist perspective might add to public dialogues.

First, consider how our world is populated by images of types of persons such as the "mentally ill," the "alcoholic," the "battered wife," the "gifted child," the "welfare mother," and so on. While such labels are often used without reflection, a constructionist perspective draws attention to their socially constructed nature. My major argument is that images of what the public *should* do depend on our images of *types* of people. So, for example, a policy of "community mental health" is sensible given an image of "mental illness" as a more-or-less "normal" condition, and the "mentally ill" person as a more-or-less rational actor. In the same way, a policy such as "lifetime incarceration for third time offenders" is sensible given an image of the "third time offender" as a person who most certainly will harm others if ever allowed freedom. Of course, other images would justify other types of public responses.

But *any* particular image will *never* encompass the heterogeneity of practical experience. At any one time, popular images of "mental illness," for example, will not likely encompass the range of possible characteristics and behaviors that could, conceivably, be contained within this label. In practical experience, individual characteristics and behaviors can range from those that an overwhelming majority of social actors would label as "normal," to those most persons would label as odd, strange, or bothersome, to those most persons would label as frightening, bizarre, and intolerable. In the same way, persons who have been convicted of three violent crimes range from those who pretend to have weapons in order to steal cigarettes, to those who use weapons and engage in repeated murders or rapes. My point is *not* that any one of such constructions is "the" reality, nor is it to argue which experiences should be encompassed by one or another label. On the contrary. My point is that the greater the disjunctures between images informing policy and the characteristics of persons who are the targets of policy, the greater the likelihood of policy failure (Loseke 1989). Public policy therefore would benefit by explicit attention to the often vaguely articulated images informing policy.

Second, this chapter illustrates how rights are not enshrined in the Constitution, nor fixed in legal codes that can, and often do, change. Legal changes depend, in part, on images. For the case at hand, while some claimsmakers argue that lawyers should be blamed for making it too difficult to involuntarily hospitalize persons who are "mentally ill" (White 1992), legal changes came primarily in the 1970s and their justifications were built on earlier claims that had criticized institutions in general and mental hospitals in particular, that had emphasized the right to self-determination for all persons, and that had normalized a variety of behaviors including those called "mental illness." While law typically is examined as a cause of social change, a constructionist perspective can examine the law as a *reflection* of change.

Third and finally, this chapter can be read as an example of a social trend in the 1990s to *limit* individual rights.Some claims and mandates, such as those promoting wearing motorcycle helmets and seat belts, are justified in terms of how they are good for the subjects of the policies. Other claims are justified not in terms of help, but by rhetorics constructing persons who need to be controlled for the good of *others*. Claims that "criminals" have too many rights, which makes prosecution difficult, and claims that the "homeless mentally ill" befoul public space form a general "public" as the beneficiary of controlling individual behavior. Claims promoting incarceration of pregnant drug-abusing women are justified in terms of what is good for a fetus. Claims surrounding "wife abuse" and "child abuse" form defenseless women and children as policy beneficiaries; a proposed policy called "workfare" for welfare recipients constructs "taxpayers" as the beneficiaries of decreased welfare spending, and so on.

What all of these recent claims have in common is that they define as public matters what previously had been defined as matters of individual choice. We increasingly live in an era where persons cannot "choose" to live on the streets, where persons cannot choose where they want to smoke cigarettes, where absent parents cannot "choose" to pay child support, where employers or teachers cannot "choose" to use language that is offensive to others, and so on. Clearly and most certainly, I am *not* arguing that these behaviors—or many others now subject to claimsmaking—should be matters of individual choice. My point is that policies promoting involuntary confinement for persons living on the streets can be read as an example of a larger social trend. Just as claims that came together in the postwar decades tended to promote increasing individual freedom and decreasing social control, now the pendulum is swinging toward promoting increasing social control and decreasing individual freedom. The question for social constructionists is *how* the pendulum rhetorically swings; the question for public policy is how far the pendulum *should* swing.

NOTES

1.   The themes of social control and help are explicit throughout academic examinations of public policy. For these themes in relation to "mental illness" see Rothman (1971), Holstein (1993), and McLeod and Milstein (1993).

2.   See Case and Taylor's edited volume (1979) for examples of how disenchantment with traditional institutions pervaded the social scene during this era.

3.   See Snow and Anderson (1993), for a recent review of the various claims about the cause of "homelessness."

4.   Some claimsmakers argue that community mental health would have worked if only governments had adequately funded the community centers that were to take the place of mental hospitals (Bassuk and Gerson 1985:133; Coates 1990:156). Others argue that the reforms themselves were wrong because they were based on little evidence (e.g., Ilchman and Rosenblatt 1987) or faulty logic (e.g., *Time* 1985). It remains that while the policy of community mental health was supported by all and criticized by none in *theory*, belief in it eroded simultaneously with its *implementation*.

5.   The articles were indexed under the major category of "homeless persons." I chose all articles for which the index abstract included the terms of deinstitutionalization, involuntary confinement, or Project HELP, which became the organization responsible for carrying out policies of involuntary hospitalization. Three brief methodological notes are in order. First, newspapers are only

one of multiple sites constructing images of types of conditions and persons, and the *New York Times* is a particular newspaper in a specific city. Second, as with any text, what appears in a newspaper is the end result of complicated bureaucratic and political processes. Here I will bracket these issues of how articles were assembled. Third, in this section all references are to the *NYT*. Here I will cite only the date of the reference. A separate reference list for the *NYT* articles also cites these sources by date and notes their by-lines.

6. Mayor Koch reports great pride in leading efforts to reinstitutionalize the "homeless mentally ill," declaring in 1993 that it was "one of the ten best things I did in my 12 years of service as mayor" (Koch 1993:xiii).

7. Careful readers might note that such a construction collapses the category of "street homeless" into the category of the "homeless mentally ill." By definition, persons who live on the street in winter become the "homeless mentally ill."

REFERENCES

Bassuk, E. L., and S. Gerson. 1985. "Deinstitutionalization and Mental Health Services." Pp. 127–144 in *Mental Health Care and Social Policy*, edited by P. Brown. Boston: Routledge & Kegan Paul.

Best, J. 1989. "Dark Figures and Child Victims: Statistical Claims about Missing Children." Pp. 21–37 in *Images of Issues: Typifying Contemporary Social Problems*, edited by J. Best. Hawthorne, NY: Aldine de Gruyter.

———. 1990. *Threatened Children: Rhetoric and Concern about Child-Victims*. Chicago: University of Chicago Press.

Brown, P. 1981. "The Mental Patients' Rights Movement, and Mental Health Institutional Change." *International Journal of Health Services* 11:523–540.

Case, J., and R. Taylor. 1979. *Co-Ops, Communes & Collectives: Experiments in Social Change in the 1960s and 1970s*. New York: Pantheon Books.

Castle, R. 1988. *The Regulation of Madness: The Origin of Incarceration in France*. Berkeley: University of California Press.

Clark, C. 1987. "Sympathy Biography and Sympathy Margin." *American Journal of Sociology* 93:290–321.

Coates, R. C. 1990. *A Street Is Not a Home: Solving America's Homeless Dilemma*. Buffalo, Prometheus Books.

Conrad, P., and J. Schneider. 1985. *Deviance and Medicalization: From Badness to Sickness*. Columbus: Merrill Publishing Company.

Fuller, T. E. 1988. *Nowhere to Go: The Tragic Odyssey of the Homeless Mentally Ill*. New York: Harper & Row.

Glazer, N. 1968. "Beyond Income Maintenance—A Note on Welfare in New York City." *The Public Interest* 16:102–120.

Grob, G. N. 1987. "Public Policy and Mental Illness: A Retrospective Analysis." Pp. 103–132 in *Coping and Caring: New York in an Era of Deinstitutionalization*, edited by A. Rosenblatt and W. F. Ilchman. Albany, NY: The Nelson A. Rockefeller Institute of Government.

Holstein, J. A. 1993. *Court-Ordered Insanity: Interpretive Practice and Involuntary Commitment*. Hawthorne, NY: Aldine de Gruyter.

Ilchman, W. F., and A. Rosenblatt. 1987. "Coping and Caring: An Overview." Pp. 1–37 in *Coping and Caring: New York in an Era of Deinstitutionalization*, edited by A. Rosenblatt and W F. Ilchman. Albany, NY: The Nelson A. Rockefeller Institute of Government.

Isaac, R. J., and V. C. Armat . 1990. *Madness in the Streets: How Psychiatry and the Law Abandoned the Mentally Ill*. New York: Free Press.

Koch, E. I. 1993. "Foreward." Pp. xiii–xvii in *Intensive Treatment of the Homeless Mentally Ill*, edited by S. E. Katz, D. Nardacci, and A. Sabatini. Washington, DC: American Psychiatric Press.

Loseke, D. R. 1989. "Evaluation Research and the Practice of Social Services: A Case for Qualitative Methodology." *Journal of Contemporary Ethnography* 18(2):202–223.

———. 1992. *The Battered Woman and Shelters: The Social Construction of Wife Abuse*. Albany: State University of New York Press.

———. 1993. "Constructing Conditions, People, Morality, and Emotion: Expanding the Agenda of Constructionism." Pp. 207–216 in *Constructionist Controversies: Issues in Social Problems Theory*, edited by G. Miller and J. A. Holstein. Hawthorne, NY: Aldine de Gruyter.

Margolin, L. 1994. *Goodness Personified: The Emergence of Gifted Children*. Hawthorne, NY: Aldine de Gruyter.

Marin, P. 1987. "Helping and Hating the Homeless: The Struggle at the Margins of America." *Harpers Magazine* January:39–49.

McLeod, M., and V. Milstein. 1993. "Impact of the Legal System on Treatment." Pp. 25–50 in *Intensive Treatment of the Homeless Mentally Ill*, edited by S. E. Katz, D. Nardacci, and A. Sabatini. Washington: American Psychiatric Press.

Mechanic, D., and D. A. Rochefort. 1992. "A Policy of Inclusion for the Mentally Ill." *Health Affairs* 11:128–150.

Merelman, R. M. 1984. *Making Something of Ourselves: On Culture and Politics in the United States*. Berkeley: University of California Press.

Morrissey, J. P., and H. H. Goldman. 1987. "Reform Cycles in the Care of the Chronically Mentally ill. Pp. 133–147 in *Coping and Caring: New York in an Era of Deinstitutionalization*, edited by A. Rosenblatt and W. F. Ilchman. Albany, NY: The Nelson A. Rockefeller Institute of Government.

Morse, S. J. 1982. "A Preference for Liberty: The Case Against Involuntary Commitment of the Mentally Disordered." Pp. 69–109 in *The Court of Last Resort: Mental Illness and the Law*, edited by C. A. B. Warren. Chicago: University of Chicago Press.

Newsweek. 1987. "Forcing the Mentally Ill to Get Help." 110(November 9):47–48.

Rothman, D. J. 1971. *The Discovery of the Asylum: Social Order and Disorder in the New Republic*. Boston: Little, Brown.

Siegel, N. H., R. L. Kahn, M. Pollack, and M. Fink. 1962. "Social Class, Diagnosis, and Treatment in Three Psychiatric Hospitals." *Social Problems* 10:191–196.

Snow. L., and L. Anderson. 1993. *Down on Their Luck: A Study of Homeless Street People*. Berkeley: University of California Press.

Stern, M. J. 1984. "The Emergence of the Homeless as a Public Problem." *Social Services Review* 58:291–301.

Time. 1985. "When Liberty Really Means Neglect." 126 (December 2):103–104.

Wagenaar, H., and D. A. Lewis. 1989. "Ironies of Inclusion: Social Class and Deinstitutionalization." *Journal of Health Politics, Policy and Law* 14:503–522.

White, R. W. 1992. *Rude Awakenings: What the Homeless Crisis Tells Us*. San Francisco: ICS Press.

REFERENCES FOR THE *NEW YORK TIMES*

1963

2-6   "Kennedy Seeks Funds to Reduce Mental Illness." (Robert C. Toth) I 1:1.

1981

3-27   "Koch Seeks Law for Roundups to Aid the Homeless." (Molly Ivins) II 3:4.

3-28   Editorial: "Scoring the Mayor." I 22:2.

1982

1-27   "Woman Refuses Aid, Dies in Carton on Street." (Robin Herman) I 1:1.

1-29   Editorial: "Rebecca Smith, Who Said No." I 26:1.

2-8   Letter from Dr. Mark Schoenberg and David Winkler. I 18:4.

2-16   Opinion Editorial: "The Lady in the Box." I 19:1.

2-19   Editorial: "Forced Shelter." I 30:1.

1983

3-25   "Mayor Offers Aid and Hand To Homeless." (Ronald Sullivan) II 1:1.

1984

8-24   Editorial: "A Street Is Not a Home" I 24:1.

10-10   "The City Sees No Solutions for Homeless." (Deirdre Carmody). I 1:4.

12-17   "The Tangled Life and Mind of Judy, Whose Home Is the Street." (Deirdre Carmody). II 1:1.

1985

1-23   "Police to Roundup Homeless When Cold Wave Grips City." (Joyce Purnick) I 1:1.

1-24   Editorial: "In From the Cold." I 24:1.

2-3   "Interview: Senator Frank Padavan on the Street People: Private Rights, Public Fears." IV 9:1.

10-25   "Koch and Rivals Clash in Debate." (Frank Lynn) II 1:5.

11-14   "Homeless in City Facing Koch Edict." (Josh Barbanel) I 1:3.

11-15   "On the Streets: Tough Test for New Homeless Policy." II 1:1.

11-22   "Mentally Ill Homeless: Policy at Issue." (Josh Barbanel) II 4:4.

11-27   "At 28, a Prologue of Promise, but a Life in Rags." (Sara Rimer). II 4:3.

12-4   "8,084 Jam City Shelters; 157 Taken Off Streets." I:1:1.

12-7   "Saving Homeless from Themselves: A New Policy Creates New Dis-
       putes." (Josh Barbanel) I 29:1.
12-8   "Weighing the Risks and Rights of Homelessness." (David Margolick) IV
       6:3.
12-17 "Helping New York City's Homeless." I 27:3.
1986
3-12   "Policy Extended of Hospitalizing the Homeless." (Barbara Basler) II 1:1.
11-14 "Homeless Brought to Shelters in Record Cold." (John T. McQuiston) II 2:4.
1987
8-29   "New York Expands Treatment Policy for the Homeless." (Suzanne
       Daley) I 1:1.
9-1   "Psychologists Back Koch's Policy on Hospitalizing Homeless People."
       (Bruce Lambert) I 1:2.
9-2(a) Editorial: "Calcutta, N.Y.: A Revolving Door." I 26:1.
9-2(b) "Lack of Beds Called Flaw in Koch's Plan for Homeless Mentally Ill."
       II:5:1.
9-4   Opinion: "Across the Street." (A. M. Rosenthal) I 27:5.
9-5(a) "In New York, Cautious Help for the Helpless." (Suzanne Daley) I 1:2.
9-5(b) "Hospital Union Is Wary of Plan for Ill Homeless." I:26:1.
9-6   "Koch Presses His Plan to Hospitalize Some Homeless." IV 6:1.
9-8   "Koch and Public Opinion: Getting the Homeless off the Street." II 3:1.
9-17   Opinion: "Koch's Mishandling of the Homeless." (Norman Siegel and
       Robert Levy) I 35:1.
10-29 "Mentally Ill Homeless Taken Off New York Streets." (Josh Barbanel) I 1:1.
11-2   "Woman Battles Koch's Program for Mentally Ill." (Josh Barbanel) II 3:1.
11-6   "In Hospital Courtroom, Plea for Freedom." (Josh Barbanel) II 1:3.
11-9   "Vallone Urges Jail for Homeless People Who Decline Help." II 2:6.
11-11 "Koch's Plan Faces a Test." (Josh Barbanel) II 1:2.
11-13 Court transcripts: "Though Homeless, She Copes, She is Fit, She Sur-
       vives." II 2:2.
11-14 Editorial: "Bring the Others in From the Cold." I 26:1.
11-26 Letter to the Editor: "Can't We Aid New York's Homeless Without Lock-
       ing Them Up?" I 30:4.
11-27 Opinion: "Psychiatrists as Puppets of Koch's Roundup Policy." (Robert
       E. Gould and Robert Levy) I 35:2.
12-19 "Court Backs Treatment of Woman Held Under Koch Homeless Plan."
       (Kirk Johnson) I:1:1.
1988
1-16   "Joyce Brown Obtains a Ban on Medicine." (Josh Barbanel) I 29:1.
1-22   Opinion: "The Mayor and Joyce Brown." (A. M. Rosenthal) I 31:1.
2-13   Letter to the Editor: "It's Time We Stopped Blaming the Homeless." I
       26:4.
1989
1-26   Opinion: "Homeless: Craziness, Dope and Danger." (Myron Magnet)
       I:31:1.

1-28 Editorial: "The Subway Killing's Lesson." IV 20:1.
6-29 "Poll Shows New Yorkers Fault City Efforts for the Homeless." (Josh Barbanel) I 1:4.
8-14 Editorial: "Help the Homeless, and Win Votes." I 14:1.
11-18 "Doors Closing as Mood on the Homeless Sours." (Sara Rimer) I 1:2.

1990
11-23 Opinion: "Park Avenue Lady." (A. M. Rosenthal) I 37:1.

1991
6-22 "Evicting the Homeless." (Sam Roberts) I 1:1.
10-28 "What Led to Crackdown on Homeless." (Sam Roberts) II 1:2.
11-28 Editorial Notebook: "Reinstitutionalize the Homeless? Opening Hospitals Would Cost a Fortune." I 26:1.

1992
8-26 "Fear Returns to Sidewalks of West 96th Street Along with Homeless Man." (Eben Shapiro) II 3:1.
11-15 Column: "Refusing to Overlook the Homeless." (Michael Winerip) I 41:1.

13

Creativity, Conflict, and Control:
Film Industry Campaigns to Shape Video Policy

DAVID F. LUCKENBILL

Technological development has been pivotal to the production and distribution of creative works. Advances in the technologies of information processing and transmission, for example, let authors produce new works (such as computer software and databases) and distribute these and more conventional works to larger audiences with greater efficiency. At the same time, technological development has hurt authors. Advances in the technologies of information reception and reproduction have enabled people to acquire and copy works without the authors' authorization or remuneration. These developments have made some members of the creative community concerned about the integrity of their works and their rights to them, and some creators have vigorously resisted threatening information technologies (Office of Technology Assessment 1986, 1992).

This chapter examines resistance to a new technology that threatened one segment of the creative community. In particular, it examines two legal campaigns by the film industry to control the unauthorized reproduction of audiovisual works following the introduction of the home videocassette recorder. Before examining these campaigns, I will describe some aspects of the legal context governing creative works.

CREATIVITY, CONFLICT, AND EXPLOITATIVE TECHNOLOGY

The relationship between people who create works of art and literature and people who use them is complex. To be sure, authors and consumers support one another. Authors inform, enlighten, and divert, and consumers reward them for doing so. On the other hand, authors and consumers conflict. A significant point of conflict involves the consumer's relationship to creative works. Basically, authors and consumers differ over how consumers should use these works (Ploman and Hamilton 1980).

Conflict over the use of creative works flows from discordant principles embodied in the law. Works of art and literature are protected by copyright law. On the one hand, copyright law gives an author a number of exclusive rights, such as to exhibit a work, reproduce the work, and distribute copies of it. Here, copyright law embraces the principle that an author has the right to remuneration. The basic purpose of copyright law is to nurture the production and dissemination of intellectual works; if people are to pursue creative endeavors, they must have an economic incentive for doing so. Accordingly, law should grant authors exclusive rights, a monopoly over their works. Yet, on the other hand, copyright law also limits the author's rights. Under the rubric of fair use, for example, the law permits people to reproduce works for purposes of criticism, news reporting, teaching, or research (Strong 1993). These limitations derive from a different principle: citizens have the right to as much information as they deem appropriate. If people are to lead rich, meaningful lives, they must be able to draw upon the creative accomplishments of others; accordingly, law should grant citizens free and unimpeded access to intellectual works. These discordant principles cause friction between authors and consumers (Fisher 1989; Horowitz 1986).

Ambiguity within copyright law exacerbates conflict over the use of creative works. Consider the concept of "fair use," the idea that one should be free to use another's work so long as the use does not exploit its commercial value. The courts established fair use in the nineteenth century, and Congress codified it in the 1976 Copyright Act. However, neither the courts nor Congress offered a clear definition of fair use (Cohen 1955; Timberg 1980). In section 107 of the Copyright Act, Congress listed four criteria for deciding whether a particular use is fair:

1. the purpose and character of the use, including whether such use is of a commercial nature or is for nonprofit educational purposes;
2. the nature of the copyrighted work;
3. the amount and substantiality of the portion used in relation to the copyrighted work as a whole; and
4. the effect of the use upon the potential market for or value of the copyrighted work.

But Congress failed to define these criteria, stipulate the order in which they are to be applied, or specify their relative weight. Such ambiguity thrusts certain uses of a work into a legal penumbra, causing discord over what constitutes appropriate use (Seltzer 1978; Timberg 1989).

Consumers' possession of creative works and their ignorance of copyright complicate conflict between authors and consumers. In many cases, the consumption of creative works requires possession; to read a book, for example, one must have a copy. While possession makes consumption possible, it also gives consumers an opportunity for wrongful exploitation; someone with a copy of a book can turn around and use it in ways that violate the author's rights. It is in an author's interest to have a work consumed by as large an audience as possible; a book's success can be measured by the number of copies sold. Yet the larger the number of people who possess a work, the larger the number who can misuse it. Thus, the author has a problem: success requires that a work be distributed to people who can proceed to abuse it.

Widespread ignorance of copyright compounds this problem. What consumers of creative works typically possess are tangible objects in which intellectual expressions are fixed—volumes, cassettes, diskettes, and so on. Law provides that consumers can do anything they want with the tangible object they purchase; they can, for instance, sell, loan, or destroy their copy of a book. However, ownership of the object is not ownership of the expression fixed in it; consumers cannot reproduce the text and sell copies. The author owns the intellectual expression, and only the author has the right to reproduce and distribute copies of it. While the copyright industry recognizes the distinction between intellectual expressions and the tangible objects in which they are fixed, most consumers do not. They view these objects the way they do other possessions: ownership of the object is taken as ownership of its contents (Office of Technology Assessment 1986). Thus, the author's problem is even more troublesome: success requires that a work be distributed to people who have few reservations about abusing it.

With regard to the use of creative works, then, there is conflict between authors and consumers. However, such conflict does not become truly problematic unless there is a technology of exploitation—a means of using creative works in ways that threaten an author's rights. If such a technology does not exist, or if it is generally unavailable, conflict over the use of a work remains pretty much academic. It is with the introduction of an exploitative technology that consumers can begin to misuse creative works, and it is with the technology's diffusion that misuse can grow. The prospect of abuse, in turn, may stimulate efforts among authors to maintain control over their works.

Controlling the Use of Films

We can see this pattern in the history of film consumption. Until recently, consumers could view films only at times and in forms determined by copyright owners (usually film studios and production companies). These limitations reflected, in large part, the lack of technologies that might have let consumers govern their use of films. As such technologies developed, consumers began to assume some control, using films in ways owners considered troublesome. One such use was unauthorized reproduction.

Through the 1960s, the unauthorized reproduction of films was technically difficult. It not only required access to special locations—such as a film vault—which housed legitimate film prints, but it also required special tools—such as an optical reduction printer—and special skills—such as knowing how to convert a 35-mm theatrical print into a Super-8 print. Not surprisingly, the operation usually involved people in the entertainment industry—film librarians, lab technicians, projectionists, and the like. And by most accounts unauthorized reproduction was rare. Some persons borrowed theatrical prints and made copies for their private collections; others borrowed or stole theatrical prints or found discarded prints, duplicated them, and sold the copies to collectors or exhibitors (Monaco 1978).

In the 1970s, unauthorized reproduction became comparatively easy. This decade witnessed the development of the videocassette recorder (VCR), a simple device that enabled almost anyone to copy a film. One merely hooked a VCR to a television set and recorded a film broadcast over the air ("off-air recording") or hooked two VCRs together and recorded a film that had been prerecorded on a videocassette ("back-to-back copying"). Video recorders began to appear in the early 1970s. However, the early systems had limited recording capability and serious technical flaws, and they were expensive. In 1975, Sony introduced the Betamax, a technically superior, relatively inexpensive system, and it did considerable business. By November 1976, approximately 25,000 Betamax units were in American homes (*Business Week* 1976). A number of Japanese and American firms followed Sony's lead, marketing longer-recording, lower-priced machines, and VCR sales climbed (Klopfenstein 1989). As VCRs became more prevalent, so did the unauthorized reproduction of films and other programs. Studies showed growing numbers of people engaged in increasing amounts of off-air recording and back-to-back copying (Agostino, Johnson, and Terry 1979).

Copyright owners saw the development of the VCR as a significant threat, and they sought to maintain control over the use of their works (Lardner 1987). In 1975, the Motion Picture Association of America (MPAA), a trade association consisting of the nation's largest film studios, established a security office to monitor the distribution of theatrical prints and to identify and prosecute film pirates (individuals engaged in unauthorized reproduction for commercial gain).[1] In 1976, two studios sued the manufacturer, distributors, and owners of the Betamax, charging that off-air recording of films and other programs was an infringement of copyright. In the late 1970s, film distributors began to treat prerecorded videocassettes so that consumers could not copy them. In the early 1980s, the MPAA promoted legislation to increase the penalties for piracy, and in the mid-1980s it urged Congress to consider legislation to modify VCRs so that consumers could not use them for back-to-back copying. Around the same time, the MPAA conducted a campaign to educate people about the wrongfulness of piracy, and the Video Software Dealers' Association (VSDA) conducted a drive to teach video dealers about the costs and consequences of the activity. The MPAA and VSDA also established piracy hotlines, toll-free numbers that people could call to report cases of piracy, and they offered rewards for the identification and apprehension of pirates.

Central to the copyright owners' efforts to maintain control were legal actions. Many film studios and production companies had legal departments, and they were organized to define matters of concern as legal problems and respond by taking legal action. Moreover, the situation seemed to demand state assistance. Owners could not effectively monitor the use of their works; while mass consumption of films and other programs required their wide distribution, owners had limited supervisory resources. Accordingly, they had difficulty keeping consumers with the means of reproduction from copying their works. It made good sense, then, to ask the state to enjoin consumers from reproducing films and sanction them for doing so.

The following analysis focuses on two film industry efforts, both legal campaigns against unauthorized reproduction. It examines them because they were among the first systematic attempts by the creative community to control reproductive technologies and because they received a good deal of attention in the press and legal circles, making them accessible for analysis. I ask two questions. First, how were these campaigns organized? Since the campaigns sought to persuade lawmakers that particular forms of reproduction must be controlled, this question concerns the rhetoric of claims (Best 1990). Second, what were the consequences of these campaigns?

TWO CAMPAIGNS AGAINST UNAUTHORIZED REPRODUCTION

Between 1975 and 1985, copyright owners mounted two campaigns against the unauthorized reproduction of audiovisual works. One focused on controlling off-air recording, while the other sought to control piracy. Both campaigns stemmed from the development of the VCR and the perception among copyright owners that the VCR could be used in ways that threatened their rights. However, these campaigns treated the technology differently, and they had different outcomes.

Off-Air Recording

Approximately one year after Sony introduced the Betamax to the American public, the film industry launched a massive legal campaign against unauthorized reproduction. This campaign involved battles on both judicial and legislative fronts.

In 1976, Universal Studios and Walt Disney Productions filed a suit in the U.S. District Court in Los Angeles charging the manufacturer, distributors, and individual owners of the Betamax with copyright infringement. The plaintiffs advanced two basic claims. First, they asserted that off-air recording of their programs for home use[2] was infringement, for it violated their exclusive right to reproduce these works. If Congress wished to permit home recording, they noted, it would have established a suitable exemption in copyright law. Moreover, off-air recording was not fair use, largely because it would cause the owners irreparable harm. The plaintiffs observed that Betamax owners commonly used the machine for both time-shifting—recording a program, viewing it at a convenient time, then erasing the program in order to use the tape again— and librarying—recording a program and saving the tape for multiple viewings. Both practices, they said, posed significant threats. Time-shifting would reduce the audience for an original telecast, reduce the audience for live television at the time of viewing a recording, and decimate the audience for reruns, while librarying would reduce the audiences for television and other entertainments. These losses would depress copyright owners' revenues because lower ratings meant smaller fees paid to producers. The plaintiffs also observed that Betamax owners commonly used the machine to avoid commercials—deleting them when recording or passing over them when playing back—and said this would further depress their revenues because advertisers would not support programs if commercials did not reach the entire audience. Second, the plaintiffs asserted that the corporate defendants were liable for contributory infringement. They stated that the manufacture, promotion, demonstration, and sale of the Betamax caused, induced, or encouraged the unauthorized reproduction of copyrighted works. In fact, according to the plaintiffs, the primary use for which the machine was designed and marketed was to record protected works.

Defining off-air recording and the manufacture and distribution of the VCR as unlawful, the plaintiffs asked the court to enjoin the defendants from distributing the Betamax and order them to recall the machines that had been sold.

The defendants countered that off-air recording for home use was not infringement. Although copyright law did not address off-air recording expressly, the legislative history of the 1976 Copyright Act showed that Congress did not intend to prohibit the home recording of either sound recordings or audiovisual works. Indeed, there was an "implied exemption" for home recording in the law. Further, they argued that even if home recording were infringement, the corporate defendants could not be held liable. Challenging allegations of contributory infringement, the defendants asserted that the VCR was a "staple article of commerce," a tool that could be used for legitimate purposes, and that the manufacturers and distributors of such articles could not be held liable for infringement by consumers.

The District Court decided in favor of the defendants (*Universal* v. *Sony* 1979). It concluded that off-air recording for home use was not infringement because there was an implied exemption for home recording in copyright law. Noting that Congress exempted home audio recording when it passed the 1971 Sound Recording Act, the court reasoned that Congress intended to exempt home video recording as well when it passed the Copyright Act. The court added that home recording qualified as fair use because home recordings were used for private, noncommercial purposes and because home recording did not appear to reduce the market for copyrighted works. Moreover, the court concluded that even if home recording were infringement, the corporate defendants could not be held liable for contributory infringement. It declared that suing defendants because they manufacture and distribute a product capable of various uses, some allegedly infringing, was unwise:

> Selling a staple article of commerce—e.g., a typewriter, a recorder, a camera, a photocopying machine—technically contributes to any infringing use subsequently made thereof, but this kind of "contribution," if deemed sufficient as a basis for liability, would expand the theory beyond precedent and arguably beyond judicial management. (p. 461)

The court also suggested that holding the defendants liable was dangerous. It noted that in patent law, the manufacturers and distributors of staple articles of commerce could not be held liable for contributory infringement, as doing so would "block the wheels of commerce." The court found the rationale for this law meaningful here: "Commerce would indeed be hampered if manufacturers of staple items were held liable as contributory infringers whenever they constructively knew that some purchasers on some occasions would use the product for a purpose which a court later deemed . . . to be an infringement" (p. 461).

The studios appealed to the Ninth Circuit Court in San Francisco, and it reversed the decision (*Universal* v. *Sony* 1981). The court held that home video recording was infringement. It reasoned that Congress did not intend to create a blanket exemption for home recording, that the basic rationale for exempting audio recording was not applicable to video recording, and that home video recording was not fair use because large portions of works were copied and mass copying would hurt the market for copyrighted works. Further, the court held that the corporate defendants were liable for contributory infringement. It argued that the District Court's reliance on the staple article of commerce principle was inappropriate. According to this principle, the sale of an item is not contributory infringement if the item is suitable for substantial non-infringing use. The court stated that the VCR lacked this feature: "Videotape recorders are manufactured, advertised, and sold for the primary purpose of reproducing television programming. Virtually all television programming is copyrighted material. Therefore, videotape recorders are not suitable for substantial noninfringing use" (p. 975).

This decision surprised a good many people. Copyright experts said the reversal was unexpected, though many thought it was appropriate. Thomas McCarthy, a law professor, called the decision "courageous" and believed that a contrary finding "might lead to unraveling the rights of creative people" (*Los Angeles Times* 1981a:1). Editorials and commentaries in major newspapers expressed appreciation for the importance of both protecting an author's rights and providing consumers with access to information, and they pressed lawmakers to find a solution satisfying both needs. On the other hand, political cartoons lampooned the decision. One showed a "Betamax squad" raiding the home of an otherwise respectable VCR owner (*Chicago Tribune* 1981). Another asked why the courts have not found firearm manufacturers liable on the same grounds as Sony (*Los Angeles Times* 1981b). And letters to the editors expressed indignation; one man accused the court of contemporary Luddism and hoped the U.S. Supreme Court would bury the decision alongside Edison's attempt to control the phonograph and AT&T's efforts to throttle network radio (*New York Times* 1981:34).

Within days, a number of bills aimed at overturning the decision were introduced in Congress. These bills exempted off-air recording for private, noncommercial use from infringement. The film industry was not pleased with these bills, and it urged legislators to present bills more to its liking (Cohodas 1982, p. 629). Some legislators answered the call, introducing "compensation bills" that exempted off-air recording but created a system of compulsory licensing in which the manufacturers of

VCRs and blank tapes would pay a royalty on each machine and tape for distribution to the appropriate copyright owners. These different bills received lengthy hearings and generated considerable debate.

The film industry backed the compensation bills. Appearing before various House and Senate committees, industry members acknowledged that off-air recording for home use should be permitted. Jack Valenti, representing the MPAA and the Coalition to Preserve the American Copyright, stated: "no one wants to prevent taping in the home. . . . I want very much to permit noncommercial taping in the home" (U.S. Senate 1982:459). At the same time, the industry continued to regard off-air recording of copyrighted works as illegitimate and insisted that copyright owners be compensated. The industry justified this demand in terms of the perceived harmfulness of off-air recording, observing that consumers commonly used the VCR for librarying and time-shifting, and arguing that these practices hurt the industry. Librarying displaced the purchase and rental of prerecorded cassettes and decimated the audiences for crucial aftermarkets, while time-shifting reduced the audiences for live telecasts and lessened viewer contact with commercials. These effects reduced industry revenues, and depressed revenues would weaken the industry. Some producers would cut their investments to make a profit, while others would abandon the creative enterprise because their incentive was gone. A shrinking industry would put thousands of people out of work and hurt the economy. Valenti stated that the film industry had been a significant trade asset, returning to the United States up to $1 billion a year in surplus balance of trade (U.S. Senate 1984:287–288). A shrinking industry also would hurt the public, for people would have fewer programs, and even fewer quality programs, available for enjoyment.

The compensation bills, members concluded, provided a reasonable way to offset the harm caused by off-air recording. Compensation would furnish the revenues the industry required and help preserve the incentive producers needed. At the same time, these bills enabled consumers to engage in off-air recording without paying extra for it. Indeed, they provided that the manufacturers of VCRs and blank tapes pay the royalties. This was deemed not only practical, for the manufacturers were best positioned to pay, but fair, for the only party to have benefitted from the VCR was the home recording industry. "Built on the backs of copyright owners," Valenti said, this industry was "swollen with profits" and "blind to the basic principles of fairness and equity underlying our copyright system" (U.S. Senate 1984:299).[3]

In contrast, the home recording industry supported the pure exemption bills. Members of this industry regarded off-air recording for home use as legitimate, and they insisted that it be free from government restraint. In particular, they opposed efforts to establish a compensation system. Members argued that the film industry's demand for compensation lacked merit. The VCR, they observed, was not the beast the film industry portrayed it as being. They noted that consumers often used the VCR for purposes other than recording programs, such as viewing prerecorded cassettes and home movies. When consumers engaged in off-air recording, they usually did so for purposes of time-shifting, not librarying, and time-shifting was harmless. It did not reduce program ratings, for ratings services counted running VCRs as "viewers," and it did not lessen viewer contact with commercials, for most time-shifters watched most commercials. Accordingly, some copyright owners—like the National Football League—did not object to off-air recording of their programs. Moreover, members observed that the VCR offered many benefits. They noted that the film industry profited from the technology. Charles Ferris, representing the Home Recording Rights Coalition, an association formed in 1982 and consisting of the manufacturers and distributors of VCRs and blank tapes, declared that the VCR created lucrative new markets for motion pictures and greatly increased the film industry's revenues (U.S. Senate 1984:341).[4] The nation benefitted too. Joseph Lagore, president of Sony Consumer Products, reported that the home recording industry employed thousands of Americans in the manufacture and distribution of VCRs and tapes and contributed some $3 billion a year to the economy (U.S. Senate 1982:32). And the public gained. As Ferris stated:

> VCRs have become a critical element in the revolution taking place in home communications. This technology will free people from the artificial confines of network scheduling, permit them to receive new and diverse sources of information and ultimately open up a vast and still largely unexplored frontier of additional uses for video recorders. (U.S. House 1983:158)

Members added that compensating copyright owners for off-air recording was unfair and harmful. Instead of collecting a fee for services rendered, as the term "compensation" implied, the compensation bills would levy a tax, a charge on property. And such a tax was wrong. In the first place, consumers, not manufacturers, would foot the bill. Carol Tucker Foreman, representing the Home Recording Rights Coalition, called the consumer's exemption from liability a "sham." If the compensation bills were passed, the consumer would bear the burden, for the manufacturers and distributors of VCRs and blank tapes would pass the costs on to consumers (U.S. Senate 1984:475). In the second place, copyright owners did not deserve the revenues the tax would produce. Ferris noted that existing market mechanisms fully compensated owners:

"Any additional tax or royalty would be a huge windfall for Hollywood producers by requiring consumers to pay twice for the same program" (U.S. House 1983:159). Almost as troubling would be "the inequity of a royalty as applied to those who are not taping copyrighted materials" (U.S. Senate 1982:574). Members also maintained that compensation would hurt the home recording industry and the public. By increasing the cost of machines and tapes, the tax would stunt the industry, "threatening the very existence of the nearly 25,000 small businesses that are totally dependent upon its vitality and impeding new business opportunities for broadcasters and independent producers" (U.S. Senate 1982:558). Nina Cornell, an economist retained by the Coalition, reported that the tax would divert manufacturers from developing the technology of video cameras, divert entrepreneurs from developing new video services for the public, and slow the development of the VCR as a medium for distributing programming (U.S. Senate 1984:400). Thus, members of the home recording industry argued that the VCR posed little danger and offered numerous benefits, while compensation for off-air recording was unfair and harmful. The only sensible policy, they concluded, was absolute exemption of off-air recording for home use.

The competing bills attracted considerable interest, not only in Congress but also in the press. Despite this interest, none of the bills came to a vote. They died in large part because, in early 1984, the U.S. Supreme Court decided in favor of the home recording industry (Witt 1984).

In a 5–4 decision, the Supreme Court reversed the Circuit Court's ruling, vindicating off-air recording for home use and exonerating the manufacturers and distributors of VCRs (*Sony* v. *Universal* 1984). The court determined that home recording did not constitute infringement. Reviewing the evidence, it concluded that consumers commonly used the VCR for time-shifting, and it agreed with the District Court that time-shifting was permitted under fair use. Time-shifting qualified as fair use because it was a noncommercial activity and did not appear to harm or threaten the market for copyrighted works. In addition, the court determined that the manufacture and distribution of the VCR did not constitute contributory infringement: "The sale of copying equipment, like the sale of other articles of commerce, does not constitute contributory infringement if the product is widely used for legitimate, unobjectionable purposes. Indeed, it need only be capable of substantial noninfringing uses. . . . One potential use of the Betamax plainly satisfies this standard, however it is understood: private, noncommercial time-shifting in the home" (p. 442).

In sum, off-air recording was a subject of contention. The film industry sought to control the activity by controlling the VCR, while the home recording industry sought to block such efforts and provide for the unbridled distribution and use of the VCR. The opponents pursued their objectives in both judicial and legislative arenas, presenting competing arguments. The film industry claimed that off-air recording and the manufacture and distribution of the VCR were illegitimate activities, that the harm caused by these activities warranted legal intervention, and that off-air recording could be controlled by prohibiting or at least regulating the distribution of the VCR. In contrast, the home recording industry claimed that off-air recording and the manufacture and distribution of the VCR were legitimate activities, that the benefits from these activities warranted legal protection, and that these activities could be preserved by legally absolving them. Despite its diligence and its offer to permit off-air recording in return for royalty payments, the film industry's campaign to control the activity failed.

Film Piracy

In the early 1980s, the film industry launched a second legal campaign against unauthorized reproduction. This campaign targeted film piracy—a type of criminal infringement involving unauthorized reproduction for commercial gain.

In the mid-1970s, film piracy became increasingly visible. Newspapers and magazines began to run stories on the nature and scope of piracy as well as on the apprehension of pirates and seizure of pirated works. Officials began to discuss the incidence and growth of piracy, the complexity of the piracy industry, their attempts to combat piracy, and the problems they encountered. Members of the film industry began to publicize the harmfulness of piracy and their efforts to capture and prosecute pirates.

In 1981, two bills were introduced in the House and Senate aimed at strengthening the laws against piracy and counterfeiting. Copyright law already provided that anyone who engaged in a criminal infringement of a copyright of a sound recording or motion picture was eligible for a fine of not more than $25,000 and/or imprisonment for not more than one year for the first offense, increasing to $50,000 and/or two years for a subsequent offense. Criminal law further provided that anyone who used counterfeit packaging to distribute copies of such works was eligible for a fine of not more than $10,000 and/or imprisonment for not more than one year for the first offense, increasing to $25,000 and/or two years for a subsequent offense. The two new bills defined grades of piracy and raised the penalties for counterfeiting and the more serious grades of piracy; they held, for example, that anyone who used counterfeit labels or packages for records or audiovisual works and anyone who reproduced or distributed, during any 180-day period, at least 1,000 copies of one or more sound recordings or 65 copies of one or more audiovisual works would be fined up to $250,000 and/or imprisoned for up to five years.

These bills targeted relatively large-scale commercial operations, those in which offenders produced large numbers of illicit copies for sale or lease and used counterfeit packaging to pass them off as legitimate. The proponents of these bills maintained that large-scale piracy was a genuine problem. Appearing before House and Senate committees, members of the film and record industries reported that piracy often involved sophisticated operations with skilled personnel, special equipment for duplicating works and producing counterfeit packages and labels, and substantial capital (U.S. House 1981:785–787; U.S. Senate 1981:44–45). Accordingly:

> multimillion dollar piracy and counterfeiting operations are not at all uncommon. For example, one counterfeiting ring raided in 1977 was alone responsible for producing and disseminating more than 25 million counterfeit records a year, reaping an annual profit of more than $30 million. (U.S. House 1981:771)

Further, members reported that lured by the promise of huge profits, organized crime was heavily involved in piracy. Indeed, James Bouras, testifying on behalf of the MPAA and the Recording Industry Association of America (RIAA), asserted that organized criminals "control" piracy. (U.S. Senate 1981:54)

Proponents also maintained that piracy had become an increasingly serious problem. David Ladd, the Register of Copyrights, stated that "film and record piracy has become epidemic around the world" (U.S. House 1981:990). Bouras observed that piracy was "a massive worldwide problem" and that "film and record piracy—and particularly counterfeiting—are growing by leaps and bounds" (U.S. Senate 1981:20, 41). In support of the latter point, he cited a government report:

> The Department of Justice has recognized the epidemic proportions of piracy and counterfeiting. In August 1980, the Attorney General published the results of a survey of FBI field offices throughout the nation which ranked the problem areas in all forms of white-collar crime, including corruption, financial crimes, and various frauds. Of the 44 crime areas listed in the survey, the FBI ranked copyright violations—that is, film and record piracy and counterfeiting—as the third most troublesome. (pp. 42–43)

Similarly, Renee Szybala, testifying on behalf of the Department of Justice, said that piracy was "a major white-collar crime" that had experienced "dramatic growth" (U.S. Senate 1981:11).

The industry blamed piracy's apparent growth on the weak penalties. Clearly, some proponents recognized that the evolution of reproductive technologies and the maturation of markets for prerecorded tapes and cassettes fostered increased levels of piracy. They noted, for example, that the development of the VCR contributed to the growth of film piracy, for the VCR was an easily accessible, reasonably affordable instrument for producing as well as consuming counterfeit tapes (U.S. Senate 1981).[5] Still, most proponents glossed over technology in favor of law, contending that the existing penalty structure encouraged piracy. They insisted that the penalties for piracy were too mild to deter offenders. Szybala maintained: "the dramatic growth of this problem has been encouraged by the huge profits to be made, while the relatively lenient penalties provided for by current law have done little to stem the tide" (U.S. Senate 1981:11). They added that the penalties discouraged officials from taking piracy seriously. Bouras told legislators that copyright law treated a first offense as a misdemeanor, and he asserted that "the misdemeanor penalty is so mild a sanction that it discourages prosecutors from pursuing cases" (U.S. Senate 1981:47).

Explaining why piracy warranted further legislative attention, proponents offered two justifications. First, they declared that piracy was costly and that many segments of society bore the costs. In presenting his bill, Senator Strom Thurmond stated: "Record and film counterfeiting and piracy combined drained an estimated $650 million annually from legitimate sales and rentals in these industries" (*Congressional Record* 1981a:4264). Testifying in support of the House bill, Bouras reported that "pirates and counterfeiters siphon more than a billion dollars a year from the legitimate industries" (U.S. House 1981:769). The victims of piracy included consumers, who were cheated by the poor quality of counterfeit goods; legitimate manufacturers and vendors of records, tapes, and cassettes, who were deprived of original sales and forced to replace shoddy counterfeits; writers, composers, film studios, and record companies, who were cheated out of the money they should have received from the sale or rental of works; and the government, which lost significant tax revenues. But there were other costs of piracy. Piracy harmed the creative enterprise. Members of the film and record industries argued that a film studio or record company depends on its few hits to cover its costs, develop talent, subsidize losing projects, and make a profit. By stealing hits, pirates deprived the studio or company of the capital needed to support creative ventures and survive in a risky business.[6] Accordingly, "motion picture studios and recording companies are forced to cut their losses by committing to fewer releases and concentrating on known artists and material" (U.S. Senate 1981:33). This meant fewer opportunities for new artists and diminished support for avant-garde projects. It also meant a reduction in the diversity of the films and recordings available to the public.

Second, proponents declared that state intervention was necessary. Some legislators suggested that piracy could be handled privately or as a civil matter, as many other forms of infringement were handled, but proponents opposed this line of thinking. They argued that piracy had increased despite the best efforts of the film and record industries:

> Both the motion picture and recording industries have established special anti-piracy offices. Each industry is spending more than a million dollars a year in that effort. But industry efforts to curb the growth of record and film piracy have met with only limited success. This is because, on their own, copyright owners, such as the members of MPAA and RIAA, can only file civil infringement actions. Such civil actions have no effect on the sophisticated criminals who engage in pirate and counterfeiting activities. They simply set up new operations in another location and ignore the injunctions issued by the civil courts. (U.S. Senate 1981:41)

Only the state, with its vast investigative resources and potent social control methods, could effectively fight piracy. Moreover, Szybala reminded legislators that piracy was in fact a crime—"the theft of intellectual property"—and asked that it be recognized and treated as such (U.S. House 1981:764).

Proponents concluded that, consistent with the relevant bills, large-scale piracy should be upgraded to a felony and subject to increased penalties. They believed that the penalties should be raised so that they fit the seriousness of the offense. While the incidence of piracy was growing and its costs were mounting—trends signifying heightened seriousness—the law continued to treat piracy as a trivial offense. There was a need to bring the penalties for piracy in line with its gravity. Bouras reviewed the laws dealing with other forms of theft and fraud and found their penalties consistent with those being proposed for piracy and counterfeiting. Indeed, the bills "would bring the penalties for these crimes up to the norm." He argued that by making large-scale piracy a felony with stiffer penalties, "sophisticated and organized criminals would be forced to recognize that their offenses will be punished under a statute which appreciates that such crimes constitute a grave threat to creative activity and a massive fraud on the public" (U.S. House 1981:775, 779).

Proponents also believed that the penalties should be raised to control the offense. They asserted that increased penalties would deter people from large-scale piracy. They portrayed offenders as rational, involved in piracy because it was profitable, producing large returns with few costs. Accordingly, they would refrain from piracy if it was unprofitable, and the obvious way to reduce the profits was to increase the costs by increasing the penalties. "Civil remedies and sanctions have proved ineffective in dealing with large-scale pirates and counterfeiters," Bouras testified. "Only strong criminal sanctions can serve as a deterrent in these cases" (U.S. House 1981:779). How severe the penalties should be was a matter of debate, but no one questioned the argument's logic that the incidence of piracy would fall if the penalties were raised.

The two bills encountered little opposition. No one testified against them, submitted letters of opposition, or expressed displeasure through their elected representatives. When legislators raised questions in the course of deliberations, they did so out of curiosity more than opposition. At the same time, the bills had the support of the Justice Department, Copyright Office, MPAA, and RIAA. They also enjoyed the support of the media. Press coverage described the nature, magnitude, and costs of piracy and the various efforts to control it, including industry and congressional efforts. Newspaper stories drew on statements by representatives of the film and record industries and the Justice Department, and they advanced images of piracy consistent with those advanced by the bills' proponents. None of the news stories questioned the "problem" of piracy, the dimensions of the crime, or the value of punishment as a means of controlling it.

Not surprisingly, the bills moved through their respective houses with ease. Each had a short, uneventful committee hearing, and each received a strong, positive recommendation. Following a brief floor discussion, each house passed its particular bill. The Senate bill—the Piracy and Counterfeiting Amendments Act of 1982—was sent to the President and won prompt approval.

In sum, a second legal campaign targeted large-scale piracy for control. The film and record industries and the Department of Justice claimed that such piracy was a genuine problem of growing proportions, that the costs of piracy and the need for state intervention warranted legislative attention, and that piracy could be effectively controlled by upgrading it to a felony and subjecting it to increased penalties. Encountering little opposition and receiving broad support, the campaign resulted in the passage of the Amendments Act.

DISCUSSION

With the development of the VCR, unauthorized reproduction of audiovisual works became increasingly common. The film industry grew concerned, and it launched two legal campaigns against the activity.

One tried to control off-air recording by controlling the VCR, while the second sought to control film piracy by raising the penalties for it. Whereas the former campaign failed, the latter succeeded. These different outcomes merit discussion.

The two campaigns differed in the degree to which their claims were consistent with prevailing ideologies for understanding and controlling copyright infringement. Research suggests that such differences can be important. In general, claimsmakers are more likely to get a particular condition recognized and addressed as a social problem when their claims coincide with dominant political, economic, or religious ideologies.

In the antipiracy campaign, film industry proponents constructed an argument that was consistent with conventional conceptions of infringement and methods for dealing with it. Proponents claimed that large-scale piracy was a significant problem. They did not seek to establish a new offense; piracy already was an offense, a type of criminal infringement, and proponents accepted this general definition. They merely argued that one form of piracy had become a serious problem. Using anecdotes and statistics drawn from various reports and officials, they argued that large-scale piracy was genuine and growing, a problem reaching "epidemic" proportions, and that it was intimately linked with organized crime. Proponents also claimed that large-scale piracy could be controlled by upgrading it to a felony and subjecting it to increased penalties. This strategy seemed reasonable. Piracy already was a punishable offense, and the idea of raising the penalties so as to deter hardened offenders fit conventional wisdom. Indeed, calls to control crime traditionally focus on increasing the severity of punishment.

In the antirecording campaign, however, film industry proponents devised an argument that ran counter to conventional conceptions of infringement and methods for managing it. They claimed that off-air recording and the manufacture and distribution of the VCR were illegitimate activities. This was a radical position. Proponents sought to establish these ostensibly respectable activities as unlawful, as types of copyright infringement. Yet off-air recording and the manufacture and distribution of the VCR did not fit conventional conceptions of infringement. When the courts considered the question of home recording, for example, they typically used definitions of infringement that emphasized economic harm; for them, a form of reproduction was infringement if it was designed to turn a profit at the copyright owner's expense or if it served to hurt the market for copyrighted works. Home recording did not fit this definition neatly. It was seen as a private, noncommercial activity in which an individual simply recorded a program broadcast free of charge for subsequent enjoyment. To many people (including judges), this activity seemed analogous to such respectable activities as recording a song from the radio or photocopying an article from a journal. Proponents also claimed that off-air recording could be controlled by prohibiting, or at least regulating, the distribution of the VCR. Yet banning the VCR did not resemble the way the state had dealt with other reproductive technologies, such as audio recorders and photocopiers. Historically, the state prohibited people from using these technologies in certain ways (such as to make numerous copies of a work) and for certain purposes (such as to make fraudulent documents). But it never prohibited the distribution of the technologies. To have banned the VCR, then, would have been extraordinary.

The difference in outcome also reflected differences in the structure of claimsmaking. The campaigns differed in the degree to which they encountered opposition. The antipiracy campaign faced little, if any, opposition. Members of the film and record industries presented their case to Congress without counterclaims from pirates or their representatives.[7] But the antirecording campaign met with considerable opposition. In both Congress and the courts, the film industry confronted a powerful adversary, the home recording industry. Like the film industry, the home recording industry included a number of large, prosperous organizations represented by a vigorous trade association able to mobilize a corps of attorneys, consultants, and public relations experts to attack its enemy and further its position (Pressman 1983). These differences in opposition may have shaped the different outcomes by influencing the manner in which the film industry presented its claims as well as the types of claims that were made.

Lacking opposition, the antipiracy proponents were free to present their case in their own terms, tailoring statements so as to increase the likelihood of success. Examination of their statements reveals that many were problematic. Some exaggerated matters. For example, proponents commonly portrayed pirates as career criminals who ran large, sophisticated operations affiliated with organized crime. They ignored more "respectable" pirates, such as the owners of video rental stores who made extra copies of hit films for lease. Other statements were erroneous. The claim (noted above) that FBI field offices ranked piracy as "the third most troublesome" white-collar crime misinterpreted the data. The offices had not rated the relative troublesomeness of piracy; rather, "copyright violations" (which included but were not limited to piracy) were noted by the third largest number of offices as "a problem area" (U.S. Department of Justice 1980, p. 14a). And many statements lacked support. Proponents declared that the incidence of piracy was growing and its costs were mounting and that organized crime was heavily involved in piracy, yet they treated these observations as matters of fact, rarely bothering to furnish evidence for them. While these claims were problematic, they formed a clear, consistent, and compelling argument—that piracy was a serious problem and that state action was needed to control it. Moreover, because these claims lacked opposition, they also had an air of truthfulness. Not surprisingly, prominent legislators accepted them. Speaking on behalf of the House bill, Representative Robert McClory called piracy "a serious problem of ever increasing magnitude," Representative Harold Sawyer agreed that piracy was "the third most troublesome" of all white-collar crimes, and Representative M. Caldwell Butler stated that organized crime was involved in piracy (*Congressional Record* 1982a).

Confronted with opposition, the antirecording proponents presented their case in a more conservative manner. They could not afford to make exaggerated, inaccurate, or unsupported statements; to do so would have invited severe counterattacks by the home recording industry. Accordingly, their claims were more prudent than those made in the antipiracy campaign. Key statements appreciated the complexities of matters. Proponents acknowledged, for example, that consumers used the VCR in various ways, only some of which threatened their interests, and they admitted that off-air recording had not yet caused any harm. Key statements also had documentation. Proponents supplied legal analyses showing that off-air recording was infringement, and they submitted scientific evidence showing that consumers commonly used the VCR for librarying and time-shifting. In addition, they furnished expert witnesses to make their position credible and celebrity witnesses (such as Charlton Heston and Clint Eastwood) to help bolster it. In advancing their case, proponents also challenged the home recording industry. For example, speaking in support of the compensation bills, Jack Valenti maintained that despite the home recording industry's assertions, the manufacturers of VCRs and blank tapes could easily absorb the royalty fees, that the Copyright Royalty Tribunal was capable of determining and distributing the fees, and that compensation would not affect the sales of VCRs and tapes (U.S. Senate 1982:490–496). Opposition, then, encouraged the antirecording proponents to present their case prudently, yet it also served to weaken their argument. The prospect of criticism forced proponents to adjust their statements to fit known facts and, in doing so, hindered them from tailoring statements to coincide with prevailing ideologies about infringement.

At the same time, members of the home recording industry presented their case. They claimed that off-air recording and the manufacture and distribution of the VCR were legitimate activities, that these activities called for legal protection, and that they could be preserved by formally absolving them. They too supplied legal analyses and scientific evidence to support their position and furnished expert witnesses to make it credible. And they attacked the film industry. Speaking against the compensation bills, Charles Ferris questioned the film industry's concerns and attributed them to ignorance:

> We submit that what we are seeing here is the not unexpected "sky is falling" response of an old, firmly entrenched industry to a young new technology that it does not yet fully understand or know how to use. Dramatic change in communications media is always accompanied by fear, confusion, and overreaction by the established industry players. . . . As Hollywood . . . learns to harness and work with the VCR industry, the studios will come to recognize the enormous opportunities that this new technology affords them. (U.S. Senate 1984:358)

Thus, opposition not only blunted the film industry's case, but it also provided lawmakers with compelling counterclaims about off-air recording and appropriate ways of dealing with it.

These fundamental differences in claimsmaking may well have contributed to the different campaign outcomes. Indeed, a growing body of work shows that rhetoric affects the results of claimsmaking (Best 1989; Holstein and Miller 1993). Still, there was another important difference between the campaigns. They differed greatly in their substantive implications, and this may have contributed to their disparate outcomes.

The two campaigns advanced different plans of action. The antipiracy campaign sought to control large-scale piracy by increasing penalties, while the antirecording campaign sought to control off-air recording by controlling the VCR. These actions differed in the number of people they would adversely affect. The antipiracy measures targeted people involved in the production and distribution of illicit tapes—a fairly small number of people who specialized in making vast quantities of counterfeit tapes for sale and a somewhat larger number who made extra copies of prerecorded tapes for lease. The antirecording measures would have affected many more people. In 1979, when the District Court rendered its decision, a ban on VCRs would have hurt not only the manufacturers of VCRs and blank tapes but some 25,000 businesses that marketed VCRs, some 3,000 to 5,000 businesses that rented prerecorded tapes, and more than 1 million VCR owners. Further, these actions differed in the amount of harm they would inflict. The antipiracy measures punished offenders, reduced their income, and jeopardized their investment in the equipment used to make tapes. The antirecording measures, in contrast, would have disrupted businesses and threatened the livelihoods of respectable people, and they would have destroyed huge, legitimate investments in developing and improving VCR technology, manufacturing VCRs and tapes, and establishing businesses for marketing VCRs and renting tapes. They also would have threatened the privacy of VCR owners. The District Court noted that enforcing a ban would have been "nearly impossible and in any event highly intrusive" (p. 468). Given the many people affected and the substantial losses they would suffer, many lawmakers were reluctant to endorse the antirecording measures (*Congressional Record* 1981b, 1981c, 1982b, 1983a, 1983b).

Moreover, the campaigns differed in their implications for technological innovation. The antipiracy measures did not threaten the process; they sought to control certain uses of a technology, not the technology itself. But the antirecording measures could have threatened innovation; seeking to control a technology, they could have set a dangerous precedent. In particular, controlling the VCR by prohibiting its distribution could have been consequential for innovation. Inventors might have been deterred from developing new technologies for fear that, given certain uses, these technologies also would be banned and their investment would be lost. In turn, technological retardation could have lowered creative output and thus weakened the nation's economic position (see Katzenbach 1987). Further, banning the technology could have helped create a climate of hostility to "Research and Development," a climate contrary to the one supported by the federal government (Office of Technology Assessment 1985).[8]

In contrast, controlling the VCR through a compulsory licensing system might have had few harmful consequences. Indeed, efforts to install this system probably failed because of their timing. Through the early 1970s, the film industry's assessment of home video was ambiguous, though it seemed rather positive. After witnessing demonstrations of Sony's early home video units, Charles Levy, representing Walt Disney Productions, told Mr. Disney, "I saw a demonstration and was very much impressed," and Berle Adams, an MCA executive, wrote Mr. Akio Morita of Sony and declared, "it sounds like an exciting breakthrough for both the motion picture and television industry. May I wish you success" (U.S. Senate 1982:168). A number of studios also hoped to exploit the technology by marketing their films to a home audience (Lardner 1987). When the industry generally decided around 1976 that the VCR posed a threat and should be controlled, an infrastructure for the production and distribution of VCRs and blank tapes had been established and plans for expansion had been cast. By 1981, when the Circuit Court decided in favor of the studios and Congress began to consider the compensation bills, home video had grown into a large industry with millions of patrons (Cahill 1988). To have approved a compulsory licensing system that would have hiked the cost of equipment some 10 to 15% would have been politically awkward.[9]

The history of the digital audio tape (DAT) recorder—a device that allows consumers to make almost perfect copies of sound recordings—is consistent with this explanation. In 1992, Congress passed the Audio Home Recording Act. This act reaffirmed the consumer's right to copy sound recordings for home use. But it also created a system in which the manufacturers of DAT recorders and blank tapes paid royalties on each recorder and tape for distribution to the relevant copyright owners, and it required the manufacturers to modify recorders so as to prevent multi-generational copying of recordings. These regulatory arrangements evolved from agreements between the music industry and home recording industry. The Recording Industry Association of America and the National Music Publishers' Association threatened to sue the first manufacturer to sell DAT recorders in the United States and to withhold their product from the DAT market. Wanting to avoid litigation and the loss of a lucrative new market, the manufacturers delayed entry until suitable agreements could be reached, agreements reflected in the act (Gow 1992; U.S. Senate 1992).

CONCLUSION

Virtually every technological innovation alters existing arrangements and threatens people with a stake in them. These people sometimes resist, and their resistance sometimes affects the technology. This was the case with the home videocassette recorder. The VCR enabled consumers to reproduce audiovisual works, threatening one of the principal rights of copyright owners and disrupting an otherwise tenuous balance between owners and consumers. Owners pressed lawmakers to create or modify laws controlling the activity, and their efforts had mixed results. The success of owners' efforts—the degree to which their conduct produced legal change—depended on several things: the degree to which their claims were consistent with prevailing ideologies for understanding and controlling infringement, the degree to which their rhetoric encountered opposition, and especially the substantive implications of their proposals for dealing with the exploitative technology. Efforts to control reproduction by banning the VCR may have failed to gain approval because they threatened existing arrangements as well as technological innovation. However, efforts to control reproduction by regulating the VCR—permitting its distribution and use in return for compensation—might have succeeded had they been made before an infrastructure for the production and distribution of the technology was established. And efforts to control reproduction by raising the penalties for piracy gained approval because they did not threaten existing arrangements or technological innovation.

NOTES

1.   This security office was a descendent of the Film Theft Committee, formed in 1919 by the dominant film companies and designed to combat film piracy. In the early twentieth century, there were a number of cases in which people stole theatrical prints and sold them or copies of them to exhibitors. While the Film Theft Committee did not eliminate piracy, its activities seemed to bring the problem under control: "Hollywood was more or less content with this state of affairs. Losses from piracy didn't appear on year-end balance sheets, and as long as the companies were highly profitable, film bootlegging proved only a minor irritant" (Monaco 1978:58).

As 16-mm projectors began to find their way into private homes following World War II, a new market for pirated prints developed. However, the studios did not seem especially concerned. Populated primarily by film collectors, the market was small and collectors tended to prefer older films, which, of course, did not compete with the studios' fare.

Through the 1960s, then, the studios did relatively little to control the reproduction of their films.

2.   The District Court defined "home-use recording" as the operation of a VCR in a private home to record a program, broadcast free over the public airwaves, for subsequent home viewing.

3.   Sidney Sheinberg, president of MCA (which owned Universal), was especially concerned by the involvement of Japanese interests. Speaking against S 1758, a pure exemption bill, he asserted that "the current bill gives manufacturers of video recorders, all of whom are foreign, and manufacturers of videotape, almost all of whom are also foreign, a free ride on the backs of the American creative community. The foreign manufacturers of these machines would have no real market for their product without the ability to copy our films—our property, American property" (U.S. Senate 1982:55–56).

4.   While Ferris called the VCR "one of the best friends Hollywood ever had" (U.S. House 1983:165), Valenti exclaimed, "the VCR is to the American film producer and the American public as the Boston strangler is to the woman home alone" (U.S. House 1983:8).

5.   Addressing the International Tape Association in early 1978, Bouras referred to film piracy as "the dark underside of the video revolution" (*Variety* 1978:42).

6.   Appearing on behalf of the RIAA, Jules Yarnell testified: "I believe that every single record company has been forced to cut down very substantially on its employees and curtail their activities, curtail their number of different types of performers whom they contract with, and try to produce recordings for, because their general volume of business has shrunk so drastically. I think that a very, very large share of that is due to the increase in counterfeiting, which deprives them of the income" (U.S. House 1981:791).

7.   The possibility of opposition was not inconceivable. In the early 1970s, record pirates testified against bills aimed at including sound recordings under the canopy of copyright (U.S. House 1971).

8.   It is not surprising, then, that bills aimed at banning "black boxes"—devices that promise to remove the interference caused by anticopying treatments and at the same time defeat these treatments and enable one to copy encrypted works—never came to a vote, despite the fact that they had the support of the film industry, the Copyright Office, and the Bush administration and were not vigorously opposed by the home recording industry (*TV Digest* 1989; U.S. Senate 1991).

9.   Shortly after the Supreme Court ruled against the studios, Representative Don Edwards, an ally of the studios and sponsor of a compensation bill, said that there was little chance Congress would pass legislation providing compensation for copyright owners: "It's the most politically unpopular issue I've ever been mixed up in. Nobody understands what I'm saying" (*U.S. News and World Report* 1984:10).

REFERENCES

Agostino, D.E., R.C. Johnson, and H.A. Terry. 1979. "Home Video: A Report on the Status, Projected Development and Consumer Use of Videocassette Recorders and Videodisc Players in the United States." Appendix 1 of *Preliminary Report on Prospects for Additional Networks*, volume 3, prepared by Network Inquiry Special Staff, Federal Communications Commission. Washington, DC: U.S. Government Printing Office.

Best, J., editor. 1989. *Images of Issues*. Hawthorne, NY: Aldine de Gruyter.

———. 1990. *Threatened Children*. Chicago: University of Chicago Press.

Business Week. 1976. "Why Sony's Betamax Has MCA Seething." November 29:29–30.

Cahill, P.E. 1988. "United States of America and Canada." Pp. 125–158 in *Video Worldwide*, edited by M. Alvarado. London: Jibbey.

Chicago Tribune. 1981. Editorial cartoon. November 10:I.17.

Cohen, S. 1955. "Fair Use in the Law of Copyright." *American Society of Composers, Authors and Publishers Copyright Law Symposium* 6:43–71.

Cohodas, N. 1982. "Clash Looming in Congress over Home Video Recording." *Congressional Quarterly* March 20:629–630.

Congressional Record. 1981a. "S 691." 127: 4264-65. March 12.

———. 1981b. "Home Video Recording." 127: 24428. October 20.

———. 1981c. "Home Videotape Recorders in Violation of Federal Copyright Laws." 127: 24429. October 20.

———. 1982a. "Piracy and Counterfeiting Amendments Act of 1982." 128: 9157-60. May 10.

———. 1982b. "Exemption of Home Recording of Television Programs for Personal Use from Copyright Law." 128: 9862-63. May 13.

———. 1983a. "S 175." 129: S 668. January 26.

———. 1983b. "On Home Recorders and the Rights of Movie Producers." 129: E 483. February 15.

Fisher, F. 1989. "The Electronic Lumberyard and Builders' Rights: Technology, Copyrights, Patents, and Academe." *Change* 21:13–21.

Gow, J. 1992. "The 'Trouble' With Digital Audio Tape." *Popular Music and Society* 16:31–48.

Holstein, J.A., and G. Miller, editors. 1993. *Reconsidering Social Constructionism.* Hawthorne, NY: Aldine de Gruyter.

Horowitz, I.L. 1986. "The Protection and Dissemination of Intellectual Property." *Book Research Quarterly* 2:4–13.

Katzenbach, N.B. 1987. "The International Protection of Technology: A Challenge for International Law Making." *Technology in Society* 9:123–139.

Klopfenstein, Bruce C. 1989. "The Diffusion of the VCR in the United States." Pp. 21–39 in *The VCR Age*, edited by M. Levy. Newbury Park, CA: Sage.

Lardner, J. 1987. *Fast Forward*. New York: Mentor.

Los Angeles Times. 1981a. "Appeals Court Ruling Stirs up the Video Recording Market." October 21, IV:1.

———. 1981b. Editorial cartoon. October 21:II.4.

Monaco, J. 1978. "Stealing the Show: The Piracy Problem." *American Film* 3:57–67.

New York Times. 1981. "Letters to the Editor." October 30:34.

Office of Technology Assessment. 1985. *Information Technology R&D*. Washington, DC: U.S. Government Printing Office.

———. 1986. *Intellectual Property Rights in an Age of Electronics and Information.* Washington, DC: U.S. Government Printing Office.

———. 1992. *Finding a Balance*. Washington, DC: U.S. Government Printing Office.

Ploman, E.W., and L.C. Hamilton. 1980. *Copyright*. London: Routledge and Kegan Paul.

Pressman, S. 1983. "Lobbying 'Star War' Flares as Movie Industry Fights Invasion of Video Recorders." *Congressional Quarterly* June 4:1099–1103.

Seltzer, L.E. 1978. *Exemptions and Fair Use in Copyright*. Cambridge, MA: Harvard University Press.

Strong, W.S. 1993. *The Copyright Book*, fourth edition. Cambridge, MA: MIT Press.

Timberg, S. 1980. "A Modernized Fair Use Code for the Electronic as well as the Gutenberg Age." *Northwestern University Law Review* 75:193–244.

———. 1989. "A Modernized Fair Use Code for Visual, Auditory, and Audiovisual Copyrights: Economic Context, Legal Issues, and the Laocoon Shortfall." Pp. 305–336 in *Fair Use and Free Inquiry*, edited by J. Lawrence and B. Timburg. Norwood, NJ: Ablex.

TV Digest. 1989. "Anti-Black Box Bill." 29 (November 6):13.

U.S. Department of Justice. 1980. *National Priorities for the Investigation and Prosecution of White Collar Crime*. Washington, DC: U.S. Department of Justice.

U.S. House of Representatives. 1971. *Prohibiting Piracy of Sound Recordings*. Hearings before Subcommittee Number 3, Committee on the Judiciary. 92nd Congress, 1st session. Washington, DC: U.S. Government Printing Office.

———. 1981. *Copyright/Cable Television*. Hearings before the Subcommittee on Courts, Civil Liberties, and the Administration of Justice, Committee on the Judiciary. 97th Congress, 1st and 2nd sessions. Washington, DC: U.S. Government Printing Office.

————. 1983. *Home Recording of Copyrighted Works*. Hearings before the Subcommittee on Courts, Civil Liberties, and the Administration of Justice, Committee on the Judiciary. 97th Congress, 2nd session. Washington, DC: U.S.
Government Printing Office.

U.S. News and World Report. 1984. "Home TV Taping Gets All-Clear." January 30:
10.

U.S. Senate. 1981. *Act of 1981—S 691*. Hearing before the Subcommittee on
Criminal Law, Committee on the Judiciary. 97th Congress, 1st session.
Washington, DC: U.S. Government Printing Office.

————. 1982. *Copyright Infringements*. Hearings before the Committee on the
Judiciary. 97th Congress, 1st and 2nd sessions. Washington, DC: U.S. Government Printing Office.

————. 1984. *Video and Audio Home Taping*. Hearings before the Subcommittee
on Patents, Copyrights and Trademarks, Committee on the Judiciary. 98th
Congress, 1st session. Washington, DC: U.S. Government Printing Office.

————. 1991. *Motion Picture Anti-Piracy Act of 1991*. Joint hearings before the
Subcommittee on Technology and the Law and the Subcommittee on Patents, Copyrights and Trademarks, Committee on the Judiciary. 102nd Congress, 1st session. Washington, DC: U.S. Government Printing Office.

————. 1992. *Audio Home Recording Act of 1991*. Report 102-294. 102nd Congress,
2nd session. Washington, DC: U.S. Government Printing Office.

Variety. 1978. "See Early Ruling on Betamax Right to Copy TV Shows." March
15:7, 42.

Witt, E. 1984. "No Copyright Violation Seen in Home Video Recording. "*Congressional Quarterly* January 21:95–96.

CASES

Sony Corporation of America et al. v. Universal City Studios, Inc., et al., 464 U.S. 417
(1984).

Universal City Studios, Inc. v. Sony Corporation of America, 480 F. Supp. 429 (1979).

Universal City Studios, Inc. v. Sony Corporation of America, 659 F. 2d 963 (1981).

14

Cold Wars, Evil Empires, Treacherous Japanese: Effects of International Context on Problem Construction

LAWRENCE T. NICHOLS

We often speak of social problems as though they are features of, and limited to, particular societies. But in today's global village, social problems frequently transcend national boundaries. Claimsmakers increasingly link local social problems to other nations. For example, U.S. corporations market tobacco in Latin America, and developed nations export hazardous waste around the world (Stebbins 1994, 1992). Such issues highlight the importance of the international context for understanding the construction of contemporary problems.

The perception that Japanese trade practices have created social problems in the United States has become widespread during the last two decades. Public opinion polls from the early 1990s, for example, indicated that less than half of U.S. citizens held friendly attitudes toward Japan (Oreskes 1990; *Gallup Poll Monthly* 1992). The Bush administration officially labeled Japan an unfair trading partner in 1989, and imposed economic penalties (Powell 1989b). The Clinton administration took an even tougher stance several years later, breaking off negotiations on trade due to its dissatisfaction with Japanese policies (Butler and Impoco 1994). During the same period, popular novels and films (Crichton 1992; Clancy 1994) portrayed Japanese corporations, business leaders, and politicians as evil conspirators bent on harming the United States.

How did this definition of the Japanese threat emerge and evolve? How did the international context affect the content of social-problems claims and audience responses to those claims? How did changes in that context affect the initial construction of the Japanese threat and later reconstructions of the problem? How did the effects of the international context compare with those of the domestic context? This chapter will explore these issues.

313

CONTEXTS AND CONSTRUCTION

Constructionist sociologists disagree over the relationship between claims and contexts. The central issue is methodological: whether and how sociologists should use their understanding of context in analyzing claimsmaking. The so-called "strict constructionists" insist that analysts avoid making judgments about context, because such judgments divert analysis away from the examination of claims, and toward an investigation of conditions. In contrast, "contextual constructionists" insist that some understanding of context is indispensable for interpreting claimsmaking.

This chapter adopts the latter approach and presumes that *claims about the Japanese threat cannot be understood apart from the contexts in which they are made.* Indeed, neither social problems claims nor any other statements can be understood entirely in their own terms; they are comprehensible only in relation to something beyond themselves. Audiences and analysts require knowledge of situations or contexts to decode the literal meaning of what they hear or read. Knowledge of context is even more indispensable for understanding connotations, emotional tone, symbolism, and other nonliteral aspects of statements or claims (Best 1990, 1993).

Types of Context

Contexts have multiple, perhaps innumerable, dimensions that are inseparable in everyday life but that can be distinguished for purposes of analysis. This discussion will focus on two dimensions of context: international and domestic, and institutionalized and situational. Both dimensions are important for understanding the construction of social problems. The effects of context vary over time. For example, the international context may shape claims during one period, but have little impact at another time.

Domestic context refers to features of the individual societies within which social problems emerge. While some analyses of social problems construction focus on a local context, e.g., within a neighborhood or town, most studies treat domestic context as national, e.g., attributing features the United States as a whole. International context, by contrast, refers to relationships among at least two nations, and may involve groups of nations (e.g., "the Pacific rim" or "the Third World").

Institutionalized context involves relatively longlasting features of societies or international social systems, especially basic social and cultural structures (e.g., economy, science, law) and the social psychologies that accompany them (e.g., individualistic attitudes in modern societies). Situational context, by contrast, refers to relatively temporary arrangements or combinations of social elements, either within particular societies or among societies. American capitalism, for example, has been a feature of the domestic, institutionalized context for economic problems in the United States, while economies dependent upon producing raw materials and importing manufactured goods is part of the international institutionalized context for many Third World countries' economic and social problems.In the same way, the "bull market" of 1982–1987 was a domestic situational context for such U.S. problems as insider-trading on Wall Street, while the 1990–1991 crisis in the Persian Gulf was an international situational context for various problems confronting many nations.

The relationship between context and claims can take several forms. Researchers should focus, first, on the ways in which contexts determine the content of claims, the identities of claimsmakers, and the rhetorical tactics that claimsmakers employ. Constructionists also need to investigate the ways in which contexts affect responses to claims, and how such effects differ according to audiences. It is also possible for claims to alter context, and thereby affect the probability of other claimsmakers coming forward, as well as the likelihood that audiences will accept or reject their assertions.

This analysis will focus on the ways context affects the content of claims and the responses of audiences to claims. In particular, I shall argue that the international context of the Cold War between the United States and the Soviet Union worked to suppress perceptions of—or at least minimize responses to claims about—a Japanese threat during the 1970s and early 1980s. As the Cold War subsided in the late 1980s, this suppressive effect vanished and claims about a major Japanese problem quickly gained widespread acceptance. Interestingly, the Cold War experience facilitated the later constructions of the Japanese threat by providing a language and imagery that could be transferred from the Soviets to the Japanese.

The analysis will also show that the effects of the Cold War context were not uniform. The suppressive effects were most evident in the executive branch of the federal government, especially the White House and the Departments of State and Defense. Other groups, including business, organized labor, and the Congress, were more likely to take the early claims of a Japanese threat seriously. The perceptions of the executive branch, however, dominated policy and thus determined how the nation would respond to Japan.

Method

Given the scope of the issues and the multitude of claimsmakers, it is
not possible to study a representative sample of claims about the Japanese threat. Rather, my analysis draws from a wide variety of sources,
including official documents, news reports, business journals and industry publications, scholarly works and documentary films, as well as
popular culture, including novels and movies. I did make a systematic
search of coverage by the *New York Times* and the *Wall Street Journal*. In
short, this chapter reflects an exploratory effort to summarize claimsmaking about Japan. I limited my research to the period 1971 to 1994.
Prior to 1970, there is scant evidence that Japan was considered either an
economic or a national security threat.

DISCOVERING THE JAPANESE THREAT: UNFAIR TRADE

As the 1970s began, the United States seemingly stood alone as the
world's dominant economic and military power. Japan and Europe had
recovered from the devastation of World War II, but their expanding
economies could not rival America's prosperity. The Soviet Union had
achieved relative equality in strategic nuclear weapons, but lagged far
behind the United States in other areas, especially economics and technology.

Once social problems claims involving Japan began to appear, however, they became fairly widespread. Since 1965, the United States had
experienced a bilateral trade deficit with Japan, meaning that Americans
bought more from the Japanese than the Japanese purchased from
Americans. Claimsmakers, especially in business, organized labor, and
government, began to define these deficits—and their alleged causes—
as serious matters requiring remedies.

The U.S. Electronic Industries Association had actually raised the issue in 1968, charging that Japanese exports of televisions violated the
U.S. Antidumping Act. Its lawsuit claimed that Japan was setting the
price of exported televisions unfairly low to capture market share. In
1971, the Tariff Commission of the U.S. Treasury Department concurred, ruling that the entire Japanese television industry was breaking
American law (*Wall Street Journal* 1971b:2). The same claims appeared in
lawsuits against Japanese manufacturers filed by National Union Electric
Corporation and 12 of its workers who had lost their jobs (*Wall Street
Journal* 1971a:9).

Similar claims were advanced by representatives of the U.S. textile
industry. Ely Callaway (1971:14) of Burlington Industries, for example,

asserted that "Prices for Japanese textiles in the United States market are generally lower than prices for comparable textiles sold and consumed by their own people." Foreshadowing claims of the following decade, Callaway concluded: "Only a major change in United States trade policy will enable American industry . . . to stay ahead in this contest . . . that really is a race for economic survival."

Other claimsmakers focused on the closure of Japanese markets. Automobile industry representatives, for example, complained: "American cars exported to Japan face a 10 per cent tariff, a commodity tax that raises the price from 30 to 40 per cent, a licensing fee, and an enormous road tax that is about five times higher than that of a Japanese car" (Flint 1971:42).

The Nixon administration and Congress increasingly accepted such claims. George Shultz, Director of the Office of Management and the Budget, told Congress that a tougher position on trade was necessary (*New York Times* 1971a). Secretary of State William Rogers likewise complained in a public speech that the bilateral trade deficit with Japan had doubled from 1970 to 1971 (*New York Times* 1971b). The Senate Finance Committee, headed by Democrat Russell Long, voted shortly thereafter to give the President power to declare a "balance-of-payments emergency" under which he could impose quotas or surcharges of up to 15% on imports (*Wall Street Journal* 1971c).

President Nixon gave further credence to such claims by imposing a 5% surcharge on all imports entering the United States. This action was so unexpected that it became known in Japan as "Nixon shock." The effect of the surcharge was to make all foreign products and services more expensive, and thus less attractive to American consumers.

Nixon's action shows that claims of a Japanese threat had gained his attention, but also suggests that he regarded the problem as relatively minor. The administration did not consult with Japan prior to imposing its surcharge, an insult that the Japanese felt deeply according to many observers. Nixon's foreign policy was oriented toward regional powers, especially Europe, the Soviet Union, and China—rather than Japan.

The measures adopted by Nixon make sense in the context of the domestic politics of reelection. The President had built a strong base of support in the South, which had previously been solidly Democratic. This region was the site of many textile firms complaining about Japan; those firms benefitted from the import surcharge. Nixon had also gained votes from groups that had long supported Democratic candidates, including blue-collar workers in the automobile and related industries, who stood to gain from the surcharge. Thus, domestic situational context facilitated the acceptance of claims about Japan. Such acceptance was also reflected in the U.S. Trade Act of 1974, which had bipartisan support. This law included Section 301, establishing penalties that the President might impose on unfair trading partners.

During the mid-1970s, however, changes in the domestic political context suppressed perceptions of a Japanese threat. The Watergate scandal preoccupied Americans and led to Nixon's resignation in 1974. For two years, the Ford administration focused on managing the domestic crisis and restoring trust in government. Issues involving Japan ranked low on its policy agenda.

Claims about the Japanese threat became prominent once again during the Carter presidency. Although the Cold War between the United States and the Soviet Union continued, the level of conflict between the two nations had subsided, as a result of the Nixon administration's policy of "detente" (lessening tensions), that had culminated in the Strategic Arms Limitation Treaty (SALT I), and the end of armed conflict between the United States and North Vietnam, a Soviet ally.

Claims about the Japanese threat in the late 1970s were similar to the earlier claims. There was, however, a more urgent tone to the rhetoric. The bilateral trade deficit became an increasingly dominant concern. Claimsmakers noted that the gap had risen from a billion dollars per year in 1971 to some $4 billion in 1976, and then had ballooned to nearly $12 billion in 1978. Numerous articles about the trade deficit appeared in business periodicals, while an article in the *Harvard Business Review* asked, "Can U.S. business survive our Japanese trade policy?" (Nevin 1978). The Joint Economic Committee of Congress (1980) held hearings on the deficit, at which one witness warned that "the American semiconductor industry stands exposed to the same Japanese target industry strategies which decimated the American color TV and steel industries" (U.S. Congress 1980:15).

The Carter administration responded by making the Japanese threat the subject of diplomatic negotiations. In 1977, the administration reached an agreement with Japan under which Japanese companies would voluntarily limit the number of televisions shipped to the United States. A year later, special trade representative Robert Strauss negotiated an accord under which the Japanese government promised to provide reciprocal access to its markets, while increasing imports of American goods (Malcolm 1978). Thus, for the second time in a decade, it appeared that the Japanese threat might be perceived as one of the nation's most important social problems.

THE COLD WAR INTERVENES

Once again, however, a shift in the international context influenced and suppressed constructions of problems with Japan. In December

1979, the Soviet Union sent thousands of troops into Afghanistan, generating shock and outrage in the United States. President Carter took a series of actions: recalling the ambassador to the Soviet Union, delaying action on a major arms control agreement (SALT II), condemning the Soviets in the United Nations, imposing an embargo on grain sales to the USSR, and calling for a boycott of the 1980 summer Olympics scheduled to be held in Moscow. In a briefing to members of Congress, Carter claimed that "The Soviet invasion of Afghanistan is the greatest threat to peace since the second world war" (Matthews 1980b:24).

News organizations supported this definition of the problem. *Newsweek* ran four cover stories on the invasion and spoke of "a new cold war." *Time* (1980:10) contended that the Soviet action "had plunged the world back into an earlier and more dangerous era." *U.S. News and World Report* (1980a:24) claimed that the invasion showed the Soviets had exploited detente to gain military superiority, and (1980b:24) quoted Senator Charles Percy's warning that a "possible third world war" was closer than at any time since 1945.

Importantly, while constructing the new Soviet threat, these and other claimsmakers linked the well-being of the United States with that of Japan, and sometimes spoke as though the interests of the two nations were nearly identical. *Newsweek* (Matthews 1980a:22), for example, asserted:

> the Soviet thrust into Afghanistan represented a severe threat to Western interests. Control of Afghanistan would put the Russians within 350 miles of the Arabian Sea, the oil lifeline of the West and Japan.

U.S. News and World Report (1980a:20) likewise concluded that "the Russians are posing the most serious threat to American interests in a quarter of a century—namely, oil supplies vital to the U.S., and even more so to its European and Japanese allies." In this way, claims about serious economic problems with Japan were replaced by a rhetoric of unity that defined the two nations as allies, and referred to Japan as "western."

Claims about the new Soviet threat also became an important feature of presidential politics in 1980. The Democratic party platform charged that Soviet actions "have violated all norms of international law and have been thoroughly condemned by the international community" (*Congressional Quarterly Almanac* 1981a:115B). The party platform redefined recent conflicts with Japan:

> Our relations with Japan have moved to a new level of maturity and cooperation. The United States is able to deal with patience . . . on a range of difficult and contentious economic issues. In the foreign policy and security area, Japan's record in support of U.S. foreign policy is second to none. (*Congressional Quarterly Almanac* 1981a:118B)

This rhetoric portrayed claims against Japan as misunderstandings. Far from inflicting economic damage, Democrats implied, Japan was "cooperating," and providing more foreign policy "support" than any other nation!

In their 1980 platform, Republicans emphasized the Soviet threat, but did not mention Japan. Condemning Carter for reductions in nuclear forces, delegates asserted that "the United States faces the most serious threat to its survival in the two centuries of its existence" (*Congressional Quarterly Almanac* 1981c:75B). Republicans also portrayed the USSR as aggressively expanding in Africa, Asia, and the Western Hemisphere. In his acceptance speech, Presidential nominee Ronald Reagan claimed: "America's defense strength is at its lowest ebb in a generation, while the Soviet Union is vastly outspending us" (*Congressional Quarterly Almanac* 1981b:38B).

After being elected President, Reagan continued to define the Soviet threat as the greatest problem confronting the United States. When the Soviets shot down a Korean airliner in 1983, Reagan denounced the action as barbaric. In a speech to the National Association of Evangelicals, the President called Soviet Communism "the focus of evil in the modern world" and denounced the USSR as an "evil empire" (Clines 1983). Its leaders, he asserted, "have openly and publicly declared that the only morality they recognize is that which will further their cause, which is world revolution."

During 1983, Reagan also introduced his controversial proposal for a defensive shield in outer space, which he claimed would render nuclear weapons obsolete. This Strategic Defense Initiative, which gained the popular nickname "Star Wars," began to receive massive budget appropriations. The Soviets denounced the plan, arguing that it would escalate the arms race, but the President defended the action as one of the most important steps toward peace taken by his administration (Reagan 1985).

Claims about Japan

Despite the emphasis on problems with the Soviet Union, claims about problems with Japan continued. Among the most vocal claimsmakers was the automobile industry, which had been losing market share to imported cars. Thus, in 1982, Douglas Fraser, president of the United Auto Workers, told the House Foreign Affairs Committee that "our trade relationship with Japan is a one-sided, lopsided discriminatory trade agreement" (U.S. House of Representatives 1982:643).

The machine tool industry also complained of Japanese practices. Nathaniel Howe, chairman of the National Machine Tool Builders Association, told the House Ways and Means Committee that "we cannot compete with Japan, Inc." (U.S. House of Representatives 1983:449). Howe testified that Japan's share of the United States import market had more than doubled in less than a decade. Similar concerns were voiced by Robert Blinken, of the Metalworking Fair Trade Coalition. Blinken charged the Japanese with formulating a blueprint for the complete takeover of the American industrial fasteners industry. Both witnesses accused the Japanese government of giving unfair financial advantages to corporations selected to export particular products.

These and other claimsmakers also alleged that American products were comparable in quality to their Japanese competition. The problem was simply that the Japanese would not buy, despite their repeated promises to increase imports. In those cases where the Japanese did buy American goods, their purpose was said to be merely to copy the technology so that they might begin exporting the products themselves. Thus, John Latona, a vice-president of a large machine-tool company, told the Ways and Means Committee:

> The facts are these: Japanese machine tools are not . . . superior to those made in the United States . . . virtually all Japanese machine tools are copied from U.S. designs. . . . The competitive advantage developed by the Japanese [is] . . . the result of a cartel with a deep pocket, in this case, the pocket of the government of Japan. (U.S. House of Representatives 1983:163)

Testimony at the 1983 hearings also introduced a theme that would become prominent several years later, namely, that Japan's trade practices threatened American security. Thus, Howe, who was vice-president of Litton Industries, a major defense contractor, claimed:

> The national security of the United States is clearly being impaired by current levels of machine tool imports. These imports threaten to debilitate the domestic tool industry, which is critical to the U.S. defense. (U.S. House of Representatives 1983:328)

Loss of the machine-tool industry, he warned, would make the United States dependent on supplies from other nations, which could prove disastrous in wartime.

Both the Carter and Reagan administrations, however, rejected such appeals. Carter turned down the plea of the metal fasteners industry in 1980. Reagan refused to intervene in the widely publicized case of Houdaille Industries, a manufacturer of machine tools. Houdaille filed a petition urging the President to revoke tax credits given to Japanese machine tool exporters. The U.S. Senate took the unusual step of passing a unanimous resolution supporting Houdaille's petition. Nevertheless, Reagan would not grant the request, and Houdaille closed its U.S. plant (Prestowitz 1988).

There are indications that the refusals of Carter and Reagan to grant relief to American businesses were influenced by their constructions of the Soviet threat. In the hearings of the House Committee on Foreign Affairs discussed above, for example, witnesses from the Reagan administration portrayed the U.S. relationship with Japan very differently than had been done by representatives of business and labor. John Holdridge, Assistant Secretary in the State Department's Bureau of Asian and Pacific Affairs, declared that the U.S. bond with Japan was "our most important bilateral relationship in the world." He provided the following rationale:

> The U.S. ability to maintain forces and bases in Japan permits power projection elsewhere in Asia. . . . Were it not for our bases in Japan and the support we enjoy from the Japanese Government . . . we would be unable to maintain this burden. (U.S. House of Representatives 1982:5)

Francis West, Assistant Secretary for Internal Security Affairs in the Department of Defense, likewise asserted: "Japan is the cornerstone of the U.S. forward defense strategy in the Asian-Pacific region" (U.S. House of Representatives 1982:17). A similar logic was advanced by Lionel Olmer, Undersecretary for International Trade in the Department of Commerce. Olmer argued quite explicitly that the Japanese trade threat had to be considered less critical than the Soviet military threat:

> We value Japan as a trading partner and as a security ally for many reasons which, in my judgment, transcend the importance of our bilateral trade relationship. . . . We do have to put our problems in the trade area in the context of the larger relationship. (U.S. House of Representatives 1982:775)

It is also important to note the significance of the Strategic Defense Initiative in this rationale. The Reagan administration intended to involve Japan as a partner in the development of its space-based shield (Armstrong 1986), and therefore did not wish to alienate the Japanese by attacking their trading practices.

Claims about the Japanese threat in the early 1980s were not, however, confined to the federal government or special interest groups among business and labor. There is also evidence that public opinion was turning against the Japanese. In 1982, for example, a Gallup poll found that favorable attitudes toward Japan had "declined noticeably in the last year, largely as a result of perceptions that trade between Japan and the United States has become a one-way street" (Lindsey 1982). The poll indicated that 63% of Americans held favorable attitudes toward Japan, down from 84% favorable in a 1980 survey.

Such data indicate that domestic and international contexts can have conflicting effects on social problems construction. In this case, the situational context of the domestic economy fostered concern about Japan among many groups. The early 1980s was a time of serious economic recession—in fact, the most severe economic crisis since the depression of the 1930s. There had been a wave of plant closings, and tens of thousands of Americans were unemployed. Government policymakers, however, were personally shielded from the adverse effects of economic problems, allowing them to focus on the international context and the alleged Soviet threat. This focus tended to suppress their awareness of problems involving Japan.

THE COLD WAR ENDS

In 1985, Mikhail Gorbachev became General Secretary of the Soviet Communist Party. To the astonishment of U.S. officials, he quickly proposed reducing tensions and the complete abolition of nuclear weapons. Gorbachev also surprised observers with proposals for the reform of the Soviet system that would lead ultimately to democracy and a market economy.

Gorbachev's efforts led to several summit meetings with Presidents Reagan and Bush. The first, in 1985, broke the ice sufficiently for the participants to schedule two more conferences. The second meeting, in 1986, reduced tensions further. The Soviets mollified American concerns by pledging to remove their troops from Afghanistan. This summit nearly produced a dramatic breakthrough agreement on arms control, but ended in stalemate when Reagan refused to delay the development and testing of Star Wars defenses (*Time* 1986). It was nevertheless widely viewed as a breakthrough in U.S.–Soviet relations (Shultz 1986).

The third summit proved far more successful. Indeed, Gorbachev's visit to Washington, D.C. in December 1987 was a personal triumph for the Soviet leader, who was warmly received by numerous representatives of government, as well as by public figures and the mass media: "Something extraordinary was taking place: four decades of often truculent cold-war rhetoric were giving way to dispassionate discourse and high-level rapport" (*Time* 1987b:17).

Increasingly positive attitudes toward the Soviets were reflected in opinion polls. Over 70% of respondents approved of the nuclear reduction treaty signed by Gorbachev and Reagan (*Newsweek* 1987b), and Americans approved of the Soviet leader by a margin of two to one, "a standing that lumps him alongside the top tier of presidential candidates" (*Time* 1987a:17). At the conclusion of the meetings, the President announced that an entirely new relationship had been established.

Six months later, the arch-anticommunist Reagan was strolling with his friend Gorbachev through Red Square and greeting well-wishers in a massive crowd. The President himself expressed amazement that his visit to Moscow was really happening. Gorbachev and Reagan concluded their final summit by signing a series of agreements, and pledging to continue lower-level talks on a broad range of issues. At this point, relations between the two countries had become normalized (Wilson-Smith 1988).

Positive relations continued for the next several years, a time of great upheaval throughout the Soviet system. In 1989, the Berlin Wall was torn down. Gorbachev pushed forward with his economic and political reforms but proved unable to control the changes he had helped to unleash. Two years later, he resigned from the government, an action that elicited a statement of regret from President Bush (1992). A year later, the Soviet Union went out of existence, replaced by a loosely integrated entity, the Confederation of Independent States. The evil empire was no more (Mandelbaum 1992).

RECONSTRUCTING THE JAPANESE THREAT: NATIONAL SECURITY

As perceptions of a Soviet military threat diminished in the late 1980s, claims about dangers from Japan increased in volume and began to be widely accepted. The Japanese threat began to assume crisis dimensions as it was qualitatively transformed. Interestingly, this transformation redefined the Japanese problem in terms of familiar Cold War rhetoric.

The Toshiba Controversy

The reconstruction was partly accomplished in 1987, through revelations that the Toshiba Machine Company had sold high-tech products with military applications to the Soviet Union. These sales violated agreements signed by Japan and 15 other nations that restricted exports to the Soviet bloc. The technology in question consisted of computer-controlled lathes that could be used to build ultraquiet propellers for nuclear submarines. Falsified export papers filed with the International Coordinating Committee on Export Controls (COCOM) indicated that Toshiba Machine Company knew its actions were illegal.

Congress reacted with outrage. In a symbolic gesture widely reported by mass media, several members demolished a Toshiba boombox on the steps of the Capitol. Within a month, the Senate approved a resolution calling for a ban on all Toshiba imports for a period of 2 to 5 years (Fuerbringer 1987). The House meanwhile voted to seek compensation in the courts. Senator Dale Bumpers apparently spoke for many when he said: "A lot of people are in prison in this country for doing a lot less than Toshiba did" (*Newsweek* 1987a).

Similar responses appeared in popular periodicals. *Time* claimed that the illegal sales were part of an organized conspiracy (Koepp 1987). *Newsweek* asserted that the United States would have to spend $40 billion on its antisubmarine forces as a result of the sales (Copeland 1987). *U.S. News and World Report* referred to the transactions as the most harmful transfer of sensitive technology in more than 10 years (Cook 1987). *Reader's Digest* called the sales "the anatomy of a betrayal" (Bennett 1987). *Business Week* warned that as a result of Toshiba's action, Soviet submarines could hit U.S. targets with nuclear missiles in a matter of minutes (Kapstein 1987).

In December 1987, Congress passed a punitive law (PL 100-202) that President Reagan immediately signed. This measure prohibited the Department of Defense from purchasing imports from Toshiba, unless the Secretary of Defense determined that the goods or services were necessary for national security.

The combative attitudes generated by the Toshiba controversy continued during the presidential politics of 1988, as rhetoric of self-defense or protectionism. In the spring, Representative Richard Gephardt won the Democratic presidential primary in Iowa largely by campaigning on this issue. He then introduced the "Gephardt Amendment" in legislative debates, a proposal to require penalties against nations like Japan that continually ran bilateral surpluses with the United States. Although the amendment was not enacted into law, it shaped much of the year's electoral debate (Kuttner 1988).

Most importantly, the Gephardt proposal appears to have been partly responsible for the passage of the U.S. Trade Act of 1988, and especially its section on unfair trade (known as "Super 301"). This law required the Office of the U.S. Trade Representative to identify publicly any unfair trading partners. It also stipulated penalties and corrective measures to be taken, including import restrictions and surcharges. A year later, Super 301 was applied to Japan by the new Bush administration (Powell 1989b).

Thus, the Toshiba incident helped crystallize new perceptions of a Japanese threat, releasing strong emotions that had been suppressed during the period of conflict with the Soviets. The image of Japan selling crucial technologies to America's most dangerous enemy made it difficult, if not impossible, to retain the earlier construction of the Japanese threat as purely a matter of economic advantage. The problem, moreover, was no longer confined to particular businesses and industries; it was seen as affecting the entire nation. Japanese trading practices were being reconstructed as a matter of life and death.

Revisionist Analyses

The reconstruction of the Japanese threat in the post-Cold War context was led by experts in academia and government—as well as some journalists—who made new claims in the form of "revisionist" economics and history. These claimsmakers attacked what they considered to be three erroneous assumptions about Japan that had shaped American attitudes and policy: (1) standard Western economics adequately explained Japanese behavior, (2) Japan would eventually become similar to other modern Western nations, and (3) U.S. national security was rooted in military power. For some revisionists, this critique became a moral crusade similar to the Committee on the Present Danger's (1984) efforts, a decade earlier, against the alleged Soviet menace.

Having rejected conventional views, the new claimsmakers asserted, first, that Japan's economics did not fit the model of free markets and rational consumers acting to maximize their own happiness. In the bestseller, *Trading Places*, for example, former trade negotiator Clyde Prestowitz (1988) analyzed how the Japanese government guided its nation's economy, and how economic gains were passed on to major corporations rather than to consumers or stockholders (see also Kuttner, 1991). In *Japan's Unequal Trade*, Edward Lincoln (1990:1) contended: "Left to itself, Japan's behavior on imports will remain peculiar and unsatisfactory to its trading partners." Economist Lester Thurow (1992) argued that Japan practiced "producer economics," an approach that tapped into the deep human desire to participate in the victories of a group. These claims earned their advocates the nicknames "trade hawks" and "technonationalists" (Powell 1989a).

Revisionists also insisted that Japan would not become increasingly similar to Europe or the United States, but would remain unique and continue to value its own uniqueness. Claimsmakers pointed out, for example, that Japan had an entire literary genre, called *nihonjinron*, celebrating the distinctiveness of Japanese culture and experience. The need for Americans to recognize this sense of difference became the theme of a series of influential articles by James Fallows (1987, 1989, 1994) in *The Atlantic Monthly*. Prestowitz (1988) also developed this claim, noting that a psychology of uniqueness provided the basis for discrimination and the deliberate exclusion of outsiders (e.g., foreign-owned businesses). Thus, the Japanese came to be perceived as "alien," an image often utilized in times of war and that had previously been applied to the Soviet Union.

Finally, and most importantly, revisionists championed the claim that national security has an economic, rather than a military, foundation. They therefore charged that the enormous spending on Cold War weaponry had weakened the United States. Prestowitz, for instance, argued that the Japanese were surpassing the United States because they correctly saw industrial capability as the source of national strength. Thurow presented a similar argument in his influential book, *Head To Head*:

> History is clear. . . . Eventually military power depends on having a successful economic base. America's success in the War in the [Persian] Gulf proves that it is, and will be, a military superpower. . . . But its success in the Gulf in no way guarantees that it will be an economic superpower in the twenty-first century. (1992:21)

Taken together, the three basic revisionist claims meant that Japan's trade policies had to be understood primarily in terms of political power, rather than economics. As the Japanese conquered markets in America, claimsmakers asserted, the United States was losing its independence—even though the nation might think that it was simply getting the best available products. Whole industries were being destroyed, while the United States also fell behind in the development of new products and services. If the trend were not reversed, the United States might never be able to compete successfully again. Even its military arsenal would eventually fall, since the best weapons are based on the best technology, which was increasingly becoming Japanese technology.

As further support for their claims, revisionists frequently cited a controversial book, *The Japan That Can Say No*, by Shintaro Ishihara, a Japanese politician, and Akio Morita, chairman of Sony Corporation (1989). This work argued that Japan could tip the balance of power between the United States and the Soviets by deciding where to sell its high technology. Never again, the authors proclaimed, could Japan be taken for granted by the superpowers. Appearing only 2 years after the Toshiba case, the book evoked outrage in the United States (Borrus 1989).

By the early 1990s, there were many indications that Americans were "rethinking Japan" (Magnusson 1991). Popular opinion polls, for example, showed that Americans regarded the economic threat from Japan as a greater danger than the military threat from the Soviet Union (*Gallup Poll Monthly* 1991). The Clinton administration made revisionist doctrines the basis for its negotiations with Japan, and the President himself acquired the public image of a "trade hawk" (Cooper and Impoco 1993). Even the top executives of American automobile manufacturers began to support revisionist views, which had formerly been associated with the protectionism of organized labor. Chrysler's Lee Iacocca (1992), for example, after participating in President Bush's trade mission to Japan, complained that the Japanese were playing by different rules and causing unemployment in the United States.

> Bipartisan support for revisionist claims also started to appear in national elections: Japan bashing is prevalent in the 1992 U.S. presidential campaign. From Pat Buchanan on the Republican Right to Senator Tom Harkin on the Democratic Left, almost the entire field of challengers is talking tough about trade with Japan. (Shapiro 1992:23)

The spread of such sentiments can help us understand the most astonishing claim about the reconstructed threat, namely, that the United States and Japan might fight another major war in the near future.

War Scares

As the Cold War with the Soviet Union came to an end, American fears about military conflict with the Soviets began to be transferred to conflicts involving Japan. Among the issues raised by claimsmakers was an alleged infiltration of the American government by persons and groups working for the Japanese. The most explicit statement of this position was provided in Pat Choate's *Agents of Influence* (1990). Choate claimed that the United States was being harmed by lobbyists hired to represent Japanese interests, as well as by various groups funded by the Japanese, including politicians, think tanks, and even universities.

A more scholarly treatment of alleged military dangers appeared in *The Coming War With Japan*, by George Friedman and Meredith Lombard (1991), who contended:

> there are underlying reasons—economic, political, and military—that must put the United States and Japan on a collision course. . . . Japan needs to control access to its mineral supplies . . . and have an export market it can dominate. . . . It must force the United States out of the western Pacific. The United States will see this . . . as Japanese aggression . . . both will engage in a cold war . . . which will . . . spill over into a hot war. (1991:13–14).

Claims about Japanese-economics-as-warfare also began to appear in popular culture. Michael Crichton's 1992 novel *Rising Sun* (which also became a 1993 movie) presented a detective story that warned about alleged dangers of Japanese policies. The book's hero, Captain Connor, cautions: "The Japanese can be tough. . . . They say, 'business is war,' and they mean it" (1992:152).

Another positive character, Professor Philip Sanders, repeats this message:

> In Japan, patenting is a form of war. . . . It takes eight years to get a patent in Japan, but your application is made public after eighteen months. . . . It's one of the ways they keep their edge. (1992:202)

Rising Sun also included references to the Houdaille Industries decision and the Toshiba controversy, claiming that in both cases aggressive and unfair Japanese practices seriously injured American interests (1992:109, 228).

The theme of imminent danger of warfare between Japan and the United States was further developed in *Debt of Honor* by Tom Clancy (1994), in which a group of powerful Japanese businessmen and their political allies launch a simultaneous attack on American financial markets and the U.S. Pacific fleet. The novel's hero, National Security Adviser Jack Ryan, realizes that the seemingly unrelated events are parts of an intricate plan to seize power from the United States. In the following exchange (1994:487), Ryan informs top government officials:

> "We're at war with Japan. They've sunk two of our submarines and crippled two aircraft carriers," Ryan said, and the room changed a lot.
> "Are you serious?" Winston asked.
> "Two hundred-and-fifty-dead-sailors serious. . . . They've also seized the Mariana Islands. . . . We have upwards of ten thousand citizens in Japan as potential hostages, plus the population of the islands, plus military personnel in Japanese custody."
> "But the media—"
> "Haven't caught on yet, remarkably enough," Ryan explained.
> "Maybe it's just too crazy."
> "Oh." Winston got it after another second. "They wreck our economy, and we don't have the political will to . . . has anybody ever tried anything like this before?"
> The National Security Adviser shook his head. "Not that I know of."

Such representations of the Japanese threat were poles apart from official pronouncements in the mid-1980s that Japan was America's closest ally and the cornerstone of U.S. defenses in the Pacific. Indeed, the depictions by Crichton and Clancy revived images of Japan as an aggressor nation fully capable of launching another Pearl-Harbor-style sneak attack.

Japan as Global Threat

While reconstructing the Japanese threat in terms of national security, claimsmakers began to attribute global dimensions to the problem. An early statement (Rich 1985) characterized Japan's trade surplus with less developed nations as "a prime cause of the worldwide debt crisis" that "could lead to a collapse of the world financial system." As the 1980s ended, an article in the *Harvard Business Review* warned that, as a result of Japan's policies:

> We face the frightening possibility of a second Great Depression . . . caused by the world's inability to pay for Japanese goods, which have now become critical, irreplaceable components in industry after industry. (Murphy 1989:80)

A few years later, U.S. Trade Representative Laura Tyson (1994:A14) would claim that Japanese practices must be reformed to "preserve the health of the global trading system."

At the same time, in rhetoric strikingly reminiscent of the Cold War, claimsmakers began to assert that the entire world had a shared interest in "containing Japan" (Fallows 1989). A Central Intelligence Agency report (leaked to the press) provided additional support by labeling Japan an "amoral" nation (*Newsweek* 1991). Increasingly, America's former staunchest ally was portrayed as an emergent Soviet-style evil empire.

CONCLUSION

Contextual constructionism has created a new agenda for social problems research. For the promise of this approach to be fully realized, however, sociologists need to make context a central consideration in all aspects of their analysis. Awareness of context is indispensable for understanding the content of claims, the identities of claimsmakers, rhetorical tactics, and audience responses. This chapter has attempted to meet this need by tracing the effects of shifting international and domestic contexts on perceptions of a Japanese threat to the United States.

In the early 1970s, claimsmakers began to construct a Japanese problem in terms of unfair trade practices. Two decades later, other claimsmakers portrayed a Japanese threat to national security that had the potential to erupt into open warfare. This chapter showed how domestic and international contexts affected this claimsmaking. The context of the Cold War between the United States and the Soviet Union suppressed perceptions of a Japanese economic threat, especially within the executive branch of government.The end of the Cold War, however, both permitted perceptions of a Japanese threat to spread rapidly and facilitated the redefinition of that threat in terms of national security.

The history of these claims suggests that the United States may need to perceive a foreign enemy, although this issue lies beyond the scope of this chapter. It may be that any nation that aspires to be the economic and political leader of the world, as the United States has in recent times, will tend to construct challenges to its ambitions. Perhaps only by constructing and overcoming such challenges can such a nation maintain a sense of preeminence. If so, then perhaps a key aspect of context may be the situational priorities of national ambition.

The available data strongly suggest that Japan will be perceived as a competitor to the United States for the foreseeable future. It is possible that a cold war with Japan will indeed develop over the next few decades, even that Japan will someday be regarded as America's major adversary. But it is also possible, in an increasingly global village bound together by peaceful negotiations, that perceived conflicts between the two nations will be resolved without the fearsome costs of an earlier Cold War.

REFERENCES

Armstrong, L. 1986. "Nakasone Goes Marching Off to Star Wars." *Business Week* (March 31):44–45.

Bennett, R. K. 1987. "The Toshiba Scandal: Anatomy of a Betrayal." *Readers Digest* 128 (December):95–100.

Best, J. 1990. *Threatened Children*. Chicago: University of Chicago Press.

———. 1993. "But Seriously, Folks: Limitations of the Strict Constructionist Interpretation of Social Problems." Pp. 129–147 in *Reconsidering Social Constructionism*, edited by J. A. Holstein and G. Miller. Hawthorne, NY: Aldine de Gruyter.

Borrus, A. 1989. "The Book That's Creating a Firestorm." *Business Week* (October 23):78+.

Bush, G. 1992. "President Bush Remarks on Mikhail S. Gorbachev's Resignation." *Vital Speeches of the Day* 58:195–196.

Butler, S., and J. Impoco. 1994. "Clinton to Tokyo: No More Nice Guy." *U.S. News & World Report* (February 21) 110:54.

Callaway, E. 1971. "U.S. Trade Policy." *New York Times* (March 7):Sec. 3; 14.

Choate, P. 1990. *Agents of Influence*. New York: Knopf.

Clancy, T. 1994. *Debt of Honor*. New York: Putnam's Sons.

Clines, F. X. 1983. "Reagan Denounces Ideology of Soviet As 'Focus of Evil.'" *New York Times* (March 9):A1, A18.

Committee on the Present Danger. 1984. *Alerting America: The Papers of the Committee on the Present Danger*. Washington, DC: Pergamon Brassey's.

Congressional Quarterly Almanac. 1981a. "Democratic Platform Text." 36:91B–118B.

———. 1981b. "Reagan's Acceptance Speech." 36:38B.

———. 1981c. "Republican Platform Text." 36:58B-84B.

Cook, W. J. 1987. "An Illegal Deal's Noisy Repercussions." *U.S. News and World Report* (June 15) 102:42.

Cooper, M., and J. Impoco. 1993. "The Making of a Trade Hawk." *U.S. News and World Report* (July 12):28–29.

Copeland, J. B. 1987. "The Battle over Toshiba." *Newsweek* (July 13):40.

Crichton, M. 1992. *Rising Sun*. New York: Ballantine Books.

Fallows, J. 1987. "Playing By Different Rules." *Atlantic Monthly* (September):260:22+.

———. 1989. "Containing Japan." *Atlantic Monthly* (May) 263:40–48+.

———. 1994. "What Is An Economy For?" *Atlantic Monthly* (January) 273:76–78+.

Flint, J. M. 1971. "U.S. Auto Men See Unfairness in Tokyo's Export-Import Policy." *New York Times* (August 23):42.

Friedman, G., and M. Lombard. 1991. *The Coming War with Japan*. New York: St. Martin's Press.

Fuerbringer, J. 1987. "Senate Backs Import Ban in Soviet Trade Deal." *New York Times* (July 1):A1, D17.

Gallup Poll Monthly. 1991. "Favorable Attitudes towards Japan Declining." (December):11–18.

———. 1992. "Americans Show Mixed Reactions to Japan." (February):2–6.

Iacocca, L. 1992. "Taking Care of Business: The Japanese Must Open Their Markets." *Vital Speeches of the Day* (March):295–299.

Ishihara, S., and A. Morita. 1989. *The Japan That Can Say No*. New York: Kodansha.

Kapstein, J. 1987. "A Leak That Could Sink the U.S. Lead in Submarines." *Business Week* (May 18):65–66.

Koepp, S. 1987. "Beware of Machines in Disguise." *Time* (September 21) 130:53.

Kuttner, R. 1988. "Gephardt Is Asking the Right Questions about Trade." *Business Week* (February 22):18.

———. 1991. *The End of Laissez-Faire*. Philadelphia: University of Pennsylvania Press.

Lincoln, E. J. 1990. *Japan's Unequal Trade*. Washington, DC: Brookings Institution.

Lindsey, R. 1982. "Resentment of Japanese Is Growing, Poll Shows." *New York Times* (April 6):Sec. II, p. 12.

Magnusson, P. 1991. "Rethinking Japan." *Business Week* (August 7):44–52.

Malcolm, A. H. 1978. "U.S. and Japan Pressing for Accord in Trade Dispute." *New York Times* (January 10):45, 49.

Mandelbaum, M. 1992. "Coup de Grace: the End of the Soviet Union." *Foreign Affairs* (Special Issue):164–183.

Matthews, T. 1980a. "The Chill of a New Cold War." *Newsweek* (January 14):24–25.

———. 1980b. "America's Get-Tough Strategy." *Newsweek* (January 21):22–24.

Murphy, R. T. 1989. "Power Without Purpose: The Crisis of Japan's Global Financial Dominance." *Harvard Business Review* (March–April):71–83.

Nevin, J. 1978. "Can U.S. Business Survive Our Japanese Trade Policy?" *Harvard Business Review* (September) 56:165–177.

New York Times. 1971a. "Tough Trade Line Urged by Shultz." (May 22):39, 41.

———. 1971b. "Japan Urged to Lift Trade Restrictions in Rogers Speech." (July 1):74.

Newsweek. 1987a. "Making Amends: Top Toshiba Executives Resign." (July 13) 110:49.

———. 1987b. "The Last Chance We Have." (December 21) 110:15–24.

———. 1991. "A Case of Ja-Panic." (June 24) 117:33+.

Oreskes, M. 1990. "Poll Detects Erosion of Positive Attitudes Toward Japan Among Americans." *New York Times* (February 6):B7.

Powell, B. 1989a. "The Rise of the Trade Hawks." *Newsweek* (March 13) 112:46–47.

———. 1989b. "Japan Makes the Hit List." *Newsweek* (June 5) 112:48–49.

Prestowitz, C. 1988. *Trading Places: How We Are Giving Our Future to Japan and How to Reclaim It*. New York: Basic Books.

Reagan, R. 1985. "The Case for Star Wars—In Reagan's Own Words." *U.S. News and World Report* (January 14) 98:24.

Rich, T. 1985. "Japan Must Join the World." *Newsweek* (November 4) 106:50–51.

Shapiro, W. 1992. "Japan Bashing on the Campaign Trail." *Time* (February 10) 135:23–24.

Shultz, G. P. 1986. "Reykjavik: A Watershed in U.S.-Soviet Relations." *Department of State Bulletin* 86:22–25.

Stebbins, K. R. 1992. "Garbage Imperialism: Health Implications of Dumping Hazardous Wastes in Third World Countries." *Medical Anthropology* 15:81–102.

———. 1994. "Making a Killing South of the Border: Transnational Cigarette Companies in Mexico and Guatemala." *Social Science and Medicine* 38 (No. 1):105–115.

Thurow, L. 1992. *Head to Head: The Coming Competition Among Japan, Europe, and America*. New York: Morrow.

Time. 1980. "Moscow's Bold Challenge." (January 14) 116:10–17.

———. 1986. "Sunk by Star Wars." (October 20) 128:19–22.

———. 1987a. "We Meet Again." (December 14) 130:16–17.

———. 1987b. "The Spirit of Washington." (December 21) 130:16–21.

Tyson, L. D. 1994. "Japan's Trade Surplus Matters." *Wall Street Journal* (March 14):A14.

United States Congress, Joint Economic Committee. 1980. *Hearing*. Washington, DC: Government Printing Office.

United States House of Representatives, Committee on Foreign Affairs. 1982. *Hearings*. Washington, DC: Government Printing Office.

United States House of Representatives, Committee on Ways and Means. 1983. *Hearings*. Washington, DC: Government Printing Office.

U.S. News and World Report. 1980a. "How the Soviet Union Exploited Detente." (January 14) 88:19.

———. 1980b. "How Key Senators Would Handle Soviets." (January 14) 88:24.

Wall Street Journal. 1971a. "U.S. Workers Who Lost Jobs Making TV Sets Sue Japanese Firms." (March 1):9.

———. 1971b. "Japan's TV Sets Ruled Harmful to U.S. Industry." (March 5):2.

———. 1971c. "'Payments Crisis' Weapons Voted by Senate Panel." (November 5):6.

Wilson-Smith, A. 1988. "Farewell to the 'Evil Empire.'" *Maclean's* (June 13) 101:16–19.

AFTERWORD

15

Constructionism in Context

The constructionist approach to studying social problems emerged from some sociologists' dissatisfaction with the dominant, objectivist stance. Constructionists argued that defining social problems in terms of objective conditions within society had two key flaws: it ignored the fact that identifying a social condition as a social problem required subjective judgment; and, by labeling conditions with little in common as social problems, objectivism could not serve as a foundation for more general theories of social problems.

In contrast, constructionists define social problems in terms of claims-making; they focus on the subjective judgments (claims that X is a social problem) that the objectivists slighted.[1] And, as the chapters in this book reveal, the constructionist approach offers a basis for developing new theories—about claims, claimsmakers, connections among claims-making campaigns, and social policies, among other topics.

The constructionist approach to social problems is relatively new, and it remains controversial. Critics attack constructionism from several sides; some sociologists defend objectivism and criticize the constructionist stance, or they argue that objectivism and constructionism can be easily reconciled; others warn that constructionism is inherently inconsistent, that its theoretical assumptions are contradictory; while, even among sociologists who see themselves as working within the constructionist tradition, there are disagreements about what sorts of analysis ought to be called "constructionist."

This afterword offers an introduction to the recent debates over social problems theory. But it is only an introduction to a growing literature. Some readers may want to learn more about those debates by going on to explore some of the references cited in this afterword.[2]

CONSTRUCTIONISM'S CRITICS: ATTACKS FROM OUTSIDE

Constructionism offers a dramatic break from the traditional objectivist approach to studying social problems. Even the term "social problem" has a different meaning when constructionists use it. While the constructionist perspective has inspired a large body of research, it continues to be criticized by sociologists who remain within the objectivist tradition. Most objectivist critiques of constructionism can be summarized within four general arguments.

1. Constructionism and Objectivism Are Complementary

Some sociologists who remain more-or-less committed to the objectivist perspective deny that constructionism represents a genuinely different approach. They argue that objectivism and constructionism are merely "two sides of the same coin," that the two theoretical perspectives can be easily reconciled. Most often, these efforts to minimize the differences between objectivism and constructionism give only lip service to constructionist concerns. For instance, many social problems textbooks' definitions of social problems mention the role of subjective judgments in identifying problems, but constructionist issues receive no further attention in these books. Such treatments misunderstand the nature of constructionism, which involves more than acknowledging that definitions of social problems are subjective. By defining social problems in terms of claimsmaking, constructionists set a new agenda for those who would study social problems; constructionist research addresses a distinct set of questions about the nature of claims, those who make claims, and so on. Thus, a traditional, objectivist approach to homelessness might focus on measuring the size of the homeless population, learning why some people become homeless, or otherwise exploring homelessness as a social condition, while a constructionist analysis would ask whose claims brought homelessness to public attention, how those claims typified the homeless, how the public and policymakers responded to the claims, and so on.

Because the two perspectives define social problems differently and focus on different issues, it is not simple to reconcile objectivism and constructionism in a single, integrated theory. For example, Jones, McFalls, and Gallagher (1989:344) offer a "unified model" in which "three major factors—visibility (intrinsic and extrinsic), expectations, and values—[interpose] themselves between objective and subjective dimensions." For constructionists, such models depend upon objectivist assumptions about social life and sociology, assumptions that constructionist analysis begins by rejecting. As a result, integrated models receive little support from the constructionist camp.

2. Constructionism's Subject Is Relatively Unimportant

Other objectivist sociologists acknowledge that constructionism has a unique approach—one they deplore. They argue that constructionists' focus on claimsmaking ignores a far more important subject: the harmful social conditions that are the "real" social problems. Thus, an article criticizing constructionist analyses in social work is titled "Reality Exists O.K.?" (Speed 1991). The constructionist response to this call for analysts to return to their traditional subject matter is twofold: (1) while there is nothing wrong with studying particular social conditions, decades of objectivist research on social conditions have failed to lay a foundation for general theories of social problems; and (2) it is important to remember that we recognize social conditions as "really" harmful only because someone made persuasive claims to that effect. Again, objectivism and constructionism ask different questions; the relative value of the two sets of questions depends upon what we want to know.

3. Constructionism Has Moral or Political Biases

Many sociologists bring moral or political commitments to their work; often, their concerns with social issues led them to study sociology. Typically, sociologists have left-liberal sympathies, and they favor egalitarian social change. Some critics—including some sociologists who identify their approach as constructionist—worry that constructionism may somehow subvert these goals. Usually, this critique argues that because people with less power have a harder time getting heard, the constructionist focus on vocal, visible claimsmaking will overlook the concerns of society's invisible members—those too inarticulate, alienated, or powerless to voice claims. For example, Patricia Hill Collins (1989:90) argues: "Poor Black women face critical issues that merit study, yet they lack the power to make their claims known within current political structures of social problems discourse," while Leslie J. Miller (1993) suggests that analysts often ignore the claimsmaking styles favored by marginalized "underdogs." Concerned that constructionists cannot be counted upon to recognize conditions that afflict those who cannot easily make claims, these critics call for a return to objective definitions of social problems. They offer various bases for such definitions, including "moral imperatives and human needs that are trans-societal and trans-historical" (Eitzen 1984:11), "the knowledge related values of science" (Manis 1985:5), and "an overarching ethical framework" (Collins 1989:90).

The argument that constructionism springs from a particular set of moral or political values is not convincing. Reading between the lines, it is sometimes possible to infer that an analyst has made certain assumptions about how the social world works—or should work. A left-liberal bent is common among sociologists, and it is no surprise that many constructionist works seem to incorporate more-or-less liberal assumptions, yet it is possible to point to particular studies that seem to reflect very different values. Moreover, it is not clear why we ought to suspect that constructionism inevitably draws upon particular values; constructionism is a tool that can be put to many uses.

Nor does it seem probable that constructionists are especially likely to overlook the concerns of the powerless. Certainly many constructionist case studies examine social movements by people who have been marginalized and discredited. In spite of some critics' concerns, there seems to be no shortage of outlets for claims, and many scholars in sociology and other disciplines seem eager to identify and describe claimsmaking by the disadvantaged. No doubt there will always be some concerns that go unstated, unnoticed, and unanalyzed, but it is not clear why we should expect sociologists operating from objectivist assumptions to be any more likely than constructionists to identify these hidden concerns as subjects for research. Again, social conditions become topics for objectivist research only when they have been subjectively constructed as problematic.

4.   Constructionism Is Merely Debunking

Constructionism shifts the analyst's focus from social conditions to members' claims about those conditions. It is the claim, not the condition that is at issue; in fact, some constructionists carefully speak of "putative conditions" that may or may not exist. This has led some critics to equate constructionism with debunking, so that they may ask whether a particular social problem is an objective social condition, or "just" a social construction. This equates social construction with error, and defines constructionist analysis as a method of exposing mistaken or distorted claims. For instance, Forsyth and Oliver (1990:285) state: "Basically the constructionist argument is that there has been no significant change in the activity in question, but that activities which were not previously defined [sic] as problematic, have been defined as a problem."

This criticism reflects a basic misunderstanding: equating social construction with erroneous reasoning. All claims—and all other human knowledge—are socially constructed. It is wrong to assume that analyses of objective conditions deal with what is true, while analyses of socially constructed claims deal with what is false. Again, all our knowledge—including our knowledge of objective conditions—is a product of social interaction, a social construction.[3]

STRICT CONSTRUCTIONISM

The most influential critique of constructionism came not from objectivists, but from two sociologists writing from a subjectivist stance, who charged that constructionists base their analyses on hidden, objectivist assumptions. Steve Woolgar and Dorothy Pawluch (1985a) argue that constructionism is internally inconsistent. They note that while constructionists identify their focus as subjective judgments or claims, constructionist analyses usually assume some knowledge of objective conditions. Thus, a standard constructionist explanation might proceed: although social condition X remained unchanged, X became defined as a social problem when people began making claims about it. Woolgar and Pawluch point to the (sometimes unstated) assumption that X was unchanged. Although constructionists speak of claims about *putative* conditions as the proper subject for social problems analysis, implying that the nature of the social conditions is irrelevant (and perhaps unknowable), they typically assume that they do know the actual status of the social condition (as an unchanging phenomenon). For Woolgar and Pawluch (1985a:216), this contradiction is at the core of constructionism: "The successful [constructionist] social problems explanation depends on making problematic the truth status of certain states of affairs selected for analysis and explanation, while backgrounding or minimizing the possibility that the same problems apply to assumptions upon which the analysis depends." Woolgar and Pawluch call this selective attention to objective conditions "ontological gerrymandering."

Woolgar and Pawluch's critique launched a lively debate among those who saw themselves as constructionists (Gusfield 1985; Hazelrigg 1985, 1986; Pfohl 1985; J. Schneider 1985b; Woolgar and Pawluch 1985b). At issue are the analytic assumptions at the perspective's foundation. What assumptions about the social world are appropriate? Should all such assumptions be avoided, or are some acceptable? What are the consequences of making different assumptions? Constructionists give various answers to these questions.

At one extreme are those sympathetic to Woolgar and Pawluch's critique. These are the *strict constructionists*, who argue that social problems analysts should avoid making assumptions about objective reality. In their view, constructionists should examine the perspectives of claimsmakers, policymakers, and other members of society. The actual social conditions are irrelevant; what matters is what the members say about those conditions. Strict constructionists focus on claimsmaking; they seek to understand, but do not presume to judge the members' claims.

In fact, because they adopt a phenomenological perspective, strict constructionists question the analyst's ability to make judgments about social conditions. Phenomenological sociology argues that all we know about the world is a social construction. This includes the claims members make about social issues, but it also includes the analyses that constructionist sociologists write about claimsmaking. In this view, the sociologist is not specially privileged; he or she is just another actor trying to make sense of the surrounding world. A sociologist who makes statements about social conditions is simply another claimsmaker, one more participant in the claimsmaking process. Strict constructionists, then, find little attraction in reconciling constructionist and objectivist theories, since they view members' claims, rather than the validity of those claims, as the subject matter for the sociology of social problems. On the other hand, strict constructionists find considerable merit in Woolgar and Pawluch's critique, and they strive to avoid making (even implicit) assumptions about objective reality.

Once Woolgar and Pawluch drew attention to the problem of ontological gerrymandering, several leading constructionists rallied around the cause of strict constructionism (Holstein and Miller 1993; Ibarra and Kitsuse 1993; Kitsuse and Schneider 1989; Sarbin and Kitsuse 1994; Spector and Kitsuse 1987; Troyer 1992). They called for constructionist researchers to shun all claims or assumptions about social conditions, to confine their analysis strictly to claims.

The most influential advocate of the strict constructionist position is John I. Kitsuse—co-author of the classic constructionist text, *Constructing Social Problems* (Spector and Kitsuse 1977). It is worth tracing how Kitsuse's interpretation of strict constructionism has evolved. Initially, strict constructionists treated ontological gerrymandering as carelessness on the part of the analyst; a careful constructionist, they argued, could avoid making forbidden assumptions (e.g., J. Schneider 1985a, 1985b). Thus, Kitsuse and Schneider (1989:xii–xiii) insist that the strict constructionist

> does not compete with members as an arbiter of true and accurate knowledge. Instead, the theoretical task is to study how members define, lodge, and press claims; how they publicize their concerns, redefine the issues in question in the face of political obstacles, indifference, or opposition; how they enter into alliances with other claims-makers; and the myriad other activities that constitute subject matter for the study of social problems.

While this seems to imply that constructionists could (carefully) continue studying cases of social problems construction, the issue was not so simple. Even this brief passage raises questions for strict constructionist analysts. For instance, how—without making any assumptions about social conditions—can an analyst identify "political opposition, indifference, or obstacles" or "alliances"? Strict constructionists began to recognize that, in practice, background assumptions about social conditions were far more commonplace in constructionist work than even Woolgar and Pawluch had suggested.

Some strict constructionists responded to this recognition by moving away from case studies. Writing with Peter R. Ibarra, Kitsuse suggested that case studies were analytically troublesome:

> [O]ur position is that the project of developing a theory of *social problems discourse* is a much more coherent way of proceeding with constructionism than, for example, the development of a series of discrete theories on the social construction of X, Y, and Z. To develop a theory about condition X when the ontological status of X is suspended results in "ontological gerrymandering". . . which is to say flawed theory. (Ibarra and Kitsuse 1993:33—emphasis in original)

Ibarra and Kitsuse's solution was to offer a new classification of claims-making rhetoric, in which the analytic focus was not social conditions, but "condition-categories"—claims about putative conditions. But, upon inspection, even their statement of this abstract theory of social problems discourse incorporated numerous assumptions about social conditions (Best 1993).[4]

Much as earlier generations of sociologists came to question whether sociology could be "value-free," strict constructionists began to recognize that their goal of an "assumption-free" sociology was an illusion. Thus, when Kitsuse and psychologist Theodore R. Sarbin introduce their 1994 collection of constructionist cases studies, they speak of the logical desirability of strict constructionism. (They equate the strict constructionist approach with what they call "contextualism"—"tell[ing] a story about phenomena in their natural contexts" [Sarbin and Kitsuse 1994:7].) But then they confess:

> None of the chapters in this volume is an exemplar of strict constructionism. . . . It is questionable whether researchers can sustain any method that would be consistent with the requirements of strict contextualism. . . . Investigators and analysts in spite of themselves cannot help but import their interests, if not their professional agendas, into their interactions with their informants. (Sarbin and Kitsuse 1994:14)[5]

In other words, strict constructionism is an elusive, unattainable goal. All sociological analysis requires stepping back from the subjects of research, calling at least a portion of the taken-for-granted social world into question. Constructionism requires stepping back a bit further, in order to question the definitions of social conditions as social problems. And the strict constructionists advocate stepping back further still, assuming less and calling still more into question. But, however far analysts distance themselves from their subject matter, they can never jettison all assumptions. Analysis requires the analyst to use language, and a culture's assumptions are built into its language. As a result, all analysts, no matter how far they may distance themselves from their subject matter, can be attacked for ontological gerrymandering.

How should sociologists respond to the strict constructionist critique? Some strict constructionists advocate directing sociological research in new directions. Thus, Woolgar and Pawluch (1985b:12) call for sociologists to "move beyond constructivism" and refocus their analyses on the nature of sociological inquiry, although they concede that the new questions they raise "will not contribute . . . to our understanding of the world as we have traditionally conceived that pursuit." This not only shifts the analytic focus away from the social conditions studied by objectivist sociologists, but also away from the claimsmaking studied by constructionists, so that the analyst's subject becomes how sociologists purport to study others. Other strict constructionists argue that sociologists should redefine their analyses as literary products, understanding that sociology is just another form of narrative, that sociologists are storytellers, and that sociological explanation is merely another genre to be subjected to literary analysis. Of course, these new, introspective research agendas completely abandon studying what most people commonly call "social problems" (see also Holstein and Miller 1993). The strict constructionists seem to have convinced themselves of the impossibility of doing sociological—or at least social scientific—analysis.

CONTEXTUAL CONSTRUCTIONISM

While debate over strict constructionism occupied the attention of a few social problems theorists, many more sociologists tried to use the constructionist perspective to do research. The years following Woolgar and Pawluch's critique of ontological gerrymandering saw the publication of numerous constructionist studies, including pieces in such prestigious journals as the *American Sociological Review* (Block and Burns 1986), the *American Journal of Sociology* (Gamson and Modigliani 1989; Hilgartner and Bosk 1988), and the *American Political Science Review* (A. Schneider and Ingram 1993). Most of this research simply ignored the strict constructionist critique.

This does not mean that the critique of ontological gerrymandering has no merit. Strict constructionism reminds analysts that they must pay attention to the assumptions they bring to their analyses. Consider, for example, arguments—discussed earlier—that equate constructionism with debunking. We might call this *vulgar constructionism*, in which the analyst argues that social problems claims are "just" social constructions, i.e., that the claims are mistaken. Strict constructionists would argue that such debunking should not be considered a form of constructionism, that it is objectivist sociology, since the debunker presumes to know—and focuses on—the actual nature of social conditions, rather than the claimsmaking process.

But the majority of constructionist research falls somewhere between the two extremes of the strict constructionists' phenomenology, with its impossible demand that analysts avoid all assumptions about social conditions, and the vulgar constructionists' debunking, which loses sight of claimsmaking as the focus for social problems analysis. Constructionist work that occupies this middle ground—the chapters in this volume are examples—is called *contextual constructionism*.

Rather than retreating into general theories of condition categories and other abstractions, contextual constructionism seeks to locate claims-making within its context. Claims emerge at particular historical moments in particular societies; they are made by particular claimsmakers, who address particular audiences. Claimsmakers have particular reasons for choosing particular rhetoric to address particular problems. Such specific elements form claimsmaking's context, and contextual constructionists argue that understanding social problems claims often depends upon understanding their context.[6]

Consider, for example, John M. Johnson's analysis of child-abuse horror stories (Chapter 2). The context for these claims includes many elements: child abuse's emergence as a highly visible social issue during the 1960s and 1970s, the expansion of federal government influence through contingent funding of child protection programs, the women's movement's calls for increased attention to various forms of family violence, widespread cultural acceptance of a sentimental view of children as vulnerable innocents, conventions within the press for using examples to attract and maintain interest in complex stories—the list goes on and on. Johnson explicitly mentions some, but not all, of these. We can imagine that a longer, more complete analysis might explore some of the elements Johnson neglects. Nor is Johnson's chapter in any way exceptional; analogous comments could be made about each of the other chapters and, in fact, about any constructionist analysis. All claims emerge in contexts and, in their efforts to understand claims, analysts inevitably refer to these contexts.

But the key point is that any analysis of the social construction of child abuse—or any other social problem—requires locating claimsmaking within at least part of its context. Contrary to what strict constructionism demands, it is neither possible nor desirable to ignore the context of claims. And, because context has so many elements, the analyst invariably has to make assumptions about some of these elements.

Contextual constructionists, then, acknowledge making various assumptions about the social context of claimsmaking. Some of these assumptions may be explicit—announced by the analyst, others may be implicit—recognized by the analyst but not announced, and still others may never be consciously articulated by the analyst. The issue is not whether an analyst makes assumptions; analysts inevitably make assumptions. Remember that even strict constructionists have come to concede the impossibility of assumption-free analyses. Rather, the issue should be whether particular assumptions somehow damage an analysis.

Consider Woolgar and Pawluch's (1985a) initial example of ontological gerrymandering, their critique of Spector and Kitsuse's (1977) *Constructing Social Problems*. In a passage about changing claims regarding marijuana, Spector and Kitsuse (1977:43) remark: "The nature of marijuana remained constant." After quoting this passage, Woolgar and Pawluch (1985a:217) pounce: "[T]he key assertion is that the actual character of a substance (marijuana), condition, or behavior remained constant." Having been found to have made an assumption about a social condition, Spector and Kitsuse stand convicted of ontological gerrymandering. The strict constructionists accepted this as a legitimate criticism, but contextual constructionists demand something more—evidence that the assumption somehow damaged the analysis.

Was this indeed Spector and Kitsuse's "key assertion"? Was it unreasonable for them to assume that the nature of marijuana had not changed? Of course, Woolgar and Pawluch are not concerned about the marijuana problem's history; they simply use this example to identify what they see as a logical error, an unwarranted assumption bootlegged into Spector and Kitsuse's analysis. But Woolgar and Pawluch do not explain why this assumption was unreasonable; they do not, for example, hypothesize that through genetic mutation or altered cultivation practices, new strains of marijuana became available. In fact, it is not clear how Spector and Kitsuse damaged their analysis by assuming that marijuana had not changed.

In contrast, critics may find it much easier to specify what is wrong with other assumptions. Imagine, for example, an analyst who describes growing concern about illicit drug use and then assumes that "Illicit drug use remained constant." A critic who argues that illicit drug use probably did not remain constant—and who can offer convincing evidence to that effect—can argue that the analysis is flawed, that the assumption has damaged the analysis.

In other words, it is neither necessary nor possible for analysts to avoid all assumptions. But analysts must be prepared to acknowledge and defend the assumptions they do make. Critics should adopt a pragmatic standard: damage caused by an assumption must be demonstrated, rather than presumed. This is, of course, the traditional standard for evaluating social scientific inquiry: analysts report their methods and findings, and invite critics to spot flaws in the reasoning. But making an assumption is not, in and of itself, a logical flaw: making an assumption should not be considered a flaw until a critic can demonstrate why that assumption should be called into question.

It is important to emphasize that contextual constructionism remains focused on claimsmaking as a process. That is, contextual constructionists make assumptions about social conditions in order to better understand how social problems claims emerge and evolve. But this does not mean that strict constructionists are right when they equate contextual constructionism with objectivist sociology. Contextual constructionist analysts continue to ask questions that are very different from the ones asked by traditional objectivist researchers.

Suppose we study a campaign against "increasing crime in the streets." What might account for those claims? A strict constructionist might note claimsmakers' references to higher crime rates or rising fear of crime. But the strict constructionist would view these statements as claims, without making any effort to assess whether there really were increases in crime or the fear of crime. In contrast, a contextual constructionist might also look at official crime statistics or polls measuring the fear of crime—even if claimsmakers never referred to statistics or polls. Suppose, for instance, that claimsmakers campaigned against increasing crime at a time when official statistics showed no increase in the crime rate. A contextual constructionist might well choose to make something of the discrepancy between the claims and other information about social conditions. At a minimum, it seems reasonable to ask what the claimsmakers used as the basis for their claims of increasing crime, and an analyst might also ask what else could account for the timing of those claims.

Here, we see a key difference between strict and contextual constructionism. Obviously, any discussion about social conditions is a social construction. A claim that crime (or the fear of crime) is increasing is just that—a claim. But calling a statement a claim does not discredit it. Contextual constructionists argue that any claim can be evaluated. A claim may be based on various sorts of evidence, such as official criminal justice statistics or public opinion polls, which are in turn social

constructions—products of the organizational practices of police departments, polling firms, and so on. Strict constructionists often argue that
one set of claims (e.g., statistics about rising crime) cannot be used to
assess other claims (e.g., claimsmaking about "crime in the streets"). But
contextual constructionists assume that they can know—with reasonable confidence—something about social conditions. They acknowledge
the socially constructed nature of crime rates and other information
about social conditions, but they assume that such information can still
be used to (imperfectly) describe the context within which claimsmaking
occurs. Certainly, whether or not official statistics showed a rising crime
rate might affect a contextual constructionist's interpretation of claims
about rising street crime. Note that analysts can handle official statistics
and other information about social conditions in different ways. In debunking, for instance, one simply accepts the official figures as true,
accurate representations of reality—an approach more objectivist than
constructionist. But a contextual constructionist views official statistics
as social constructions, and is more likely to ask how claimsmakers use
such statistics. Are claimsmakers familiar with the official data, or do
they ignore it, or interpret it selectively in a way consistent with their
claims? Treating official statistics as accurate measures of social conditions may move an analyst outside the constructionist tradition, but the
error in treating official statistics as part of the claimsmakers' context—
and as claims in their own right—is less obvious.

The distinction between strict and contextual constructionism, then,
becomes a matter of degree. Woolgar and Pawluch helped sensitize
sociologists to the ways assumptions can creep unnoticed into analyses,
but strict constructionism's goal of assumption-free analysis can never
be achieved. Moreover, strict constructionism comes at a cost; it con-
strains analysis and limits what we can learn about the process of constructing social problems. Analysts who hope to understand how and
why social problems emerge and evolve must locate claimsmaking within its context. By default, all constructionist analysis becomes a form of
contextual constructionism.

USING THE CONSTRUCTIONIST PERSPECTIVE

The debate over the theoretical underpinnings of constructionism
may give the impression that this is a dry, academic, ivory-tower perspective of little practical value. It would be a shame to end on that note.
Once understood, the constructionist perspective can be useful, both for
would-be claimsmakers and would-be social problems analysts.

Constructionism as a Guide to Making Claims

Relatively few people achieve national recognition as claimsmakers who are invited to testify before Congress, are photographed for newsmagazines, and are interviewed on the evening network news. But not all claimsmaking occurs in the national arena. Claimsmaking also takes place in state capitols and city halls, in communities and neighborhoods, at workplaces, and on college campuses—wherever people try to draw attention to what they consider troublesome conditions.

Constructionist research offers valuable lessons for would-be claimsmakers. Claimsmakers face practical obstacles: they must attract attention, enlist support, and shape policy. Constructionist research shows how other claimsmakers have dealt with these obstacles. In a sense, constructionist case studies present guidelines for what works (and what does not), and under what circumstances. Studying sociologists' analyses of successful and unsuccessful claimsmaking can help would-be claimsmakers plan their own campaigns.

Applying Constructionism to New Topics

While insights from constructionist research can be used to help design new claimsmaking campaigns, constructionism remains most useful as an analytic tool. Constructionism is a stance, an orientation, a perspective we can apply to better understand the world around us. We live in a world where claimsmaking has become routine. The front page of a typical morning newspaper probably features three or four examples of claimsmaking. Claims account for large shares of the material presented in newsmagazines, on news broadcasts, before Congressional hearings, on radio and television talk shows, and so on. Usually these claims highlight fresh aspects of familiar social problems—say, a report that researchers have identified another cancer-causing substance. Less often, the claimsmakers say they have discovered a brand new problem.

While the media offer a steady supply of contemporary claims, it is also easy to identify historical examples of claimsmaking. American history, for instance, features campaigns for the abolition of slavery, women's suffrage, temperance, and so on. While more often described as political or social movements, these were, obviously, instances of claimsmaking.

Whether contemporary or historical, claims can be studied by adopting the constructionist perspective (see Spector and Kitsuse [1977:159–171] for practical suggestions). This requires focusing on the claims themselves, the claimsmakers, and the claimsmaking process.

Claims. The first task in constructionist analysis is to locate examples of the claims being made. Sources for claims vary, depending upon how and when the claims were made, the claimsmakers' credentials, and so on, but standard sources include (1) press coverage, both print (e.g., newspaper and newsmagazine articles) and electronic (e.g., evening network news, *60 Minutes*), (2) scholarly and professional books and periodical articles, (3) popular treatments, trade books, articles in general-interest magazines, or talk show discussions, (4) testimony before Congressional hearings, (5) pamphlets, flyers, handouts, and other ephemeral materials, (6) public opinion polls, and (7) interviews with claimsmakers.

Sometimes is it possible to trace the shifting level of interest in a social problem by measuring the frequency with which a particular type of claim appears. Sociologists often use indexes to the mass media (e.g., the *Reader's Guide to Periodical Literature*, the *New York Times Index*, or the *Television News Index and Abstracts*) to measure changing levels of media coverage of social problems.

Once a set of claims has been located, their content can be analyzed. Several questions become important: What is being said about the problem? How is the problem being typified? What is the rhetoric of claimsmaking—how are claims presented so as to persuade their audiences?

Claimsmakers.   A second focus for analysis is claimsmakers. To begin, the claimsmakers must be identified. Who actually makes the claims? Whom (if anyone besides themselves) do the claimsmakers say they represent? Are the claimsmakers leaders or representatives of particular organizations, social movements, professions, or interest groups? With whom are they allied or linked through previous contacts? Are they experienced claimsmakers, or novices? Do they reflect a particular ideology? What are their interests—in the issues they raise, in the policies they are promoting, and in the success of the campaign? How does the fact that these are the people making the claims shape the claims that get made?

The Claimsmaking Process.   Claims evoke varying responses. Some claims are ignored—the claimsmakers choose not to pursue their campaign and the matter is quickly forgotten. Occasional claimsmakers have dramatic success stories: people listen to the claims and respond quickly by adopting whatever policies the claimsmakers recommend. Most often, of course, campaigns have mixed success: only prolonged claimsmaking produces results, or the claimsmakers manage to organize an active social movement, but have difficulty changing social policy, or it becomes necessary to mount a series of campaigns, each leading to small policy changes. Obviously, claimsmaking processes are complex, and a good deal of comparative research will be needed before they can be understood. Some basic questions about any claimsmaking campaign might include: Whom did the claimsmakers address? Were other claims-makers presenting rival claims? What concerns and interests did the claimsmakers' audience bring to the issue, and how did those concerns or interests shape the audience's response to the claims? How did the nature of the claims or the identity of the claimsmakers affect the audience's response?

In addressing the various questions raised by constructionists, it is important to remain focused on claimsmaking, to avoid being distracted by the social conditions about which claims are being made. This does not mean—in spite of the strict constructionist's objections—that conditions cannot figure into the analysis, but conditions should never become the focal point. Strict constructionists prefer to ask how claimsmakers perceive and describe social conditions. Contextual constructionists may also ask how its larger context shapes claimsmaking. But neither form of constructionism treats social conditions as its analytic centerpiece.

In short, constructionism has become a useful, active research tradition—one that promises to lead to general theories of social problems. The chapters in this book reflect developments within constructionism, but they also are meant to be read as an invitation to join those doing constructionist analysis.

ACKNOWLEDGMENTS

Jun Ayukawa, Donna Maurer, and T. Memoree Thibodeau made helpful comments on an earlier draft of this chapter.

NOTES

1. Spector and Kitsuse's (1977) *Constructing Social Problems* and an earlier article by Herbert Blumer (1971) were the most influential early theoretical statements of the constructionist perspective. Joseph Schneider's (1985a) review article lists many early case studies. Holstein and Miller's (1993; Miller and Holstein 1993) recent collections include discussions that approach constructionism from a variety of theoretical orientations. The constructionist approach to social problems is related to recent intellectual movements in other disciplines, including philosophy, anthropology, communications, literary analysis, and political science, that share a concern with understanding how people assign meaning to their worlds.

2. While constructionist research appears in many sociological journals, most articles concerning theoretical issues about constructionism in particular,

and social problems theory in general, have appeared in *Social Problems*, the journal of the Society for the Study of Social Problems. In addition, the *SSSP Newsletter* has printed a number of brief but noteworthy contributions to the debate. Anyone can receive both *Social Problems* and the *SSSP Newsletter* by joining the Society (see a current issue of *Social Problems* for details—dues for students are modest).

3.   This is not to deny that some constructionist work does debunk claims. There are some "plot lines" that reoccur in many constructionist studies. One standard plot features plucky claimsmakers who draw attention to a neglected social problem. These sympathetic portraits tend to focus on social movements' struggles to bring issues to the fore. When we read between the lines, we may suspect that the analyst approves of the claimsmakers' cause. In these studies, the analytic focus is less often a critical analysis of the claims that a discussion of the practical problems claimsmakers face: how to mobilize supporters, how to generate sympathetic media coverage, how to influence policymakers, and so on. This plot's drama comes from casting the claimsmakers as underdogs, who must struggle to call attention to a neglected, albeit legitimate issue.

A second common constructionist plot line seems more critical of the claims-makers. Here, the analyst dissects claims, often calling them into question. (It is these analyses that lead some critics to equate constructionism with debunking.) The claimsmakers in these accounts are rarely underdogs: they may be powerful officials, prestigious professionals, influential members of the mass media, or other well-placed elites; if they are activists, they typically have powerful allies. In this plot, the drama comes from the analyst challenging widely accepted claims.

The choice of plot line often seems to depend upon the politics of analysts and their sociological audience. Because sociologists tend to have liberal sympathies, most analysts no doubt find it easier to adopt the first plot line to analyze campaigns for left-liberal causes. Thus, we have numerous sympathetic studies of claimsmaking by feminists, peace activists, and so on. In contrast, analysts who focus on more conservative causes, such as drug wars, tend to subject the claimsmakers' rhetoric to criticism. In contrast, there seem to be relatively fewer critical analyses of, say, the rhetoric of claimsmaking about sexual harassment, just as there are few studies celebrating the struggles of the English-only movement.

But, again, this pattern is not inherent in the constructionist stance. While analysts may seem to favor some politically charged topics and shy away from others, these values are something analysts bring to the perspective. Construc-tionism is a tool, not an ideology; it orients the analyst to forgo concentrating on the nature of social conditions and, instead, to ask questions about claimsmak-ing. People with very different values may agree that constructionism's topic—the rise and fall of social problems—is a significant feature of contemporary society and warrants study, and they may find it useful to adopt the construc-tionist approach.

4.   Holstein and Miller (1993) and Miller and Holstein (1993) present some 20

commentaries on Ibarra and Kitsuse's paper, written from a range of theoretical orientations.

5. The final sentence in this passage offers another example of the problem with strict constructionism. Even here, Sarbin and Kitsuse makes assumptions about analysts' intent, interests, and agendas. It is apparently impossible to describe strict constructionism in terms that do not violate its tenets (Best 1993)

6. Some researchers have begun identifying their work as examples of contextual constructionism (Goode and Ben-Yehuda 1994; Hallett and Rogers 1994; Rafter 1992; Sarbin and Kitsuse 1994).

REFERENCES

Best, J. 1993. "But Seriously Folks." Pp. 129–147 in *Reconsidering Social Constructionism*, edited by J. A. Holstein and G. Miller. Hawthorne, NY: Aldine de Gruyter.

Block, F., and G. A. Burns. 1986. "Productivity as a Social Problem." *American Sociological Review* 51:767–780.

Blumer, H. 1971. "Social Problems as Collective Behavior." *Social Problems* 18:298–306.

Collins, P. H. 1989. "The Social Construction of Invisibility." *Perspectives on Social Problems* 1:77–93.

Eitzen, D. S. 1984. "Teaching Social Problems: Implications of the Objectivist Subjectivist Debate." *SSSP Newsletter* 16 (Fall):10–12.

Forsyth, C. J., and M. D. Oliver. 1990. "The Theoretical Framing of a Social Problem." *Deviant Behavior* 11:281–292.

Gamson, W., and A. Modigliani. 1989. "Media Discourse and Public Opinion on Nuclear Power." *American Journal of Sociology* 95:1–37.

Goode, E., and N. Ben-Yehuda. 1994. *Moral Panics*. Oxford, UK: Blackwell.

Gusfield, J. R. 1985. "Theories and Hobgoblins." *SSSP Newsletter* 17 (Fall):16–18.

Hallett, M. A., and R. Rogers. 1994. "The Push for 'Truth in Sentencing'." *Evaluation and Program Planning* 17:187–196.

Hazelrigg, L. E. 1985. "Were It Not for Words." *Social Problems* 32:234–237.

———. 1986. "Is There a Choice Between 'Constructionism' and 'Objectivism'?" *Social Problems* 33 (October/December):S1–S13.

Hilgartner, S., and C. L. Bosk. 1988. "The Rise and Fall of Social Problems." *American Journal of Sociology* 94:53–78.

Holstein, J. A., and G. Miller (eds.). 1993. *Reconsidering Social Constructionism*. Hawthorne, NY: Aldine de Gruyter.

Ibarra, P. R., and J. I. Kitsuse. 1993. "Vernacular Constituents of Moral Discourse." Pp. 25–58 in *Reconsidering Social Constructionism*, edited by J. A. Holstein and G. Miller. Hawthorne, NY: Aldine de Gruyter.

Jones, B. J., J. A. McFalls, Jr., and B. J. Gallagher III. 1989. "Toward a Unified Model for Social Problems Theory." *Journal for the Theory of Social Behavior* 19:337–356.

Kitsuse, J. I., and J. W. Schneider. 1989. "Preface." Pp. xi–xiii in *Images of Issues*, edited by J. Best. Hawthorne, NY: Aldine de Gruyter.

Manis, J. G. 1985. "Defining Social Problems." *SSSP Newsletter* 16 (Winter):5.

Miller, G., and J. A. Holstein. 1993. *Constructionist Controversies*. Hawthorne, NY: Aldine de Gruyter.

Miller, L. J. 1993. "Claims-Making from the Underside." Pp. 349–376 in *Reconsidering Social Constructionism*, edited by J. A. Holstein and G. Miller. Hawthorne, NY: Aldine de Gruyter.

Pfohl, S. 1985. "Toward a Sociological Deconstruction of Social Problems." *Social Problems* 32:228–232.

Rafter, N. H. 1992. "Claims-Making and Socio-Cultural Context in the First U.S. Eugenics Campaign." *Social Problems* 39:17–34.

Sarbin, T. R., and J. I. Kitsuse. 1994. "A Prologue to *Constructing the Social*." Pp. 1–18 in *Constructing the Social*, edited by T. R. Sarbin and J. I. Kitsuse. Thousand Oaks, CA: Sage.

Schneider, A., and H. Ingram. 1993. "Social Construction of Target Populations." *American Political Science Review* 87:334–347.

Schneider, J. W. 1985a. "Social Problems Theory." *Annual Review of Sociology* 11:209–229.

———. 1985b. "Defining the Definitional Perspective on Social Problems." *Social Problems* 32:232–234.

Spector, M., and J. I. Kitsuse. 1977. *Constructing Social Problems*. Menlo Park, CA: Cummings.

———. 1987. "Preface to the Japanese Edition: Constructing Social Problems." *SSSP Newsletter* 18 (Fall):13–15.

Speed, B. 1991. "Reality Exists O.K.?" *Family Therapy* 13:395–409.

Troyer, R. 1992. "Some Consequences of Contextual Constructionism." *Social Problems* 39:35–37.

Woolgar, S., and D. Pawluch. 1985a. "Ontological Gerrymandering." *Social Problems* 32:214–227.

———. 1985b. "How Shall We Move Beyond Constructivism." *Social Problems* 33:159–162.

Biographical Sketches of the Contributors

Lynn Appleton is Associate Professor in the Department of Sociology and Social Psychology at Florida Atlantic University. She is working on a project on the "recovery movement" and the treatment of addiction to alcohol and other drugs. She is not sure if she has an "inner child," but is certain that she has an "inner teenager."

Joel Best is Professor and Chair of the Department of Sociology at Southern Illinois University at Carbondale. Specializing in social problems and deviance, his books include *Threatened Children* and *Organizing Deviance* (with David F. Luckenbill) and *Troubling Children* (Aldine). He received his Ph.D. from the University of California, Berkeley.

Philip Jenkins is Professor of Religious Studies and History at Pennsylvania State University. His most recent books include *Intimate Enemies: Moral Panics in Contemporary Great Britain* (1992) and *Using Murder: The Social Construction of Serial Homicide* (1994) (both published by Aldine de Gruyter). His book on the social construction of the clergy abuse problem is shortly to be published by Oxford University Press.

Valerie Jenness is Assistant Professor of Sociology at Washington State University. She earned her Ph.D. in Sociology at the University of California, Santa Barbara in 1991. She is the author of *Making it Work: The Contemporary Prostitutes' Rights Movement in Perspective* (Aldine), as well as numerous articles on the prostitutes' rights movement, the gay and lesbian movement, and the criminalization of activities commonly called hate crimes. Her current research focuses on the linkages between gender, social movements, and the social construction of deviance.

John M. Johnson is Professor of Justice Studies and Women's Studies at Arizona State University where he was named Distinguished Research Professor in 1986–87. He has founded or co-founded seven nonprofit agencies which serve the needs of domestic violence or crime victims in the Phoenix, Arizona area. During 1995–97 he serves as the President of the 350-member Unitarian Universalist Church in Chandler, Arizona, the first Buddhist elected to such an office.

Karl Kunkel is Assistant Professor of Sociology at Southwest Missouri State University, teaching courses in sociology of law and criminal justice studies. His current research involves an examination of the animal rights movement using the constructionist approach to social problems. This work emphasizes implications of this movement for constructionist theory. He is also completing a textbook in the sociology of deviance.

Harry Gene Levine is Professor of Sociology at CUNY–Queens College. He received his Ph.D. from the University of California, Berkeley, and has written extensively on alcohol and other drugs. He is co-editor of *Crack in Context: Demon Drugs and Social Justice* (University of California Press, in press).

Donileen Loseke is Associate Professor of Sociology at Skidmore College. She received her Ph.D. from the University of California, Santa Barbara. Her book, *The Battered Woman and Shelters: The Social Construction of Wife Abuse*, is published by the State University of New York Press.

Kathleen Lowney is Associate Professor of Sociology at Valdosta State University. Her current research interests include satanism; joke cycles as social problems work; how women's fear helps them construct "safe" people and places; and kudzu as a social problem.

David F. Luckenbill is Associate Professor of Sociology at Northern Illinois University. His current research focuses on the exploitation and protection of intellectual property. He is the co-author (with Edwin H. Sutherland and Donald R. Cressey) of *Criminology* (General Hall, 1992) and the co-author (with Joel Best) of *Organizing Deviance* (Prentice-Hall, 1994).

Shan Nelson-Rowe received his Ph.D. at the State University of New York at Stony Brook, and teaches sociology at the University of Wisconsin, Milwaukee. He is interested in constructions of childhood and education, and is currently researching the origins of educational toys.

Lawrence T. Nichols is Associate Professor of Sociology at West Virginia University. He has published in the areas of criminology and deviance, corporate social responsibility and business ethics, organizational policy making, dispute resolution, and the history and sociology of social science. His current research interests include the role of mass media in the construction of organizational deviance, landmark white-collar crime cases, and the development of sociology at Harvard University.

Craig Reinarman is Professor of Sociology at the University of California, Santa Cruz. He has published widely in the area of drug abuse and drug policy. He is the author of *American States of Mind* (Yale University Press, 1987), co-author of *Cocaine Changes* (Temple University Press, 1991) and co-editor of *Crack in Context: Demon Drugs and Social Justice* (University of California Press, in press). He is currently conducting cross-cultural research on drug policy.

Shirley A. Scritchfield is Associate Professor of Sociology at Creighton University. Her recent work centers on the social construction of ethics in reproduction, primarily focused on assisted reproductive technologies. She also is trying her hand at applied sociology, having assumed a position in Institutional Research at Creighton in 1995.

Gwyneth I. Williams is Associate Professor of Political Science at Webster University, St. Louis, Missouri. Her research areas include family law and gender politics. She is currently working on a manuscript on the politics of joint custody law.

Rhys H. Williams is Assistant Professor of Sociology at Southern Illinois University, Carbondale. His research interests focus on the intersection of politics, religion, culture and social movements. Among his published work is, with N.J. Demerath III, *A Bridging of Faiths: Religion and Politics in a New England City*, (Princeton University Press, 1992) and "Constructing the Public Good: Cultural Resources and Social Movements," *Social Problems* (February, 1995).

Index